No Stress Tech Guide To Crystal Xcelsius 4.5

For people that want to learn how to turn Excel spreadsheet data into an interactive dashboard for Business Intelligence analysis or how to enhance PowerPoint presentations

By Dr. Indera Murphy

Tolana Publishing
Teaneck, New Jersey

No Stress Tech Guide To Crystal Xcelsius 4.5: For people that want to learn how to turn Excel spreadsheet data into an interactive dashboard for Business Intelligence analysis or how to enhance PowerPoint presentations

Published By:
Tolana Publishing
PO Box 719
Teaneck, NJ 07666 USA

Find us online at www.tolanapublishing.com
Inquiries may be sent to the publisher: tolanapub@yahoo.com

Our books are available online at www.amazon.com, www.barnesandnoble.com, www.alibris.com and www.biblio.com. They can also be ordered from Ingram.

ISBN-13: 978-1-935208-02-0
ISBN-10: 1-935208-02-0

Library of Congress Control Number: 2009903338

Printed and bound in the United States Of America

Cover by Mary Kramer, Milkweed Graphics, www.milkweedgraphics.com

v1.0b

Who The Book Is For

This book is for anyone that wants to learn Crystal Xcelsius, version 4.5. People that are upgrading from a previous version of the software will have a refresher of the basics and then learn about the features and options that are new in this version of Crystal Xcelsius.

About The No Stress Tech Guide Series

The No Stress Tech Guide To Crystal Xcelsius 4.5, is part of a growing series of computer software training books that are designed to be used in a classroom setting, an online class or as a self-paced learning tool. The books contain an abundance of screen shots to help reduce the "stress" often associated with learning new software.

Tolana Publishing believes that the following principals are important when it comes to computer software training books:

⇒ The print should be large enough so that the reader does not have to squint.
⇒ The step-by-step instructions should really work and not leave something out.
⇒ Features or options that do not work as intended should be pointed out, not to bash the software company, but so that you do not think that you are crazy <smile>.
⇒ That there should be a realistic mix of theory, real world examples and hands-on exercises. It is important to know the past, because it helps you transition into the future with ease and dignity.

Other Titles In The No Stress Tech Guide Series

Microsoft Works 7	ISBN-13: 978-0-9773912-2-6
Microsoft Works 8 & 8.5	ISBN-13: 978-0-9773912-1-9
Windows XP	ISBN-13: 978-0-9773912-0-2
Crystal Reports XI For Beginners (2nd Edition)	ISBN-13: 978-1-935208-00-6
OpenOffice.org Writer 2	ISBN-13: 978-0-9773912-4-0
ACT! 2007	ISBN-13: 978-0-9773912-5-7
Microsoft Works 9	ISBN-13: 978-0-9773912-7-1
Crystal Reports For Visual Studio 2005	ISBN-13: 978-0-9773912-6-4
Crystal Reports Basic For Visual Studio 2008	ISBN-13: 978-0-9773912-8-8
Crystal Reports 2008 For Beginners	ISBN-13: 978-0-9773912-9-5
What's New In Crystal Reports 2008	ISBN-13: 978-1-935208-01-3
ACT! 2009	ISBN-13: 978-1-935208-07-5

Forthcoming Titles

OpenOffice.org Writer 3

About The Author

Dr. Indera Murphy is an author, educator and IT professional that has over 20 years of experience in the Information Technology field. She has held a variety of positions including technical writer, programmer, consultant, web designer, course developer and project leader. Indera has designed and developed software applications and web sites, as well as, manage technology driven projects in several industries. In addition to being an Executive Director and consultant, Indera is also an online adjunct professor. She teaches courses in a variety of areas including project management, technical writing, information processing, Access, HTML, Windows, Excel, Dreamweaver and critical thinking.

Why I Wrote This Book

After not finding a book for this version of the software and reading the description of the only book for the previous version of Crystal Xcelsius, I quickly realized that there is definitely a need for this book. Not only does this book teach a beginner, through step-by-step instructions and hundreds of illustrations, it provides examples of when to use certain features to make the dashboard more visually appealing and professional.

I felt that users, especially new users of the software, would prefer to have more assistance in learning how to get the most out of Crystal Xcelsius. The Users Guide that comes with the software provides a starting point of reference, but does not provide a sufficient amount of examples to demonstrate the core features of the software, nor does it provide hands-on exercises.

Crystal Xcelsius is an exciting software package that is used to enhance presentations that have numerical data. With a little guidance, you will be able to create meaningful dashboards. This book contains exercises in step-by-step format, so that if you have never used Crystal Xcelsius before, you can learn how to use the software. This does not mean that only the basic features of Crystal Xcelsius are covered.

I have been told and sometimes criticized for having an eye for detail (being picky). I believe that my eye for detail helps me write better books. I am not purposely looking for things that do not work right. I am looking for outcomes that are different then what I was expecting to see or have happen. Having said that, by no means is this meant to indicate that I see or catch every nuance of a software package, but I try.

I know that many books claim to have "step-by-step instructions". If you have tried to follow the instructions in a book that make this claim and you got lost or could not complete a task as instructed, it may not have been your fault. When I decided to write computer books, I vowed to really have step-by-step instructions that actually included every step. This includes steps like which file to open, which menu option to select, when to save a file and more. In my opinion, it is this level of detail that makes a computer book easy to follow, which reduces the "stress" of learning software. I hope that you agree.

TABLE OF CONTENTS

INTRODUCTION TO CRYSTAL XCELSIUS 4.5

LESSON 1

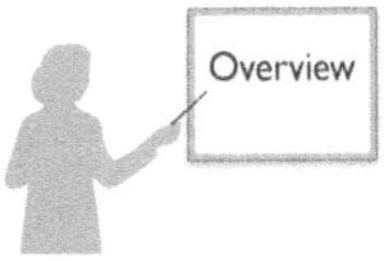

The goal of this lesson is to familiarize you with Crystal Xcelsius and what it offers. Crystal Xcelsius is gaining in popularity as another way to present and analyze spreadsheet data in a dashboard format.

In addition to becoming familiar with what Crystal Xcelsius has to offer, you will gain a better understanding of how intricately linked Crystal Xcelsius and Microsoft Excel really are. The last major concept covered in this lesson is to learn the basics of Business Intelligence and how Crystal Xcelsius can be used as a key tool for Business Intelligence analysis.

Excel has been around for a long time and has been a primary way to analyze data, provide data in chart format and provide what-if functionality. The good news is that Crystal Xcelsius is not going to cause Excel to go away. In fact, Crystal Xcelsius requires Excel spreadsheets. Crystal Xcelsius is used to provide interactive functionality for data in spreadsheets.

Having said all of that, please be assured that the focus of this book is teaching you how to use Crystal Xcelsius. The extent that Excel and Business Intelligence are covered is in an overview format, so that you can start to understand how and why they work well together, as well as, what you can or should do to the data in an Excel spreadsheet to make it more Crystal Xcelsius friendly.

What Is Crystal Xcelsius?

Crystal Xcelsius is a software package that allows you to visually organize and present data from Excel spreadsheets in a meaningful way. The primary goal of Crystal Xcelsius is to take the data from an Excel spreadsheet and put it in a visual format that will be used as part of a presentation or for business analysis purposes. Crystal Xcelsius provides several options for how the data can be viewed, including what-if analysis, drill-down charts and other interactive features.

While Excel allows you to present the data in chart format, Pivot Tables and even some types of dashboards, if you need to redisplay the data based on changing one of the variables, you could be stuck if you are in the middle of a live presentation or meeting. You may have to create another chart during the presentation in front of a roomful of people. No stress there <smile>. For example, if the Excel chart displayed the mortgage data based on a specific interest rate, but people in the meeting ask to see the mortgage data in a chart based on several interest rates, you would have to modify the spreadsheet on the spot during the meeting to display the mortgage data with several interest rates instead of one.

This is where Crystal Xcelsius is very beneficial and the better tool for the task. You could add a component for the mortgage interest rate cell to accommodate a wide range of internet rates in one dashboard. By adding a component like slider to the mortgage interest rate cell, different interest rates could be selected. Each time that a different interest rate is selected, the chart would change immediately to reflect the interest rate that is selected. With Crystal Xcelsius you could go one step further and hide one of the charts initially displayed and allow users to display it when they want or need to, with the click of a button on the dashboard.

This functionality is done in real time in Crystal Xcelsius, which makes the dashboard **DYNAMIC** (ever changing), instead of **STATIC** (never changing). Using Crystal Xcelsius to present spreadsheet data in an interactive, visual format is the next level up from using Excel and PowerPoint to present data. Two of the biggest advantages Crystal Xcelsius has over Excel are discussed below.

① The people using a dashboard that was created in Crystal Xcelsius, do not have to have Crystal Xcelsius or Excel installed on their computer, nor do they have to know how to use either software package.

② A dashboard that is created in Crystal Xcelsius can be distributed in several formats including PowerPoint, Adobe PDF and Flash.

If you have been struggling trying to get your Excel data into a PowerPoint presentation or struggling to make the presentation look better or more professional, those days are just about over because the dashboards that you create in Crystal Xcelsius can also be incorporated in a PowerPoint presentation.

I started writing this book during the most exciting campaign of my lifetime, for the highest office in the country. The one thing that I have heard Barack Obama say over and over is that it is time for a change. His mission is to change the landscape of America so that more people have access to better jobs, as well as, the goods and services that they need. The mission of Crystal Xcelsius is to change how spreadsheet data is presented, by turning it into a meaningful and interactive dashboard.

In one sentence to answer what Crystal Xcelsius is, I would say "Crystal Xcelsius is a good way to visually, spice up spreadsheet data and allow the person using the dashboard to control what is displayed".

What's New In Crystal Xcelsius 4.5?

What you will notice that's new, depends on the previous version and edition of Crystal Xcelsius that you used, if any. The older the version of Crystal Xcelsius (version 3 or 4) that you are upgrading from, the more new features you will notice. For example, if the previous version that you used was the standard edition of version 3 and you now have version 4.5 professional, you will see a lot more new features then if you are upgrading from the professional edition of version 4. Some of the new features are discussed below.

⇒ **Animation Enabled** This option is available for all chart types except the Area chart. When the dashboard is run, parts of the chart will change in size or have animated movement, as the data changes. The animation options are similar to some of the ones PowerPoint has.
⇒ **OHLC and Candlestick Charts** These two chart types are primarily used to display stock market data. Each marker on the chart corresponds to a different value of the stock, including the opening and closing value of the stock for a particular day.
⇒ **Export Model** This option exports a copy of the Excel spreadsheet data that was used to create the dashboard.
⇒ **List View Component** This component displays a group of cells from the spreadsheet in a table layout format. It has more functionality than the Table component that Crystal Xcelsius already had.
⇒ **Export To Word** Exports the model to a Microsoft Word document.
⇒ **Panel Set Component** This component provides navigation in the dashboard by allowing more than one dashboard to be part of a larger dashboard.
⇒ **Skins** Three skins have been added: Graphite, Halo and Windows Classic. Skins change the appearance of dashboard components.

How This Book Is Organized

Topics and exercises build on ones covered in previous lessons. To get the most out of this book, it is not advised that you skip around unless you have used Crystal Xcelsius in the past. The first reason is because some of the files used in later lessons are created in exercises earlier in the book. The other reason is that a topic or option may have been covered in more detail earlier in the book. If you decide to skip around and cannot complete an exercise because there is something that you do not understand, you will have to go back and find the section that covers the topic in question. Below is an overview of what is covered in each lesson.

Lesson 1 covers the conventions used in this book, so that you will know what certain things mean. You will learn how to check for software updates. Some of the terms that are used extensively in this book and in the Business Intelligence community, are explained in detail.

Lesson 2 introduces you to Crystal Xcelsius by explaining the workspace environment and its options. This includes menu options, the toolbar, the Components Explorer and Object Browser. The types of dashboards that Crystal Xcelsius can produce are explained and illustrated.

Lesson 3 provides a walk through of the dashboard design process so that you have a foundation to build on for creating effective, more so than dazzling, dashboards. You will learn how to import data into a Crystal Xcelsius model. Common options on the Properties dialog box are explained. You will see that you cannot create a dashboard without these options, so pay attention <smile>. And probably most important to you, is that you will learn how to create your first dashboard if you have never used Crystal Xcelsius before.

Lesson 4 covers Excel topics that you should understand so that you can ensure that the spreadsheets that you need to use will work smoothly in Crystal Xcelsius. You will also learn how cells, rows and columns of data in the spreadsheet are linked to components in a dashboard. Don't worry, you do not need a scientific calculator to complete this lesson.

Lesson 5 covers Single Value components like sliders and gauges in detail. This is one technique that is used to control or select the data that appears on the dashboard. You will also learn how to create interactive maps to display spreadsheet data geographically.

Lesson 6 covers probably more than you ever wanted to know about charts. If you did not know before, you will see that a large number of dashboards have charts. Some of the charts created in this lesson are the foundation for other features covered later in the book. So make sure that you complete all of these exercises.

Lesson 7 shows you how to create a variety of menus. Menus are used to control other components on a dashboard, like which chart data to display. For all intensive purposes, if you needed to create 25 dashboards that each need two charts and used data from 25 spreadsheets, you could combine all of that data into one spreadsheet, using 25 tabs on the spreadsheet. You could create one menu that would have options for each of the 25 dashboards and display the dashboards one by one. Some may call this cheating, but I just wanted to let you know the possibilities that a good menu design can handle.

Lesson 8 covers alerts, which is a way to conditionally change the color of components at run time. Alerts are a visual technique used to emphasize certain data or make the data stand out.

Lesson 9 covers several ways to enhance dashboards, including refreshing the data, using the Art and Background components, as well as, linking information on the Internet to components on a dashboard. You will also learn how to let users update the data in a spreadsheet and have the data changes that they make incorporated in the dashboard, the next time that the model is published.

Lesson 10 covers the features that are only in Crystal Xcelsius Professional. This includes drill down charts, interactive calendars and picture menus.

Lesson 11 goes beyond the basics and covers functionality that some would put in the advanced category. This includes password protecting dashboards and having the ability to display and hide components on a dashboard as needed. The secret behind many of the "cool" features is Dynamic Visibility, which is covered in detail.

Lesson 12 covers global customization options and techniques. All of the export options to turn a model into a dashboard that you can distribute to other people to use are discussed. Yes, I know that you are sad to see it end <smile>.

Objectives

Step-by-step instructions are included throughout this book. This book takes a hands-on, performance based approach to teaching you how to use Crystal Xcelsius and provides the skills required to create efficient and effective dashboards. After completing the exercises in this book, you will be able to perform the following tasks and more:

- ☑ Implement good dashboard design techniques.
- ☑ Add interactive and animated functionality to dashboards.
- ☑ Use the features that come with the professional edition of Crystal Xcelsius, including drill-down charts, accordion menus and interactive calendars.
- ☑ Use advanced options including password protection and creating help options in a dashboard.
- ☑ Refresh data in a dashboard.
- ☑ Publish dashboards to several output formats including PDF, HTML and PowerPoint.

Helpful, But Not Required

This book is written to accommodate classroom and online training, as well as, to be used as a self-paced training course. The previous section discussed the objectives that are covered in this book. If you have not used Crystal Xcelsius before or have not created dashboards before, don't panic. In my opinion, the keys to learning software or most things in life, is having the patience and the desire to accomplish the task. While there are no required prerequisites to successfully complete the exercises in this book, having a general knowledge of any of the following would be helpful, but not required.

- ☑ Using formulas and cell references in Excel.
- ☑ The basics of a PowerPoint presentation.
- ☑ The purpose of dashboards.
- ☑ Business Intelligence.
- ☑ What-If analysis.

Lesson 1 Objectives

After reading and completing the exercises in this lesson you will understand the following:

- ☑ What Crystal Xcelsius is designed to do.
- ☑ What dashboards are.
- ☑ The requirements and the process of importing data into a Crystal Xcelsius model.
- ☑ How to get help if you get stuck.
- ☑ What a visual model is and its purpose in Crystal Xcelsius.

Conventions Used In This Book

I designed the following conventions to make it easier for you to follow the instructions in this book:

- ☑ The `Courier font` is used to indicate what you should type.
- ☑ **Drag** means to hold down the left mouse button while moving the mouse.
- ☑ **Click** means to press the left mouse button once, then release it immediately.
- ☑ **Double-click** means to quickly press the left mouse button twice, then release it.
- ☑ **Right-click** means to press the right mouse button once, which will open a shortcut menu.
- ☑ Click **OK** means to click the OK button on the dialog box.
- ☑ Press **Enter** means to press the Enter key on your keyboard.
- ☑ Press **Tab** means to press the Tab key on your keyboard.
- ☑ Click **Save** means to click the Save button on the toolbar or dialog box.
- ☑ **SMALL CAPS** are used to indicate an option to click on or to bring something to your attention.
- ☑  This icon indicates a tip or additional information about the topic that is being discussed.
- ☑  This icon indicates a shortcut or another way to complete the task that is being discussed.
- ☑  This icon indicates something important that you need to be aware of.
- ☑  This icon represents a question that I posted a the Crystal Xcelsius forum, but either did not receive an answer to by the time this book went to print or the answer that I received did not resolve the problem or question that I had.
- ☑  This icon indicates that after testing the steps several times on different computers, the results vary. This doesn't mean that I have done something wrong, only that there can be differences in the results that you see.
- ☑ [See Lesson 2, Object Browser] refers to a section in a different lesson that you can use as a reference for the topic that you are currently reading.
- ☑ [See Lesson 2, Figure 2-8] refers to an illustration (screen shot) in a different lesson that you can use as a reference for the topic that you are currently reading.
- ☑ The section heading **EXERCISE X.Y:** (Where X equals the lesson number and Y equals the exercise number) represents exercises that have step-by-step instructions that you should complete. You will also see sections that have step-by-step instructions that are not an exercise. Completing them as you go through the book is optional.
- ☑ When you see "**THE DIALOG BOX SHOULD HAVE THE OPTIONS SHOWN IN FIGURE X-X**", or something similar in the exercises, check to make sure that your dialog box does look like the figure. If it does, continue with the next set of instructions. If your dialog box or screen does not look like the figure, redo the steps that you just completed so that your dialog box or screen does match the figure. Not doing so may cause you problems when trying to complete exercises later in the book.
- ☑ When you see, "Hover the mouse pointer", it means to place the mouse pointer over the component referenced in the instruction, but do not click.
- ☑ "Clear the (name of option)" means to remove the check mark from the option specified in the instruction.
- ☑ "Select the range" means to select the cell(s) in the spreadsheet that was imported into the model that you are currently working on.

- ☑ "Save the (name of model) as" means to open the (name of model) file and save it with the new file name that is specified in the instruction. Doing this lets you keep the original file as is.
- ☑ **FORMAT ⇒ ALIGN ⇒ TOP** means to open the **FORMAT** menu, select the **ALIGN** option, then select the **TOP** option, as illustrated in Figure 1-1.

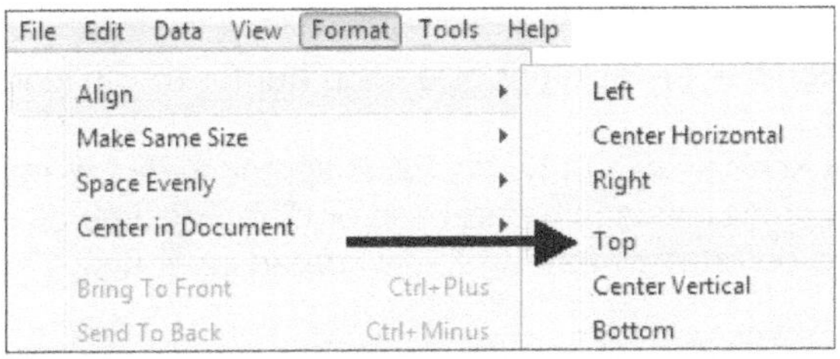

Figure 1-1 Menu navigation technique illustrated

Assumptions

(Yes, I know one should never assume anything, but the following assumptions have been made.) It is assumed that . . . .

- ☑ You know that the operating system used to write this book is Windows Vista Home Premium.
- ☑ You know that Crystal Xcelsius 4.5 Professional is the edition used to write this book.
- ☑ You know that the version of Word, Excel, Outlook and PowerPoint used or referenced in this book is 2003.
- ☑ That you have Crystal Xcelsius 4.5 (any edition) and Microsoft Excel installed. Excel must be installed before installing Crystal Xcelsius.
- ☑ You understand that if you have a different version of any of the software packages referenced above, that what you see on your computer screen will be slightly different then some of the illustrations in this book.
- ☑  You know that this button will minimize the open window and place an icon for the open window on the Windows taskbar. When you want to view the window again, click the button on the taskbar and the window will reappear.
- ☑  You know that this button will open the current window to the full size of your computer screen.
- ☑  You know that this button will close the window that is open.
- ☑ You are familiar with the Windows environment including Windows Explorer and are comfortable using a mouse.
- ☑ When you see C1:E14, you know that it means to select (highlight) the range of cells from C1 to E14 on the Excel spreadsheet.
- ☑ You understand that the following terms are used interchangeably: Visual model, model and visualization. They refer to the file that is used to create and modify what will eventually become the dashboard, which is the finished product that you can distribute to other people.
- ☑ You have access to the Internet to download the practice files needed to complete the exercises in this book and to download any updates to Crystal Xcelsius that are available.

☑ You know that Crystal Xcelsius requires that the Flash Player or plug-in be installed. When Crystal Xcelsius is installed, there is a prompt to install the player if it is not already installed on your computer or if the version of the player or plug-in that is installed on your computer is too old. If an acceptable version of the player is installed, you will not be prompted to install it. If for some reason you discover that the Flash Player is not installed on your computer, you can download and install it for free from www.adobe.com.

☑ When you see <smile>, it signifies my attempt at adding humor to the learning process.

☑ You understand that Crystal Xcelsius can only use Excel spreadsheets to import data. If the data that you need to use is in a database or different type of spreadsheet, the data has to be brought into an Excel spreadsheet first.

Interactive Message Symbols

Like many other software packages, Crystal Xcelsius will display interactive messages that require a response from you to confirm an action. Table 1-1 explains the three types of interactive message symbols and what they mean.

Symbol	Name	This interactive message type . . . . .
	Information	Provides information about an action that you just performed.
	Warning	Usually requires you to make a decision. (1)
	Critical	Requires you to make a decision before moving on to the next step. (1)

Table 1-1 Interactive message symbols explained

(1) I have seen a message box with the warning or critical symbol and no text, as shown in Figure 1-2. This is probably a bug that has not been documented.

Figure 1-2 Critical warning message

Differences Between The Standard And Professional Editions

Table 1-2 primarily shows the differences between the Standard and Professional editions of Crystal Xcelsius 4.5. The table below only includes features that are different between the editions, so that if you are using the Standard edition you know which features are not available. The Workgroup features are included in the table, in case you are thinking about upgrading at a later date. Now that Xcelsius 2008 is available, you may have to look really hard to find any Crystal Xcelsius 4.5 edition for sale.

Feature	Standard	Professional	Workgroup
Accordion Menu	N	Y	Y
Fish-Eye Picture Menu	N	Y	Y
Sliding Picture Menu	N	Y	Y
External Slide Show	N	Y	Y
Drill Down Chart	N	Y	Y
Interactive Calendar	N	Y	Y
Source Data Component	N	Y	Y
Export To Adobe PDF	N	Y	Y
List Builder	N	N	Y
Ticker	N	N	Y
Web Service Coordinator	N	N	Y
XML Data Button	N	N	Y
XML Map Refresh	N	N	Y
Connection Light	N	N	Y
Login	N	N	Y
People List	N	N	Y
Remote Scenarios Buttons	N	N	Y

Table 1-2 Crystal Xcelsius edition differences

As you can see, there are not many features in the Professional edition that are not in the Standard edition. If you have the Standard edition you will be able to complete almost all of the exercises in this book. The professional features are covered in Lesson 10. If you have the Standard edition, you can skip this lesson, unless you want to read about the features to determine if you have a need for them. If you have the Workgroup edition, you have all of the features shown in the table and can complete all of the exercises, just like you can with the Professional edition. The benefit primary of using the Workgroup edition is that it supports connections to live data.

What This Book Does Not Cover

The topics that are not covered in this book are listed below:

① Features only found in the Workgroup edition of Crystal Xcelsius.
② XML functionality and connectivity.
③ Excel spreadsheets created with Live Office.
④ Integrating dashboards into Crystal Reports.

Exercise 1.1: How To Check For Software Updates

This exercise will show you how to check for and install updates for Crystal Xcelsius. The software does not have any built-in option that will notify you that an update is available. This means that you will have to check the web site periodically, to see if there are any updates.

1. Go to www.sdn.sap.com/irj/sdn/businessobjects-downloads. Could they make the link just a little bit longer? <smile>

2. Click on the link for Xcelsius downloads.

3. Open the **SOFTWARE PRODUCT** drop-down list and select Xcelsius.

4. Open the **PRODUCT VERSION** drop-down list and select 4.5, then click the Search button. You will see a web page similar to the one shown in Figure 1-3.

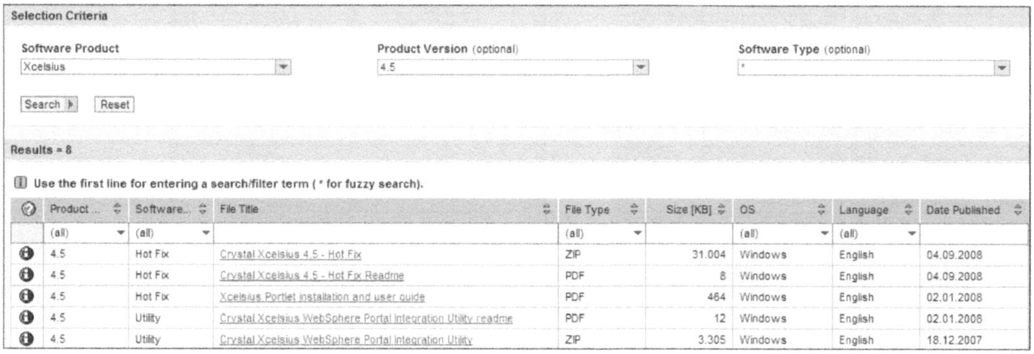

Figure 1-3 Selection Criteria web page

5. Click on the link for the update file that you need, then save it to your hard drive.

> I save update files to my desktop so that they are easier to find. After I install it, I remove it from my desktop, mainly because fewer items on the desktop means the computer will boot faster.

6. Extract the files from the zip file.

7. Double-click on the **SETUP.EXE** file and follow the installation instructions.

Getting Help

There are four primary ways to get help if you have a question on how to use a feature or option in Crystal Xcelsius, as discussed below.

① Read this book from cover to cover. Many of the basic questions that you may have are probably covered in this book. If you have a question that you think should be covered, please let me know so that I can consider including it in the book for the next version of the software.

② The Online Help file. This is the electronic version of the Users Guide. It is helpful for the basic definitions of properties.

③ Xcelsius forums. You can post questions and learn how other people are using the software. The forums are also a great way to keep up on the latest trends of the software and to get ideas on how to enhance your dashboards.

④ Hire an Xcelsius consultant. Need I say that this is the most expensive option and you probably will not get an answer to your question as fast as you would like.

The Online Help File

When you open the Help file, it opens in a new window instead of opening on the right side of the Crystal Xcelsius workspace. To open the Help file, follow the instructions below.

1. Help ⇒ Contents.

   You will see the window shown in Figure 1-4.

   The **CONTENTS** tab is like a table of contents.

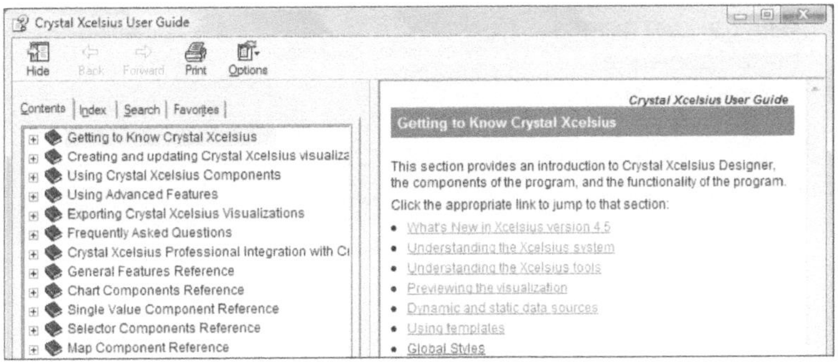

Figure 1-4 Contents tab options

Clicking on the plus sign in front of the topic that you want to know more about will display additional topics. You may have seen this style of help in other software applications. Each of the tabs (Contents, Index, Search and Favorites) provide help in a different way.

Figure 1-5 shows the options on the Index tab.

You can type in a keyword, then click the **DISPLAY** button that is illustrated, or you can scroll down the list of keywords and select the topic that you want.

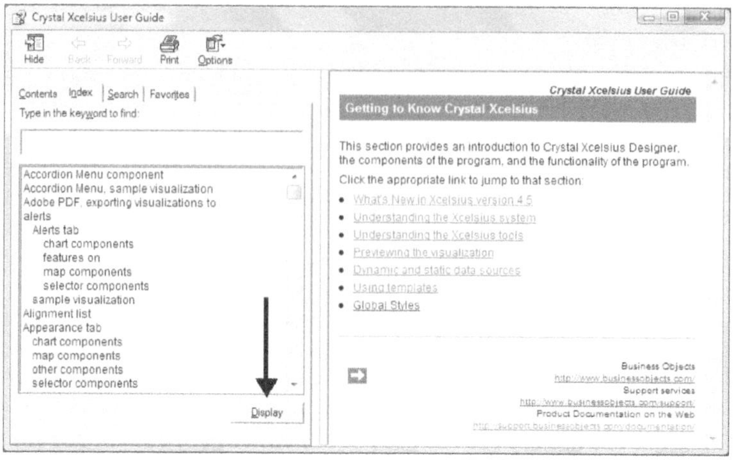

Figure 1-5 Index tab options

2. Click on the **SEARCH** tab.

   If you type in a keyword on this tab and then click the **LIST TOPICS** button shown in Figure 1-6, you will see a list of topics that relate to the keyword that you typed in.

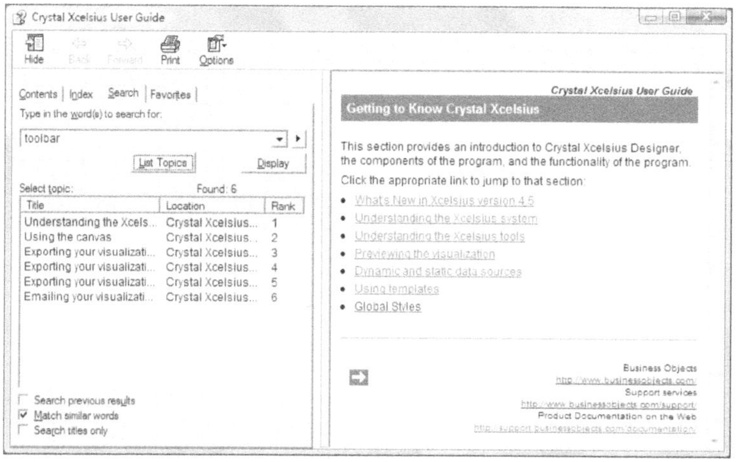

Figure 1-6 Search tab options

3. Select the topic that is closest to what you are looking for, then click the **DISPLAY** button or double-click on the topic.

4. Click on the **FAVORITES** tab.

   This tab is used to view a list of the help topics that you have bookmarked, as shown in Figure 1-7.

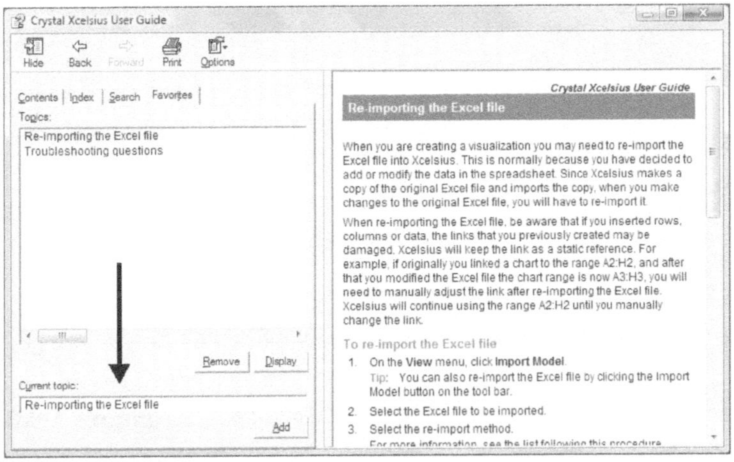

Figure 1-7 Favorites tab options

> **How To Add A Topic To The Favorites Tab**
>
> 1. To add a topic to the Favorites tab, display the topic on the right side of any help window.
> 2. Click on the Favorites tab. You should see the topic name in the **CURRENT TOPIC** field at the bottom, on the left side of the window, as illustrated above in Figure 1-7.
> 3. Click the **ADD** button.

There are five buttons at the top of the help window, as shown in Figure 1-8. The toolbar buttons are explained below.

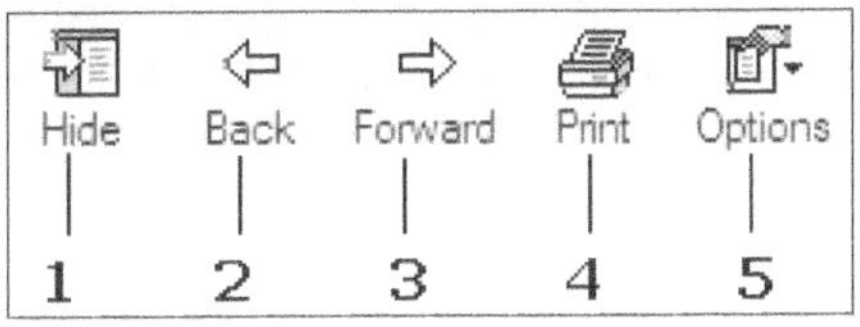

Figure 1-8 Help toolbar buttons

① The **HIDE/SHOW** button will close the left side of the help window, as shown in Figure 1-9. Compare this to the window shown earlier in Figure 1-7. To restore the left side of the window, click the **SHOW** button shown in Figure 1-9.

② The **BACK** button displays the previous topic that you viewed. This option is only available after you have displayed at least two help topics.

③ The **FORWARD** button works similar to the Back button. The Forward button will also display topics that you have already viewed.

④ The **PRINT** button will print the help topic that is displayed.

⑤ The **OPTIONS** button provides ways to customize the help window. The options are shown in Figure 1-10. The **SEARCH HIGHLIGHT** option turns the keyword highlighting shown in Figure 1-9, on and off.

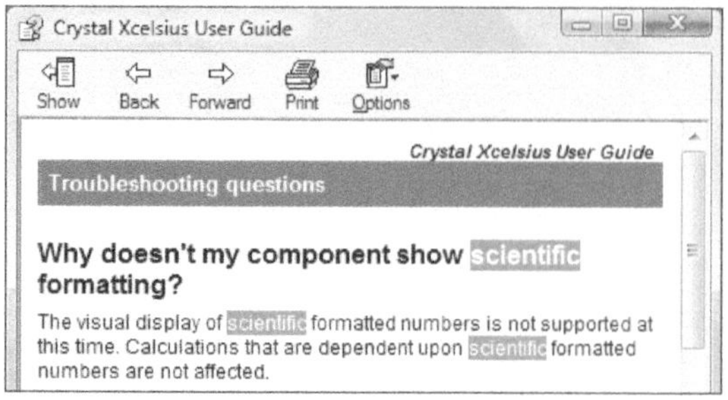

Figure 1-9 Left side of the help window hidden

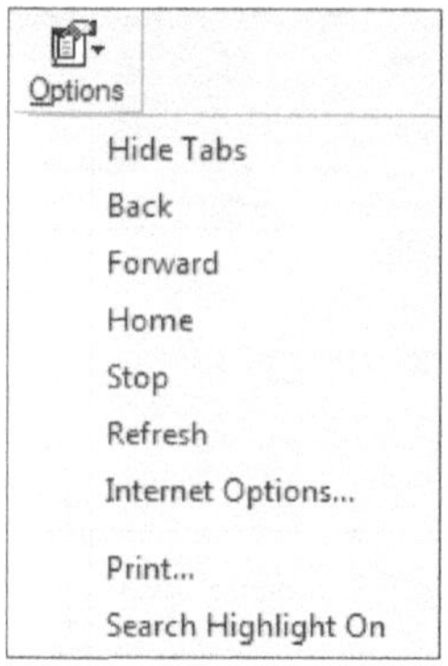

Figure 1-10 Help customization options

Crystal Xcelsius Forums

If you have a question about Crystal Xcelsius you can post a message in one of the forums listed below. This is the best place to go for help if you are having trouble installing the software or have a question on how to use an option. If you do not already have an account, you will be prompted to create one. The account is free.

The questions are answered by other users and forum moderators. Before posting your question, you should search the forum because the answer to your question may already be there. The two forums that I visit are listed below.

SAP Xcelsius forum www.sdn.sap.com/irg/sdn/forums
Scroll down to the Crystal Reports and Xcelsius section, then click on the Xcelsius link.

Business Objects Board www.forumtopics.com/busobj/

If you plan to participate in forums, in my opinion, you should not use your primary email address. Most people that use their primary email address in online public places, like a forum, suddenly wind up with more spam then they can handle after they join. My advice is to set up a free email account and use that email account to post messages in forums and newsgroups. If your ISP offers multiple email accounts, you can create another account under your primary account and use that one. In their defense though, it appears that SAP (The parent company of Business Objects) has gone to greater lengths to protect our privacy, then a lot of other companies that host forums have.

Exercise 1.2: Create A Folder For Your Files

You will use several spreadsheets as the basis for the models and dashboards that you will create in this book. Some of these spreadsheets are ones that I created for this book and others are the spreadsheets for the sample dashboards that come with Crystal Xcelsius.

All of the files that I created start with cx_. All of the files that you need for this book are in a zip file named cx45.zip. I did this to make it easier for you to have all of the files needed for this book in one place, but you can use the spreadsheet files for the sample dashboards, from the folder that they are already in, on your hard drive, if you want. In addition to the spreadsheets, there are model files that I created and image files that you will need to complete the exercises. Some of the files that are in the zip file are used to demonstrate a concept.

Throughout the book I will refer to the folder that you will create in this exercise as "Your folder". You will create the folder at the root of the C drive to store the files that you download, as well as, the models and dashboards that you create.

To obtain the files send an email to cx45@tolanapublishing.com. If you do not receive an email in a few minutes with the subject line Crystal Xcelsius 4.5 Files, check the spam folder in your email software.

1. Open Windows Explorer, then click on the C drive or the primary drive that you save files on.

2. File ⇒ New ⇒ Folder.

3. Type `Xcelsius Book` as the folder name, then press Enter.

4. Go to the web page listed in the email that you received and download the zip file into the folder that you just created.

5. In Windows Explorer, click on the folder that you just created.

   Right-click on the zip file and select **EXTRACT TO HERE**, as illustrated in Figure 1-11.

   The files will be copied to your folder.

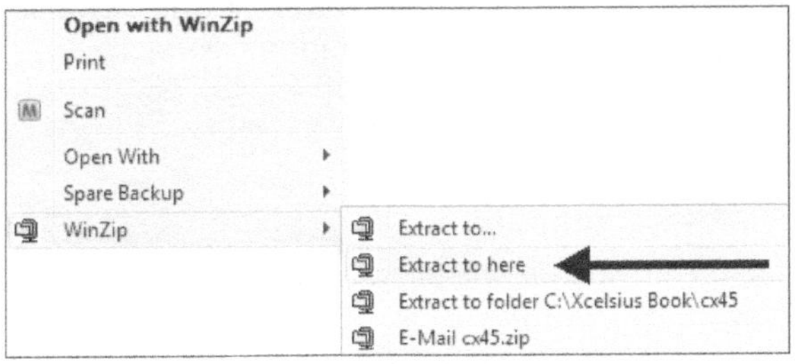

Figure 1-11 How to extract the files

File Naming Conventions

Like many things in life, there are rules that you have to follow. Below are the rules for the files that you will create.

① The file name cannot contain any of the following characters:
~ ! @ # $ % ^ & * ( ) + { } | : " < > ? ` - = [ ] \ ; ' , . /

② The file name can have a combination of letters, numbers and the under score. The underscore is often used in place of a space in the file name.

As you read earlier, the files that I created for this book have the underscore as part of the file name instead of spaces. I acquired this habit in my former life as a programmer. Many IT people still follow this practice today, especially for any file that will be accessed on the Internet.

The models and dashboards that you create will be saved with prefix "My". That way they will all be grouped together in the folder, so that you will know which files you created.

Okay Already, Can I See What Crystal Xcelsius Can Do With Spreadsheet Data?

Given all of the types of databases, enterprise tools and reporting packages that are available, you have to admit that it is interesting that Excel is still being used as much as it is. I am by no means down playing Excel, just the opposite. I think that it is fantastic that for over 20 years Excel is still growing, holding its own and still going strong.

Even better that Crystal Xcelsius came along and will take data from an Excel spreadsheet and turn it into something visually appealing to look at and use. Excel is a widely used software application. If you do not believe me, search the book section of Amazon's web site for books on Excel. Crystal Xcelsius is a great boost to business intelligence analysis because it takes what many call "boring data" and transforms the data into an interactive dashboard, that can display the data in summary format, as well as, display the underlying detail data.

Usually, one PowerPoint slide would be created for each region shown in Figure 1-12, especially if you also needed to display a chart and show the detailed data for each region. Using Crystal Xcelsius, all of that data including the detail data and chart, can easily be incorporated into one dashboard.

If you wanted to go a step further, the dashboard could be exported to PowerPoint. In PowerPoint, the dashboard would only be one slide in the presentation.

	A	B	C
1	Actual Sales vs Projected		
2			
3		Last Years Actual Sales	Projected Sales
4			
5	North	$147,000	$150,000
6	South	$472,000	$375,000
7	East	$515,000	$500,000
8	West	$280,000	$405,000
9			
10		Current Actual Sales	Projected Sales
11			
12	North	$123,000	$150,000
13	South	$424,000	$400,000
14	East	$394,000	$375,000
15	West	$210,000	$225,000

Figure 1-12 Spreadsheet data

If you have ever come close to not wanting to create a PowerPoint presentation because of the large amount of spreadsheet data and charts that need to be placed in a format that is easy to use and understand, help is here. With Crystal Xcelsius and this book, those days are just about over because this software will turn the static spreadsheet data into an interactive visual presentation that people will want to look at and use.

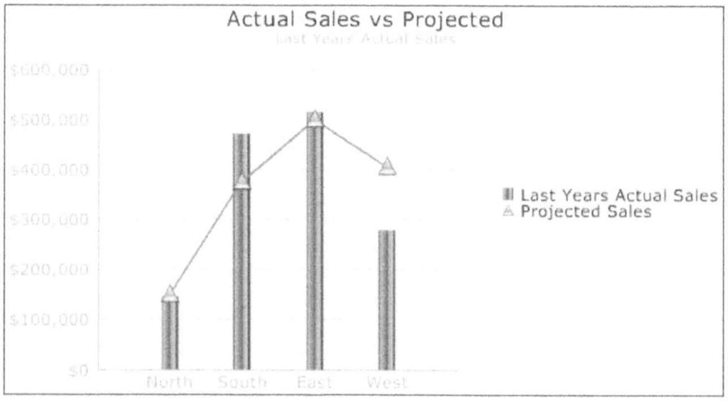

Figure 1-13 Dashboard created from the data shown in Figure 1-12

You can take some of the data in the spreadsheet and create a visualization like the one shown above in Figure 1-13. You could also create a chart for the current and projected sales, create a menu with options to select the charts, all in one dashboard.

In each lesson, you will learn about different types of components that are used to create dashboards. I understand how easy it is to want to incorporate as many features as possible. That's fine as long as they are well placed and easy to understand. I hope that you keep in mind that the majority of dashboards that you create will be used to make business decisions.

Terms That You Need To Understand

Before you go any further, there are some terms that you need to understand to get a better idea of how dashboards can aid in the decision making process, display trends and much more. You will also start to understand how powerful Crystal Xcelsius is. There are terms that you may have heard before, but are not exactly sure what they mean: Business Intelligence, Metrics, Key Performance Indicators, What-If Analysis, Components, Visual Model and Dashboard. The goal of this section is to explain the terms and their relationship to Crystal Xcelsius.

Business Intelligence is often called BI for short. Business intelligence is the process of analyzing data, raw or otherwise and converting the analysis into knowledge (intelligence). Business intelligence, in the broad sense, is a collection of technology and applications that are used to gather, store, access and analyze data, often in an enterprise environment. This process is usually used to make business decisions or track trends and changes. The typical business intelligence uses include querying, reporting, forecasting, data mining and statistical analysis.

Some of the goals of business intelligence analysis include being able to easily find new business opportunities, making decisions on existing processes, looking for ways to save money and having the ability to recognize where improvement is needed. Crystal Xcelsius presents the data in a visual format. While not the traditional type of report, the dashboards that are created in Crystal Xcelsius produce reports on a higher and more interactive level than what can be created in Excel. There are entire books on the Business Intelligence practices and techniques.

Metric A metric is one piece of data. Examples are the number of cars made in a month or quarterly sales per region. These values can be manually entered into a spreadsheet or a formula can be created to calculate the metric.

Key Performance Indicators are often called KPI's for short. KPI's are a way to measure the performance of a process. The goal of KPI is to uncover performance that is not in the normal, acceptable range. Many dashboards are created around this concept because key performance indicators are one tool used to make business decisions, strategic or otherwise.

For example, during the course of a month, a car manufacturing plant may produce 10,000 cars. Each car needs a steering wheel. On a dashboard that monitors the quantity of steering wheels and other car parts on hand, one can monitor if the quantity of a product drops below the number of cars produced on any given day. If the quantity of steering wheels drop below the required on hand amount, the process of producing cars slows down.

The lack of a sufficient number of steering wheels indicates that at least one of the following is true: Enough steering wheels are not being ordered, the production of cars was increased without enough notice, the delivery time is too long, the product is not being ordered soon enough or something else. Whatever the reason, the end result is the same, the car manufacturer loses revenue because production stops or at least slows down. Car dealers do not get the cars on time, so they can potentially lose sales. Should this happen, the KPI's need to be reviewed and a business decision has to be made that will prevent a shortage or car parts going forward.

Another way to explain KPI is that it is a metric that is tied to a target. This target can be a single value or a range of values. In the example above, the target (10,000 cars a month) is a single value. The metric is the current number of cars that have been produced. This metric can be presented by day or by week. On the 24th of the month, the metric value should be larger than the metric value for the fifth of the month because more cars should have been produced later in the month then in the first week.

What-If Analysis This type of analysis is used to see how changing the value in one field effects other values that are being used in the analysis. The example most used to explain what-if analysis is how changing the interest rate changes the monthly mortgage payment. In this example, the what-if value, if you will, is the interest rate. When the interest rate is changed, the monthly mortgage payment is automatically recalculated to show the new mortgage payment.

If you have used Excel for a while, you know that one of its strong points is being able to create what-if analysis scenarios. One of the ways that this is accomplished in Excel is through the use of Pivot Tables. The functionality in Crystal Xcelsius will let you take what-if analysis to a completely different level and allow you to make changes to the what-if fields in the dashboard, in real-time. This means that during a presentation, you will have the ability to demonstrate what-if this or what-if that, without having to modify the Excel spreadsheet. For many, just being able to turn the what-if analysis functionality into a visual presentation is worth the price of Crystal Xcelsius.

Components are objects like gauges, maps, charts and toggle buttons that are used in Crystal Xcelsius to add interactive functionality to dashboards. Some components are used to display data, while other components are used to select data or used to get data from the user at run time.

Visual Model This is the working version file of what will become the dashboard when the model is compiled and published. This is the file that you import the spreadsheet data into, as well as, add components to. Visual models, or models, as I refer to them, make the raw spreadsheet data shown earlier in Figure 1-12, easier to understand. In Crystal Xcelsius, you will spend almost all of your time working with visual model files. In addition to designing the dashboard layout, the model can be used for testing, before the actual dashboard is created and distributed.

What Is A Dashboard?

More than likely, if you have read any literature on Crystal Xcelsius, it had the word "Dashboard" in it. In general, a dashboard is a visual or graphical representation of the data behind a performance indicator. In Crystal Xcelsius, a dashboard is the finished product. Okay, I know what you are asking. You are asking "What is the finished product?" The finished product is the output of the **VISUAL MODEL**, which contains interactive objects like menus, sliders, charts and the data from the spreadsheet that these components represent.

The finished product is a standalone file that can be distributed and used by people, which does not require Crystal Xcelsius or Excel to be installed on their computer.

Unlike scorecards (2), dashboards are very closely tied to providing data (usually operational) in a visual format that is easy for the user to understand. From a high level perspective, a dashboard is one tool used to determine whether or not a business strategy is meeting expectations.

(2) The primary function of a **SCORECARD** is to aid in keeping the company (or a department) on track by monitoring the progress of KPI's that have been determined as necessary to meet a business objective. To me, scorecards are a type of project plan, which contains a list of tasks that must be completed, tested and implemented before the project can be considered complete.

Sample Dashboards

Figures 1-14 to 1-16 show some of the sample dashboards that come with Crystal Xcelsius.

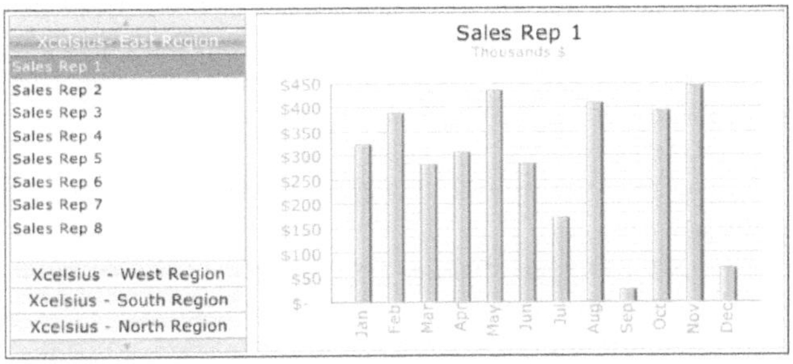

Figure 1-14 Accordion Menu dashboard

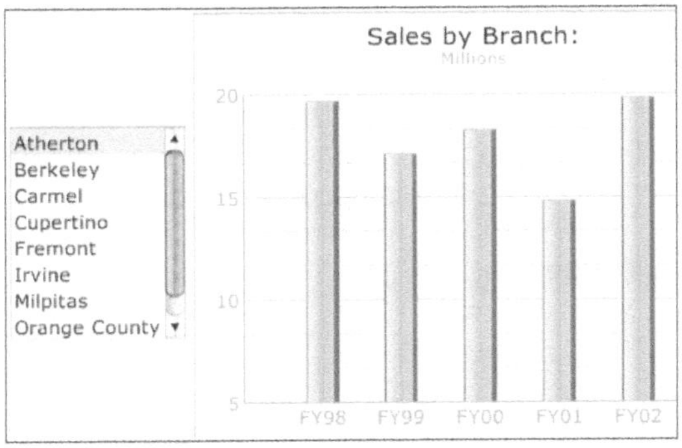

Figure 1-15 List Box dashboard

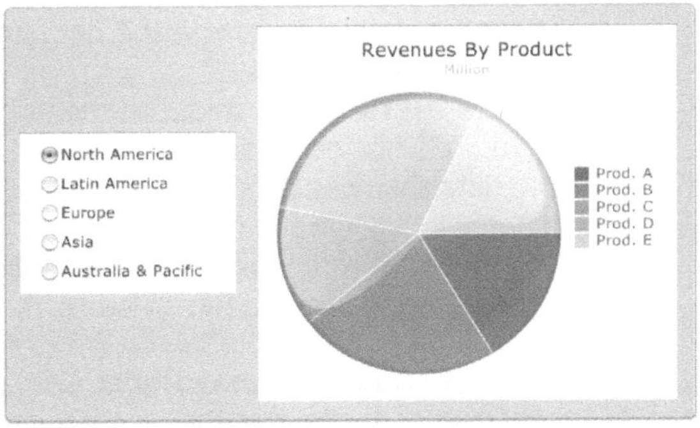

Figure 1-16 Status List dashboard

How Crystal Xcelsius Does What It Does

The prior sections have explained what Crystal Xcelsius is and what it is capable of doing. Hopefully, you are somewhat excited about using Crystal Xcelsius to create dashboards. I suspect though, that you are a bit curious about how Crystal Xcelsius does what it does, especially because you can create a dashboard for the most part, using point and click techniques. Translated, that means very little typing is required to use Crystal Xcelsius.

What I find interesting is that for all that this software can incorporate in a dashboard, the file size of a dashboard is very small. The three main tasks that are needed to create a dashboard are explained below.

① **IMPORT THE DATA** from an Excel (**.XLS**) spreadsheet into a Crystal Xcelsius model. A model can only use one spreadsheet. If the data that you want to use to create the dashboard is in another format, like a database or word processing document, you will have to export the data to an Excel spreadsheet.

Yes, I know that it is often reported that Crystal Xcelsius only uses data created in Excel spreadsheets, but trust me, as a lot of companies have data in Enterprise databases, they could not use Crystal Xcelsius if they could not access and use some of their core data that is in other formats, relatively easy.

As long as you can import data from another source into Excel, you can use the data in Crystal Xcelsius. Crystal Xcelsius can use data that is pulled into Excel from an XML file format that Excel can recognize. Using XML is beyond the scope of this book. If you need to use enterprise data and cannot or do not want to set up an XML file to import the data into Excel, you can use a tool like Microsoft Query. You can also look into the Workgroup edition of Crystal Xcelsius 4.5 or upgrade to one of the Enterprise editions of Xcelsius 2008, which is available now.

When the spreadsheet data is imported into the model, the import process creates a copy of the Excel spreadsheet and uses the copy in the model. The cell formatting and formulas in the spreadsheet are also imported. Nothing is changed in the original spreadsheet. If data is changed in the original spreadsheet, it is not picked up automatically by the model. The spreadsheet would have to be re-imported, so that the changes would be incorporated in the dashboard. This is how the dashboard can function as a stand alone file. Having said that, a dashboard can be configured to use live data at run time, through XML or the Workgroup edition. The closest solution to using live data is to refresh the data and publish the model again.

② **CREATE THE MODEL** by selecting the appropriate components for the data. The model is your dashboard in design mode. This is the file used to add and link components to the data that was imported. The model is also the file that is used to edit and test what will become the finished product (the dashboard). If you need to change the dashboard or re-import data, the model is the file that you use. The dashboard file cannot be modified. It has to be recreated after you make changes to the model file.

③ **COMPILE AND PUBLISH THE MODEL** Compile the model for testing and previewing purposes to make sure that it produces the expected outcomes. The compiled file makes sure that the dashboard can be run on any computer, regardless of the computers operating system. Publishing the model is how the dashboard file is created. Publishing is the process of exporting the model file, into a stand alone file that does not require having Crystal Xcelsius installed to run the dashboard. As you will learn, there are several output formats that you can select from. Keep in mind that Crystal Xcelsius is a Windows-based product, which means that some of the file output options are Windows specific, like Word and Excel.

Backing Up Your Work

I cannot stress how important it is to back up your work frequently. Doing so will save you frustration in the event an electrical power failure occurs and you are using a desktop computer or if your computer has a hardware failure. If you are using a laptop, an electrical power failure may not be as critical because the battery in the laptop should automatically start working. The majority of times that you lose work, it cannot be recovered or if it can, it may cost you a few hundred dollars or more to recover it. Never mind the stress and aggravation.

If you aren't already, you should be saving a copy of your work to an external device like an external hard drive, USB drive, CD or DVD. Windows has a backup utility that you can use. Even better then creating a backup copy of your files is to create an image of the entire hard drive. For more information on images, see www.tolana.com/tips/image.html. In the workplace, you can save a copy of your files to a network drive. I tell my students to back up their work and it never fails that a student loses some, if not all of their work. Don't say that I didn't warn you <smile>.

My Wish List

While Crystal Xcelsius provides a lot of features and bang for the buck, there are some things that I wish were fixed or improved. You can view my wish list by clicking on the wish list link on the homepage for this book on www.tolanapublishing.com.

GETTING STARTED WITH CRYSTAL XCELSIUS

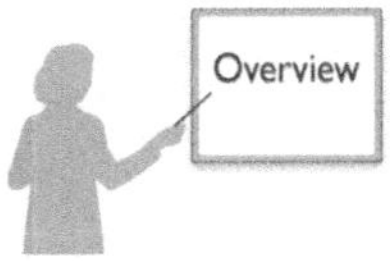

In this lesson you will learn your way around Crystal Xcelsius by learning about the following:

- ☑ The workspace
- ☑ The canvas
- ☑ The menu
- ☑ The toolbar
- ☑ Components Explorer
- ☑ Object Browser
- ☑ Formatting options
- ☑ Selecting components

LESSON 2

Crystal Xcelsius Workspace

When you open Crystal Xcelsius you will see the workspace shown in Figure 2-1. This is where you create the model that will become the dashboard.

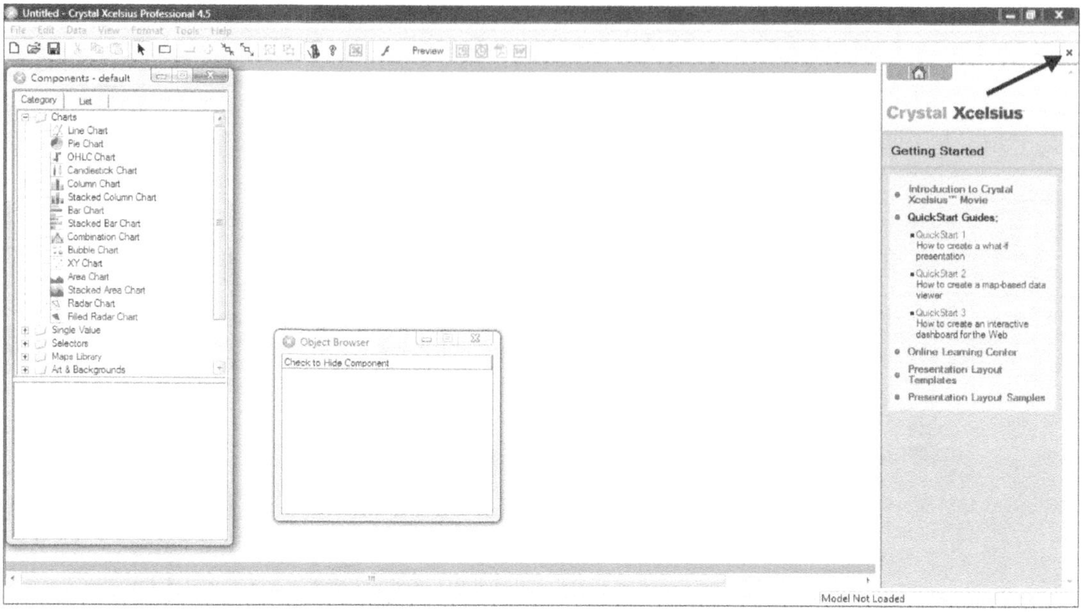

Figure 2-1 Crystal Xcelsius Workspace

By default, the Getting Started Window, Components and Object Browser dialog boxes are opened automatically, as shown above. To close the Getting Started window, click on the X at the top of the window, as illustrated above, in the upper right corner of Figure 2-1.

If you see the dialog box shown in Figure 2-2, you have to decide how you want to close the Getting Started Window.

The second option will keep the Getting Started Window from opening automatically every time that you open Crystal Xcelsius.

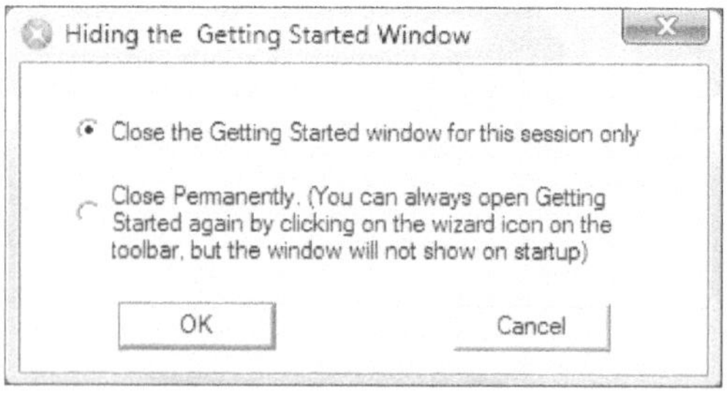

Figure 2-2 Hiding the Getting Started Window dialog box

The Canvas

The white space in the middle of the Xcelsius workspace is called the **CANVAS**. This is where you place the components, backgrounds and other objects needed to build the model for the dashboard.

Adding A Component To The Canvas

There are two ways to add a component to the canvas as discussed below.

① Drag the component from the Components dialog box and place it on the canvas.
② Click on the component in the Components dialog box, then click on the canvas.

Canvas Size

The canvas that you saw earlier in Figure 2-1 is the default canvas size. You can change the canvas size at any time. You can change it before you start creating the model, when you are finished creating the model or anytime in between. I tend to leave the canvas size large until I am finished creating and testing the model. [See Lesson 9, Resize The Canvas]

Crystal Xcelsius Menu

Many of the options on the menus are the same as options in spreadsheet or word processing software. The options explained below in Tables 2-1 to 2-6 are the options on each menu that are either specific to Crystal Xcelsius or provide different functionality then what you may expect.

File Menu Options

The options on the File menu in addition to opening models are used to create models, view the sample dashboards that come with Crystal Xcelsius, update the data for dashboards and compile the model to create a dashboard.

Menu Option	Description
New From Template	Opens the dialog box shown in Figure 2-3. You can select a template to use as the basis for the dashboard that you want to create. To me, using templates is only helpful if you have data that fits the components used in the template. What I do find them helpful for is getting ideas for my own dashboard layouts.
Samples	Opens the dialog box shown in Figure 2-4. The options in the **ITEMS** list are the sample dashboards that come with Crystal Xcelsius.
Document Properties	Opens the dialog box shown in Figure 2-5. The options on this dialog box are used to change the size of the canvas. The options in the **PRESET SIZE** drop-down list are different display sizes. You can also enter any information about the model that you think is helpful or important in the **DESCRIPTION** field.

Table 2-1 File menu options explained

Menu Option	Description
Font	Used to change the fonts that the components use. Figure 2-6 shows the font options. The default font is Verdana. This is where you can change the default font. Clicking the **UNICODE FONT OPTIONS** button opens the dialog box shown in Figure 2-7. The options on this dialog box are explained below. The **USE NON-EMBEDDED FONTS** option allows any font to be used. This option is used to select fonts for the components. Selecting this option means that all of the fonts installed on your computer will be available on the Appearance tab of the Properties dialog box. The downside is that if the font that you select is not on the computer that is running the dashboard, the dashboard will probably not have the look that you intended, because the fonts will be substituted with fonts installed on the computer that the dashboard is being run from. This means that the text on the dashboard can vary from computer to computer. **USE EMBEDDED FONTS** is the default option even though it increases the file size and load time of the dashboard. The file size is increased because a copy of the True Type fonts that are used in the model are placed in the SWF file. The benefit of selecting this option is that the fonts display properly in the dashboard whether or not the computer that the dashboard is run from has the fonts installed that you used.
Export Settings	Opens the dialog box shown in Figure 2-8. The options shown at the top of the figure are used to select how the data for the model will be updated. ① **USE CURRENT EXCEL DATA** This is the default option. It will use the same spreadsheet that was originally used to create the model, when the data in the model is updated. ② **USE ANOTHER FILE** This option is used to select a spreadsheet, other then the one that was used when the model was first created to use as the data source for the model when the data is updated.
Export Preview	Compiles the model, creates a temporary SWF file and displays the model in your web browser. This is one way that you can test the model.
Export	Displays the submenu shown in Figure 2-9. Each option compiles and exports (publishes) the model to a different file format. For example, if you select the Adobe PDF option, the model will be saved in a PDF file, which is the dashboard file that you would distribute.
Snapshot	Exports the data that is currently displayed in the model. This is a subset of the data that was imported into the model. I did not find this option to work as intended.

Table 2-1 File menu options explained (Continued)

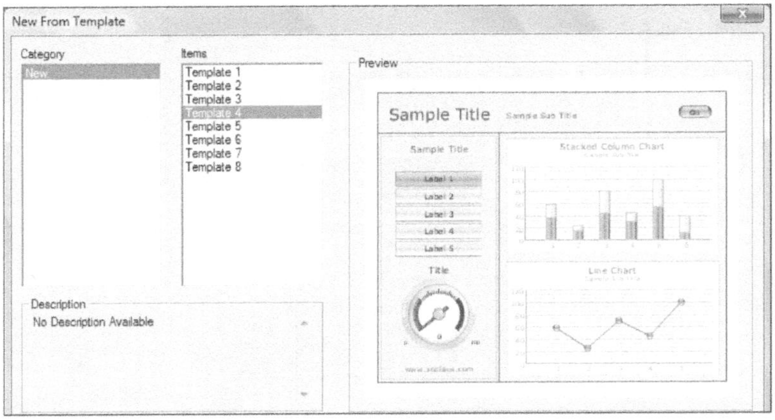

Figure 2-3 New From Template dialog box

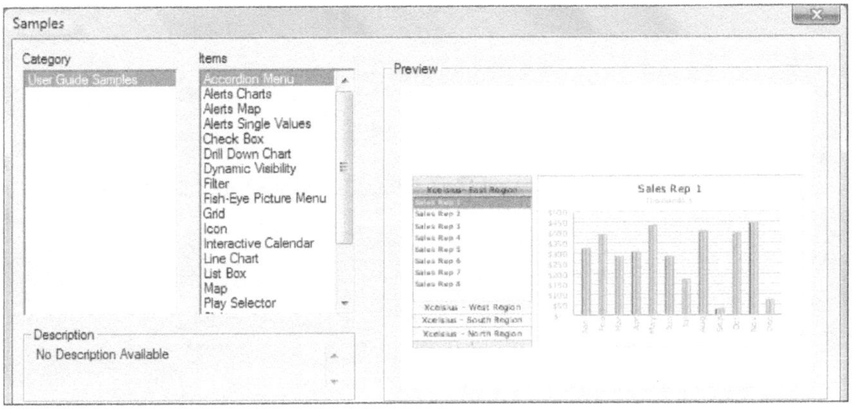

Figure 2-4 Samples dialog box

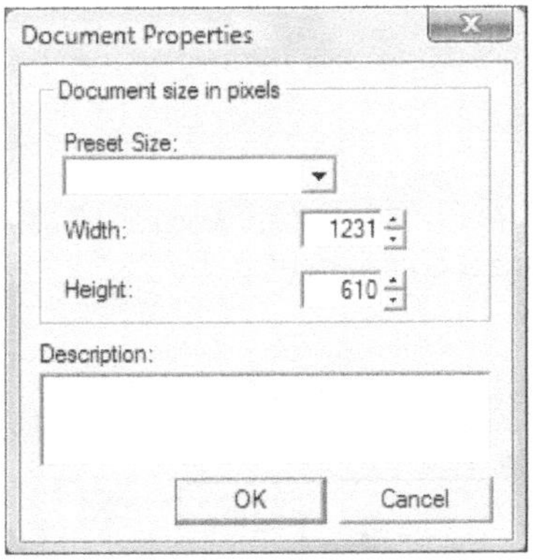

Figure 2-5 Document Properties dialog box

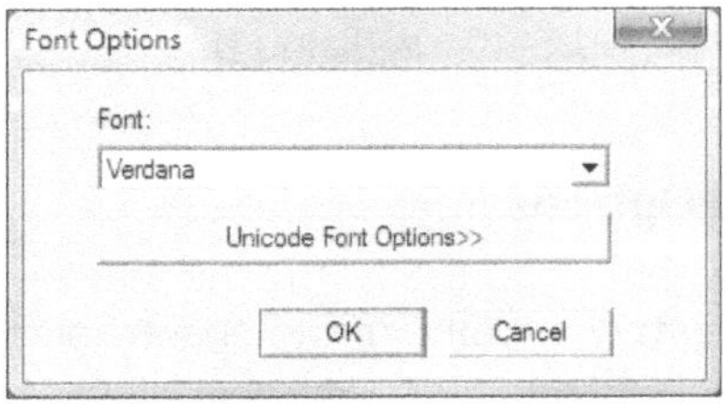

Figure 2-6 Font Options dialog box

> Not all components support non-embedded fonts.

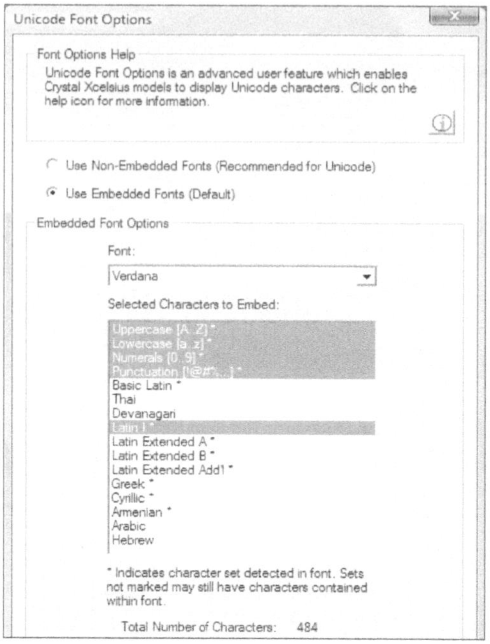

Figure 2-7 Unicode Font Options dialog box

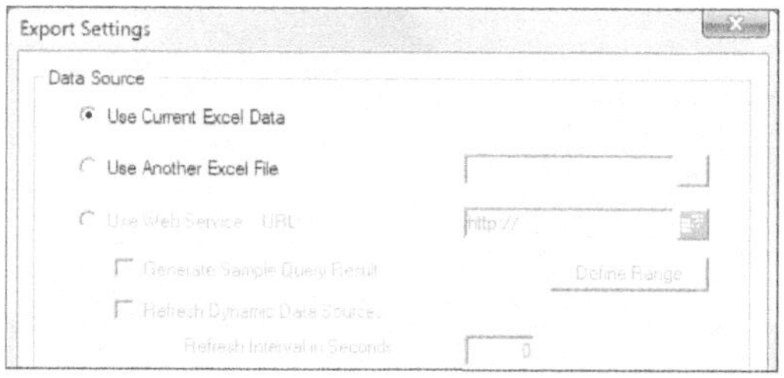

Figure 2-8 Export Settings dialog box

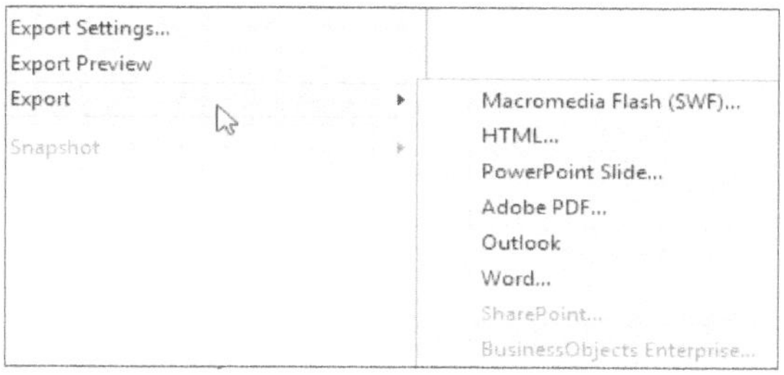

Figure 2-9 Export submenu options

Edit Menu Options

Many of the options on the Edit menu may be familiar, especially if you have used word processing software. Some of the options on the Edit menu require a component to be selected before the menu option is available.

Menu Option	Description
Select All	Selects all of the components on the model that are not hidden.
Properties	Opens the Properties dialog box. Some of the options on this dialog box change, based on the component that was selected before opening the dialog box. As you will see, starting in Lesson 3, you will spend a lot of time using this dialog box.

Table 2-2 Edit menu options explained

Data Menu Options

The options on the Data menu allow you to work with the spreadsheet data.

Menu Option	Description
Import Model	Adds the data from an Excel spreadsheet to the model.
Export Model	Exports a copy of the Excel spreadsheet that was used to create the dashboard. It does not matter whether or not the model was created on your computer or another computer, because the data is part of the model.
Replace Data Selection	This option is used to update the value in a single cell or some cells in the spreadsheet that was imported into the model, while leaving the data in other cells in the model unchanged. Figure 2-10 shows the dialog box used to configure data that will be replaced. The options on this dialog box will check a spreadsheet and bring the values from it, into the model.
XML Map Options	This option uses the Excel 2003 XML Map functionality to connect to XML compliant databases. This allows the data to be updated on the fly when the dashboard is run, without having to export the model each time the data changes.
Maximum Rows	The option on the dialog box shown in Figure 2-11 is used to select the maximum number of rows of data that will be bound to the components in the model. If the model has a lot of components that are bound to 700 rows of data for example, this option would need to be increased. Business Objects recommends 512 rows or less per tab, which is the default. The larger the number, the longer it will take for the model to open. If more than 512 rows of data are bound, you may see a warning message.

Table 2-3 Data menu options explained

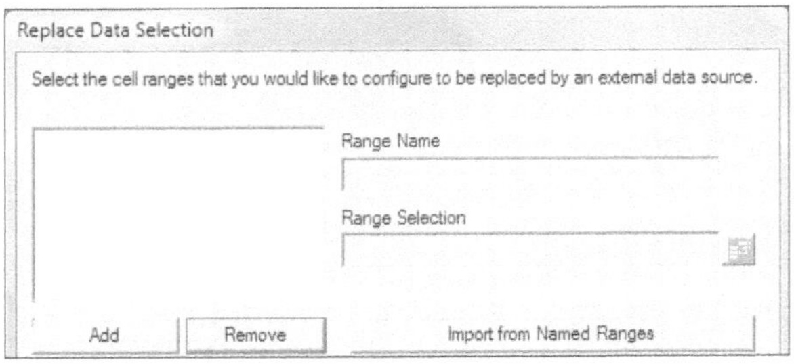

Figure 2-10 Replace Data Selection dialog box

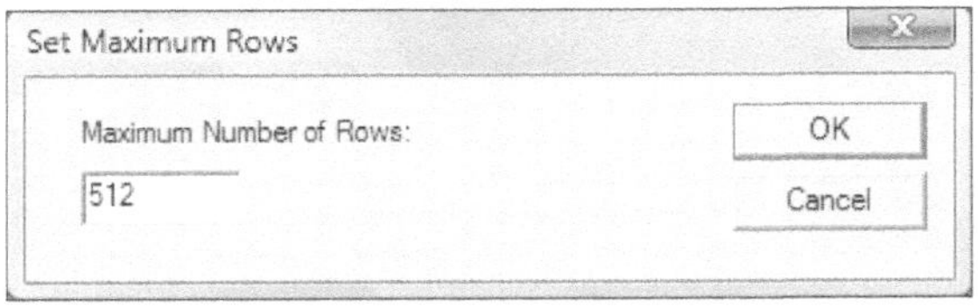

Figure 2-11 Set Maximum Rows dialog box

> At first I found the Maximum Rows option confusing. I thought that it was the maximum number of rows of data in a spreadsheet that could be imported into the model. After reading the messages in the forum, I discovered that I was not the only one that thought this.

View Menu Options

The options on the View menu are used to select many of the tools in Crystal Xcelsius.

Menu Option	Description
Grid	Provides a way to align objects on the canvas. (1)
Components	Opens the Components Explorer dialog box. (1)
Components Preview	This option is used to view or test the model.
Object Browser Window	Opens the Object Browser Window. (1)
Change Style	Opens the Global Styles dialog box. The options are used to change the default appearance of components. There are several predefined styles that you can select. There are also options on this dialog box to change text labels, buttons and backgrounds. [See Lesson 12, Using Global Styles]
Change Skin	Opens the Skins dialog box, which is used to select a predefined color scheme for Crystal Xcelsius. [See Lesson 12, Using Skins]
Switch To/Retry Dialog	Selecting this option will toggle the Switch To/Retry dialog box shown in Figure 2-12, off and on. This dialog box appears in Crystal Xcelsius, when Excel is busy. Clearing this option will cause Crystal Xcelsius to wait for Excel to not be busy, before it will continue processing data. Clearing this option will cause the "**EXCEL IS BUSY**" dialog box to appear. (2)

Table 2-4 View menu options explained

(1) You will learn more about this option later in this lesson.

(2) I had this error message on my Windows XP laptop and Excel was not running. If you get this error message, open the Task Manager in Windows by pressing the CTRL + ALT + DEL keys, while Crystal Xcelsius is open. On the Applications tab, look for Excel, as shown in Figure 2-13. If it's there, select it, then click the End Task button. On the Processes tab, look for the Excel.exe, as shown in Figure 2-14. Select it, then click the End Process button. If you do not see Excel on either of these tabs, you have the same problem I did, that I could not resolve or get a resolution to. My only saving grace is that I have two laptops.

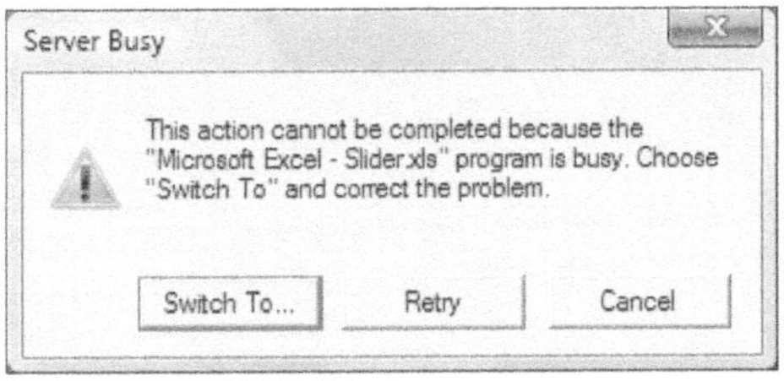

Figure 2-12 Switch To/Retry dialog box

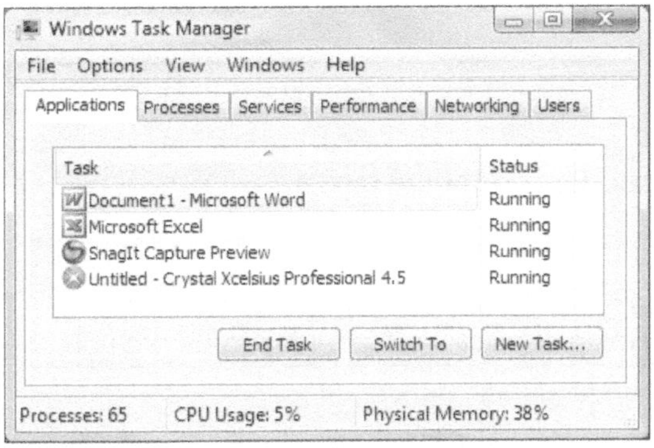

Figure 2-13 Applications tab on the Task Manager dialog box

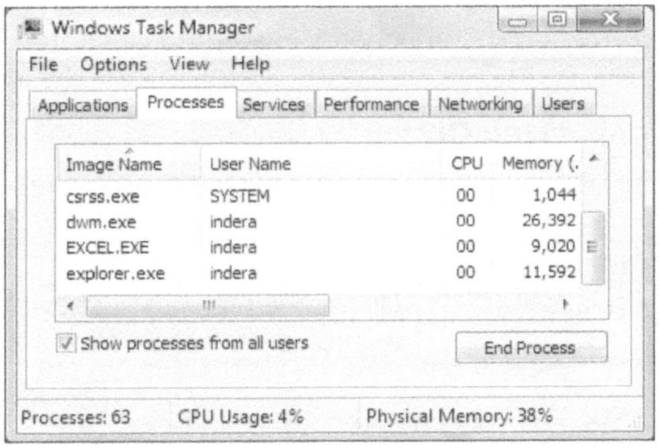

Figure 2-14 Processes tab on the Task Manager dialog box

Format Menu Options

The options on the Format menu are used to modify the components in the model, including changing the size of the components. The first four options on this menu are explained later in this lesson.

Menu Option	Description
Bring To Front	Moves the selected component(s) to the top layer. (3)
Send To Back	Moves the selected component(s) to the bottom layer. (3)
Bring Forward	Moves the selected component(s) up one layer. (3)
Send Back	Moves the selected component(s) back one layer. (3)
Group	Places the selected components in a folder in the Object Browser, as illustrated in Figure 2-15. This may make finding components that you need to work with easier to find, if the model has a lot of components.
Ungroup	Removes the group option from components in the selected group.

Table 2-5 Format menu options explained

(3) Layers are invisible and automatically created when components are stacked on top of each other. This option is used to change the components position in the stack.

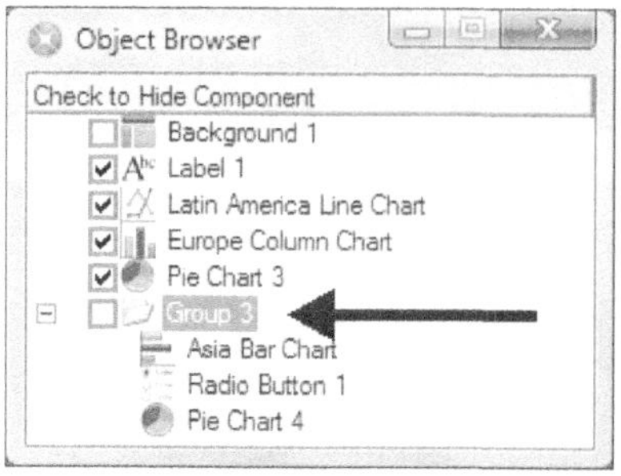

Figure 2-15 Components in a group illustrated

Tools Menu Option

The option on the Tools menu is used to create a backup copy of the model.

Menu Option	Description
Options	Opens the dialog box shown in Figure 2-16. Selecting the **ALWAYS CREATE BACKUP COPY** option allows a backup copy of the model file to be created.

Table 2-6 Tools menu option explained

Figure 2-16 Options dialog box

Crystal Xcelsius Toolbar

The toolbar shown in Figure 2-17 contains buttons for the menu options that you will probably use the most. The buttons on the toolbar are a subset of the menu options. Table 2-7 explains the buttons on the toolbar.

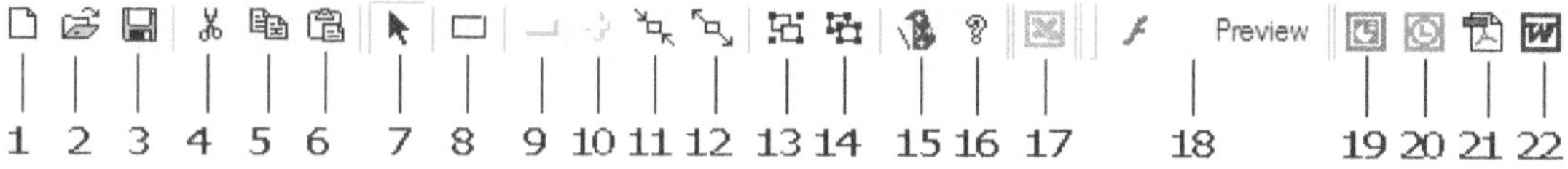

Figure 2-17 Crystal Xcelsius toolbar

Button	Purpose
1. New	Opens a blank canvas to create a new model.
2. Open	Opens an existing model.
3. Save	Saves the open model. If the model has not been saved before, you will be prompted to provide a file name.
4. Cut	Deletes the selected component(s).
5. Copy	Copies the selected component(s) and places them in the Windows clipboard.
6. Paste	Places the components in the clipboard into the model.
7. Selection Tool	Takes the focus to the selected component(s).
8. Component tool	Takes the focus to the Components dialog box.
9. Decrease canvas	Makes the canvas size smaller in increments.
10. Increase canvas	Makes the canvas size larger in increments.
11. Fit canvas to components	Resizes the canvas to the size of the components. Usually, this decreases the canvas size.
12. Fit canvas to window	Resizes the canvas to the size of the window. Usually, this increases the canvas size.
13. Group components	Places the selected components in a folder in the Object Browser, as shown earlier in Figure 2-15.
14. Ungroup components	Removes the group option from components in the selected group.
15. Show/Hide Quick Start Wizard	Opens or closes the Getting Started Window on the right side of the Crystal Xcelsius workspace, shown earlier in Figure 2-1.
16. Help	Opens the Help application.
17. Import Model	Adds the data from an Excel spreadsheet to the model that is open.
18. Enable Macromedia Flash (SWF) preview mode	Switches between the **PREVIEW MODE**, which is used for testing the model and the **DESIGN MODE**, which is used to create and modify the model.
19. Send to PowerPoint	Exports the open model to a PowerPoint slide. (4)
20. Send to Outlook	Creates a Flash file, then opens a new email window in Microsoft Outlook and attaches the Flash file to the email.
21. Send to Adobe Acrobat PDF	Exports the model to an Adobe PDF file. (4)
22. Send to Microsoft Word	Exports the model to a Microsoft Word document. (4)

Table 2-7 Crystal Xcelsius toolbar buttons explained

(4) You will not be prompted to enter a file name for the dashboard by selecting this toolbar button, like the File ⇒ Export menu option does. Selecting this button creates a temporary SWF file, that you can use for testing purposes. You should delete the temporary files after you have completed the dashboard.

Crystal Xcelsius File Types

Crystal Xcelsius produces two types of files. Each file type has a different extension, as discussed below.

① **.SWF TEMPORARY FILES** This is the model file in a compiled format.

② **.XLF FILES** This is the model file that is used to create the dashboard. XLF stands for **X**ce**L**sius **F**ile.

Temporary Files

Crystal Xcelsius creates a variety of temporary files when data is imported and when models are compiled and previewed. Unfortunately, Crystal Xcelsius does not delete these files when you close the software or turn the computer off like some software packages do. You will have to delete them from the Temp folder on your hard drive manually. In Windows Vista, the location of the temp folder is C:\Users\Your account\AppData\Local\Temp. The majority of temporary Crystal Xcelsius file names start with **IM#** and **GEN#**. The file names are in numbered sequential order, as shown in Figure 2-18. PowerPoint and .bmp temporary files that Crystal Xcelsius creates are also placed in this folder.

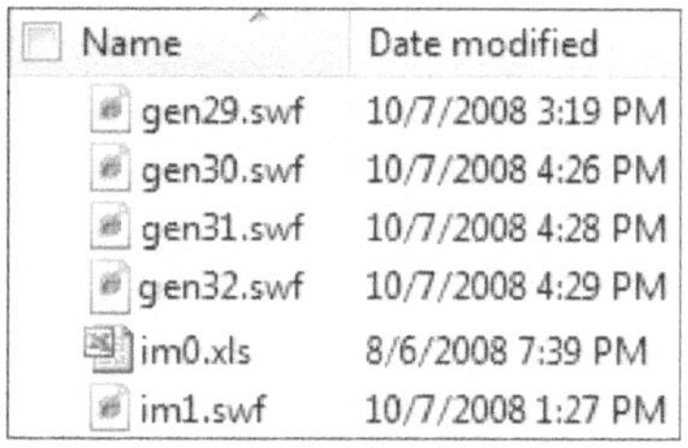

Figure 2-18 Crystal Xcelsius temporary files that can be deleted

Components Explorer

This is one of the most used tools in Crystal Xcelsius. This tool contains the objects, which are called components, that are added to the canvas to create a dashboard. As shown in Figure 2-19, the components are organized by category.

They are grouped by their functionality. Unlike the Getting Started Window, there is no option to prevent the Components Explorer window from automatically opening every time that Crystal Xcelsius is opened.

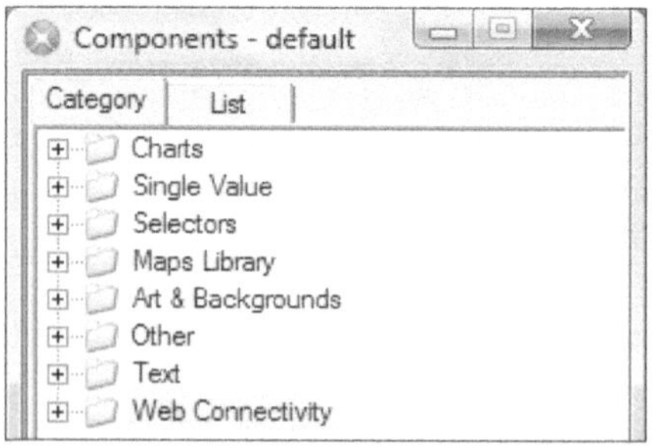

Figure 2-19 Category view of the Components Explorer window

If you do not want to memorize which folder a component is in, click on the **LIST** tab at the top of the Components dialog box. The components are listed in alphabetical order on this tab, as shown in Figure 2-20.

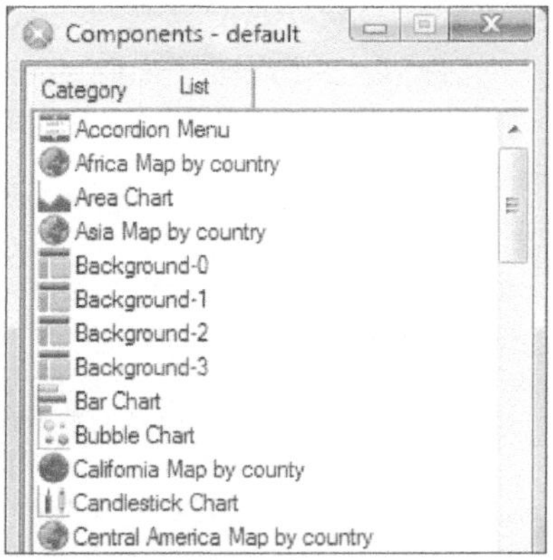

Figure 2-20 List view of the Components Explorer window

Object Browser

When you open Crystal Xcelsius, the Object Browser opens by default. The order that components are added to the canvas is the order that they appear in the Object Browser. The Object Browser window, shown earlier in Figure 2-15 is used to perform a variety of tasks like selecting, grouping, renaming or hiding components. There is no option to prevent the Object Browser window from automatically opening every time that Crystal Xcelsius is opened.

Selecting Components In The Object Browser

Below are two ways to select a component in the Object Browser.

① To **SELECT ONE COMPONENT** in the model, click on the icon or component name. You will see a frame around the component in the model.

② To **SELECT MORE THAN ONE COMPONENT**, click on the first component that you need, then press and hold down the CTRL key and click on the other components that you want to select.

If the components that you want to select are next to each other, you can click on the first component, press and hold down the SHIFT key, then click on the last component that you want to select. Usually, the reason to select multiple components is because you need to make the same change to all of the selected components, like making all charts the same size or deleting all of the labels.

Object Browser Features

Four of the more popular tasks that can be accomplished in the Object Browser are discussed below.

① **DELETING MULTIPLE COMPONENTS AT ONE TIME** Select all of the components that you want to delete, then press the Delete key or select Delete on the shortcut menu.

② **HIDING COMPONENTS** Clicking in the check box in front of a components name will hide the component on the canvas. This may be useful if there are a lot of components on the canvas and you need space to work.

③ **RENAMING COMPONENTS** Some of the component names that you saw earlier in Figure 2-15 are the default component names that are automatically assigned when a component is added to the canvas. This is the same name that appears at the top of the Properties dialog box. If the dashboard only has a few components, using the default component names may not be such a bad thing. If there are several of the same component in the model, it will be difficult to know which component is which. In that case, renaming the components is a good idea.

④ **GROUPING COMPONENTS** While all types of components can be grouped, the best reasons that I can think of to group components is because they are the same component type and you need to change their properties. When you make a property change, it is changed for all of the components in the group. The other reason is for setting up Dynamic Visibility functionality.

Another reason to group components is if you will have the need to move several components at the same time. An example of this would be a dashboard that has several toggle buttons. The buttons may currently be at the top of the dashboard, but they now need to be moved to the bottom of the dashboard. You do not have to select each toggle button component individually. You can select the group, which allows you to move all components in the group at the same time.

When components are grouped, they appear in a group folder in a tree structure, like the one shown earlier in Figure 2-15. As you can see, the default group name does not indicate anything about the components in the group. You can change the group name by following the steps in the Renaming Components section below.

> You do not have to group components in order to change an option for several components at one time. You can select all of the components on the canvas that you need to modify before opening the Properties dialog box.

Renaming Components

If there are several of the same type of component in the model, it will be confusing to know which component is which, if you use the Object Browser. One time that I can think of when renaming components is a good idea is when you need to place several of the same type of component on top of each other in the model. An example would be if you had three charts and based on a condition, a different chart would be displayed. If this is the case, without moving the components around on the canvas, you have no way to access the second or third component because they are covered up. To rename a component that is not marked as hidden in the Object Browser, follow the steps below.

1. Slowly click twice on the component name. You will see a border around the name.

   This will put the Name field in **EDIT MODE**, as illustrated in Figure 2-21.

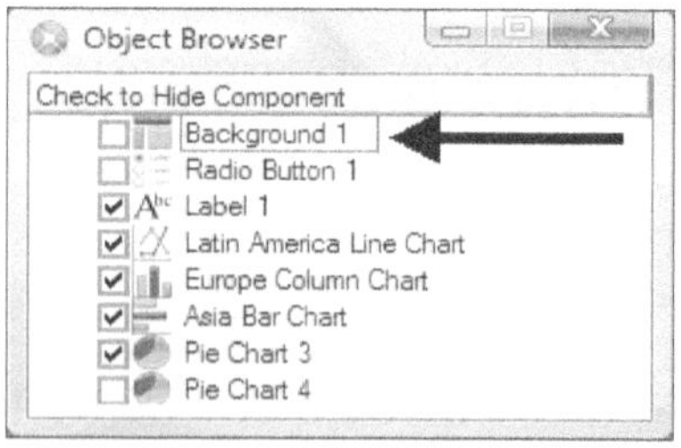

Figure 2-21 Component name in edit mode

2. Type in the new name, then press Enter.

Shortcut Menu

The shortcut menu shown in Figure 2-22 is the same shortcut menu that is available when you right-click on a component on the canvas.

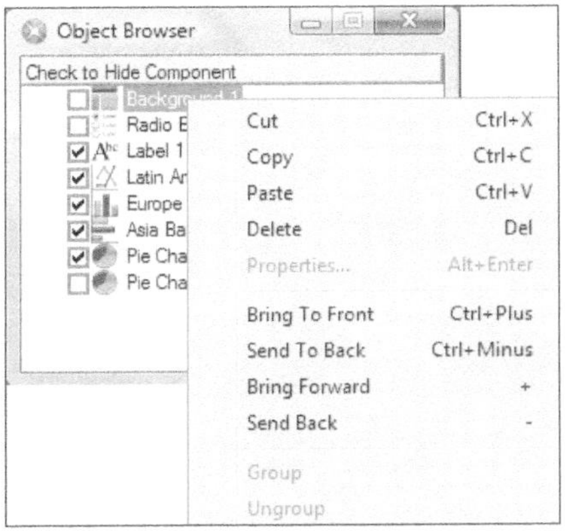

Figure 2-22 Shortcut menu

Sample Dashboards

The section discusses three examples of how dashboards can be used to take static data in a spreadsheet and turn it into interactive data in a dashboard. As you read earlier, Crystal Xcelsius allows you to create What-If analysis functionality.

Dashboard Example #1

Figure 2-23 shows a spreadsheet that has profit margin data for books. The Marketing department has a big book promotion project that they need to get approval for. The Vice President of Marketing asked to see the projected income if the number of copies sold increased by 500, 1,500 and 4,000 copies per region. Having this information would help determine if the book promotion project should be approved. Unless someone in the marketing department is a human calculator, they could not answer this question off the top of their head or while giving a presentation to pitch the promotion project.

If the data shown in Figure 2-23 was turned into the dashboard shown in Figure 2-24, it would be easy to answer what the projected income would be, based on the number of additional copies sold.

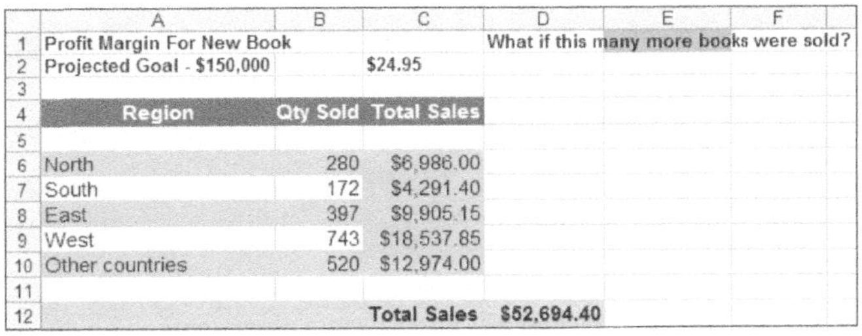

	A	B	C	D	E	F
1	Profit Margin For New Book			What if this many more books were sold?		
2	Projected Goal - $150,000		$24.95			
3						
4	Region	Qty Sold	Total Sales			
5						
6	North	280	$6,986.00			
7	South	172	$4,291.40			
8	East	397	$9,905.15			
9	West	743	$18,537.85			
10	Other countries	520	$12,974.00			
11						
12			Total Sales	$52,694.40		

Figure 2-23 Profit margin spreadsheet

That is because the person using the dashboard could use the slider at the bottom to select the number of copies sold (the what-if).

Changing the number of copies sold, increases or decreases the profits accordingly.

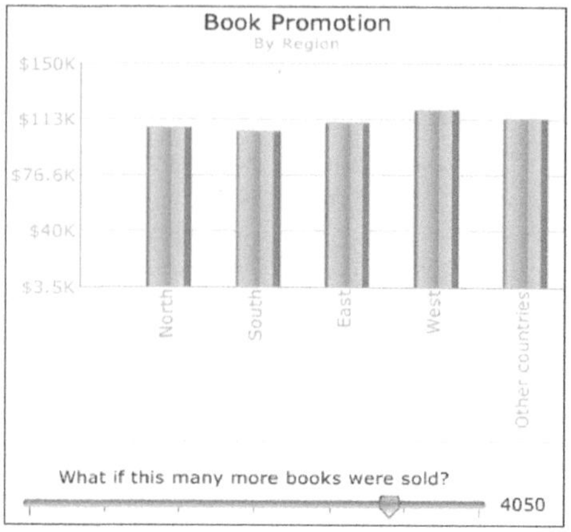

Figure 2-24 Profit margin dashboard

Dashboard Example #2

Figure 2-25 shows the revenues for five products that are sold in five parts of the world. A column chart like the one shown above in Figure 2-21 could be used to display all of the product data in the Revenues By Product spreadsheet at one time. A better solution in my opinion would be to create five different charts, one for each region.

I know what you may be thinking. You are thinking that displaying five charts on the dashboard at the same time is too much. If that is what you are thinking, you are correct. Rather than display all five charts at one time on the dashboard, a menu could be added. The options on the menu shown in Figure 2-26 allow the user to click on a button to display the data for the region. Figure 2-26 shows the data for Latin America. Figure 2-27 shows the data for Asia.

	A	B	C	D	E	F	G
1	Revenues By Product		Rev				
2							
3		Status List	Prod. A	Prod. B	Prod. C	Prod. D	Prod. E
4	North America		$ 14.22	$ 20.12	$ 12.18	$ 25.49	$ 15.64
5	Latin America		$ 21.05	$ 19.54	$ 15.88	$ 18.73	$ 15.02
6	Europe		$ 21.06	$ 20.45	$ 14.49	$ 16.78	$ 13.61
7	Asia		$ 12.25	$ 17.12	$ 20.99	$ 16.79	$ 12.07
8	Australia & Pacific		$ 15.36	$ 25.74	$ 13.17	$ 19.42	$ 12.70

Figure 2-25 Revenues By Product spreadsheet

Figure 2-26 Latin America Revenues By Product dashboard

Figure 2-27 Asia Revenues By Product dashboard

Dashboard Example #3

1. Open Crystal Xcelsius if it is not already open. If you see the windows illustrated earlier in Figure 2-1, close them.

2. File ⇒ Samples. Click on the **USER GUIDE SAMPLES** category. Select the **ALERTS SINGLE VALUES** item, then click OK.

The dashboard shown in Figure 2-28 allows the user to select a different dollar amount for three line items (sales, inventories and cost of goods sold) in the budget.

The three colors on each gauge represent whether or not the forecast number is acceptable. Forecast numbers that are in the red section of the **GAUGE** component are not acceptable.

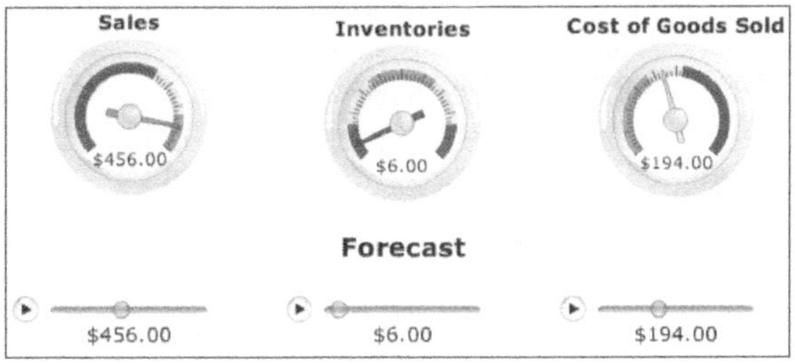

Figure 2-28 Alerts Single Values dashboard

Numbers in the yellow section indicate that caution should be noted. Numbers in the green section are an acceptable forecast amount for the line item. Notice that the needle on each gauge changes color. To change the value on the gauge, use the sliders at the bottom of the dashboard.

Can you believe that this dashboard was created from the data in the spreadsheet shown in Figure 2-29?

	A	B	C	D
1	Summary Report			
2	Corporate Health Measures			
3				
4		Sales	Inventories	Cost of Goods Sold
5	Actual Value	$ 456.00	$ 78.00	$ 256.00
6	Target	$ 435.00	$ 54.00	$ 220.00

Figure 2-29 Alerts Single Values spreadsheet

Formatting Options

Crystal Xcelsius has four main ways that components can be formatted. The options are at the top of the Format menu shown in Figure 2-30. The first three formatting options require that at least two components on the model be selected before they can be used. As you can see, each formatting option on the menu has a right arrow which means that there is a submenu of options.

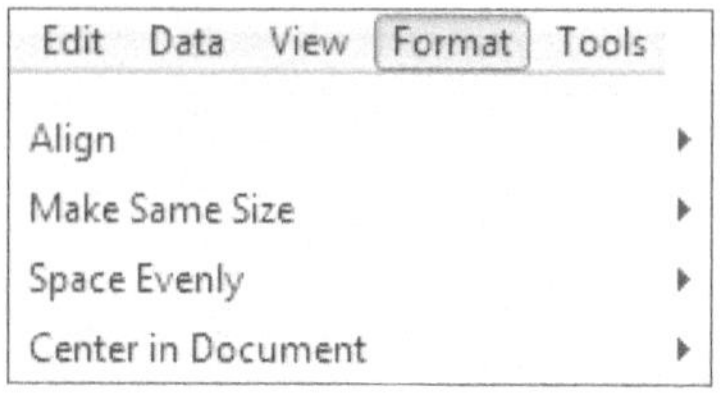

Figure 2-30 Format options

Tables 2-8 to 2-11 explain the options on each submenu.

> When multiple components are selected, they are aligned or resized based on the first component that is selected.

Align Options	Description
Left	Aligns on the left side of the component.
Center Horizontal	Aligns on the center of components horizontally.
Right	Aligns on the right side of the component.
Top	Aligns on the top of the component.
Center Vertical	Aligns on the center of components vertically.
Bottom	Aligns on the bottom of the component.

Table 2-8 Align options explained

Size Options	Description
Width	Makes the selected components the same width.
Height	Makes the selected components the same height.
Both	Makes the selected components the same width and height.

Table 2-9 Make Same Size options explained

Space Options	Description
Across	Adds or removes space between the components from left to right.
Down	Adds or removes space between the components from top to bottom.

Table 2-10 Space Evenly options explained

> The **CENTER IN DOCUMENT** options explained in Table 2-11 do not move the components to the center of the model.

Center Options	Description
Vertical	Centers the component between the top and bottom sides of the canvas vertically, where it is in the model. The component will not be moved left or right.
Horizontal	Centers the component between the left and right sides of the canvas horizontally, where it is in the model. The component will not be moved up or down.
Both	Centers the component between the top and bottom of the canvas vertically and left and right horizontally, where it is on the canvas.

Table 2-11 Center in Document options explained

Selecting Components

You will spend a lot of time selecting components on the canvas to create the perfect dashboard. Like many features, there is more than one way to select components on the canvas, as discussed in the following two sections.

Selecting A Single Component

To select a single component, click on it with the left mouse button.

When selected, you will see a (blue) frame around it, as illustrated in Figure 2-31. You will also see squares on the frame.

These squares are called **SIZE HANDLES**. They allow you to change the size of the component to make it wider, longer, shorter or smaller. You will learn how to resize components later in this lesson.

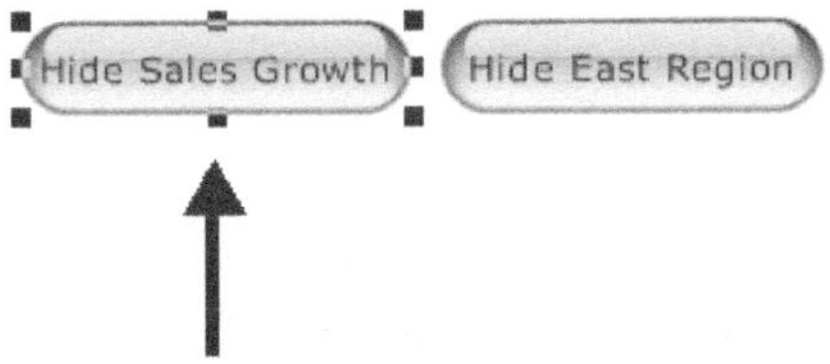

Figure 2-31 Component selected and size handles illustrated

Selecting Multiple Components

There will probably be times when you need to apply the same option to more than one component in the model. You can also use this technique to change the same option on more than one component at the same time. A lot of the editing that you will do requires multiple components to be selected. There are two primary ways to select the components on the canvas that you need, as discussed below.

① Click on one component. Press and hold down the **CTRL** key, then click on the other components that you need to select.

② Draw what is called a **MARQUEE** or **LASSO** around the components with the mouse, as shown in Figure 2-32. To do this successfully, the components need to be near each other, either side by side or up and down from each other. To use this technique, no components can already be selected. Click outside of the first component. Hold the left mouse button down and draw around the components that you need to select. You will see a frame being drawn. When you are finished selecting the components and release the mouse button, you will see that several components have been selected.

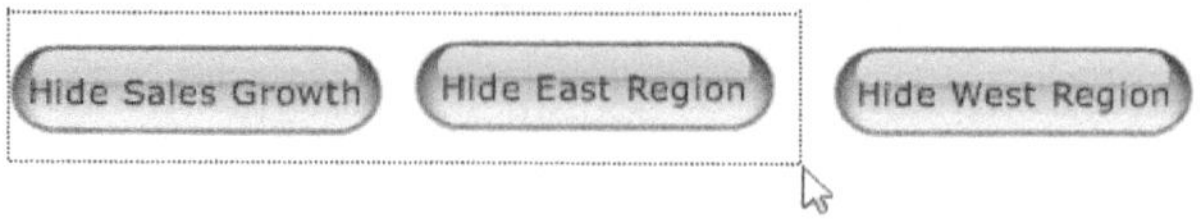

Figure 2-32 Marquee or lasso effect

Nudging Components

So far in this lesson you have learned how to move and resize components using the mouse. You can also move and resize components using the keyboard and touchpad. This is helpful if you use a laptop and do not use a mouse. Using the keyboard and touchpad to move or resize components is known as **NUDGING**.

How To Move A Component By Nudging It

1. Without using the mouse, select the component that you want to move.
2. Use one of the four arrow keys on the keyboard to move the component in the direction that you need to reposition it.

Using The Grid

Selecting options on the dialog box shown in Figure 2-33 can help in aligning components on the canvas. When you need to have greater precision over lining up objects on a model then doing it manually provides, you can turn on the **SHOW GRID** option. This option is not on by default.

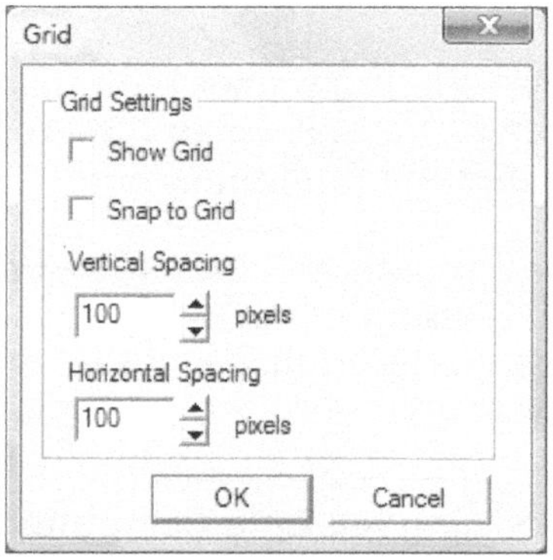

Figure 2-33 Grid dialog box

View ⇒ Grid ⇒ Show Grid, will display the grid on the model, as shown in Figure 2-34.

The grid is the dot pattern in the background. The smaller the number that is entered in the **VERTICAL** and **HORIZONTAL SPACING** options on the Grid dialog box, the smaller the grid will be.

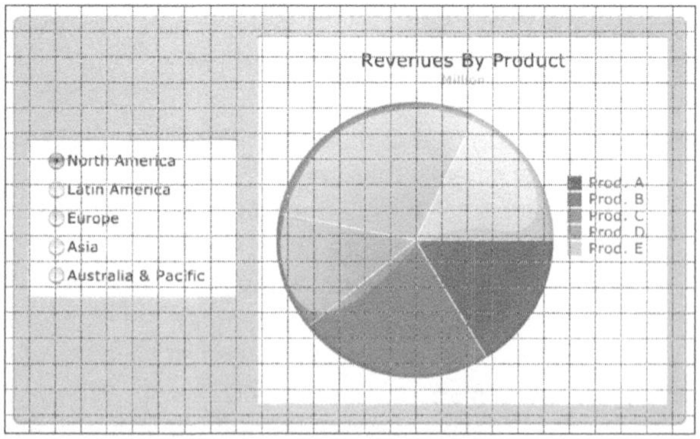

Figure 2-34 Grid feature on a model

Usually, when components are added to a workspace and the **SNAP TO GRID** option is enabled, the components are automatically placed on the closest grid position to where you release the mouse button. When this option is selected nothing seems to happen in Crystal Xcelsius.

CREATE YOUR FIRST DASHBOARD

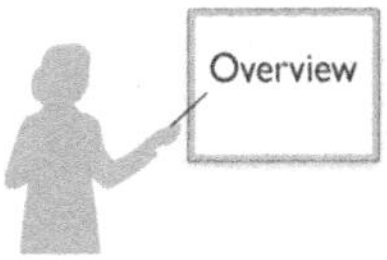

In this lesson you will learn how to create a basic dashboard. While learning how to create a dashboard, you will learn about the following:

- ☑ The dashboard design process
- ☑ Properties dialog box
- ☑ Single Value components
- ☑ Other components

LESSON 3

Dashboard Design Overview

Yes, I know that you are anxious to create your first dashboard, but having a foundation of effective dashboard layout and design principles and techniques is important because if you start off wrong, you will end up wrong or worse <smile>. Many of the layout and design concepts that I discuss in this lesson are very similar to those used for creating reports. However, keep in mind that reports are usually paper based and dashboards are not. If you have used a report writer like Crystal Reports, you may already be familiar with some of the design topics.

Designing For Scalability

This term refers to the process of trying not to limit the functionality of the end product. Scalability allows a product to have modifications made without significantly altering the structure of the underlying data. Even though the user may only request the functionality for a, b and c, you should analyze their request and think "What-If", with each item that they are requesting. Some call this thinking outside of the box.

Even when you give the user exactly what they asked for, they will often come back and say "What about this?" or "What about that?". If the spreadsheet or dashboard design has limitations, you may find it difficult and at the very least, extremely time consuming, to make the changes needed to incorporate any new functionality that may be requested. If this happens, it means that you did not design with scalability.

Keep in mind that even though the data in a spreadsheet is in a **FLAT FILE** format, it can be designed to allow a dashboard to have the "relational" aspect that is often required. The reason that data in a spreadsheet is flat file is because often, the same information is entered in the same column for several records. If you are sitting there shaking your head, pay close attention in Lesson 4, because it sheds light on the differences between flat file and relational data.

Dashboard Design Process

There are several items that need to be addressed and worked out before you create a dashboard, whether this is your first dashboard or your 100th dashboard. This section is an overview of the dashboard design process. Dashboard design could be an entire lesson or two all by itself, but I am giving you the abridged version. The dashboard design process is part of what is known as the "Business Requirements" phase of a project. As you gain experience, you will see that if you do not get the business requirements right, the project will be delayed, potentially be over budget and not produce the results that the business owner (requestor) or client is looking for. Many call this a "bad career move".

When you learn the concepts presented in this lesson, it will be easier for you to create dashboards. Out in the real world, you should write down the answers to the questions that will be covered in the dashboard design process sections of this lesson. The more planning that you do before you create the dashboard, the less that you will have to modify a dashboard after it is created. There are four primary steps to the dashboard design process. Each step can have multiple tasks.

You will see how these steps come together through the exercises in this book. When creating dashboards, especially ones that other people will use, it is imperative that you fully understand the requirements, which often includes asking a lot of questions. This is not a task that you can be bashful about. Not asking questions, or worse, asking the wrong questions, will more than likely cause you grief down the road.

Step 1: Define The Purpose Of The Dashboard

Yes, I know what you are saying; "How hard can it be to figure out the purpose of a dashboard?". The answer is that it depends on how well the person or group of people are able to explain what they want the dashboard to provide and how well you understand what they tell you.

It is possible that the majority of dashboards that you create will be used by someone else, which means that you should meet with the person or group of people that will use the dashboard. These meetings are part of the requirement gathering process. You may have to have more than one meeting to get a good idea of what the dashboard needs to include, because the users may not tell you or be able to clearly articulate their needs in one meeting.

Dashboards are often used as a decision making tool, which means that poor decisions will be made or the decision making process will be ineffective, due to missing or incorrect data that is presented on the dashboard. The data must be correct and presented in a logical manner in order to be an effective decision making tool.

> One dashboard can be used by people at different levels in the company. This means that at each level, people can have slightly different needs. If this is the case, you will have to plan and design the dashboard accordingly, so that it meets the needs for all of the users.

Your role as the dashboard designer is to gather the information needed, which will help the user(s) of the dashboard to be able to use it easily, as well as, understand the data that is presented on the dashboard. If the information is not presented in a way that works for the users, trust me, they will let you know and you will be spending a lot of time modifying the dashboard(s).

In my opinion and based on the experiences that I have had, the more that users have you modify a dashboard, the faster your credibility goes down hill. That is not something that you want to happen. What I have discovered, is that if you create a prototype (which is discussed later in this lesson) for the users, they can discuss what they like and do not like about the prototype. Usually, you will gain valuable information that is often hard to get users to discuss. The worst thing that you can do in many cases, is give the users the impression that you know more about their needs or data then they do. I am not saying that in some cases that you will not know more about their needs or data, just don't give them that impression, if you know what I mean.

To define the expected outcome of the dashboard, write a descriptive sentence or two about the purpose of the dashboard or what the dashboard needs to accomplish. Below are some sample purpose statements.

① The purpose of the dashboard is to compare last years sales data to this years sales data, by region.
② The purpose of the dashboard is to show products that are low on inventory and need to be reordered.

What I am about to say may sound a little off of the beaten path, but please hear me out. When you ask questions, try to think of the component(s) that will be needed. For example, the first purpose statement above indicates that a chart is needed. At the very least, the dashboard needs a chart that can display a trend of two series of data.

The dashboard needs a combination or area chart. To allow the user to select the region (more than three or four regions could make the chart cluttered or hard to read), the dashboard needs a menu component or a toggle component that allows a specific region to be selected. Being able to narrow down the component options will help you understand how the data in the spreadsheet needs to be laid out.

In addition to defining the expected outcome(s) of the dashboard, you have to take into consideration who will be using the dashboard. It is very possible that managers and their staff will request similar dashboards. In many cases, it is better to create separate dashboards, even if there is only one component that is different, then to try and get multiple parties to try and come up with one dashboard that works for both groups of users. If you are responsible for supporting the dashboards, the down side to creating multiple dashboards that are similar is that you may have to make future changes to multiple dashboards. As you gain dashboard design experience, understand business requirements and know the requestors, you will be able to quickly determine which is the best solution.

Step 2: Determine The Layout Of The Dashboard

Now that you have determined the purpose of the dashboard, you need to determine where each piece of data should be placed on the dashboard.

Task 1

In addition to determining where the data should be placed, you need to determine some or all of the following:

① Create a list of fields (cells) that need to be displayed on the dashboard. If you know what spreadsheet each field is in, include that on the list. If the data does not currently exist, include it on the list also. You will use this list to complete tasks in future steps in the design process.
② If necessary, create a list of fields that will be used to select what other components display.
③ An important question to answer during this step is what format(s) the dashboard needs to be in. This is known as the **DELIVERY METHOD**. For example, does the dashboard need to be in PDF format or does it need to be web based. The way that a dashboard needs to be distributed can influence the layout of a dashboard. You should also determine if the dashboard needs to be distributed in more than one format.
④ What is the appropriate title for the dashboard? Is the title in a field or do you have to type it in?

⑤ Does the dashboard need dates? If so, what format should they be in and where should they be placed on the dashboard.

Task 2

If you are creative you will like this task. This task involves selecting the components, backgrounds etc. Yes, I know that it is early in the design process, but there is no point waiting, because making decisions like this can help structure the data in the spreadsheet better. If you followed my advice in step 1 about the components, you may be well on your way to completing the component selection process. Keep in mind that as fun and exciting as it is to create a dashboard in Crystal Xcelsius, that it is a business decision tool, not something that can be framed as artwork.

Step 3: Find The Data For The Dashboard

This step is very important because without the data there is no dashboard. As the person creating the dashboard, life will be much easier for you if you are familiar with the data needed for the dashboard and how the data is organized. If you are not familiar with the data or are not technical, you may have to rely on the users or Information Technology specialists, to help you with the tasks in this step. There are three tasks that you have to work on to complete this step successfully. Keep in mind that when you finish all of the tasks in this step, that you have all of the data in one spreadsheet. The data can be on more than one tab as needed.

Task 1

The first task that you have to complete is to find out which spreadsheets and possibly other data repositories, like a database, contain the data for the dashboard. Use the list of fields that you created in Step 2, to find the spreadsheets and databases. You may also have to find out what servers the data is on. This task is known as finding the **DATA SOURCE**.

Task 2

This task involves selecting the actual fields in the spreadsheets that are needed for the dashboard. Use the list that you created in Step 2. Once the fields are selected, determine the formatting for each field and how the fields need to be displayed on the dashboard. You also have to determine if the current column or field names are the best choice for the dashboard. One example of when a column or field name needs to be changed on a dashboard is for fields that are known as ID fields. Using ID fields as the name on a dashboard has no meaning to most users.

Task 3

Now that you have found some of the data, there may be fields left on the list that you created in Step 2 that you have not found. More than likely, many of the fields that are left on the list are calculated fields. This task involves writing out the formulas for the calculated fields. Some calculated fields may use a built-in Excel function and others will require you to write the formula. Examples of calculated fields include:

① Sales price times quantity.
② Number of days between the order date and the ship date.
③ How long the person has been employed at the company.

If you, as the dashboard designer, come to the conclusion that some data that the users are requesting does not exist, they or someone other then you, needs to create the data if the user plans to stick to their original request.

Step 4: Organize The Data

This step involves organizing all of the data. Many of the options that you decide on in Task 1 below, will automatically dictate which type of component (ie. chart, menu, slider) each field will have to use.

Task 1

To complete this task you have to organize all of the data, from the spreadsheets and calculated fields, as well as, any other data source. Organizing the data means that at a minimum, answering the following questions is necessary.

① Does the data need to be grouped? If so, which field(s) should the data be grouped on? [See Lesson 4, Grouping Data]

② Does the dashboard need to have any data flagged? If so, how should the data be flagged? The primary reason data would be flagged is so that it can be easily identified on a dashboard. Make a list of any data that needs to be flagged. Crystal Xcelsius has several options including alerts (Covered in Lesson 8), borders, symbols, changing the font size and other formatting techniques that you can use to indicate that the data is flagged.

Task 2

To complete this task you have to determine which type of component each field should use. Task 1 had you make decisions on how to organize the data at a high level. There are several types of components that can be used to display data. You also have to determine if the component should be an input (requests data from the user) or output (displays data) component.

Task 3

One way that you organize the data is selecting which rows of data will actually be used as the data source. This is important because it is not a requirement that all of the data in a spreadsheet appear on the dashboard. For example, if the dashboard needs to display sales (orders) for a specific sales rep, you would select a component that would allow the user to select the particular sales rep whose data will appear on the dashboard. Another example would be to display all customers that purchased a specific product or group of products.

In addition to data selection, it may be necessary to create filters which will make the dashboard more flexible in terms of record selection. Filters allow the user to select the criteria that will be used to retrieve the data that will appear on the dashboard. Filters allow one dashboard to be run with a variety of selection criteria. An example of this would be an order dashboard. This dashboard could have filters for the order date, order amount and sales rep fields. One dashboard could display all of the following.

① All orders on a specific date.

② All orders for a specific sales rep.

③ All orders for a specific product.

④ All orders on a certain date for a specific sales rep.

Task 4

Depending on the company, it may be necessary to have the person or group of people sign a document that states that all of the tasks discussed above will produce the dashboard(s) that they need.

Refreshing Data

Unlike reports that are run off of live data all the time, dashboards usually do not. While not a part of the actual dashboard design process this task must be addressed. As you have read, once the data is imported into the model, the spreadsheet is disconnected from the model.

Dashboards become outdated, when they use old data. The process of refreshing data is covered in Lesson 9. If you will be the one responsible for re-exporting the model to get the revised data, you need to set up a schedule that works for you and the users. Remember, that they do not have Crystal Xcelsius installed on their computer, so they cannot update the data in a dashboard on their own.

Dashboard Prototype

Even though you will go through the entire dashboard design process, it is very possible that the users are still somewhat unclear or cannot visualize what the finished dashboard will look like. No pun intended. If that is the case, creating a dashboard prototype will be a life saver. A prototype can be hand drawn on paper or you can create a sample dashboard that displays the data based on the information that you gather during the dashboard design process. This sample dashboard is known as a **PROTOTYPE**.

Some dashboard designers create this prototype as each of the steps and tasks that were discussed above are completed. Other dashboard designers will create the prototype right after the dashboard design process is over. The reason prototypes are helpful is because the users will get a pretty good idea of what the finished dashboard will look like, based on the information that they have supplied.

The feedback that you receive from the users about the prototype is invaluable because users get to "see" what they asked for. I have found this process to be a very effective way for users to tell me what they like, don't like, need and don't need.

Ways To Create A Dashboard

There are two ways to create a dashboard: Using an existing model and from scratch. Each has pros and cons, as discussed in the next two sections.

Create A Dashboard Based Off Of An Existing Model

If a dashboard exists that is similar to the dashboard that you now need to create, select this dashboard creation option. Save the existing model with a new file name and make the necessary changes to create the new dashboard.

An example of when to create a dashboard based off of an existing dashboard would be when two groups of people need to see the majority of the same data and one group needs additional information that the other group does not need, or when one group needs the same data, just in a different layout. A different layout could be something as easy as using a different type of chart. You can also use one of the templates that come with Crystal Xcelsius to format the dashboard differently.

Create A Dashboard From Scratch

This option provides the most flexibility to create a dashboard. You start with a blank canvas (no pun intended, again) and add the components. For many, this can be intimidating, especially in the beginning, but being the fearless person that you are, I am sure that you will do just fine.

Learning To Create Dashboards

For some, learning to create dashboards can be intimidating. **LEARNING TO CREATE DASHBOARDS REQUIRES TIME, PATIENCE, DEDICATION, PRACTICE AND ATTENTION TO DETAIL.** Crystal Xcelsius is a very robust package and has a lot of features and options. As you go through the hands-on exercises in this book, take your time and try to understand how the concepts that you are learning can be applied to dashboards that you will create on your own. It is possible to go through this entire book in a few days if you already have above average dashboard design experience or if you have used a previous version of Crystal Xcelsius and have a pretty good foundation of the software.

The reality is that you will make some mistakes along the way. If you have a fear of making mistakes, this is the time to let go of that fear, because the fear will prevent you from learning. It is also normal to initially get confused on what to do next. Even though you may not understand why you are being instructed to do something, the steps in each exercise will allow you to achieve the expected result. This is how you will begin to build a foundation for creating dashboards and learning Crystal Xcelsius.

The first time that a concept or technique is presented, a lot of information is provided. Each subsequent time that you have to perform the same task, less and less information (aka hand holding) will occur. As you will see, there are a lot of repetitious tasks involved in creating dashboards. These are the tasks that less and less information will be provided for as you go through the book. The purpose behind this learning technique is to allow you to start relying more on your knowledge, which in turn allows you to complete an exercise in less time, instead of flipping through this book to find the answer. Hopefully, after reading the previous pages in this lesson, you are much better prepared to create your first dashboard.

Properties Dialog Box

The Properties dialog box is how a component is modified. There are common properties that all components have. They are explained in this lesson. Overall, the options on the tabs work as discussed below.

The **GENERAL TAB** contains the properties that you will use most because they are used to select the data that the component displays. The properties on this tab are used to link a cell or range of cells to a component. All components have a General tab.

The **DRILL DOWN TAB** contains properties that allow detail data to be displayed. This detail data comes from summary data in another component on the dashboard. This tab is only available for charts and is only available in the Professional edition of Crystal Xcelsius.

The **BEHAVIOR TAB** contains properties that determine minimum and maximum data ranges, animation, default settings for the component, how the user can interact with the dashboard and whether or not a component is visible when the dashboard is first opened.

The **ALERTS TAB** contains properties that are used to dynamically change the colors on a component, based on values that are pre-selected. These dynamic color changes are used to bring certain data to the dashboard users attention.

The **APPEARANCE TAB** contains properties that are used to change how the component looks. This includes changing the color, font size or location of where a part of the component, like where a charts legend is displayed.

All components do not have all five tabs shown in Figure 3-1. The tabs have different options depending on the component. For example, the Behavior tab shown in Figure 3-2 shows the options for a **LINE COMPONENT**. Figure 3-3 shows the Behavior tab options for a **COMBO BOX COMPONENT**.

Don't worry, the options for each component are explained in this book on a tab by tab basis, not in a glossary at the end. You can thank me later <smile>.

When you add a component to the canvas, more than likely, the default functionality on the Properties dialog box is not enough for the component to perform the way that you need it to. Selecting and changing options on the Properties dialog box gives the component additional functionality.

As you will see, there are a lot of options on the Properties dialog box. You do not have to try to memorize them. Hopefully, now you understand why earlier I said to pay attention to the Properties dialog box discussions.

Figure 3-1 Properties dialog box

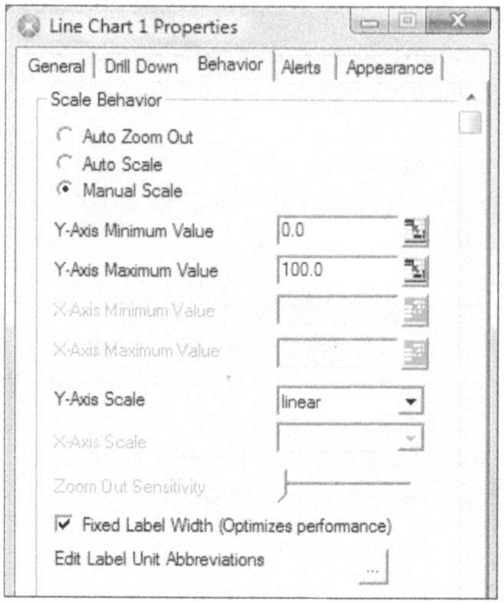

Figure 3-2 Line chart behavior tab options

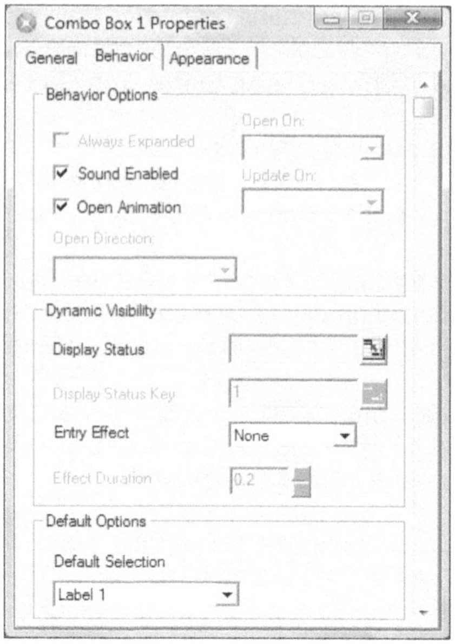

Figure 3-3 Combo Box behavior tab options

Crystal Xcelsius calls each option, except for buttons, on the Properties dialog box a property. I refer to each option on the Properties dialog box as an option. For example, in Figure 3-3 above, I refer to the Default Selection property as the Default Selection option.

Some of the options on the Properties dialog box are the same for all types of components. The sections below discuss the options on each tab that are the same or used often, regardless of the component. As you have probably figured out, each category of components like charts and selectors have their own set of properties. Some components have properties that are specific to the component. These properties are also explained in the lesson that the component is covered in.

Common Buttons On The Properties Dialog Box

The buttons discussed in this section are available for most components.

Cell Selector Button This is probably one of the most used options on the Properties dialog box. Clicking this button opens the spreadsheet that was imported into the model. This is how you select the cell or range of cells that a component will use. Options on the Properties dialog box that have a cell selector button will have one or the other. You just need to know how each button functions so that there are no surprises when the data in the dashboard is updated. There are two types of cell selector buttons, as discussed below.

① **Dynamic** as shown in Figure 3-4, is used to select cells that have data that you want to have updated when the data is refreshed in the model.

Figure 3-4 Dynamic cell selector button

② **Static** as shown in Figure 3-5, is used to select cells that have static data. This means that the values in the cells will not be updated when the data is refreshed in the model.

Figure 3-5 Static cell selector button

Browse Button Clicking the button shown in Figure 3-6 will open a dialog box like the ones shown in Figures 3-7 and 3-8.

Figure 3-6 Browse Button

The dialog boxes shown in Figures 3-7 and 3-8 are used to type in a value for the option instead of selecting a cell in the spreadsheet that has the value.

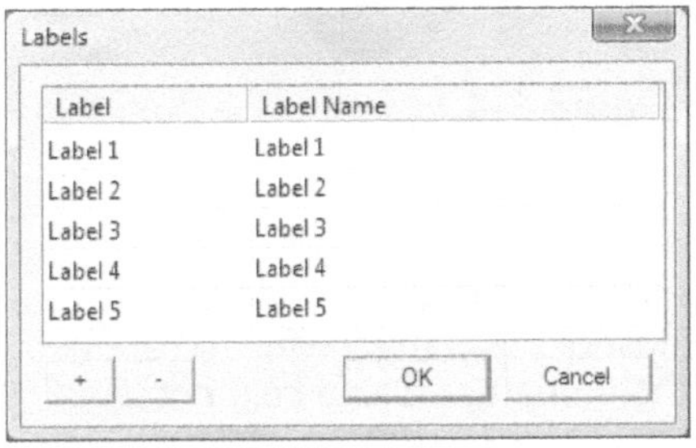

Figure 3-7 Labels dialog box

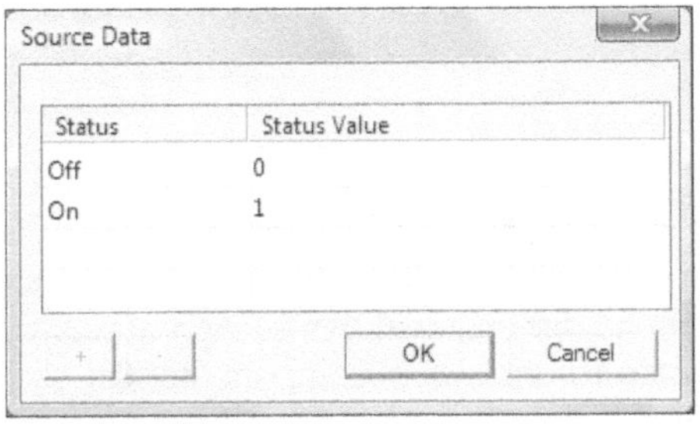

Figure 3-8 Source Data dialog box

Information Button At the end of some options you will see the button shown in Figure 3-9.

Figure 3-9 Information button

This button provides more information on how features on the Properties dialog box work together. If you click this button, you will see a window similar to the one shown in Figure 3-10. You can view an animated demo of how the component works.

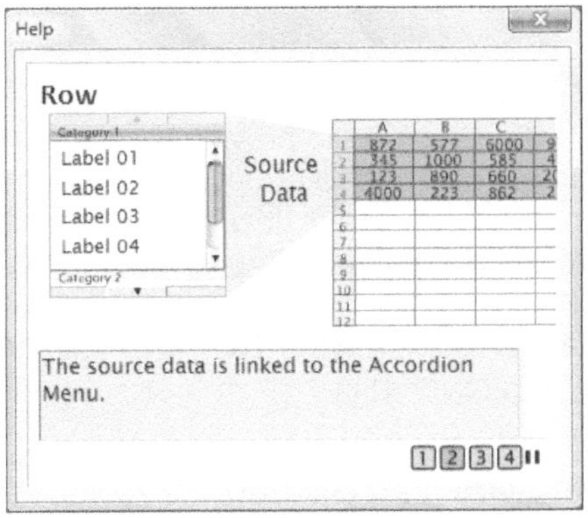

Figure 3-10 Help window

Color Selector Button

As its name suggests, clicking the button shown in Figure 3-11 will open the dialog box shown in Figure 3-12. This is how you select the color that you want to use to change the color of a portion of the component.

If you want to create a custom color, click the **DEFINE CUSTOM COLORS** button.

Figure 3-11 Color Selector button

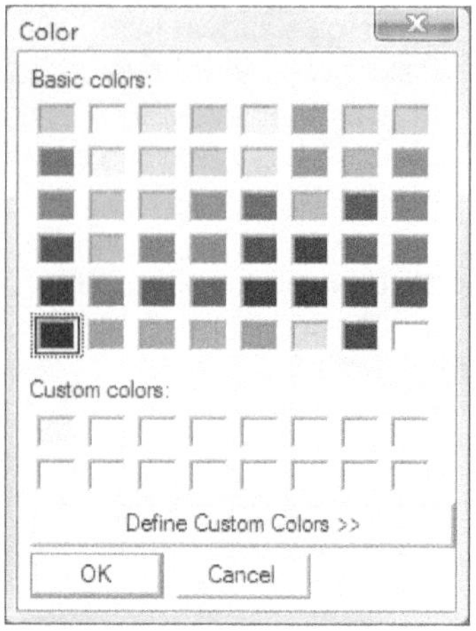

Figure 3-12 Color dialog box

Common Options On The Properties Dialog Box

This section covers the options that are common on different sections of the Properties dialog box. The options discussed in this section are available on most of the components and are not explained again for individual components. On each tab of the Properties dialog box, notice that the options are grouped into sections.

Axis Values

You will see several options on different tabs on the Properties dialog box that are for an axis on the component. They are explained below.

X Axis values are displayed horizontally across the bottom of the component.
Y Axis values are displayed vertically along the left side of the component.

Common General Tab Options

The options on the General tab provide the same functionality from one component type to another. Each type uses different options to accomplish data linking tasks. The options on the tab are used to create or select titles for various parts of a component and link cells in the spreadsheet to the component. Each component type has options on the General tab that are the same for the majority of components of that type. I refer to these as General tab common options for that component type. They are explained at the beginning of the lesson that the component type is covered in.

Common Behavior Tab Options

Like the General tab, the options on the Behavior tab vary from one component type to another. The options are used to set up parameters for the data that will be displayed on the component, like high and low values. Each component type has options on the Behavior tab that are the same for the majority of components of that type. I refer to those as Behavior tab common options for that component type. They are explained at the beginning of the lesson that the component type is covered in. Many components have dynamic visibility options.

Because the dynamic visibility options are covered in detail in Lesson 11, I do not reference them when explaining the options on the Behavior tab for any individual component.

Common Alerts Tab Options

The options on this tab are used to set conditions, both positive and negative. These options cause different parts of the component to change colors. You can also set sounds. Every component that supports alerts has the same options on this tab. Because the Alerts tab is covered in detail in Lesson 8, I do not reference the tab when explaining the options for an individual component.

Common Appearance Tab Options

The options discussed in this section are common to most components. They may appear in a different section of the Appearance tab, but they work the same from component to component. The options on this tab are used to customize how the component will look. Depending on the type of component, this tab has buttons that open what I call panels, that display additional appearance options for the component. The Appearance tab is the only tab that has buttons that display additional options. When you see a reference to a panel, know that you have to select the Appearance tab first. This tab can have up to five panels, as discussed below.

Single Value components have two panels: Titles and Layout as shown in Figure 3-13. Some selector components (Fish-Eye, Sliding Picture and Accordion) have the Titles and Layout panels also. Chart components have five panels on the Appearance tab: Series, Y-Axis, X-Axis, Titles and Layout, as shown in Figure 3-14.

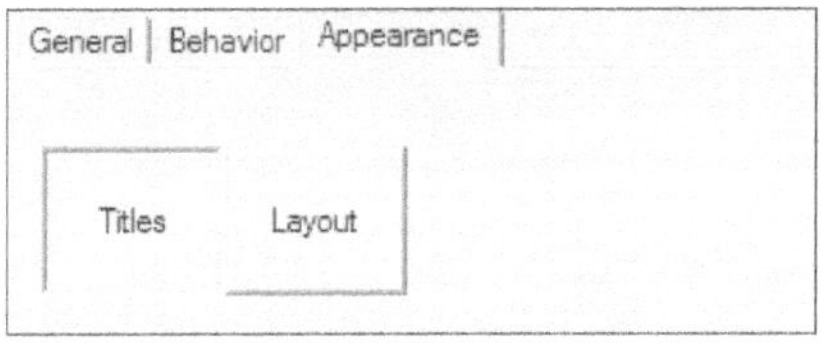

Figure 3-13 Titles and Layout panels

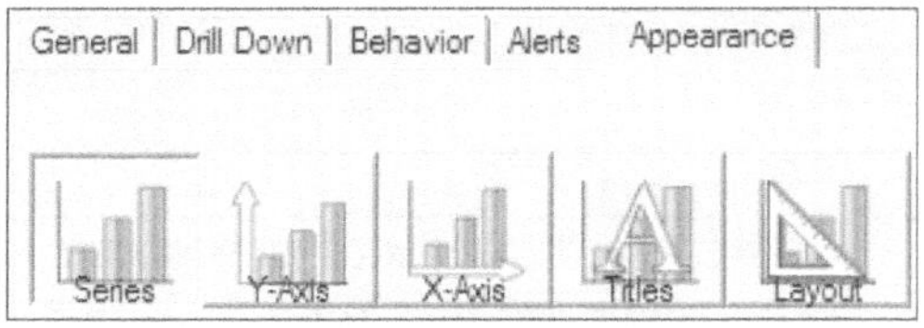

Figure 3-14 Chart component panels

The **ALIGNMENT** options shown in Figure 3-15 are used to align the text of the option that it is associated with. For example, on a chart, the alignment option is associated with the chart title, as illustrated in Figure 3-16. On a List Box component, the alignment option is associated with the labels, as shown in Figure 3-17.

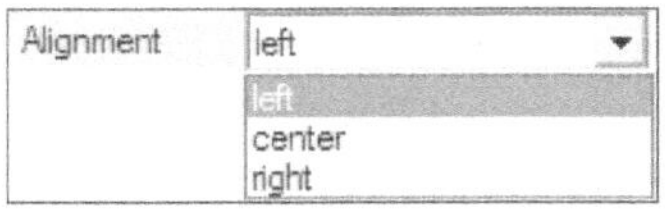

Figure 3-15 Alignment property options

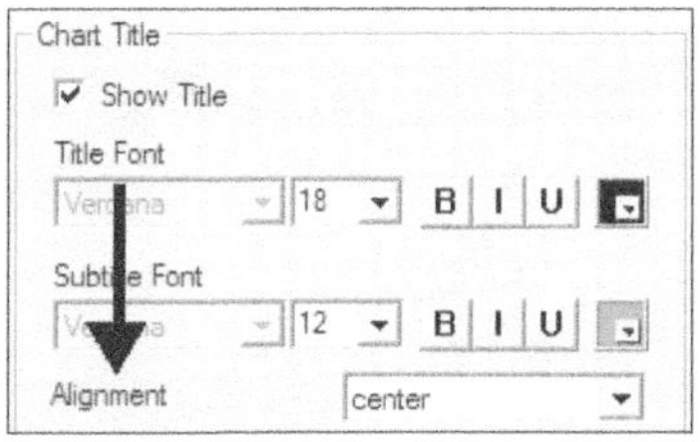

Figure 3-16 Chart Title alignment option

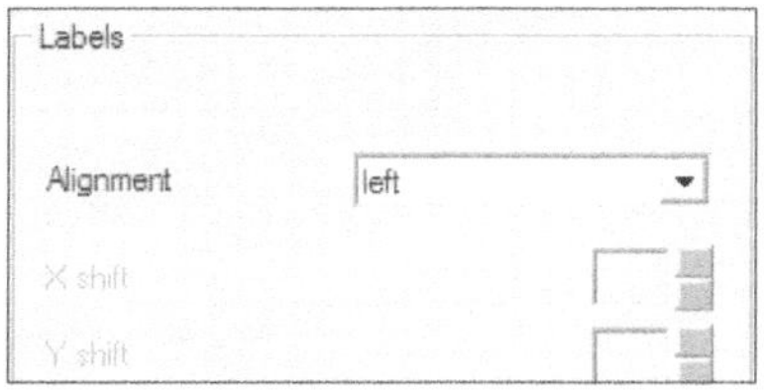

Figure 3-17 Labels alignment option

USE CUSTOM COLOR This option must be checked to be able to change the color options on the tab. Figure 3-18 shows the option on the Layout panel of the Horizontal Progress Bar component. Figure 3-19 shows the option on the Series panel of the Line Chart component.

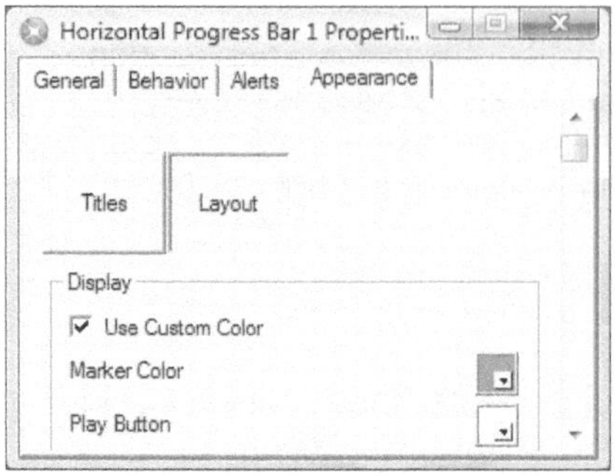

Figure 3-18 Use Custom Color option on the Horizontal Progress Bar layout panel

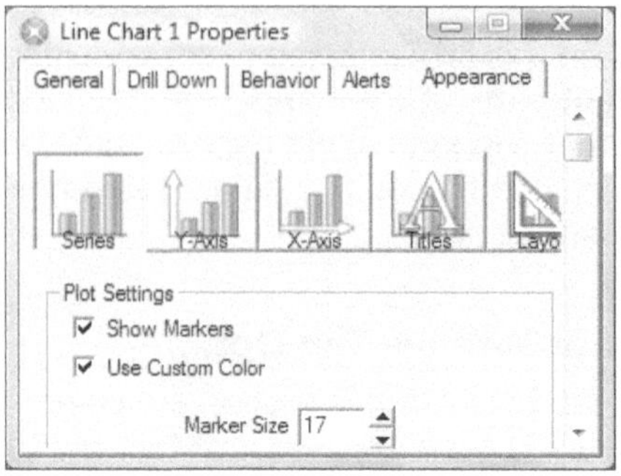

Figure 3-19 Use Custom Color option on the Line Chart series panel

Font Options

The options shown in Figure 3-20 are used to modify the font for a part of the component. They are explained in Table 3-1.

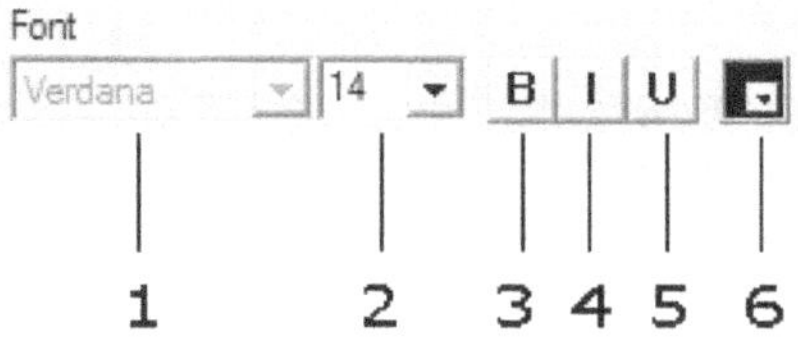

Figure 3-20 Font options

Button	Purpose
1. Font	The default font for all components is Verdana. As you see, the font option is not enabled. If you want to use a different font, you have to select it on the Unicode Font Options dialog box. If available, you can select a different font for the option, as shown in Figure 3-21. The font option is only available if the Use Mon-Embedded Fonts option is selected on the Unicode Font Options dialog box. [See Lesson 2, Figure 2-7].
2. Font Size	Is used to select the font size.
3. Bold	Makes the text bold.
4. Italic	Makes the text italic.
5. Underline	Underlines the text.
6. Color	[See Color Selector button, earlier in this lesson]

Table 3-1 Font options explained

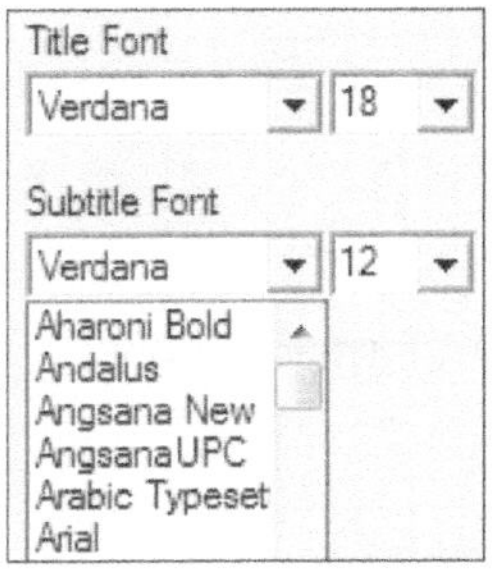

Figure 3-21 Available Fonts

Numeric Format Options

These options are built-in formats that can be applied to different types of numeric data. The eight numeric formats are explained below.

① The **GENERAL** format option displays the data as it is, as shown in Figure 3-22. (1)

Figure 3-22 General format options

② The **NUMERIC** format options shown in Figure 3-23 are used to format numbers.

The options in the **NEGATIVE VALUES** drop-down list are used to select how negative numbers should be processed.

DECIMAL PLACES Is used to select the number of decimal places to display.

Check the **USE 1000 SEPARATOR** option if you want numbers to display commas.

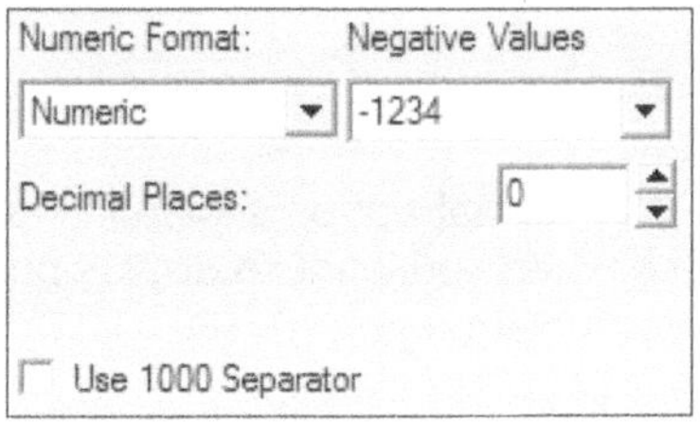

Figure 3-23 Numeric format options

③ The **CURRENCY** format options shown in Figure 3-24 are used to format monetary values.

PREFIX Is used to select a symbol to place at the beginning of currency values. The default is a dollar sign. You can type in another symbol.

SUFFIX Is used to type in a symbol to place at the end of the currency value.

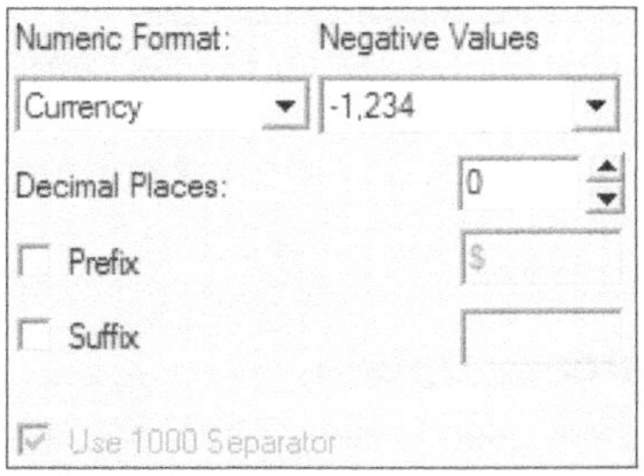

Figure 3-24 Currency format options

> The prefix and suffix options are mutually exclusive, meaning you can select one or the other, but not both.

④ The **PERCENT** format options shown in Figure 3-25 are used to format percent values.

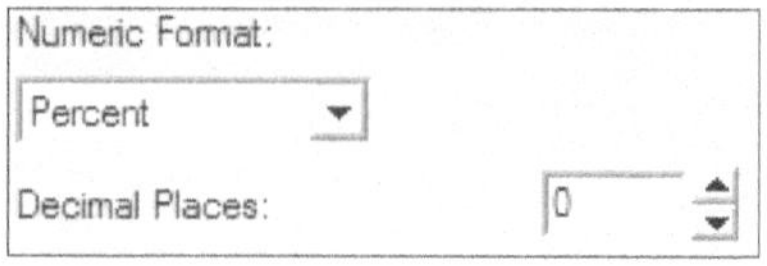

Figure 3-25 Percent format options

⑤ The **DATE** format options shown in Figure 3-26 are used to select how dates should be displayed.

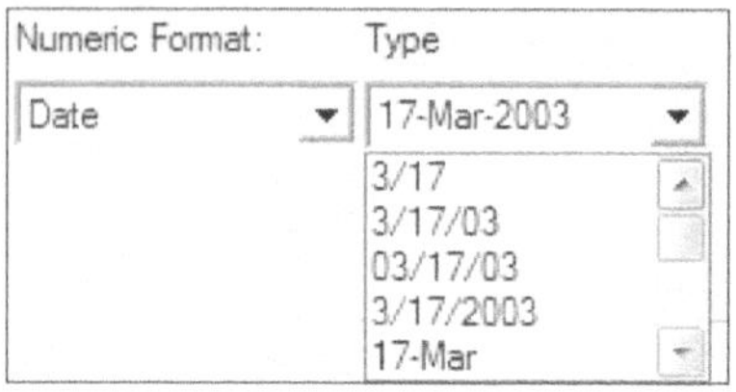

Figure 3-26 Date format options

⑥ The **TIME** format options shown in Figure 3-27 are used to select how times should be displayed.

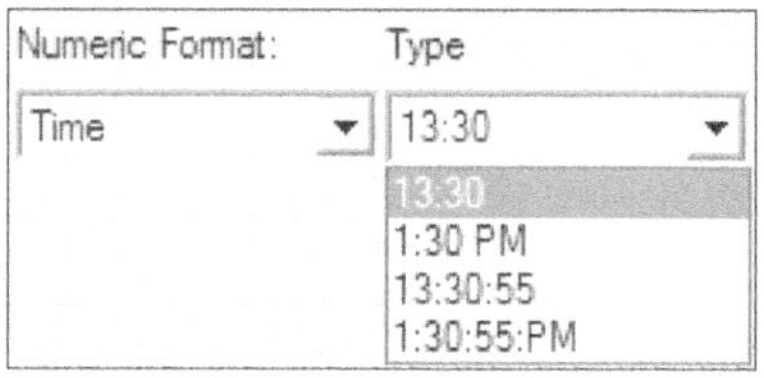

Figure 3-27 Time format options

⑦ The **TEXT** format option shown in Figure 3-28 is used when you want to display numeric values as plain text. (1)

Figure 3-28 Text format options

⑧ Select the **FROM SPREADSHEET** option shown in Figure 3-29 when you want to use formatting from the spreadsheet that Crystal Xcelsius does not support. The format that is not supported, appears in the **FORMAT STRING** field. [See Lesson 4, Custom Formatting]

Figure 3-29 From Spreadsheet format options

(1) There are no other options for this format type.

Transparency Option

This option is used to select how see through a part of the component is. Zero makes part of the component completely see through. 100 makes the part of the component solid. This field is shown in Figures 3-30 and 3-31. Figure 3-32 shows the transparency option set to 50. Figure 3-33 shows the transparency option set to 100.

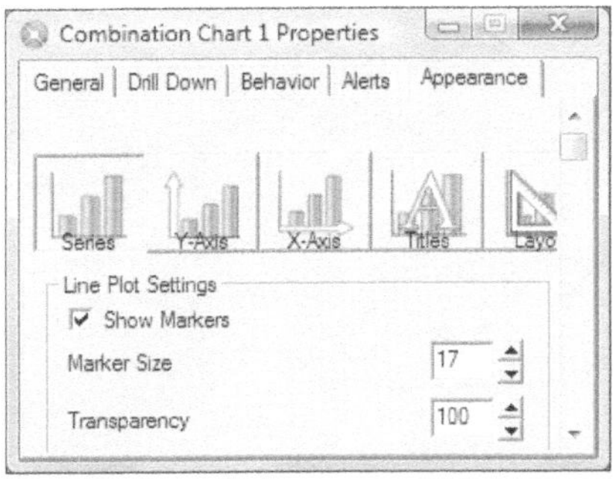

Figure 3-30 Line Plot Settings Transparency option

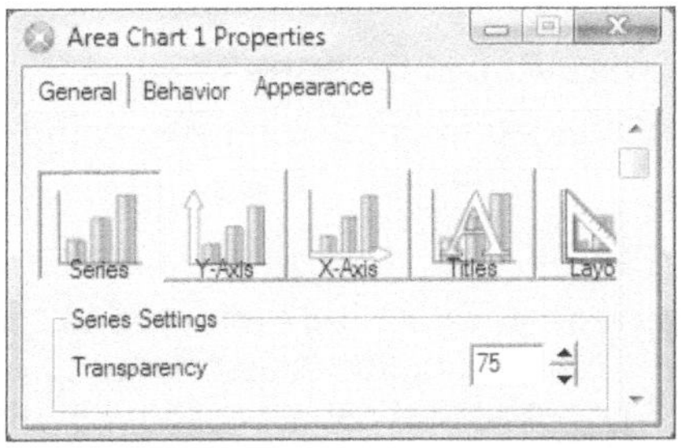

Figure 3-31 Series Settings Transparency option

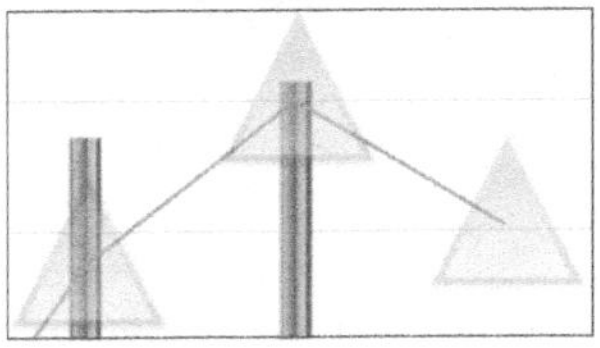

Figure 3-32 Transparency option set to 50

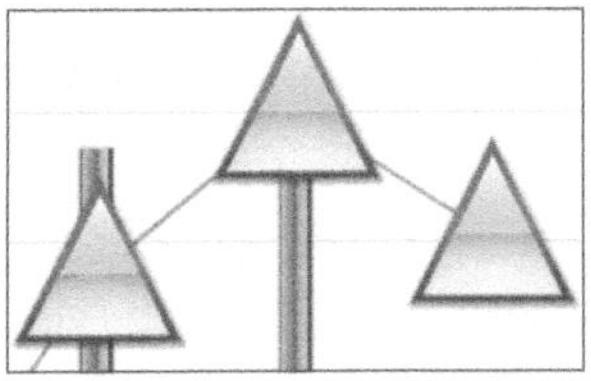

Figure 3-33 Transparency option set to 100

The **WEIGHT** option shown in Figure 3-34 is used to select the thickness of a line that is around part of the component. Zero is the thinnest line size and 100 is the thickest size that the line can be. Figure 3-35 shows the horizontal axis weight value set to 10 and the vertical axis weight value set to 1.

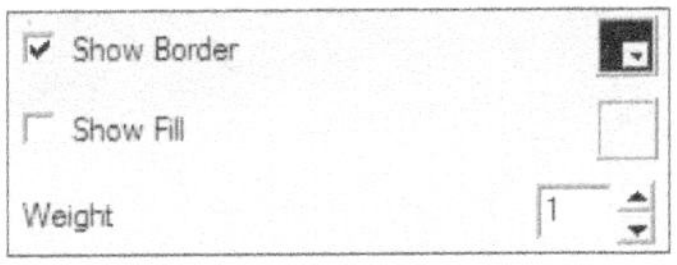

Figure 3-34 Weight option

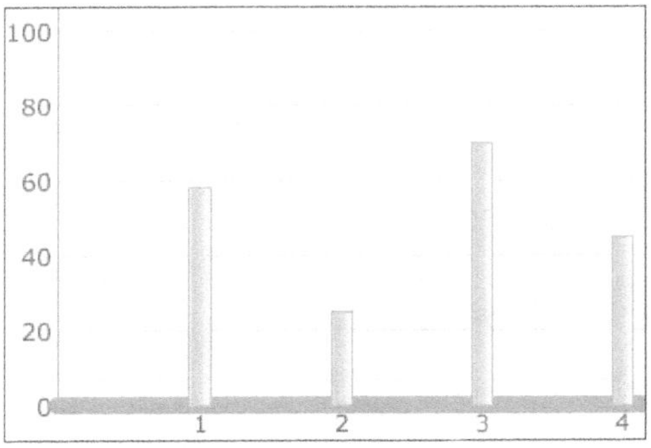

Figure 3-35 Different weight options set

The **SHOW BORDER** option shown above in Figure 3-34 or the **SHOW AXIS** option shown in Figure 3-36 must be selected, in order to use the Weight option.

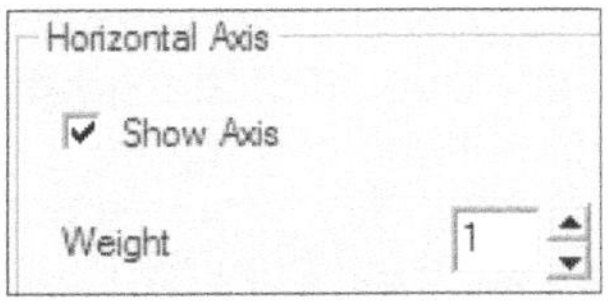

Figure 3-36 Show Axis weight option

Common Titles Panel Options

The options discussed in this section are on the Titles panel on the Appearance tab.

Position Options

The options shown in Figure 3-37 are used to select where the text that this option is associated to will appear. This drop-down list can have some or all of the following nine options: Top left, top center, top right, left, right, center, bottom left, bottom center or bottom right. The options available vary depending on the component.

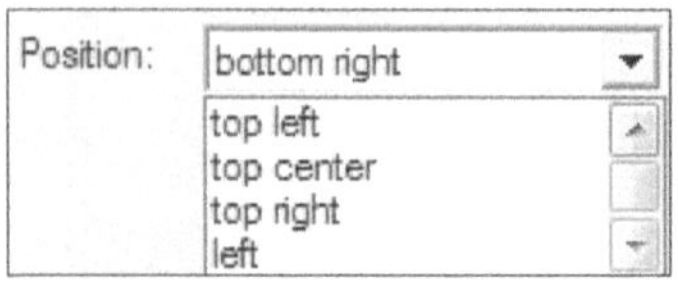

Figure 3-37 Position options

The **X SHIFT** option shown in Figure 3-38 is used to move text (that is part of the component) or values, right or left, based on the option selected in the **POSITION** option.

The **Y SHIFT** option is used to move text (that is part of the component) or values, up or down based on the option selected in the **POSITION** option shown in Figure 3-38 or by the **PLACEMENT** option, shown in Figure 3-39.

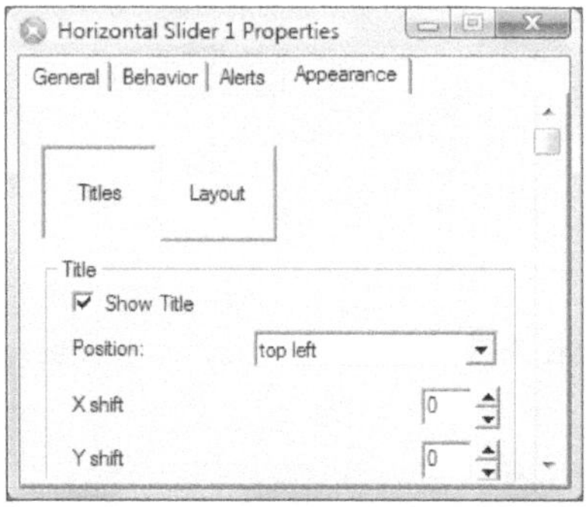

Figure 3-38 X and Y Shift options

Figure 3-39 Placement option

What Are Components?

I have used the word component a few times already in this book, but have not taken the time to thoroughly explain what a component is until now. The reason is because you are about to create your first dashboard and I wanted this concept to be fresh in your mind.

Components are the core of what makes Crystal Xcelsius the tool that it is. Components are what make a dashboard interactive and fun to use. Single Value components are just one type of component that you can use. All of the Single Value components basically provide the same functionality, meaning that if you connect a gauge or slider to the same cell, you will get the same data results and functionality. One component often looks better or is more appropriate for a particular task then another. Other types of components include charts and selectors.

Why Reinvent The Wheel?

In Lesson 2 you viewed one of the dashboards that come with Crystal Xcelsius. I do not know what you think, but I think that the sample dashboards are very good. What I thought to myself when I was learning Crystal Xcelsius was that it would be cool to learn how to create the dashboards that come with the software. Hopefully you agree, because they are some of the dashboards that you will learn how to create in this book. Did you ever try to recreate the sample files that come with software that you use? I have and sometimes it can be frustrating. This is your lucky day because I have suffered through deconstructing the majority of the sample dashboards that come with Crystal Xcelsius. Well, I am exaggerating because they were not as bad as I thought they would be to figure out.

Your First Dashboard

In Lesson 2 you previewed a little of what Crystal Xcelsius can do. You learned about the three basic tasks that need to be completed to go from spreadsheet data to finished dashboard. The primary goal of this lesson is to help you feel comfortable using Crystal Xcelsius.

As the title of this lesson states, you will create your first fully functional dashboard. Along the way of creating the dashboard you will learn about the following: Importing data, creating and testing a model, Single Value components, the Components dialog box and the Properties dialog box. Items and options that are not explained in detail in this exercise, are explained in detail in later lessons. I know how excited you are to create a dashboard and I do not want to slow the process down any further then I already have.

Exercise 3.1: Create A Basic Dashboard

This exercise will show you how to complete the following tasks, which are the basic requirements to create a dashboard.

① Import the data from an Excel spreadsheet.
② Select and configure the components for the model.
③ Test the model and publish it.

In this exercise you will learn how to create the slider model shown in Figure 3-40.

The dashboard displays the number of cars sold and the total sales amount per city (location).

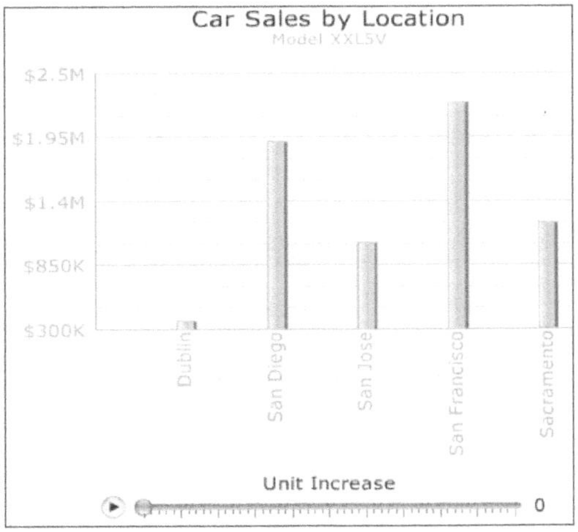

Figure 3-40 Slider dashboard

Import The Data

1. Open Crystal Xcelsius. If you see the Components window, Object Browser or Properties dialog box, close them.

2. Click the **IMPORT MODEL** button on the toolbar. (the Excel icon)

   You will see the dialog box shown in Figure 3-41.

Figure 3-41 Import Model dialog box

> **DATA ⇒ IMPORT MODEL**, will also open the dialog box shown above in Figure 3-41.

3. Click the **BROWSE** button on the Import Model dialog box to open the dialog box shown in Figure 3-42.

   Navigate to your folder and double-click on the Slider spreadsheet file.

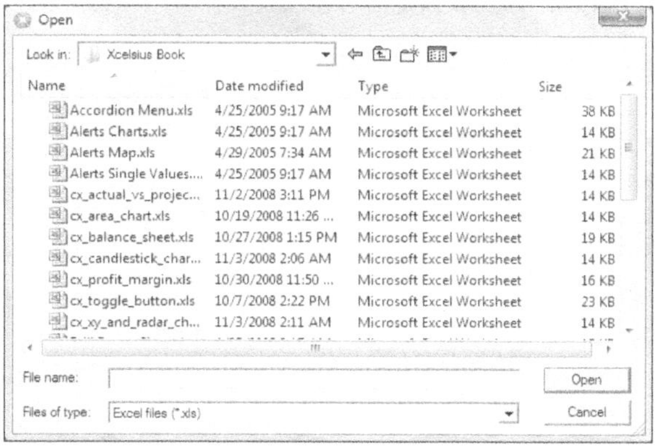

Figure 3-42 Open dialog box

4. Click OK on the Import Model dialog box. The data in the spreadsheet will be imported. When the import is finished, you will see the words **MODEL IMPORT DONE** in the lower right corner in the Status bar section of the Crystal Xcelsius workspace. This means that the data has been successfully imported into the model.

> The important thing to remember is that once the data from the spreadsheet has been imported, Crystal Xcelsius detaches (or disconnects) from the spreadsheet. If the spreadsheet that the model is based on is updated, the new or revised data will not be part of the dashboard unless the spreadsheet is re-imported.

Create The Model

Creating the model is sometimes called "Building the visual model". You will add two components to the model, a chart and a slider.

Add The Chart Component To The Model

This component will be used to create a visual representation of the data in the spreadsheet. That is a sophisticated way of saying that the chart component will be used to display the data <smile>.

1. Open the Charts category folder in the Components dialog box, then click on the Column Chart option.

   At the bottom of the Components dialog box, you will see a preview of what the component looks like, as illustrated at the bottom of Figure 3-43.

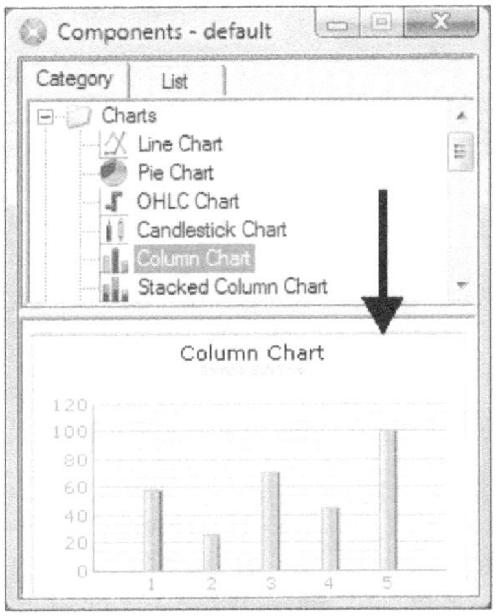

Figure 3-43 Component preview section illustrated

2. With the Column Chart component still selected, drag it to the canvas.

3. Double-click on the chart to open the Properties dialog box.

> If you right-click on the component on the canvas and select the Properties option, the Properties dialog box will open.

Select The Options For The Column Chart

All of the options that have the **CELL SELECTOR** button shown earlier in Figure 3-4 have two options for adding the text, a cell or cell range to it, as discussed below.

① You can type the data in the field. Use this option when the value is not in the spreadsheet.

② You can select the cell(s) in the spreadsheet. It is best to use this option when the data is in the spreadsheet because it helps reduce errors. If the data in the spreadsheet changes and you re-import the data, the data in the model will be updated.

Select The General Tab Options

1. Click the Cell Selector button at the end of the Chart title field.

2. Click in cell A1, as illustrated in Figure 3-44, then click OK on the Select A Range dialog box.

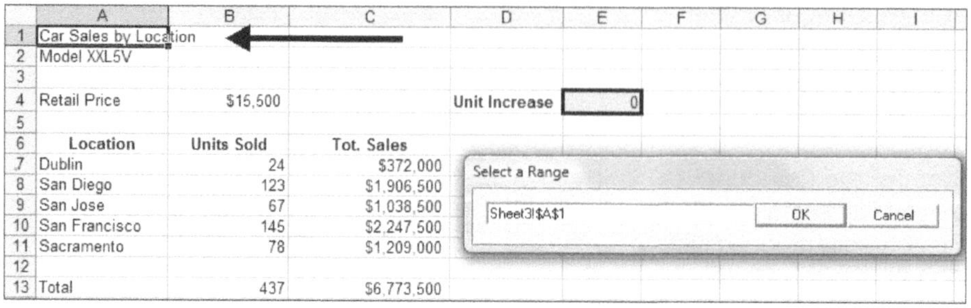

Figure 3-44 Spreadsheet data for the model

The **SELECT A RANGE** dialog box, shown above on the right side of Figure 3-44, is the tool used to link cells in the spreadsheet to the model. While you can type in the range on the Properties dialog box, it is safer and probably faster to use this dialog box to select the cell(s).

Notice that the component has displayed the data that corresponds to the cell that you selected. In this exercise that is the charts title. This feature is even more helpful when you select a large range of data because you can double check to make sure that you selected the data that you need.

3. Type `Model XXL5V` in the Chart subtitle field. This is the same data that is in cell A2 in the spreadsheet. You could have selected that cell for the Chart subtitle field.

Data Range Options

The options in this section of the Properties dialog box are used to select the values in the spreadsheet for the grid portion of the chart. In this exercise, the values that will be charted are the total sales for all locations. The Series In options, **ROWS** and **COLUMNS** are used to indicate how the series of data is laid out in the data range that was selected.

1. Click the Cell Selector button at the end of the Data Range field.

2. Select the range C7:C11, then click OK.

   You should have the options selected that are shown in Figure 3-45.

   Notice that the **SERIES NAME** and **X VALUES** fields were automatically filled in, as illustrated at the bottom of the figure.

   You can change the series name by typing it in or selecting the cell in the spreadsheet that has the name that you want to use for the series.

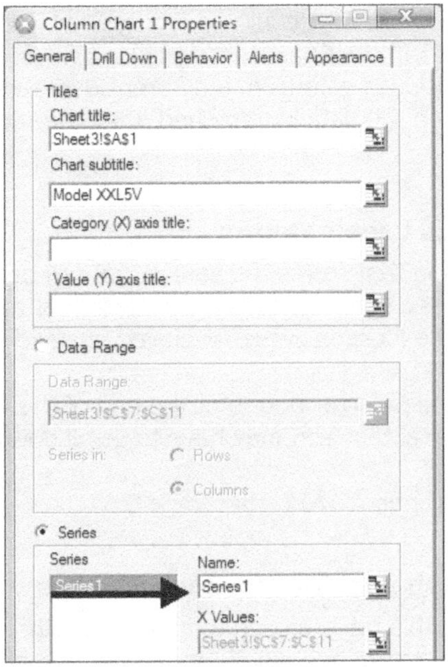

Figure 3-45 Column chart general tab options

Notice the values on the X Axis shown in Figure 3-46. They are different then the ones shown earlier in Figure 3-40. Also notice that the format of the values is different.

The options on the X Axis shown earlier in Figure 3-40 are the default options that Crystal Xcelsius automatically selected.

There is a specific range of values for the total sales, which limits the (range of) values that will be displayed on the dashboard.

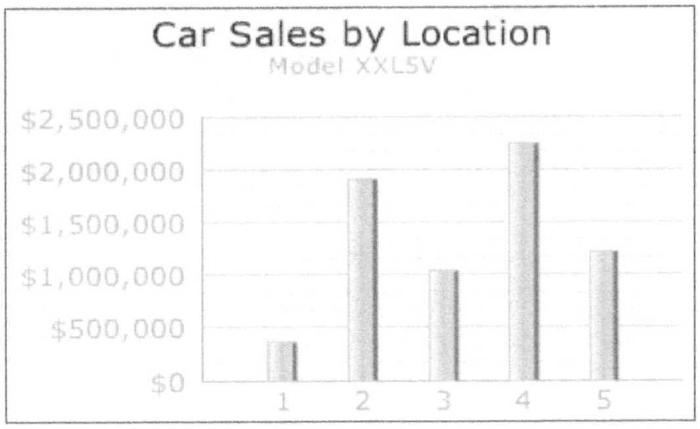

Figure 3-46 Column chart

If the spreadsheet that is being used to create the dashboard has a lot of data or data that does not need to be displayed, you could limit the range of values. I personally prefer **NOT** to limit values because doing so sometimes does not provide a true portrayal of the data in the spreadsheet. This could unintentionally be misleading to the people that use the dashboard. If you need to put limits on a range of values, I think that it is a good practice to indicate that on the dashboard. Using the Chart subtitle is a good place to put this information or you can use a label component. For example, putting a date range in the Chart subtitle field would let users know the dates that the data displayed in the dashboard is for.

In the spreadsheet shown earlier in Figure 3-44, I would put "For Jan. 1, 2008 to Jan. 31, 2008" in cell D1. In the Chart subtitle field, I would reference cell D1. If the dashboard is updated and includes data from a different date range, I would change the date range in cell D1, so that when the data is refreshed, the date range would reflect the changes. Doing this is optional.

Category Axis Labels Option

This is the option that stores the values that will be displayed across the bottom of the chart. Currently, you see numbers across the bottom of the chart. The chart would be easier to understand if the locations were displayed, instead of the numbers.

1. Click the Cell Selector button at the end of the Category Axis Labels option, at the bottom of the General tab. You may have to scroll down to see this option.

2. Select the range A7:A11, then click OK.

Select The Behavior Tab Options

The options on this tab are used to manipulate the data that is displayed on the dashboard and to select the **RUN TIME** options. To make your dashboard look like the one shown earlier, options on the Behavior tab need to be changed.

The **MANUAL SCALE** option is used to change the X and Y Axis values. You can type in the values that you want or you can select them from the spreadsheet. It is very possible that the values that you want to use are not in the spreadsheet.

1. Select the Manual Scale option on the Behavior tab.

2. Type `300000` in the **Y-AXIS MINIMUM VALUE** field.
   Type `2500000` in the **Y-AXIS MAXIMUM VALUE** field.

3. Check the **FIXED LABEL WIDTH** option. You should have the options shown in Figure 3-47.

   The Fixed Label Width option makes the axis label values uniform, which should make the values on the axis easier to read. In this exercise, the range is $300,000 to $2.5 million.

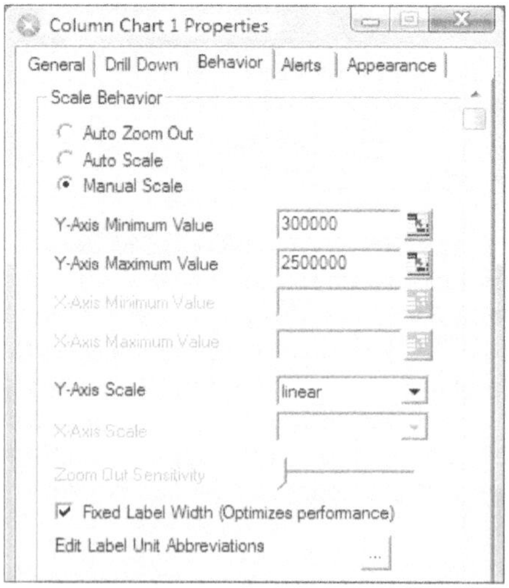

Figure 3-47 Behavior tab options

Add The Slider Component To The Model

The slider component that you add to the model will be used to increase or decrease the number of cars (units) sold.

1. Open the Single Value category folder on the Components dialog box, then open the Slider folder.

2. Drag the **HORIZONTAL SLIDER-0** component to the canvas and place it under the chart.

3. On the General tab of the Properties dialog box, click the Cell Selector button at the end of the Title field. Click in cell D4, then click OK.

4. Click the Cell Selector button at the end of the **LINK TO CELL** field.

   Click in cell E4, then click OK.

   You should have the options shown in Figure 3-48.

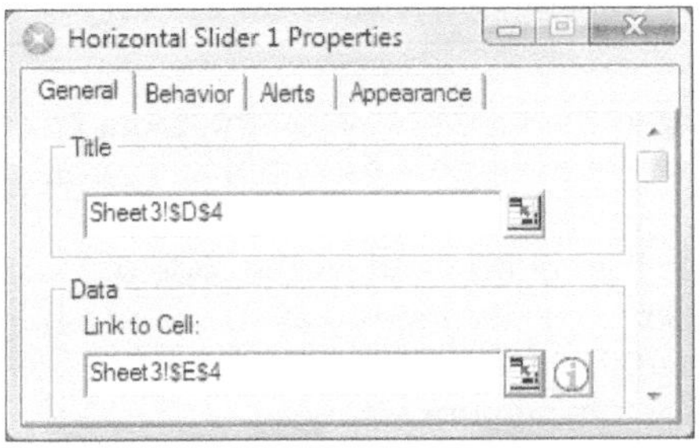

Figure 3-48 Horizontal Slider general tab options

Yes, I know that cell E4 is empty. If you were going to use the spreadsheet to perform the analysis of What If X more cars were sold per location, cell E4 is where you would type in X. In the dashboard, the slider will be used to select X.

The Total Sales field on the spreadsheet has the formula, Unit Increase plus Units Sold. Therefore, as the Unit Increase value becomes larger, the Total Sales cells in the spreadsheet and the bars in the chart will go up, as you will see shortly. The value selected on the slider is placed in cell E4 in this example, which then recalculates the values in the Total Sales column.

5. On the Behavior tab, select the **SHOW PLAY BUTTON** option.

6. On the Appearance tab, click the Layout button.

   You can type the number in or you can use the arrow buttons at the end of the field to select the number.

   Change the **NUMBER OF TICKS** option to 11.

   Change the **NUMBER OF SUBTICKS** option to 4, as shown in Figure 3-49. Earlier in Figure 3-40, you saw tick marks on the slider component.

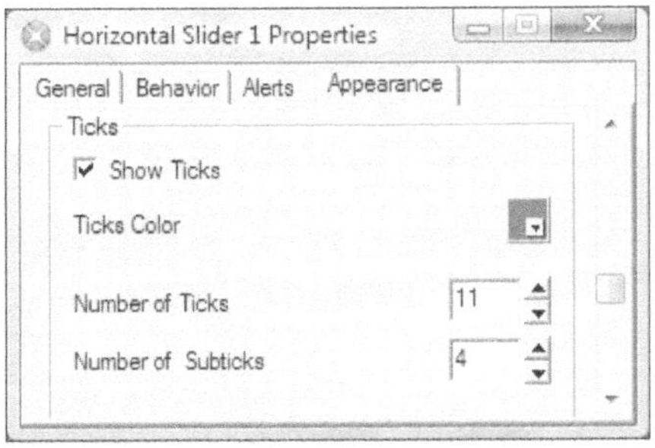

Figure 3-49 Ticks options

Save And Test The Model

In this part of the exercise you will test the model.

1. Make the chart larger and the slider longer.

2. Click the Save button on the toolbar. Type `My slider model` as the file name, then press Enter.

3. Click the Preview button. The model should look like the one shown earlier in Figure 3-40.

> Each time the Preview button is clicked, the model is compiled into a SWF file. These swf files are temporary files and can be deleted. [See Lesson 2, Temporary Files]

4. You can drag the blue button on the slider or click the **PLAY** button on the slider. Clicking the Play button a second time causes the slider to stop.

If you click the Play button and let the slider go all the way to the end, what you will notice is that the bars for some locations (cities) will reach the maximum value of $2.5 million before the slider reaches 100. This is an example of why I am not a fan of using a range for data, in particular, for the maximum amount.

5. If you need to make changes, click the Preview button to return to the design mode and make the changes. Save the changes.

Export And Publish The Model

In the previous part of the exercise you created and saved the model. In the file format that the model is currently in, the only people that could use it are people that have Crystal Xcelsius installed. Most of the time, you will need to distribute dashboards to people that do not have Crystal Xcelsius installed. The way that the dashboard is distributed is to export the model. A Flash file is automatically created and then added to the export option that you select. The Flash file can be run as is, saved in a PDF file or another output format.

In this part of the exercise you will learn how to export the model to a Flash file, which is the file that you can distribute. This is probably the part of the exercise that you have been waiting for because you will be able to let other people see your dashboard. By now, I am sure that you understand the Crystal Xcelsius provides several options for you to select from to distribute your dashboard. These options are pretty straight forward.

1. In design mode, File ⇒ Export. You will see the submenu shown in Figure 3-50.

   Depending on the edition of Crystal Xcelsius that you have installed and other software that is installed on your computer, you will see different options at the bottom of the submenu.

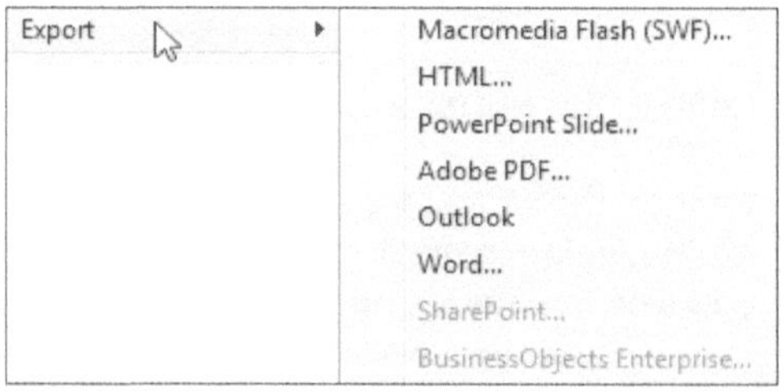

Figure 3-50 Export submenu

The options shown above in Figure 3-50 are the default export options. The ones that are not enabled means that you cannot export your model to it.

2. Select the **POWERPOINT SLIDE** option.

3. Navigate to the folder where you want to save the dashboard. In this exercise, navigate to your folder, then type `My slider dashboard` as the file name, as shown at the bottom of Figure 3-51.

   If you were going to distribute this dashboard, you will save it on a network drive instead of the hard drive on your computer. That way other people can access it.

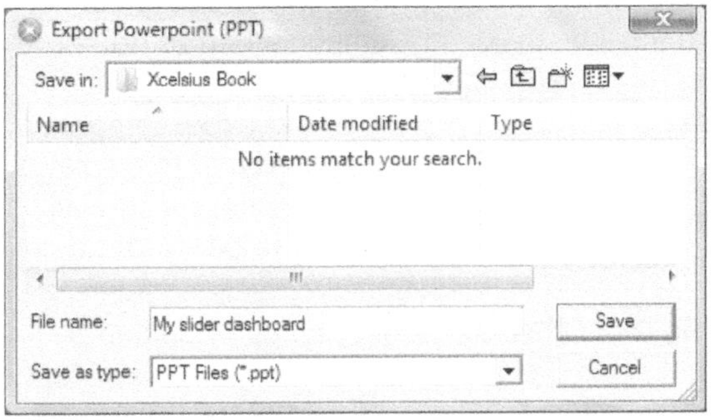

Figure 3-51 Location for the dashboard

4. Press Enter or click the Save button.

Once the dashboard is created, it will open in the format that you selected. In this exercise PowerPoint will open. As you can see, the dashboard is smaller in PowerPoint than it was in the model. In Lesson 9 you will learn how to resize the canvas, which is how the size of the dashboard is changed.

Hopefully, the process of creating the dashboard was not to painful. In the next lesson, you will learn about the data behind dashboards.

Other Component Types

As shown in Figure 3-52, Single Value components are just one type of component. There are seven other types of components, which are explained in Table 3-2. The lesson that the component type is covered in, is listed at the end of the description in brackets.

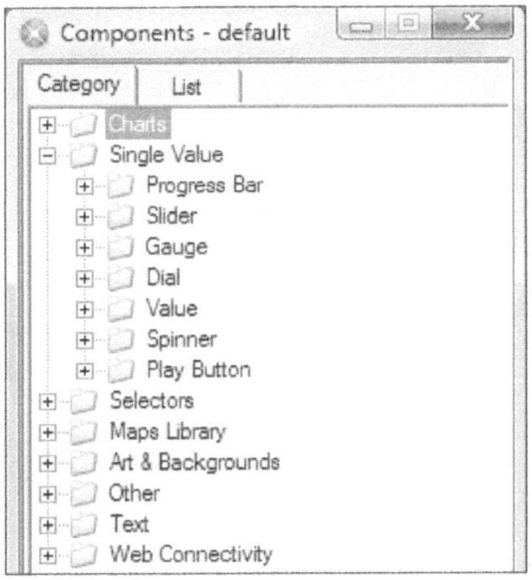

Figure 3-52 Components dialog box

Component Type	Description
Charts	Displays the data from the spreadsheet in a chart. [Lesson 6]
Selectors	A collection of components that allow the user to change at least one variable, which causes the data displayed in another component on the dashboard to change. [Lesson 7]
Maps Library	Links data geographically to different parts of the map. [Lesson 5]
Art & Backgrounds	A collection of components that can be added to the model to make the dashboard look better. They have no effect on the data or functionality of the dashboard. [Lesson 9]
Other	Components that do not fit in any of the other categories. [Lesson 9]
Text	Input and Label components that are used to pass data to the dashboard and to display text or data. [Lesson 9]
Web Connectivity	Adds Internet functionality and allows images and Flash files on the Internet to be used the dashboard. [Lesson 9]

Table 3-2 Other component types explained

PREPARING EXCEL SPREADSHEETS FOR DASHBOARDS

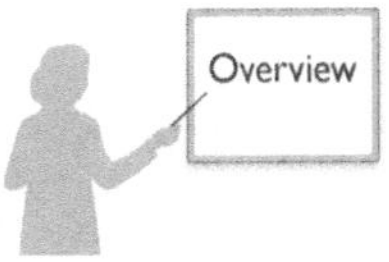

In this lesson you will learn about topics that will help you create better Excel spreadsheets for Crystal Xcelsius dashboards, including the following:

- ☑ Excel functionality not supported in Crystal Xcelsius
- ☑ Design principles
- ☑ Data modeling
- ☑ Connecting to external data sources
- ☑ Grouping data
- ☑ Chart data
- ☑ Formatting options

LESSON 4

Excel Overview

Okay, now that you have created your first dashboard in Crystal Xcelsius, this is a good time to go over topics in Excel that will help you structure that data in the spreadsheet to be more Crystal Xcelsius friendly. Before you become too excited about Crystal Xcelsius, I want to spend some time going over some Excel concepts that I think will help you create better dashboards in Crystal Xcelsius.

As I have said earlier, Excel has been around for a long time and will be here for quite some time. Some of the first dashboards were created in Excel. Many still are today. Because you purchased this book, I can conclude that at the very least, you want to see what Crystal Xcelsius has to offer that Excel doesn't, in terms of dashboard functionality.

If you have created dashboards in Excel, I think that the majority of topics covered in this lesson will be familiar. My primary goal for this lesson is to get you to start thinking about spreadsheet data in terms of what is needed to be able to create an effective dashboard in Crystal Xcelsius. In Lesson 3, you read about the dashboard design process. Some of the topics covered in this lesson expand on the topics presented in that lesson.

Another reason that at the 11th hour of writing this book that I decided to add this lesson is to let you know that most of the time the spreadsheet will not come to you from the user in the layout needed to create a dashboard.

Having written quite a few books that require sample files, every so often, I receive an email from a reader asking why is it that the data that they use at work is not ready to be used in a mail merge or a report like the sample files for the book are. Because I have or will, by the end of this lesson, addressed this topic thoroughly, I am not expecting any email like that from you. Instead, you can email me thanking me for the heads up <smile>.

I realize that some readers have already created dashboards in Excel. In this lesson, I try to point out as many similarities and differences as I can between creating dashboards in Excel and Crystal Xcelsius, to help make your transition easier.

Crystal Xcelsius Benefits

There are some benefits to using Crystal Xcelsius to create dashboards that Excel does not provide, including the following:

① By default, users cannot view, change or delete the formulas in the spreadsheet used to create a dashboard because they do not have access to the spreadsheet.

② Security of the spreadsheet data. While you can hide or protect the data and formulas in an Excel dashboard, it is much easier for someone to gain access to the protected information in Excel. Dashboards created in Crystal Xcelsius do not have this issue because the users only interaction with the data is via the dashboard. The formulas work in the dashboard but are not accessible via the dashboard.

③ Dashboards created in Crystal Xcelsius can be exported to other formats like HTML or PowerPoint and the formulas still work.

Excel Functionality That Crystal Xcelsius Does Not Support

For all that Crystal Xcelsius offers dashboard designers, there are some Excel features and functionality that Crystal Xcelsius does not support, as listed below:

① Active X Controls
② Auto Filters
③ Form Controls
④ Cells or spreadsheets that are linked to other spreadsheets
⑤ Macros
⑥ Rounding
⑦ Pivot Tables, but you can import the data displayed in a Pivot Table
⑧ Scientific formatted numbers. [See Lesson 1, Figure 1-9]

Excel Functions Supported In Crystal Xcelsius

Thankfully, the Crystal Xcelsius documentation team included a list of the supported Excel functions in the online users guide. I say thankfully, because I truly did not want to have to type them in <smile>. To view the list, follow the steps below.

1. Open Crystal Xcelsius.

2. Help ⇒ Contents ⇒ Contents tab ⇒ Supported Excel Functions.

   You should see the list shown on the right side of Figure 4-1.

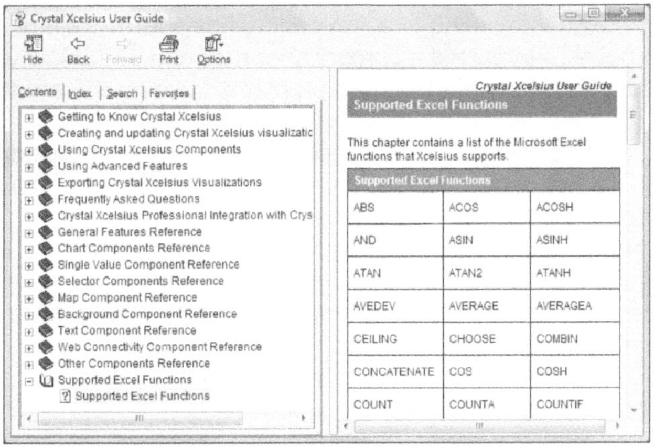

Figure 4-1 Supported Excel functions

Reports vs Dashboards

I have heard people use these words interchangeably and often it drives me nuts because they are two different ways to display data. Never mind that fact that I have written several books on Crystal Reports, the most popular report writing software currently on the market, so I think I know a thing or two about reports.

Out of all of the Business Intelligence tools, reports are probably the most used. Reports allow data to be presented in an easy to read and understand format. Reports primarily display raw data if you will. Reports also display summary and group information.

Reports present data, usually with minimal interaction between the report and person running the report. Reports often lead to further analysis. Most reports are paper based and have a broad goal and are not intended to be used to slice and dice data, as they say.

Dashboards are primarily graphical. They are usually not paper based. The graphical representation of data makes it easier to see the trends and draw conclusions. Dashboards either have the analysis built-in or allows the user to display the analysis in more than one way. Dashboards tend to present summary information, while reports tend to display more detailed information.

Crystal Xcelsius should be used to present data for analysis purposes. This means that often the data has already been summarized before it is imported into a model. Overall, Crystal Xcelsius uses less rows of data then a traditional report. Now that I have cleared up the differences between reports and dashboards, lets move on.

Data Modeling

In Lesson 3, I discussed the concept of designing for scalability. That is part of data modeling. A **DATA MODEL** is the structure or foundation for the data for a specific purpose. The purpose of a data model is to store data for analysis, not process data. In this case, the purpose is to import the spreadsheet data into a Crystal Xcelsius model.

I am sure that there is a limit to how many rows of spreadsheet data Crystal Xcelsius can work with, without coming to a screeching halt, but I could not find a definitive answer. For testing purposes, I imported a spreadsheet that had 15,000 rows of data. The import process took a while, but after that I had no problems building the model.

If the data model is not correct and the data is imported into Crystal Xcelsius, you will find that you cannot design the dashboard that you need. I understand that this concept may sound scary, but it is not as bad as you may be thinking. If you can visualize what the dashboard should look like and what functionality it should have, it will be easier to set up an appropriate data model. Sometimes, trying to visualize what the data for the dashboard should look like does not work. When that happens, I work backwards and will create the prototype with the data however I have it set up and see where I run into a problem. Often, for me, this is quicker and less stressful then trying to figure out the data model first. I don't advise this though, especially for people that are just starting out, because it is easy to miss something.

In Lesson 3, you learned how to gather all of the fields needed for the dashboard. Once you have the fields, you have to put them in the correct structure for the data model. One thing that may help is to keep in mind that from left to right in a spreadsheet, the data needed for a menu or filter component and data that is repeated row after row, goes in the left most columns. The data that is unique to each row, like totals or quantities, are placed in the right most columns. As shown in Figure 4-2, columns A to C contain the data the repeats, row after row, while the data in columns D to G is different from row to row.

	A	B	C	D	E	F	G
1	Sales by Sales Representative						
2							
3	*Product*	*Sales Rep*	*Account Type*	Q1	Q2	Q3	Q4
4	Product 1	Sales Rep. 1	New Customer	$ 44.2	$ 64.4	$ 55.3	$ 50.7
5	Product 2	Sales Rep. 1	New Customer	$ 39.6	$ 38.3	$ 34.7	$ 47.2
6	Product 3	Sales Rep. 1	New Customer	$ 41.9	$ 66.8	$ 55.5	$ 54.2
7	Product 4	Sales Rep. 1	New Customer	$ 41.5	$ 66.9	$ 40.8	$ 59.4
8	Product 5	Sales Rep. 1	New Customer	$ 63.2	$ 40.2	$ 58.1	$ 46.7
9	Product 6	Sales Rep. 1	New Customer	$ 50.9	$ 44.3	$ 50.1	$ 51.9
10	Product 7	Sales Rep. 1	New Customer	$ 53.7	$ 54.8	$ 39.1	$ 54.7
11	Product 8	Sales Rep. 1	New Customer	$ 62.0	$ 58.7	$ 56.6	$ 62.6
12	Product 9	Sales Rep. 1	New Customer	$ 63.8	$ 37.6	$ 48.1	$ 53.3
13	Product 1	Sales Rep. 1	Existing Customer	$ 52.8	$ 43.5	$ 44.0	$ 63.6
14	Product 2	Sales Rep. 1	Existing Customer	$ 63.7	$ 41.0	$ 45.3	$ 40.4

Figure 4-2 Appropriate data structure for a dashboard

If you are creating the dashboard in Excel, you would have to be concerned about what is known as **DATA PRESENTATION**. This is a term used to describe how the data looks. A lot of the data presentation is handled for you in Crystal Xcelsius. In a way, it doesn't matter what the data looks like in Excel, as much as it matters that the data model is correct.

How Metrics And KPI's Influence The Spreadsheet Structure

In Lesson 1 you read about these terms. Now it is time to dig deeper to understand how they will influence the spreadsheet structure. Following the KPI example in Lesson 1 of producing 10,000 cars a month, if the user needed to see the data by number of cars produced a day and by week, one section of the spreadsheet would need daily totals and another section would need weekly totals, as shown in Figure 4-3.

	A	B	C	D	E	F	G	H	I	J	K	L	M	N	O
1	Car Model	Feb. 1	Feb. 2	Feb. 3	Feb. 4	Feb. 5	Feb. 6	Feb. 7	Feb. 8	Feb. 9	Feb. 10	Feb. 11	Feb. 12	Feb. 13	Feb. 14
2															
3	Model A	12	50	40	99	130	80	50	40	99	111	68	77	52	67
4	Model B	12	123	200	99	13	81	50	200	99	333	89	49	83	15
5	Model C	8	45	75	99	110	82	50	75	99	222	79	37	95	150
6															
7	Daily Total	32	218	315	297	253	243	150	315	297	666	236	163	230	232
8															
9	Week 1 Total		1508												
10	Week 2 Total		2139												

Figure 4-3 Appropriate data structure for daily and weekly totals

Using Multiple Tabs

Many of the spreadsheets that you will come across will have one week or one month of data on a different tab. Often, spreadsheets like this have links between the tabs or to other spreadsheets, which is not supported in Crystal Xcelsius. You should be able to fit a years worth of data on one tab.

A good use of creating a dashboard from a spreadsheet that has data on multiple tabs is if the dashboard needs to display unrelated data. For example, a dashboard that would be used as part of a presentation to the Executive board could have the following requirements because you know how executives like to hear about several areas of the company at the same time <smile>.

① Display the detail and summary information for sales in North America.
② Display the healthcare costs for offices in the United States, Canada and Australia.
③ Display the number of laptops donated to charities by state.

To make it easier to keep the data needed for these three requests organized, each data set would go on a different tab.

While the data for the requirements for the dashboard is unrelated, all of the data would probably not be displayed at the same time, but it could. A menu would be created in the dashboard that let the user select which of these data sets they want to view.

Using Enterprise Data

If you have been looking around Crystal Xcelsius or Excel trying to figure out how you are going to get data from your Enterprise environment into Excel without having to get a Database Administrator to do it for you, this is the section that you have been looking for.

I cover two ways to bring your data into Excel. If the database is password protected, you will need the login information. You may also need rights to the server that the database is on.

Connecting To External Data Sources

By now you know that Excel is the tool that Crystal Xcelsius uses to import data. Many companies keep their data in databases like SQL and Microsoft Access. There are two tools that come to mind that you can use to import data into Excel, as listed below. The basics of each tool are covered in this lesson.

① The Import External Data option in Excel.
② Microsoft Query.

Using The Import External Data Option In Excel

Excel has built in functionality that allows you to connect to external data sources to import data into a spreadsheet.

The **IMPORT EXTERNAL DATA** option shown in Figure 4-4 is a wizard that walks you through selecting the database and table(s) that you want to import.

In Excel 2007, this option has been renamed to Get External Data.

The steps below show you how to import data from a Microsoft Access database. You can connect to other data sources besides Microsoft Access using this wizard.

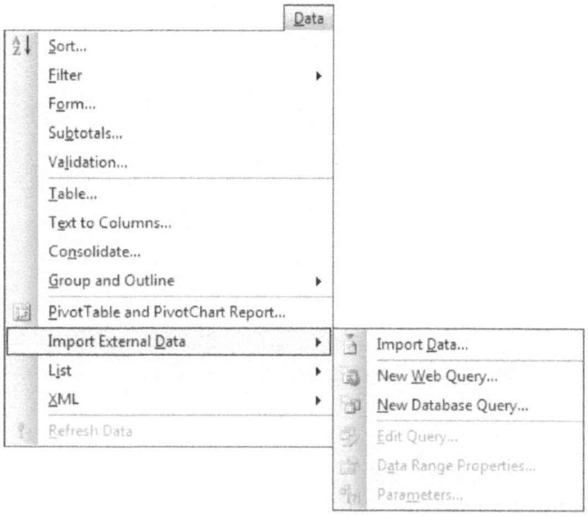

Figure 4-4 Import External Data option in Excel

1. Open a new Excel workbook, unless you want to import data into an existing workbook.

2. Data ⇒ Import External Data ⇒ Import Data, as shown above in Figure 4-4.

Database Connections

If you have never connected to a database that is the same type as the one that you want to connect to now (on the computer that you are currently using), you have to set up a connection for that type of database. For example, if you want to connect to an SQL database, but have never created a connection to any SQL database, you have to create a connection for SQL databases before you can import data from that data type.

3. If you need to create a connection, see the section "How To Create A Connection To A Remote Data Source", later in this lesson.

   If you see a connection to the database and table in Figure 4-5 that you need, go to the section "Use An Existing Connection", later in this lesson.

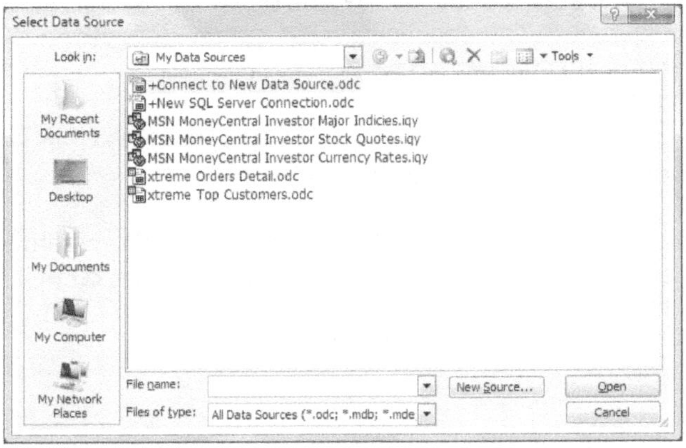

Figure 4-5 Select Data Source dialog box

4. Navigate to the folder that the database is in, in the **LOOK IN** drop-down list, shown above in Figure 4-5.

5. Double-click on the database. You will see the dialog box shown in Figure 4-6.

   If the database has queries or views, they will be listed on this dialog box also. You can select one of these as the source to import.

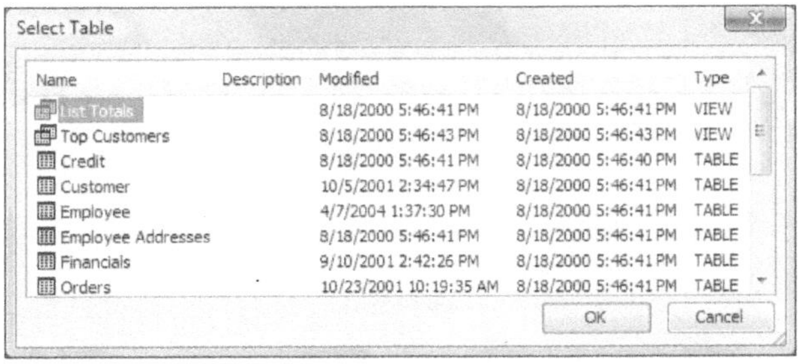

Figure 4-6 Select Table dialog box

6. Select the table, then click OK.

Import Data Dialog Box Options

On the dialog box shown in Figure 4-7, select **EXISTING WORKSHEET** if you want the data from the table to be imported to the current worksheet.

If you want the data to be imported to a **NEW WORKSHEET**, select this option.

The **PROPERTIES** button opens the dialog box shown in Figure 4-8. The options selected are the default options. If you need to change any, you can.

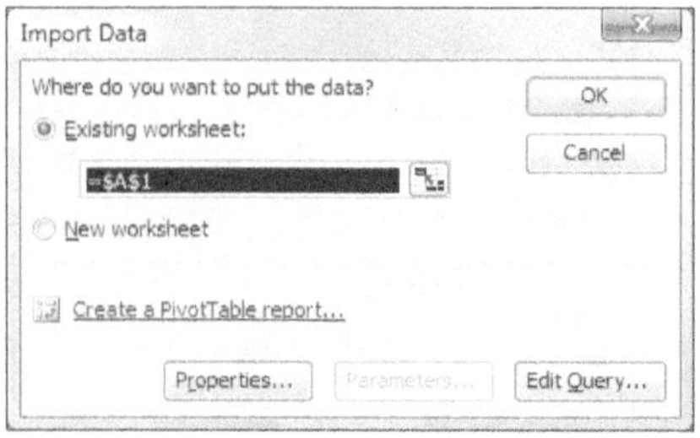

Figure 4-7 Import Data dialog box

The **EDIT QUERY** button opens the dialog box shown in Figure 4-9. If you need to edit any of the query related fields, you can.

The **CREATE A PIVOT TABLE REPORT** link opens the wizard shown in Figure 4-10. These options are used to create a Pivot Table report based on the data in the table that you selected. All of the data from the table may not be imported.

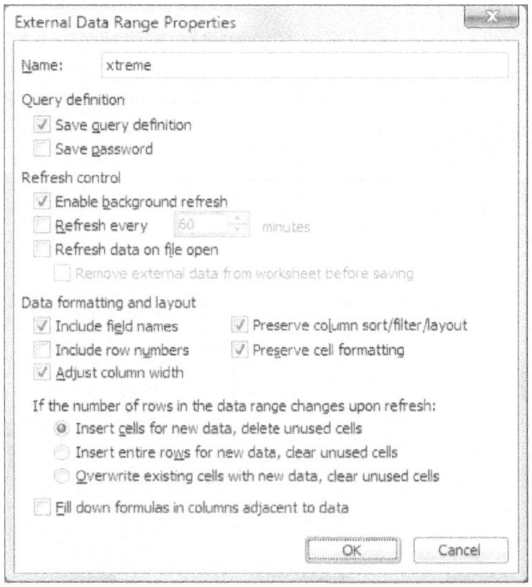

Figure 4-8 External Data Range Properties dialog box

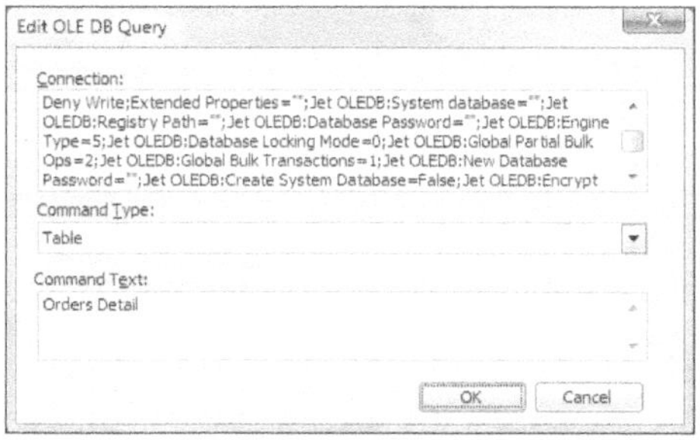

Figure 4-9 Edit OLE DB Query dialog box

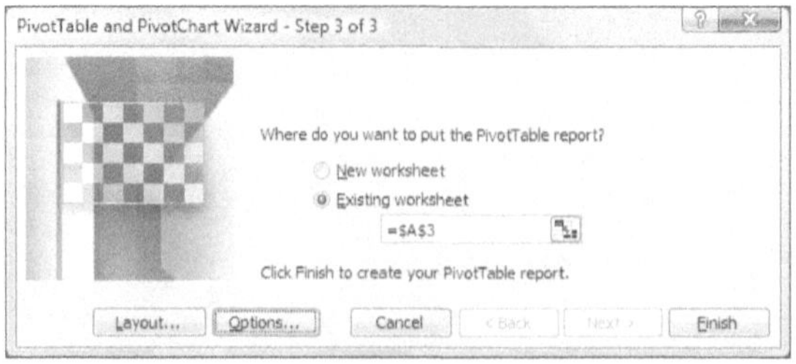

Figure 4-10 Pivot Table wizard

7. Once you have made your selections on the Import Data dialog box shown earlier in Figure 4-7, click OK. The data will be imported into the spreadsheet.

External Data Toolbar

After the data is imported, you should see the toolbar shown in Figure 4-11. When you need to refresh the data from the external data source, click the button illustrated.

Figure 4-11 External Data toolbar

How To Create A Connection To A Remote Data Source

To create a connection to a remote data source, select one of the options below on the Select Data Source dialog box, shown earlier in Figure 4-5.

① **CONNECT TO NEW DATA SOURCE**, then click the Open button. (1)

② **NEW SOURCE** button. (1)

③ **NEW SQL SERVER CONNECTION**, then click the Open button. You will see the dialog box shown in Figure 4-14.

(1) Opens the dialog box shown in Figure 4-12. Select **ODBC DSN** if you want to connect to a Microsoft Access database, then click Next. You will see the screen shown in Figure 4-13. If you need to connect to SharePoint, select the **DATA RETRIEVAL SERVICES** option shown in Figure 4-12.

Figure 4-12 Data Connection Wizard

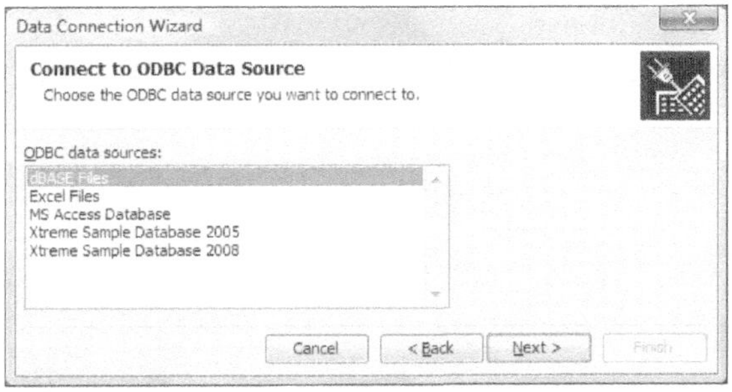

Figure 4-13 Data Connection Wizard to connect to an ODBC Data Source

Figure 4-14 Data Connection Wizard to connect to a database server

Use An Existing Connection

If the connection that you need is on the dialog box shown earlier in Figure 4-5, click on it, then click Open. Just make sure that it is the correct table.

Microsoft Query Wizard

This is a program that comes on the Microsoft Office installation CD. One of the features of the Query Wizard is to create connections to external data sources and import data into Excel. The advantage that this tool has over the Import External Data option in Excel is that you can modify the structure of the data that will be imported. By that I mean that you can do any of the following, prior to importing the data.

① Create a query to select specific records to import from the table(s).
② Join several tables.
③ Sort the data before it is imported.

Installing Microsoft Query

Depending on how Microsoft Office was installed, the MS Query Wizard may or may not already be installed. Follow the steps below to see if MS Query is installed and if it isn't, install it.
If you know that MS Query is installed, go to the section "Create A Database Connection Using MS Query".

1. Open Excel, if it is not already open.

2. Data ⇒ Import External Data ⇒ New Database Query, as shown earlier in Figure 4-4. If you see the Choose Data Source dialog box, MS Query is already installed. Go to the section, "Create A Database Connection Using MS Query".

3. If you see the message shown in Figure 4-15, click Yes, to start the installation process.

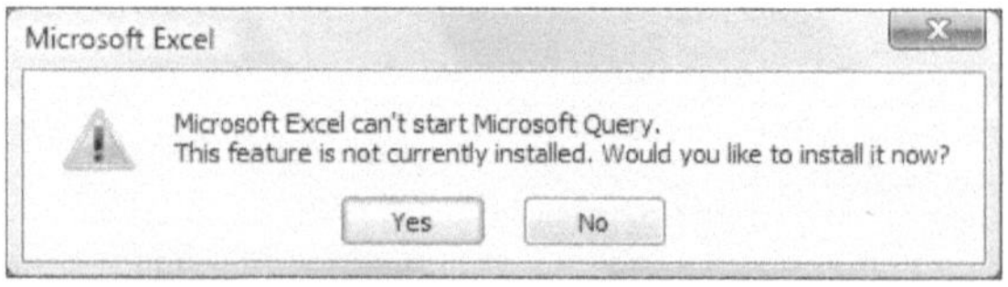

Figure 4-15 MS Query install message

You may be prompted to put the Microsoft Office CD into the drive. When the installation is completed you will see the Choose Data Source dialog box.

Create A Database Connection Using MS Query

The steps below show you how to connect to a Microsoft Access database.

1. In Excel, Data ⇒ Import External Data ⇒ New Database Query. You will see the dialog box shown in Figure 4-16.

   It is very possible that you will see different file types then the ones shown. The options that you have are from connections that you have already set up.

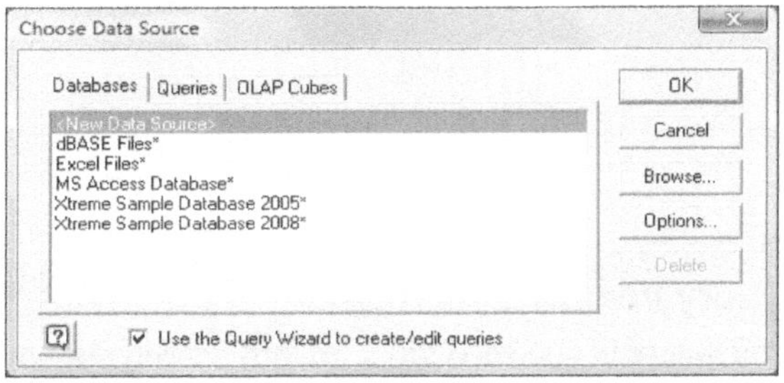

Figure 4-16 Choose Data Source dialog box

To connect to a database that has a file type (dBase Files, Excel Files and MS Access Database) in the list shown above in Figure 4-16, select the file type, then click OK. If you need to connect to an SQL or Oracle database or a database that does not have a corresponding file type in the list in Figure 4-16, select the **NEW DATA SOURCE** option, then click OK.

2. Select the MS Access Database option, then click OK.

3. If the database is not on your hard drive, open the **DRIVES** drop-down list, shown at the bottom of Figure 4-17 and select the drive that the database is on. You should also see the message box shown in Figure 4-18. This lets you know that you are in the process of creating a connection to a database.

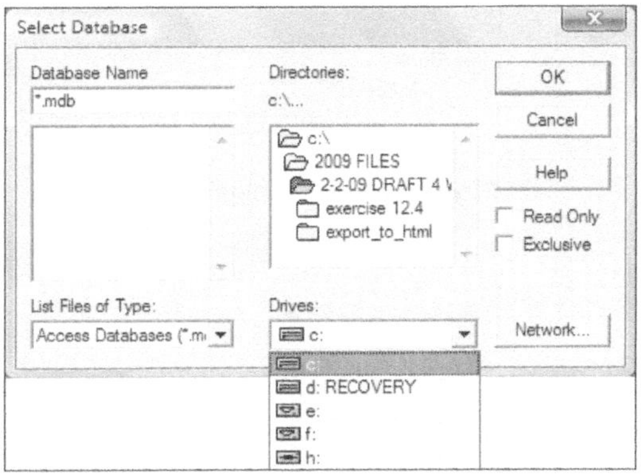

Figure 4-17 Select Database dialog box

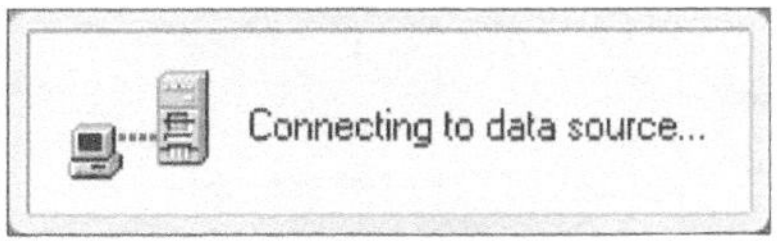

Figure 4-18 Connection message

4. In the **DIRECTORIES** section of the Select Database dialog box, navigate to and double-click on the folder that has the database that has the table(s) that you want to import.

5. In the **DATABASE NAME** list you will see a list of the databases that are in the folder that you selected.

   Click on the database that you want to connect to, as illustrated in Figure 4-19, then click OK.

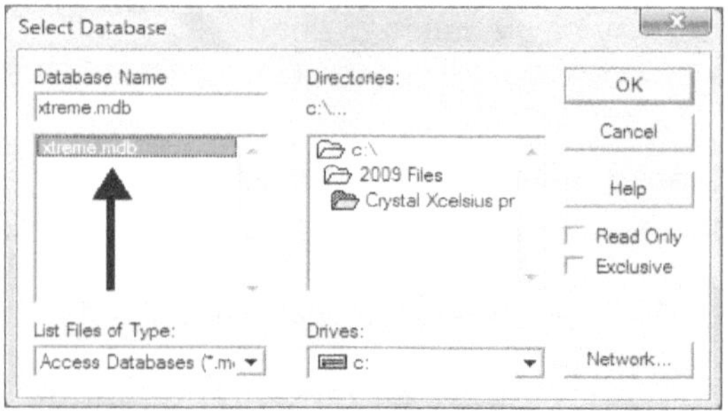

Figure 4-19 Selected database illustrated

Query Wizard Overview

You will now see the Query Wizard screen shown in Figure 4-20. This is where you select the fields from the table(s) that you want to import. If you click on the plus sign in front of a table name in the **AVAILABLE TABLES AND COLUMNS** list, you will see all of the fields in that table, as shown in Figure 4-21.

If you are not sure of the data that is in a field (which the Query Wizard refers to as a column), click on the field in the Available tables and columns or Columns in your query list, then click the **PREVIEW NOW** button. In the **PREVIEW OF DATA IN SELECTED COLUMN** field, you will see the data that is in that field.

The **OPTIONS** button opens the dialog box shown in Figure 4-22. These options control what is displayed in the Available tables and columns list.

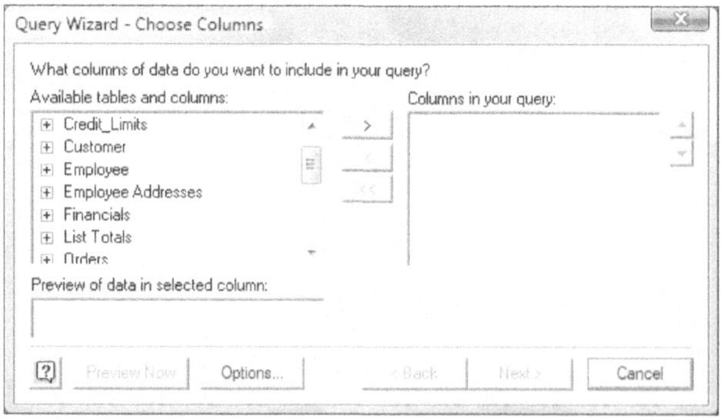

Figure 4-20 Query Wizard - Choose Columns screen

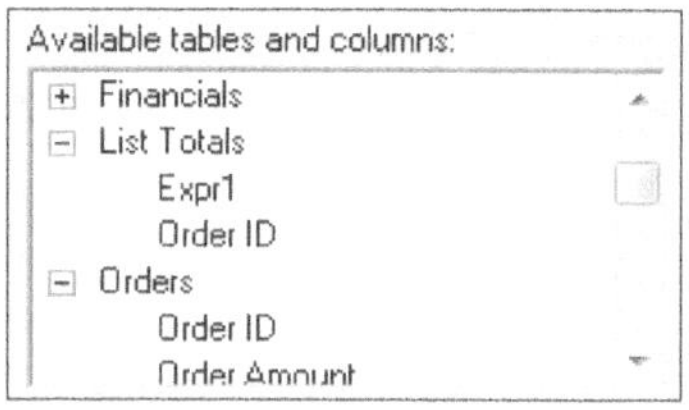

Figure 4-21 Tables expanded

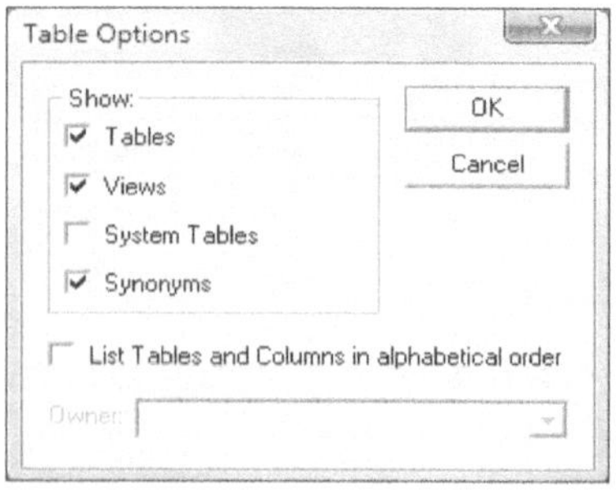

Figure 4-22 Table Options dialog box

Use The Query Wizard To Select The Data To Import

There are four steps to selecting and importing the data using the Query Wizard. Steps 2 and 3 are optional.

Step 1: Choose The Columns

1. Select a field that you want to import, then click the right arrow button. You should see the field that you selected in the **COLUMNS IN YOUR QUERY** list.

> **How To Add All Fields From A Table**
>
> If you want to import all of the fields from a table, click on the name of the table, then click the right arrow button.

> **How To Change The Order Of Fields Being Imported**
>
> If you need to rearrange the order of the fields in the Columns in your query list, click on the field that you want to move, then click the Up or Down button to the right of the list box.

2. When you have selected all of the fields that you need, click Next.

Step 2: Filter The Data

The options on this screen are used to select the criteria to filter (reduce) the number of records that will be imported into Excel. If you need to create criteria for another field, select the field name on the left, then select the criteria for the field.

Figure 4-23 shows sample filter criteria. Fields in bold in the **COLUMN TO FILTER** list indicate that you have already selected criteria for the field.

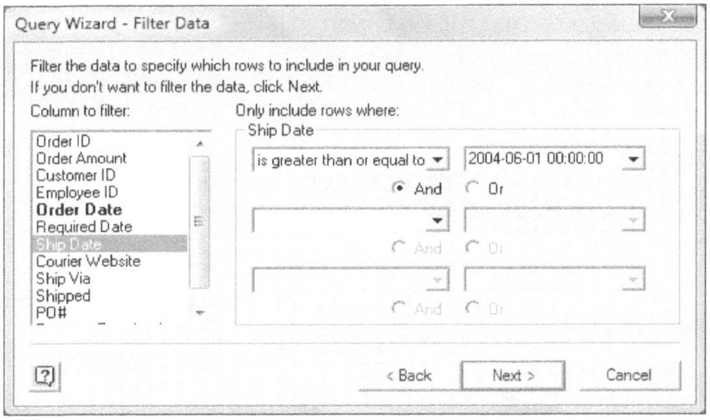

Figure 4-23 Query Wizard - Filter Data screen

1. Select the filter criteria for each field that you need.

2. Click Next.

Step 3: Sort The Records

The options shown in Figure 4-24 are used to sort the records that will be imported into Excel.

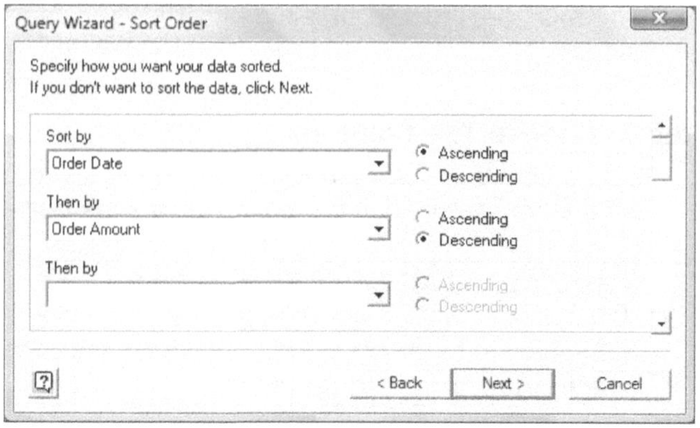

Figure 4-24 Query Wizard - Sort Order screen

1. Select the Sort Order.
2. Click Next.

Step 4: Finish The Import

The options shown in Figure 4-25 are used to select what you want to do with the records that will be imported.

The **SAVE QUERY** button lets you save the query that you just created.

Queries that you save will appear on the Queries tab, as shown in Figure 4-26.

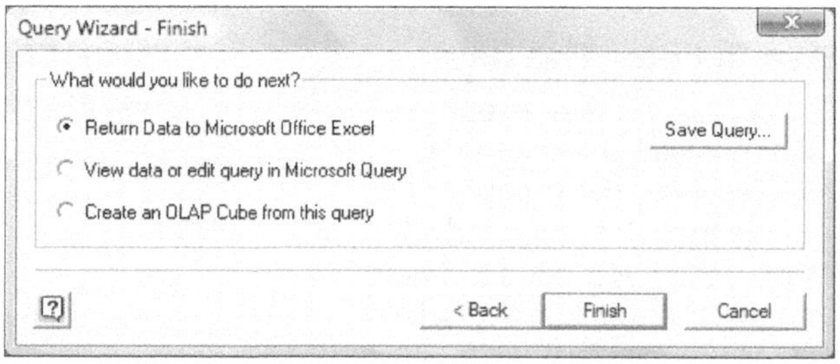

Figure 4-25 Query Wizard - Finish screen

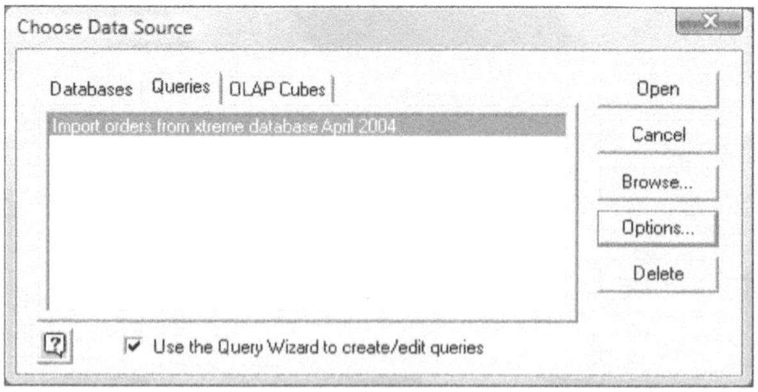

Figure 4-26 Queries tab on the Choose Data Source dialog box

The **RETURN DATA TO MICROSOFT OFFICE EXCEL** option imports the data into the current worksheet.

The **VIEW DATA OR EDIT QUERY IN MICROSOFT QUERY** option is used to view the data that will be imported or to edit the query that you created in the Query Wizard, as shown in Figure 4-27. The options discussed below are how to close the Query Tool.

① File ⇒ Cancel and Return to Microsoft Office Excel, will close the query tool and query wizard. Data will not be imported.
② File ⇒ Return Data to Microsoft Office Excel, is used to view and modify the query. This option will import the data to the spreadsheet.

The **CREATE AN OLAP CUBE FROM THIS QUERY** option will appear if you have already set up a connection to a database that supports OLAP Cubes. You will see the wizard shown in Figure 4-28. This wizard will let you import the data into an OLAP Cube structure. **OLAP** stands for On-Line Analytical Processing.

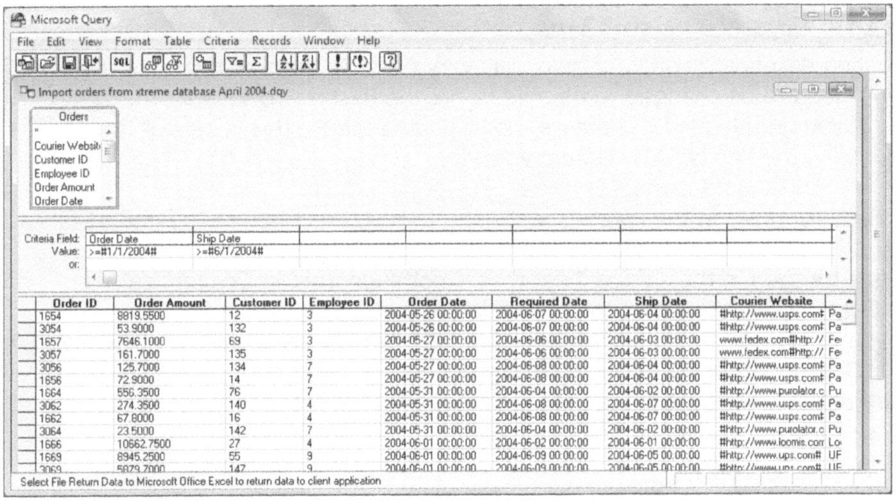

Figure 4-27 Microsoft Query tool

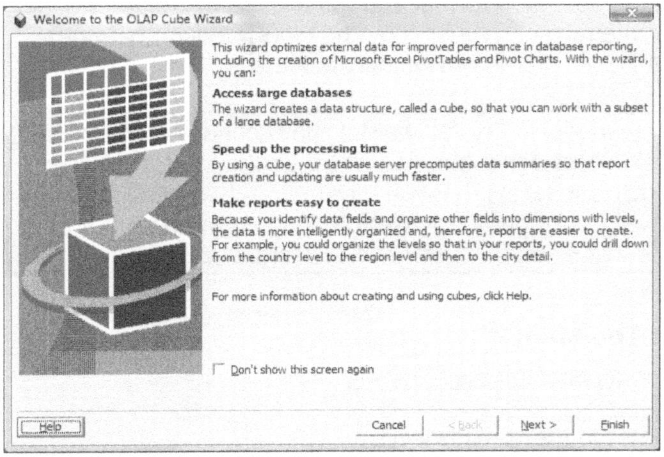

Figure 4-28 OLAP Cube Wizard

Check The Data Model

There are several tasks that need to be completed before the spreadsheet is imported in Crystal Xcelsius, as discussed below.

① Make sure that all of the data is in the spreadsheet. I know that sounds funny, but it is very easy to leave off a row or column of data.
② Check and test the formulas and functions to make sure that they reference the correct cells and are not producing any errors.
③ Include as much numeric formatting as needed. Also make sure that the numeric formatting is correct for each field.
④ For testing purposes (in Crystal Xcelsius), in the spreadsheet you should include negative numbers and data that does not belong, to see how Crystal Xcelsius handles it.

Importing Data Into Crystal Xcelsius Tips

When you start creating dashboards on your own, it is very possible that the layout of the spreadsheet data will need to be changed to be able to get the dashboard to work the way that you need it to. If you find this to be the case, don't panic because this is part of the learning curve. Hopefully, the tips below will help you.

① The data and formulas in the spreadsheet need to be correct before the import takes place.
② If there is a function in the spreadsheet that is not supported in Crystal Xcelsius, it needs to be replaced in the spreadsheet before the data is imported.
③ As best you can, make sure that the layout of the spreadsheet is correct. If you add, modify or delete rows or columns in the spreadsheet to be able to create the dashboard and then re-import the data, some of the references to cells on the Properties dialog box in Crystal Xcelsius may not work. If this type of change occurs, you will have to manually change the links in the model so that the dashboard will work with the structure changes in the spreadsheet.
④ When you import a spreadsheet, all of the tabs in the Excel workbook are imported. This allows you to select data on any tab, to link a component to in the model. If there are tabs with data in the spreadsheet that you will not use to create the dashboard, you should delete the tabs of data or copy the tab(s) of data that are needed to a new spreadsheet before starting the import process.

> Once the data is imported into the model in Crystal Xcelsius, any changes made to the data on the spreadsheet will not be captured in the dashboard unless the spreadsheet data is re-imported into the model. If it seems that you have read this already in this book, you are not crazy, you have. I have purposely written it more than once because it seems to be a step that people just learning Crystal Xcelsius forget.

How Many Rows And Columns Is Too Many?

The honest answer to that question is, it depends on the following:

① The number of rows and columns in the spreadsheet.
② The number of complex formulas the spreadsheet has.

I have create a model that has 15,000 plus rows, but only four columns of data and a few SUM formulas. I haven't tried it, but I suspect that a spreadsheet that has 15,000 rows and 12 or more columns of data will cause the dashboard to run slow.

After reading a lot of messages in forums, I found out that formulas cause a performance hit (2), more than a large number of rows of data. The more complex the formulas are, the quicker the performance of the dashboard will degrade. Excel does not process the formulas in a dashboard. Remember that once you import the data into the model, Excel is disconnected from the model. Flash actually processes the formulas in the dashboard, which is probably why all of Excels functions are not supported in Crystal Xcelsius. (I did not verify that, it is just my educated guess.)

The one function that I noticed when reading the messages in the forums that people had trouble with is VLOOKUP. Too many formulas with the VLOOKUP function in a model, causes the dashboard to take a performance hit.

(2) A **PERFORMANCE HIT** is a process that causes something, in this case, a dashboard to run slower then it would if the process was not being used.

VLOOKUP Function

VLOOKUP is an Excel function that is used to look for a specific value in the left most column of data. The value found is used to retrieve data in another cell in the row.

Grouping Or Sorting Data

Grouping data is the process of being able to put like items together. Crystal Xcelsius does not have a built in grouping or sorting option, so you will have to set up any grouping or sorting that the dashboard needs in Excel. In order to do this, you need to know what field(s) the groups are for and what component will be used. The component that comes to mind first is the filter component.

If you are or were a programmer at any time, this is one area of the dashboard design process that will truly make you cringe <smile>. In order to be able to group data for components, each row of data must have the same information in certain columns.

For example, Figure 4-29 shows the quarterly sales per rep, per product, per account type.

Fellow programmers, so far, so good. Unfortunately, Crystal Xcelsius cannot use this layout to populate the filter component shown in Figure 4-30.

	A	B	C	D	E	F	G
1	Sales by Sales Representative						
2							
3	*Sales Rep*	*Account Type*	*Product*	Q1	Q2	Q3	Q4
4	Sales Rep. 1	New Customer	Product 1	$44.2	$64.4	$55.3	$50.7
5			Product 2	$39.6	$38.3	$34.7	$47.2
6			Product 3	$41.9	$66.8	$55.5	$54.2
7	Sales Rep. 1	Existing Customer	Product 1	$52.8	$43.5	$44.0	$63.6
8			Product 2	$63.7	$41.0	$45.3	$40.4
9	Sales Rep. 2	New Customer	Product 1	$58.1	$38.3	$56.7	$61.0
10			Product 2	$48.5	$54.3	$43.3	$38.1
11			Product 3	$52.6	$26.9	$40.6	$60.1
12			Product 4	$42.5	$66.5	$44.0	$44.7

Figure 4-29 Quarterly sales

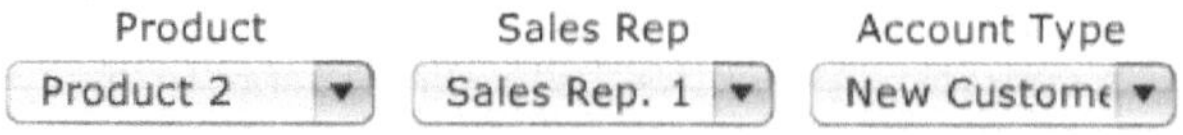

Figure 4-30 Filter component

I understand that in Excel the layout shown earlier in Figure 4-29 is a very popular format for creating reports. It is very common to use empty space for repetitive data. To populate the filter component, the data must look like the spreadsheet shown in Figure 4-31.

	A	B	C	D	E	F	G
1	Sales by Sales Representative						
2							
3	*Product*	*Sales Rep*	*Account Type*	Q1	Q2	Q3	Q4
4	Product 1	Sales Rep. 1	New Customer	$ 44.2	$ 64.4	$ 55.3	$ 50.7
5	Product 2	Sales Rep. 1	New Customer	$ 39.6	$ 38.3	$ 34.7	$ 47.2
6	Product 3	Sales Rep. 1	New Customer	$ 41.9	$ 66.8	$ 55.5	$ 54.2
7	Product 4	Sales Rep. 1	New Customer	$ 41.5	$ 66.9	$ 40.8	$ 59.4
8	Product 5	Sales Rep. 1	New Customer	$ 63.2	$ 40.2	$ 58.1	$ 46.7
9	Product 6	Sales Rep. 1	New Customer	$ 50.9	$ 44.3	$ 50.1	$ 51.9
10	Product 7	Sales Rep. 1	New Customer	$ 53.7	$ 54.8	$ 39.1	$ 54.7
11	Product 8	Sales Rep. 1	New Customer	$ 62.0	$ 58.7	$ 56.6	$ 62.6
12	Product 9	Sales Rep. 1	New Customer	$ 63.8	$ 37.6	$ 48.1	$ 53.3
13	Product 1	Sales Rep. 1	Existing Customer	$ 52.8	$ 43.5	$ 44.0	$ 63.6
14	Product 2	Sales Rep. 1	Existing Customer	$ 63.7	$ 41.0	$ 45.3	$ 40.4

Figure 4-31 Data for a three level filter component

Programmers, you may cringe now. For all of the non programmers reading this book, the reason that we are cringing at the data structure shown above in Figure 4-31 is because if we created a database that stored data this way (repeating the same data over and over, row by row), we would be fired! Sadly, this is a perfect example of what I meant earlier when I stated that you have to use an Excel structure that Crystal Xcelsius can support.

Until the time comes when Crystal Xcelsius can directly support relational databases, this is how data must be structured in a spreadsheet.

Flat File vs Relational Data Structures

For as long as I can remember, someone will state that Excel is relational. If you are one of those people, this will hopefully clarify it for you. Relational data is stored in more than one table in a database. To display relational data, more than one table is required. In order for a table to be relational, each record in the table **MUST** have a unique identifier. This identifier is usually system generated, which means that us mere mortals do not add data to the field. Excel does not have the ability to create a unique system generated field or another type of unique identifier, therefore, Excel is not relational, it is flat file.

How To Filter Data In Excel

If filtering data is a new concept to you, follow the steps below to get a feel for how filtering data works in Excel. It is very similar to how it works in Crystal Xcelsius. My goal is to help you become familiar with the data for the Filter component in Crystal Xcelsius. The steps below are based on Excel 2003. If you have Excel 2007, you will have to locate the Auto Filter option.

1. Open the Filter spreadsheet in Excel.

2. Data ⇒ Filter ⇒ Auto Filter. At the top of the spreadsheet, each column should have a drop-down list.

3. Open the drop-down list for the Account Type column and select New Customer.
   You should only see rows of data that have New Customer, as shown in Figure 4-32.
   The Filter component in Crystal Xcelsius, shown earlier in Figure 4-30, works the same way.

	A	B	C	D	E	F	G
1	Sales by Sales Repr	entative					
4	Product 1	Sales Rep. 1	New Customer	$ 44.2	$ 64.4	$ 55.3	$ 50.7
5	Product 2	Sales Rep. 1	New Customer	$ 39.6	$ 38.3	$ 34.7	$ 47.2
6	Product 3	Sales Rep. 1	New Customer	$ 41.9	$ 66.8	$ 55.5	$ 54.2
7	Product 4	Sales Rep. 1	New Customer	$ 41.5	$ 66.9	$ 40.8	$ 59.4
8	Product 5	Sales Rep. 1	New Customer	$ 63.2	$ 40.2	$ 58.1	$ 46.7
9	Product 6	Sales Rep. 1	New Customer	$ 50.9	$ 44.3	$ 50.1	$ 51.9
10	Product 7	Sales Rep. 1	New Customer	$ 53.7	$ 54.8	$ 39.1	$ 54.7
11	Product 8	Sales Rep. 1	New Customer	$ 62.0	$ 58.7	$ 56.6	$ 62.6
12	Product 9	Sales Rep. 1	New Customer	$ 63.8	$ 37.6	$ 48.1	$ 53.3
22	Product 1	Sales Rep. 2	New Customer	$ 58.1	$ 38.3	$ 56.7	$ 61.0
23	Product 2	Sales Rep. 2	New Customer	$ 48.5	$ 54.3	$ 43.3	$ 38.1
24	Product 3	Sales Rep. 2	New Customer	$ 52.6	$ 26.9	$ 40.6	$ 60.1
25	Product 4	Sales Rep. 2	New Customer	$ 42.5	$ 66.5	$ 44.0	$ 44.7
26	Product 5	Sales Rep. 2	New Customer	$ 66.0	$ 59.9	$ 57.8	$ 55.4

Figure 4-32 Data filtered in the spreadsheet

4. Open the Sales Rep drop-down list and select Sales rep 2. Only new customers for Sales rep 2 are displayed in the spreadsheet. All of the other records are hidden.

Before you fall out of the chair, as the dashboard designer, you do not have to change the spreadsheet shown earlier in Figure 4-29 to the one shown earlier in Figure 4-31. You can tell the user of the spreadsheet to change the data to the required layout. What I learned a long time ago, is that as the developer of a data driven project, you are much safer by having the data owners make changes to the data, then doing it yourself. Yes, as IT people we could probably do it faster, but that is not the point. If you do not touch a users data, they cannot attempt to blame you for data errors down the road <smile>!

If it is discovered after you have finished the dashboard and put it into production, that any of the following needs to be done, the spreadsheet and model will require modifications after you finish yelling. (Can you say scope creep?) For those of you that skimmed over the Dashboard Design section in Lesson 3, may want to revisit it before venturing out on your own to create a dashboard.

① At least one filter, as shown earlier in Figure 4-30, is in the wrong order. For example, if the sales rep filter should come before the product filter, the spreadsheet would have to be changed and column B would have to be moved to column A. No change would have to be made to the selected options in the model, only the data would have to be refreshed.

② A new group is needed. For example, the filter options shown earlier in Figure 4-30, also need an option to select the customers state. A new column would have to be added to the spreadsheet in the appropriate location. This change, in addition to having to refresh the data in the model would at the very minimum require changes to the options on the General tab on the Properties dialog box in Crystal Xcelsius to include the addition of the new column of data.

③ An existing group that is being used in the filter needs to be deleted. If the column of data for the filter that needs to be deleted is between other columns on the spreadsheet that are being used as filters, the column would have to be deleted and options on the General tab would have to be modified after the data has been refreshed.

If the column that is no longer needed for the filter is the first or last column in the filter range in the spreadsheet, you can leave the spreadsheet as is and just change the options on the General tab to not reference the column.

Cells With And Without Formulas

When cells are linked to a component, they behave differently depending on whether or not they have a formula. Single Value components that are linked to a value can be used to select other data in the dashboard. For example, a slider component that is linked to a cell with a value, as shown in Figure 4-33 can be used to select values that display in a chart. Figure 4-34 shows the spreadsheet used for the component.

A component that is linked to a cell with a formula can only be used as an output component. You need to make sure that cells that will be linked to a Single Value component that will be used to select or control data in another component on the dashboard do not have formulas.

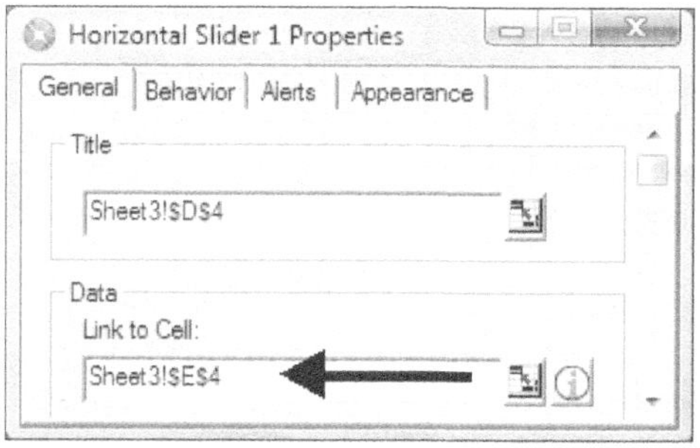

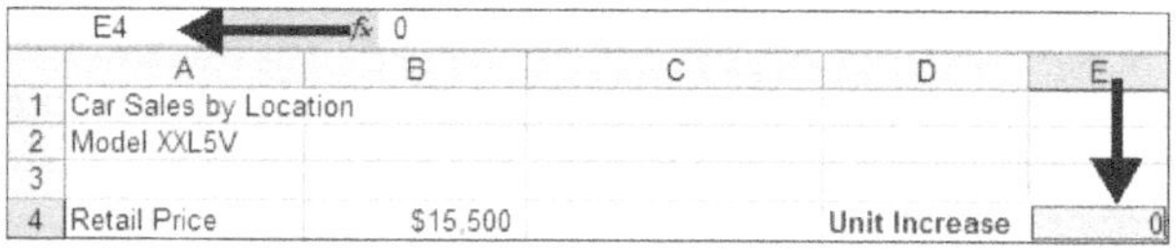

Figure 4-34 Cell for a Single Value component illustrated

Figure 4-33 Single Value component linked to a cell with a value

Charts

Charts are the core of dashboards in Excel and Crystal Xcelsius. The majority of chart types in Crystal Xcelsius and Excel are the same. Charts are covered in detail in Lesson 6. The differences that I have observed are discussed below.

① The biggest difference is that the data that is displayed in charts in Crystal Xcelsius can be changed by other components in the dashboard.

② In Excel you can modify individual parts of a chart, like a data series. While charts created in Crystal Xcelsius have data series, they cannot be customized as much. In Crystal Xcelsius, a chart does not have individual parts, other then the titles, labels and legend.

③ Crystal Xcelsius does not allow you to change the chart type once the component has been added to the canvas.

④ Another chart difference that you will notice is that Combination charts in Crystal Xcelsius only use line and column charts, unlike Combination charts in Excel, which can use an area chart as one of the chart types in a Combination chart.

Demystifying Chart Data

As if going through the dashboard design process in Lesson 3 was not bad enough and having to figure out the appropriate data model didn't push you to the edge, now you have to know how to set up the data, depending on the chart type.

The reason that I am covering this information is based on an Introduction to Excel class that I teach from time to time. I do not know what it is, but students that have an A average in the class will all of a sudden have a C average after completing the assignments on charts. It took me a while to figure out why. What I concluded was that students truly did not understand that different types of charts require the data to be set up in a specific way. I believe this is because they do not know which values in a spreadsheet, Excel uses to plot data. If you fall into this category, you are not alone.

The goal of this section is to help get you familiar with how the data layout should be for some of the more common chart types. The spreadsheets and charts used in the examples come from exercises that you will complete later in this book.

Pie Chart Data

Pie charts represent a series of data at a specific time. Figure 4-35 shows data that will allow you to create a pie chart. To create a pie chart for all products in Europe, the Data Range in Crystal Xcelsius would be C6:G6. Each value in the data range represents a slice of the pie.

The Category Axis Labels would be C3:G3. The column headings are the category labels. There is no rule that column headings have to be in row A.

The chart in Crystal Xcelsius would look like the one shown in Figure 4-36.

	A	B	C	D	E	F	G
1	Revenues By Product		Rev				
2							
3		Status List	Prod. A	Prod. B	Prod. C	Prod. D	Prod. E
4	North America		$ 14.22	$ 20.12	$ 12.18	$ 25.49	$ 15.64
5	Latin America		$ 21.05	$ 19.54	$ 15.88	$ 18.73	$ 15.02
6	Europe		$ 21.06	$ 20.45	$ 14.49	$ 16.78	$ 13.61
7	Asia		$ 12.25	$ 17.12	$ 20.99	$ 16.79	$ 12.07
8	Australia & Pacific		$ 15.36	$ 25.74	$ 13.17	$ 19.42	$ 12.70

Figure 4-35 Data for a pie chart

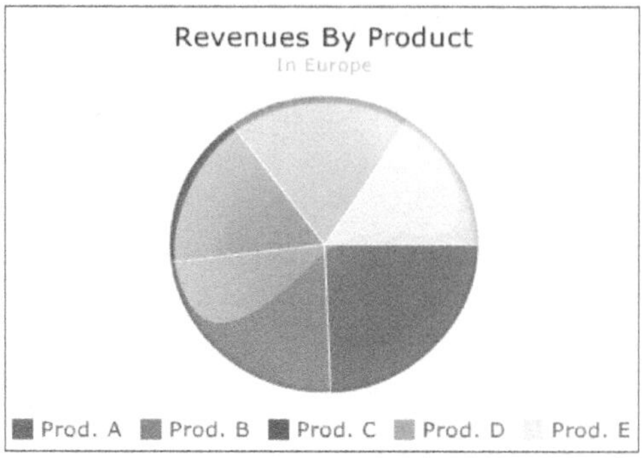

Figure 4-36 Pie chart in Crystal Xcelsius

Line Chart Data

Line charts represent data over a period of time. Figure 4-37 shows data that can be used to create a line chart. Bar, area and column charts can also be created from the data in Figure 4-37.

A line chart can be created to show one series of data, as shown in Figure 4-38. Figure 4-39 shows two series of data in an area chart. The data range for the market growth series is B4:I4. The data range for the sales growth series is B5:I5. if you were going to create a Line chart with two series, you would select the same data range.

	A	B	C	D	E	F	G	H	I
1	Sales Growth vs Market Growth								
2									
3		**1995**	**1996**	**1997**	**1998**	**1999**	**2000**	**2001**	**2002**
4	Market Growth	7.00%	5.00%	5.00%	3.50%	7.00%	8.00%	5.00%	2.50%
5	Sales Growth	9.00%	7.00%	6.00%	5.00%	8.00%	10.00%	11.00%	13.00%

Figure 4-37 Data for a line chart

Figure 4-38 Line chart for the sales growth series of data

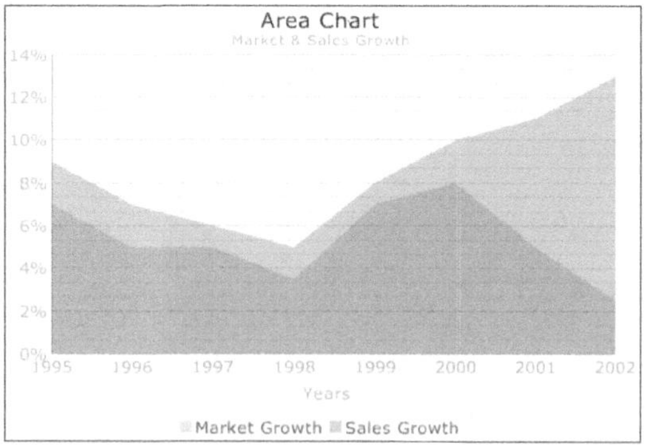

Figure 4-39 Area chart

Figure 4-40 shows the same two series of data in a bar chart that were used to create the area chart.

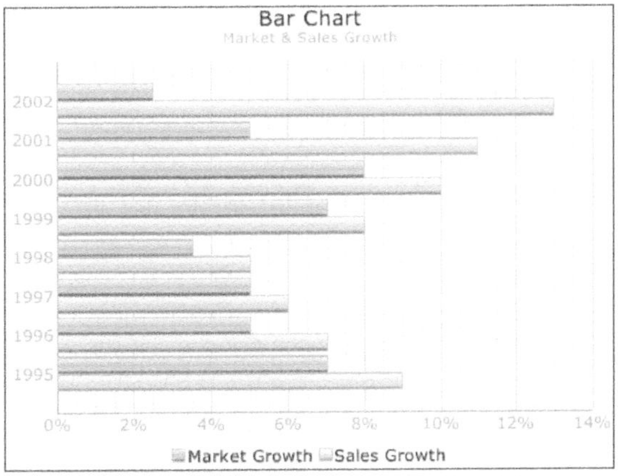

Figure 4-40 Bar chart

Bubble, XY And Radar Chart Data

These chart types are similar in terms of data structure. All three chart types plot data based on the X and Y Axis. Where the X value and Y value intersect is where the marker is placed on the chart.

Bubble charts go one step further by also using a Z value, which is used to determine the size of the bubble on the chart.

Figure 4-41 shows data that can be used to create these three chart types.

	A	B	C
1	Months on market	Asking Price	Qty
2	35	$355,000	78
3	12	$160,000	19
4	6	$150,000	89
5	25	$400,000	36
6	28	$210,000	100
7	8	$175,000	47
8	22	$360,000	51
9	15	$223,000	22
10	33	$316,000	53
11	10	$500,000	10
12	8	$429,000	44
13	4	$279,900	77

Figure 4-41 Data for several chart types

Column A is the data for the X Axis. Column B is the data for the Y Axis. Column C is the data that will determine the size of the bubble. The larger the number, the larger the bubble size will be. XY and Radar charts would not use this column of data in this scenario.

Figure 4-42 shows the Bubble chart from the data shown in above in Figure 4-41.

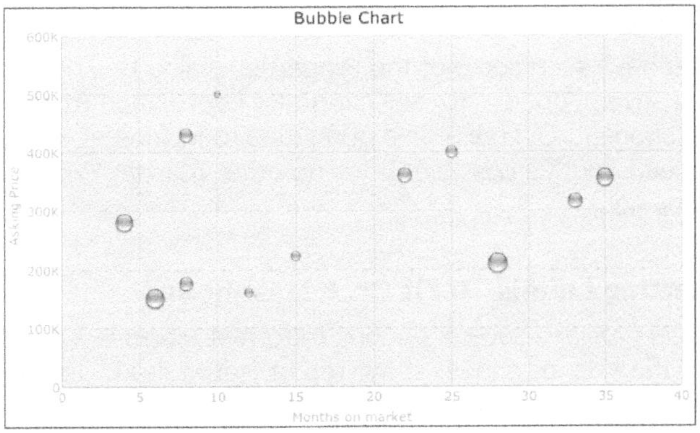

Figure 4-42 Bubble chart

Figure 4-43 shows the XY chart that could be created from the data shown earlier in Figure 4-41.

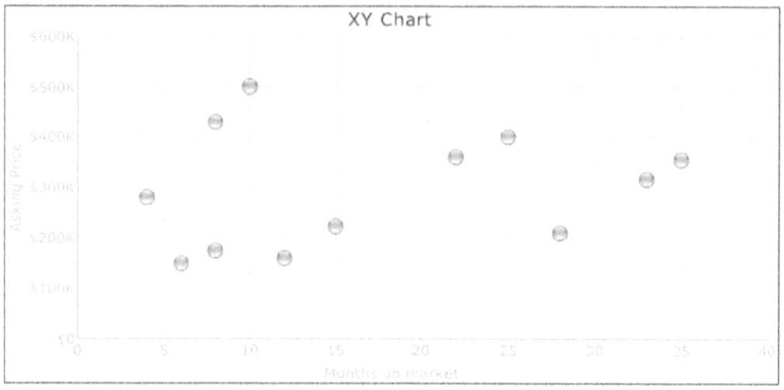

Figure 4-43 XY chart

Bubble Charts vs XY And Radar Charts

While these chart types appear similar, there are some differences, as discussed below.

① Bubble charts can only use numeric data. Usually, the X Axis data for XY and Radar charts is text.
② Bubble charts require three columns of data. XY and Radar only use two columns of data.

Form Controls

As you read earlier in this lesson, Crystal Xcelsius does not support any of Excels form controls, meaning they cannot be imported. While that is true, Crystal Xcelsius does have some options that provide the same functionality. One is the Spinner component. The majority of Excels form controls have a counterpart (ie, Check Box, Combo Box, List Box) in Crystal Xcelsius.

Formatting Options

Excel provides a variety of formatting options for text and numeric data. Most of them are not available in Crystal Xcelsius. The sections below discuss data that should be added to the spreadsheet so that it will be available in Crystal Xcelsius and formatting that you should set up in Excel.

Titles And Labels

You have seen some of the Properties dialog box options in Crystal Xcelsius. On the General tab are several options for selecting title information from the spreadsheet for various parts of a component. Overall, it is a good idea to include as many of the titles and labels in the spreadsheet as possible. If for no other reason, Excel has a spell checker and Crystal Xcelsius does not.

Getting Labels To Fit On A Dashboard

Excel provides several options to format labels in a spreadsheet when the labels are too wide for the axis, as shown at the top of Figure 4-44. Usually, this is an issue for months. I prefer the first option shown in the figure because it saves space because the month names are abbreviated. Many people prefer to use the second option in Excel.

Crystal Xcelsius does not have options that replicate the last two options. On the X-Axis if you have enough space to make the chart large enough, you can get the titles in a vertical position as shown in Figure 4-45. If you want to use the first option shown in Figure 4-44, but the spreadsheet will be used for other purposes, it is best to make a copy and use the copy. That way you can type in the abbreviated month names on the spreadsheet that will be imported.

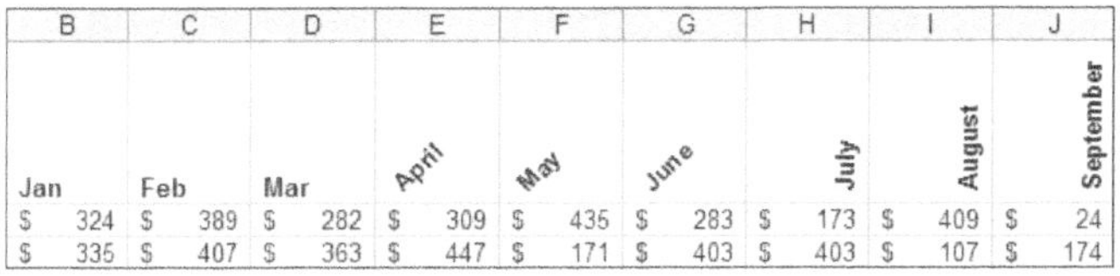

B	C	D	E	F	G	H	I	J
Jan	Feb	Mar	April	May	June	July	August	September
$ 324	$ 389	$ 282	$ 309	$ 435	$ 283	$ 173	$ 409	$ 24
$ 335	$ 407	$ 363	$ 447	$ 171	$ 403	$ 403	$ 107	$ 174

Figure 4-44 Excel label formatting options

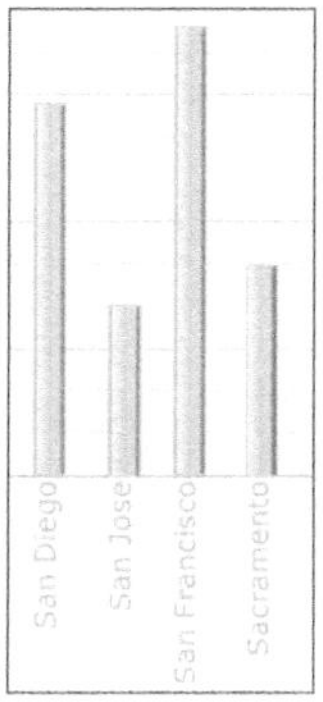

Figure 4-45 X-Axis labels

Using A Background Color In Spreadsheets

As you go through the exercises in this book, you will see that some cells in some of the spreadsheets have a background color. I take no credit for this idea. These colored empty cells will be used to store the data selected by a component that will be displayed on the dashboard. This is helpful because hopefully, it will remind you that the cells are being used, so you should not put data in them.

You will see that the cells with a colored background that are at the top of the spreadsheet are used by components to pass data. This is how one component controls the data that is displayed in another component. Cells with a colored background that are below several rows of data are used to display a series of data on a component. This helps make the cells that have been reserved stand out on the spreadsheet.

Formatting Numbers

Excel provides more numeric formatting options than Crystal Xcelsius. It is a good idea to format the numeric data in the spreadsheet as much as possible before importing it into a model.

While it is acceptable to use decimal points in Excel, as much as possible in my opinion, try to avoid them because decimal points are often hard to read in a dashboard. Commas on the other hand, make the data easier to read in a dashboard. The dialog box in Figure 4-46 shows the formatting options in Excel.

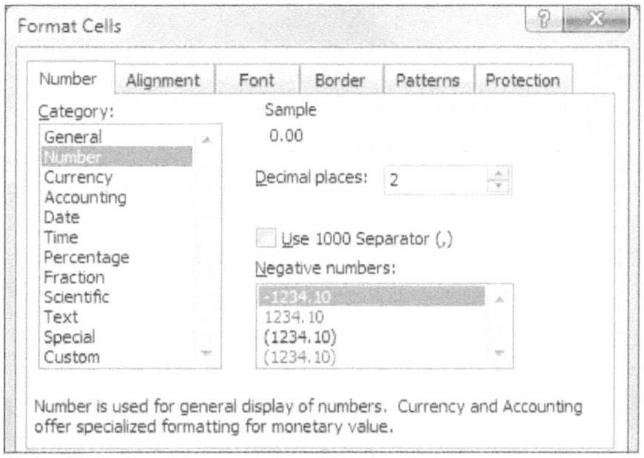

Figure 4-46 Excel Format Cells dialog box

Custom Numeric Formatting

Some of the numeric formatting that is supported in Excel does not have an equivalent formatting option in Crystal Xcelsius. This usually happens when a custom number format type is selected in Excel, as shown in Figure 4-47.

In Lesson 3, you learned about the **FROM SPREADSHEET** numeric formatting option in Crystal Xcelsius. If cells in the spreadsheet have numeric formatting that does not appear in the model, select the From Spreadsheet option on the Appearance tab on the Properties dialog box.

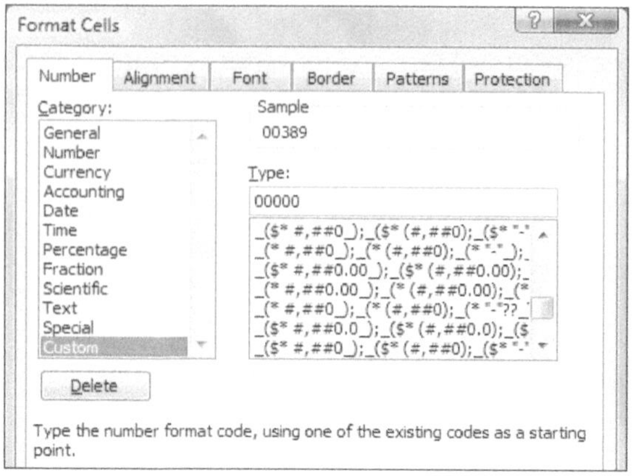

Figure 4-47 Excel Custom Number format type options

Conditional Formatting

Conditional formatting is the process of automatically changing the appearance of cells (like the background color of cells) or the values in cells (like changing the font size of the value in a cell) based on a condition that you set up. Without a doubt, Excel has the better tool set in my opinion, when it comes to conditional formatting. Excel allows you to create conditional formatting rules to change the color of cells, format bars and more. Figure 4-48 shows the conditional formatting options in Excel.

Crystal Xcelsius has alerts, which support conditional formatting. Alerts let you change the color of different parts of a component, based on whether the value in a field is below the target value, in the accepted target range or above a target value.

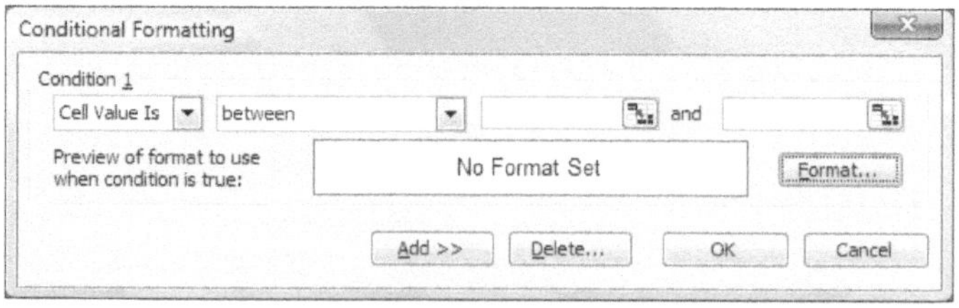

Figure 4-48 Excel Conditional Formatting dialog box

Protecting The Dashboard Data

In Excel, protecting the data in a spreadsheet can be a major decision because you do not want a user to inadvertently mess up your work. You have probably spent time protecting the data, formulas and anything else that could cause the spreadsheet to not work as intended. You may have used any or all of the following to protect the spreadsheet: Making the spreadsheet read-only, putting a password on the file or adding protection to the worksheet.

The good news is that you do not have to implement any of these protection tasks in Crystal Xcelsius because the user does not have access to your really cool formulas, nor can they peek behind the cells so to speak, to see how you put the spreadsheet together. Unless you tell a user, they will not even know the name of the spreadsheet that you used to create the dashboard. I just wanted to let you know this, so that you would not spend any time implementing any type of security on an Excel spreadsheet that will be used to create a dashboard.

USING SINGLE VALUE COMPONENTS AND INTERACTIVE MAPS

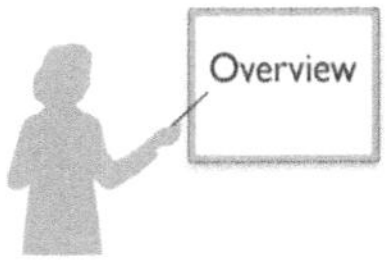

In this lesson you will learn about all of the Single Value components and how to create dashboards that use the Single Value components listed below:

☑ Value component
☑ Dial component

You will also learn how to use map components and how to configure a map to be used as an input selector.

LESSON 5

Single Value Components Overview

In Lesson 3 you learned about the common options that many components have. In this lesson, you will learn about Single Value component options. You will see that some options are the same for many Single Value components. Rather than be redundant, for options that were explained in Lesson 3, you will see a reference to the appropriate section of Lesson 3, instead of repeating the same information again here for each component.

Like the common options that you learned about in Lesson 3, each category of components has common options. They are covered at the beginning of the lesson instead of repeating them for each component that they apply to. When you see a reference like [See Common General Tab Options, earlier in this lesson], you can review that section if necessary for an explanation of the options on the tab.

Single Value components are components that link to a single cell (of numeric data) in the spreadsheet. Figure 5-1 shows the types of Single Value components.

View ⇒ Components, opens this dialog box.

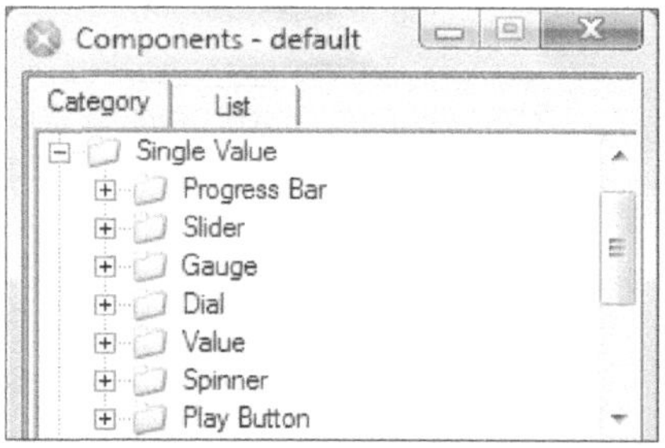

Figure 5-1 Single Value components

Single Value Component Categories

As you will see, most Single Value components fall into one of the categories discussed below.

① **INPUT COMPONENTS** allow the data that is linked to the component to be changed from the dashboard.

② **OUTPUT COMPONENTS** pass data to the dashboard.

You can use some of the Single Value components interchangeably because they have the same functionality. When this is the case, my advice is to select the component that looks best for the data that will be displayed with the component.

Some Single Value components are in both of the categories discussed above. Table 5-1 explains the Single Value components. All of the options on the General, Behavior and Appearance tabs, except the dynamic visibility options are explained in this lesson.

> **Using Multiple Single Value Components**
>
> It is possible that you will need to link more than one Single Value component to the same cell in a dashboard. If this is the case and you use different minimum and maximum values for each Single Value component, some of them will reach the maximum value quicker then others. While the dashboard will function properly, the user may not notice that at least one of the components has reached the maximum, which means that accurate data may not be displayed in another component on the dashboard.

Component	Description
Dial	This input component allows the user change the value in the linked cell. This action will automatically change the values displayed in another component in the dashboard. Figure 5-2 shows one of the dial component styles. (1)
Slider	This input component works the same as the dial component. You used this component in Lesson 3. [See Lesson 3, Exercise 3.1, Create A Basic Dashboard] (1)
Progress Bar	This output component works the opposite of the dial and slider components because it displays a cells value instead of allowing the value to be changed. It has a read-only effect. The progress bar displays the linked value in comparison to the highest value in the cells that it is linked to. Figure 5-3 shows one of the progress component styles. (2)
Gauge	This output component is similar, in terms of functionality, to the progress bar component. The gauge also measures any change in the linked cell. Figure 5-4 shows one of the gauge component styles. (2)
Value	This component can be used as an input or output component because it represents a single cell. Use it as an **INPUT COMPONENT** when it will be linked to a cell that has a formula. Use it as an **OUTPUT COMPONENT** when it will be linked to a cell that has a value. Figure 5-5 shows one of the value component styles.
Spinner	This input component works the same as the dial component because it is used to change the value in another component. Figure 5-6 shows one of the spinner component styles. (1)
Play Button	This input component allows the value in the linked cell to be increased or decreased in increments. (1)

Table 5-1 Single Value components explained

(1) This component should be linked to a cell that has data that was typed into the spreadsheet, instead of a cell that has a formula.
(2) Use this component if the cell that is being linked to has a formula. The reason is because the value in a cell with a formula cannot be changed with a component because the value in the cell is calculated.

Figure 5-2 Dial component

Figure 5-3 Progress Bar component

Figure 5-4 Gauge component

Figure 5-5 Value component

Figure 5-6 Spinner component

> If you link a component to the wrong type of cell, the component will not work as you expect. For example, if you link a dial component to a cell that has a formula, you will not be able to use the dial to select a value, thus making it an output component.

Single Value Component Options

The options discussed in this section are common to the Single Value components that you just read about in Table 5-1.

Common Single Value General Tab Options

The options on this tab are used to link cells in a spreadsheet to a component on the model. Figure 5-7 shows the General tab options for a slider.

TITLE Type in the title or select the cell in the spreadsheet that has the title for the component.

LINK TO CELL Type in or select the cell in the spreadsheet that the component should be linked to.

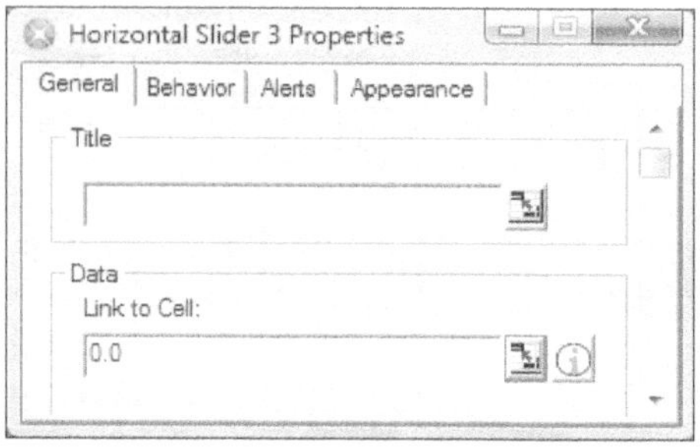

Figure 5-7 Common Single Value general tab options

Common Single Value Behavior Tab Options

Believe it or not, the options on this tab are used to limit data and functionality.

Examples of limitations include adding a range of minimum and maximum values, as shown in Figure 5-8, or only allowing certain play back options.

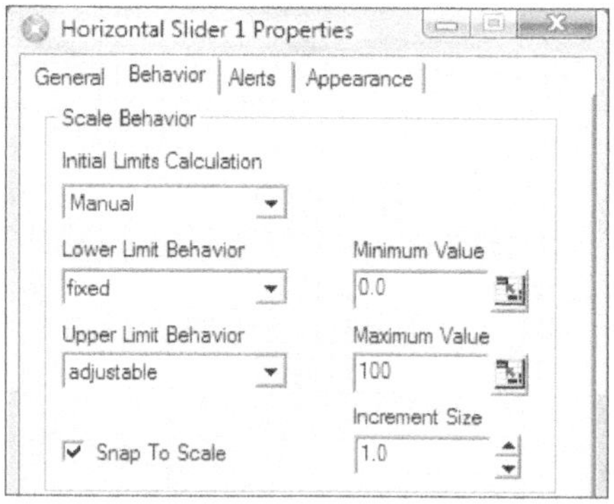

Figure 5-8 Common Single Value behavior tab options

Scale Behavior Options

INITIAL LIMITS CALCULATION This option, as shown in Figure 5-8, is used to set the minimum and maximum limits for the component by selecting one of the options discussed below, from the drop-down list.

① **MANUAL** This is the default option. Select this option when you want to set the minimum and maximum values.

② **VALUE BASED** Limits are close to the value. (3)

③ **ZERO BASED** In the range of values that is automatically selected, zero is either the lower or upper limit. (3)

④ **ZERO CENTERED** The range uses zero as the center value. This means that the component can display negative numbers. (3)

⑤ **ALERT BASED** The range covers all alert levels. The **ENABLE ALERTS** option on the Alerts tab must be selected for this option to appear in the Initial Limits Calculation drop-down list.

(3) This option is automatically selected by Crystal Xcelsius.

LOWER LIMIT BEHAVIOR Is used to select how the minimum value that the component will display will be selected. This option controls the Minimum Value option. (4)

UPPER LIMIT BEHAVIOR Is used to select how the maximum value that the component will display will be selected. This option controls the Maximum Value option discussed below. (4)

SNAP TO SCALE If checked, this option forces the pointer (the moveable part of the component) to match the value that is displayed on the component.

MINIMUM VALUE Is used to select the lowest value that the component can display. (5)

MAXIMUM VALUE Is used to select the highest value that the component can display. (5)

INCREMENT SIZE Restricts values that are manually entered in the Minimum and Maximum Value fields to be in specific increments. For example, if this value is set to 100, each tick mark on a dial will represent an increase or decrease of 100. (5)

(4) The options in this drop-down list are explained in the section "Lower And Upper Limit Behavior Options", later in this lesson.

(5) If you are entering percents in this field or any value field on any Behavior tab, they have to be entered in decimal format.

For example, you have to type in .01 for 1% and .25 for 25%. This is why by default, these fields have values with decimal points, as shown above in Figure 5-8 and in Figure 5-9.

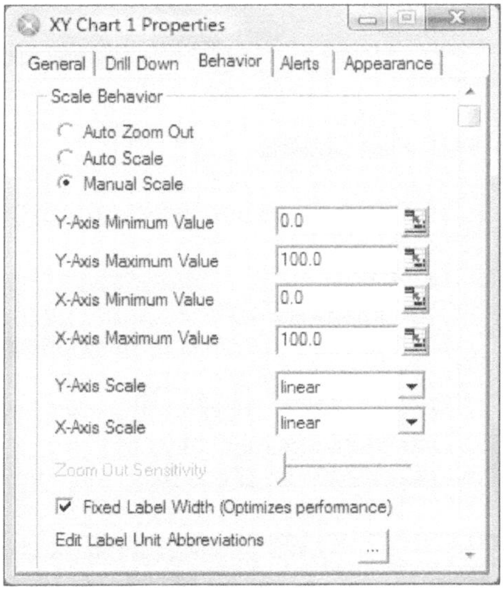

Figure 5-9 Chart behavior tab value options

Lower And Upper Limit Behavior Options

As shown earlier in Figure 5-8, these two properties have three options that can be selected, as discussed below:

① **FIXED** Select this option for the Lower Limit Behavior option if you do not want the value in the linked cell to be less than the value in the Minimum Value option. Select this option for the Upper Limit Behavior option if you do not want the value in the linked cell to be greater than the value in the Maximum Value option. This is the default option.

② **ADJUSTABLE** This option is similar to the Fixed option. The difference is that you can select the lower and upper limit values.

③ **OPEN** Use this option when you want to select any number for the limit value, as long as the number does not conflict with the number for the other limit value. For example, you could select 10 for the minimum value and 20 for the maximum value, but you could not select 20 for the minimum value and 10 for the maximum value.

Play Options

The options in this section of the Behavior tab are shown in Figure 5-10. They are used to select the automation functionality for the component. Figure 5-11 shows the Slider Single Value component with all of the play options selected. The options are explained below.

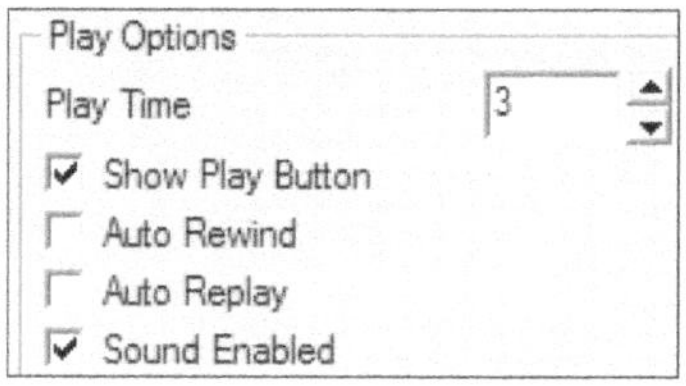

Figure 5-10 Play Options

Figure 5-11 Slider component with all play options selected

① **PLAY TIME** Is used to select how many seconds the component will run, from start to finish.

② **SHOW PLAY BUTTON** Adds a play/start button to the beginning of the component. This option enables the other options in this section.

③ **AUTO REWIND** If checked, this option will cause the slider to automatically go back to the beginning of the component, after it reaches the end.

④ **AUTO REPLAY** If checked, the component will automatically continue to run, over and over, until it is manually stopped.

⑤ **SOUND ENABLED** If checked, the component will make a sound when clicked on.

> The Dial component is the only Single Value component that supports the **SOUND ENABLED** option. Other components like the Combo Box component support sound, but not as a play option.

Common Single Value Titles Panel Options

Figure 5-12 shows the options on the Titles panel. These options are used to customize titles and values on the component.

Title Options

The options in this section are used to display the title on a component and change the titles appearance.

SHOW TITLE If checked, this option will display the title on the component.

POSITION, X SHIFT and **Y SHIFT**
[See Lesson 3, Position Options]

Value Options

The options in this section are used to customize the numeric values on the component.

POSITION Is used to select where the values will be placed on the component.

Limits Options

SHOW LIMITS Is used to display the values at the bottom of the component, that the needle represents, as illustrated in Figure 5-13.

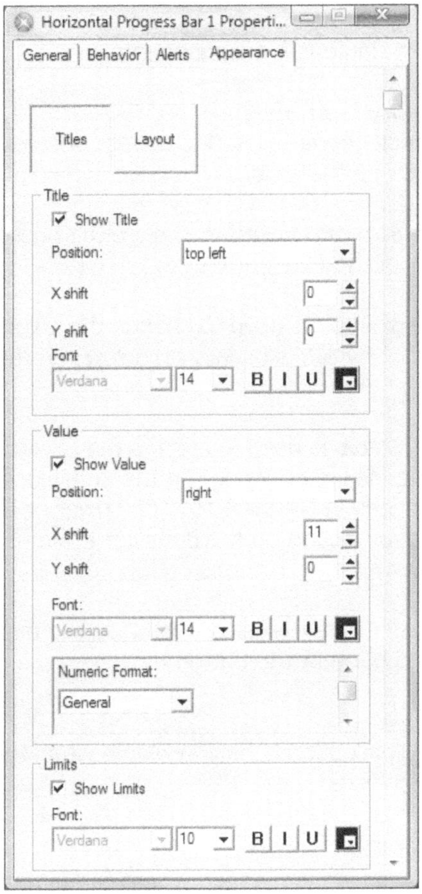

Figure 5-12 Common Single Value titles panel options

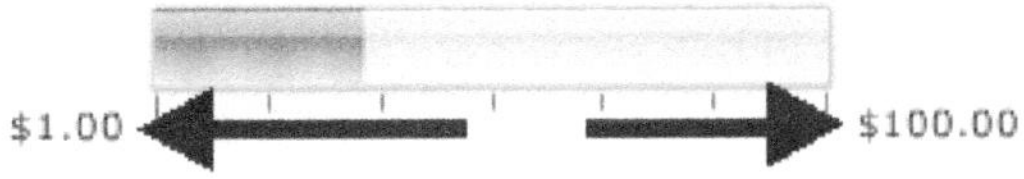

Figure 5-13 Show Limits option illustrated

Common Single Value Layout Panel Options

The options shown in Figure 5-14 are common to many Single Value components.

Display Options

MARKER COLOR Is used to change the color of the button on the slider.

PLAY BUTTON Is used to change the background color of the Play button. (6)

PLAY SYMBOL Is used to change the color of the symbol (which is usually an arrow) on the Play button. (6)

LIMITS FILL Is used to change the background color of the Maximum Value (on the Behavior tab), as illustrated in Figure 5-15. The Lower or Upper Limit Behavior option on the Behavior tab must be set to **ADJUSTABLE**, to use this option.

SLIDER GUTTER Is used to change the default color of the bar that the button moves across.

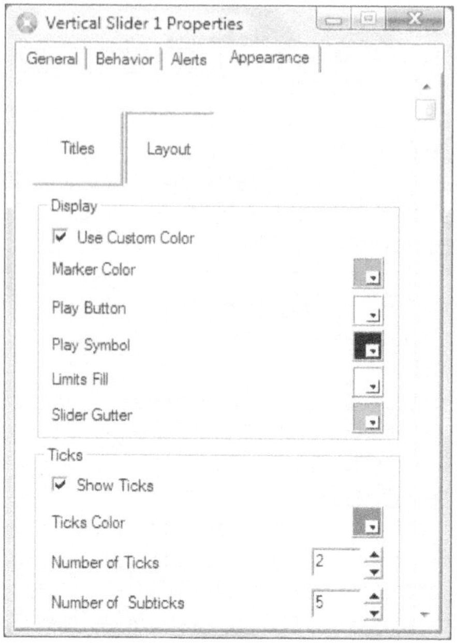

Figure 5-14 Common Single Value layout panel options

(6) This option is only available when the Show Play Button option on the Behavior tab is selected.

Figure 5-15 Limits Fill option illustrated

Ticks Options

The options in this section are used to add and customize the tick marks on a component like a progress bar or slider. Tick marks are the long and short lines on the component. Figure 5-16 illustrates the tick marks on a dual slider component.

Figure 5-16 Tick marks illustrated

SHOW TICKS This option must be selected to display tick marks on the component.

TICKS COLOR Is used to change the color of the tick marks.

NUMBER OF TICKS Is used to select how many primary (longer) tick marks are on the component. A value from 2 to 21 can be entered for this option.

NUMBER OF SUBTICKS Is used to select how many secondary (shorter) tick marks are on the component. Subticks are placed between two primary tick marks. A value from 0 to 21 can be entered for this option.

Tips For Completing The Exercises In This Book

As you will see, many of the steps are the same for each model that you will create. To avoid being extremely repetitive, the following tasks will not be repeated for each exercise.

① At the beginning of each exercise you should open a new model prior to starting step 1, unless instructed to open an existing model.
② When you see the instruction "Add the (name of) component", it means to add the component to the canvas. After you add a component to the canvas, you should open the Properties dialog box for the component that you add.
③ When instructed to open or save a file, look in or use the folder that you created.
④ Preview the model. If your model does not look like the one in the figure, you should go back and review the steps to make sure that you completed all of the tasks.
⑤ Unless specifically stated, you do not have to create (publish) the dashboard file for the remaining exercises in this book. In Lesson 12 you will learn how to publish dashboards in a variety of formats. For now, just save the model with the correct file name.
⑥ In the Property/Change To tables, like the one shown below in Exercise 5.1, step 3, you will see references to a single cell (A1, B5, etc.) or a cell range (A1:C5). This means to select the cell reference in the spreadsheet for the option.
⑦ In some of the Property/Change To tables, you will see "Select this option" in the second column. This means that you should click in the box in front of the option, so that it has a check mark.
⑧ In some of the Property/Change To tables, you will see "Clear this option" in the second column. This means that you should remove the check mark from the option.

Format For Exercises

At the beginning of this lesson, the common options for Single Value components were explained and illustrated. Before each exercise, the options that are unique for the component(s) that will be used in the exercise will be explained.

For example, Exercise 5.1 uses the Value and Play Button components. Their options are explained right before the exercise starts. Many of the Properties dialog box screen shots will only display the options that will be explained.

Excel Spreadsheets

At the beginning of many exercises, you will see an Excel spreadsheet. The spreadsheet displays the data that will be used to create the model. The reason that I display the data is to help you get a feel for how the data needs to appear in the spreadsheet for the components, which will hopefully help you to create the type of dashboard that you need, when you are on your own.

Value Component

This component is different from many of the other Single Value components because the user types in the value that is used to display the values in another component like a chart. The Value component has the option of also using a play button, which will automatically increment the number in the Value component and display the corresponding data in another component on the dashboard. Remember that a Value component can only be linked to one cell in the spreadsheet.

General Tab Options

[See Common Single Value General Tab Options, earlier in this lesson]

Behavior Tab Options

Interaction Options

The options shown in Figure 5-17 control the functionality of the Value component.

MOUSE SENSITIVITY Is used to set how the mouse movements change the values of the component. A low setting on this option means that small changes made by the mouse will increment the value of the component in small amounts. A high setting on this option means that small changes made by the mouse will increment the value stored by the component in large amounts.

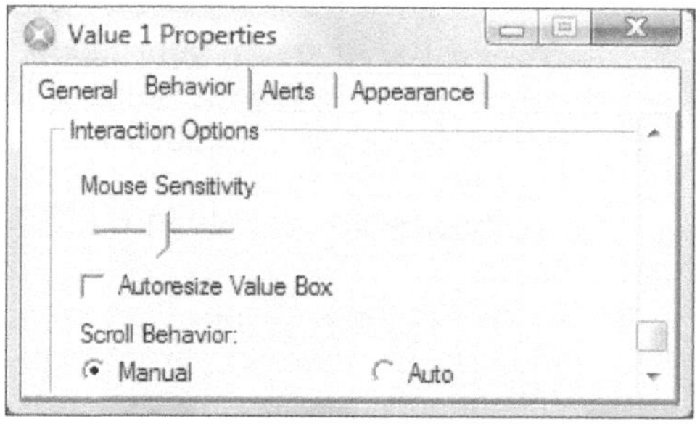

Figure 5-17 Value component behavior tab options

AUTORESIZE VALUE BOX Select this option if you want the Value component to automatically be resized to fit the number that is entered or displayed in the field.

SCROLL BEHAVIOR Is used to select how the mouse pointer is used to change the value displayed in the component. The maximum value that can be selected is equal to the value in the Maximum Value field in the Scale Behavior section on the tab. Make sure that the cells in the grid are large enough to accommodate the maximum value, otherwise, the table will look like the one shown in Figure 5-18.

1	##	3	4	5
2	4	6	8	##
3	6	##	12	15

Figure 5-18 Grid too small to support large values

① Select the **MANUAL** option if you want the user to drag the mouse pointer up or to the right on the component to change the value. This will increase the value that is displayed. Dragging the mouse pointer down or to the left will lower the value that is displayed.

② Select the **AUTO** option if you want the user to drag the mouse to the value on another component that they want.

Titles Panel Options

[See Common Single Value Titles Panel Options, earlier in this lesson]

Layout Panel Options

The Layout panel options that are used to change the color of the Value component are shown in Figure 5-19.

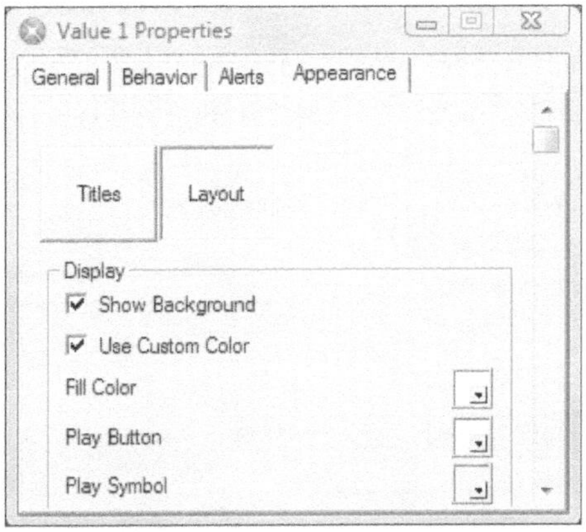

Figure 5-19 Value component layout panel options

SHOW BACKGROUND Is used to display or hide the border around the component.

FILL COLOR Is used to change the background color of the component.

PLAY BUTTON Is used to change the background color of the Play button.

PLAY SYMBOL Is used to change the color of the Play button.

Play Button Component

General Tab Options

[See Common Single Value General Tab Options, earlier in this lesson]

Behavior Tab Options

The Play Options on the Behavior tab for the Play Button are shown in Figure 5-20.

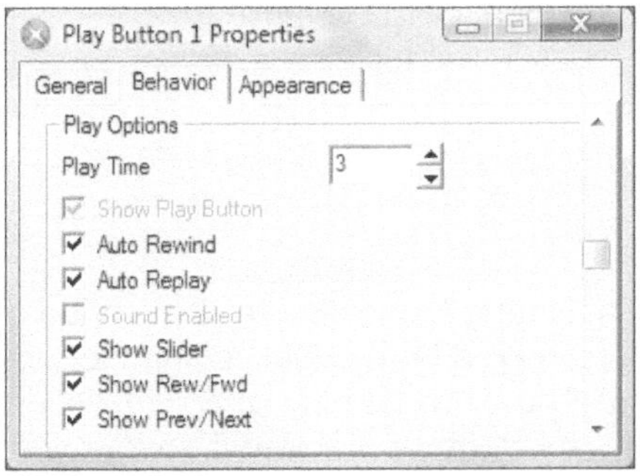

Figure 5-20 Play Button behavior tab options

SHOW SLIDER If checked, a slider will be added to the Play Button selector.

SHOW REW/FWD If checked, this option adds the rewind and fast forward buttons to the Play Button selector.

SHOW PREV/NEXT If checked, this option adds the previous and next buttons to the Play Button selector.

Titles Panel Options

[See Common Single Value Titles Panel Options, earlier in this lesson]

Layout Panel Options

[See Common Single Value Layout Panel Options, earlier in this lesson]

Exercise 5.1: Using The Value Component

In this exercise you will add the Value component to a model. This will let the user enter the Unit price for a product, which will show how different price points effect the revenue for several stores. Figure 5-21 shows the data for this exercise.

	A	B	C
1	**Price Sale Impact Over Total Revenues**		
2	Comparison by Store		
3			
4	Price per Unit	$ 45.00	
5			
6	Store Name	Quantity Sold	Revenues (Quantity * Price)
7	Store A	350	$ 15,750.00
8	Store B	125	$ 5,625.00
9	Store C	245	$ 11,025.00
10	Store D	88	$ 3,960.00
11	Store E	188	$ 8,460.00

Figure 5-21 Value component data

1. Save the cx_value_field_model file as `My value component.`

2. Add the Value -0 component above the chart in the upper right corner.

3. On the General tab, make the changes in the table.

Property	Change To
Title	A4
Link to Cell	B4

4. On the Behavior tab, make the changes in the table.

Property	Change To
Lower Limit Behavior	Fixed
Upper Limit Behavior	Open
Minimum Value (7)	0
Show Play button (8)	Select this option

(7) Setting the Minimum Value option to zero prevents a negative number from being entered in the Value component field on the dashboard.
(8) The Value Display sample dashboard that comes with Crystal Xcelsius does not have this feature. I added it so that you can see how the Play Button component works.

5. Save the changes. The model should look like the one shown in Figure 5-22.

If you see pound signs in the field that you just added, as shown in Figure 5-23, make the field larger.

Double-click in the Price per Unit field, then type in a different amount and press Enter. You will see the values in the chart change.

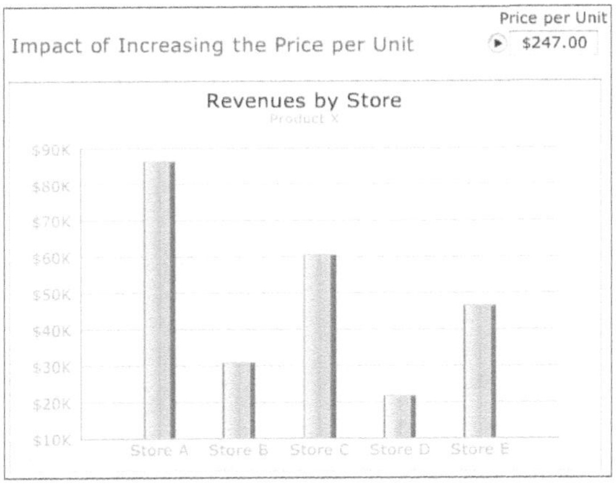

Figure 5-22 Value component model

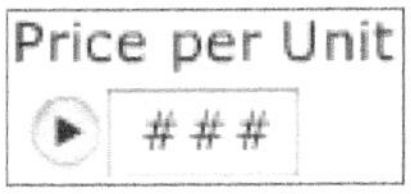

Figure 5-23 Value component that is too small

Earlier in Figure 5-21 you saw that cell B4 (the cell used in the Link to Cell option) has a value in it. This value will be displayed in the Value component by default when the dashboard is first opened. If cell B4 was empty in the spreadsheet, nothing would appear in the Price per Unit field when the dashboard is first opened.

The minimum value that can be entered in the field is zero, which may not be obvious to the user. In Exercise 11.4 you will modify this model to include a help message for this field.

6. Click the Play button. As the number in the Price per Unit field increases, notice that the values on the Y Axis on the chart increase.

Dial Component

General Tab Options

[See Common Single Value General Tab Options, earlier in this lesson]

Behavior Tab Options

Interaction Options

If you have trouble moving the needle on the dial, it is because by default, the **MOUSE TRACKING** option on the Behavior tab is set to **VERTICAL**, as shown in Figure 5-24.

When this option is set to vertical, you can only move the mouse pointer up or down. The **RADIAL** option allows the mouse pointer to use circular movement.

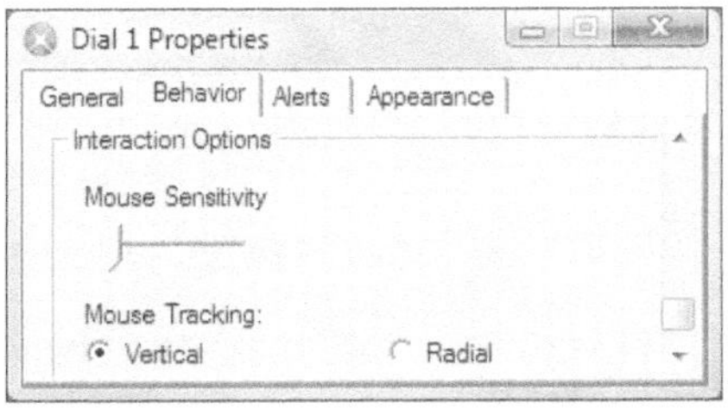

Figure 5-24 Dial behavior tab options

Titles Panel Options

[See Common Single Value Titles Panel Options, earlier in this lesson]

Layout Panel Options

The Dial component layout panel options are shown in Figure 5-25.

Display Options

PLAY BUTTON and **PLAY SYMBOL** [See Value Component Layout Panel Options, earlier in this lesson]

POINTER Is used to change the color of the needle on the dial.

KNOB Is used to change the color of the center of the dial.

GRIP Is used to change the color of the border on the dial.

Ticks Options

MINIMUM ANGLE Is used to select the lowest number that the needle on the dialog can select. This option is not available if the Lower Limit Behavior option on the Behavior tab is set to Open.

MAXIMUM ANGLE Is used to select the highest number that the needle on the dialog can select. This option is not available if the Upper Limit Behavior option on the Behavior tab is set to Open.

Figure 5-25 Dial layout panel options

Exercise 5.2: Using Dial Components

In Lesson 3 you learned about dial components. You also created a dashboard that used a slider component as the input component. Dial and slider components can be used interchangeably. In this exercise you will add a dial component to the model that you created in Exercise 3.1.

1. Save the My slider model as `My dial component`.

2. Add the Dial-0 component below the slider component, then make it larger.

3. On the General tab, make the changes in the table.

Property	Change To
Title	D4
Link to Cell	E4

4. On the Behavior tab, make the changes in the table.

Property	Change To
Maximum Value	250
Sound Enabled	Select this option

The slider component has a maximum value of 100. This means that using the dial option will let the user see how income increases as the number of cards sold changes.

5. On the Appearance tab, click the Titles button, then select the Show Limits option.

6. On the Appearance tab, click the Layout button, then make the changes in the table.

Property	Change To
Use Custom Color	Select this option
Pointer	Red
Knob	Light yellow
Grip	Green

7. Save the changes.

   If you click on the green part of the dial to increase the number of units sold, you will see that once you select a number greater than 138, all of the bars on the chart will have reached the top of the chart, as shown in Figure 5-26.

   That is because the chart has a maximum amount of $2.5 million. If this limitation was removed from the chart, the bars would not reach the top of the chart because the values on the Y Axis would keep growing.

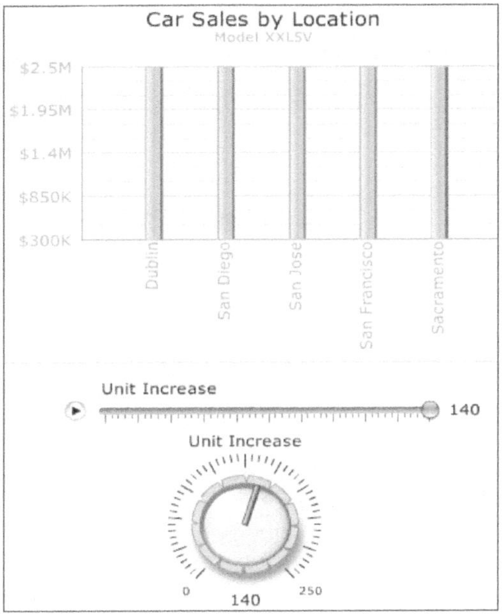

Figure 5-26 Dial component added to the chart

Horizontal And Vertical Slider Components

The horizontal and vertical slider components have the same options on the Properties dialog box.

General Tab Options

[See Common Single Value General Tab Options, earlier in this lesson]

Behavior Tab Options

[See Common Single Value Behavior Tab Options, earlier in this lesson]

Titles Panel Options

[See Common Single Value Titles Panel Options, earlier in this lesson]

Layout Panel Options

[See Common Single Value Layout Panel Options, earlier in this lesson]

Dual Slider Component

Horizontal and Vertical Slider components only have one starting point. Dual sliders have two, as shown in Figure 5-27. The numbers on the slider control the range (the starting and ending values) of values that will be displayed on another component. Each button can be moved left and right.

Figure 5-27 Dual Slider component

General Tab Options

The Dual Slider general tab options are shown in Figure 5-28.

Data Options

LOW DATA Is used to select the starting low value for the slider.

HIGH DATA Is used to select the starting high value for the slider.

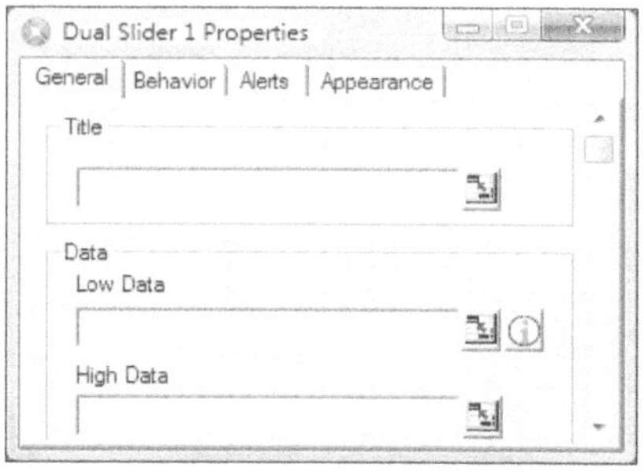

Figure 5-28 Dual Slider general tab options

Behavior Tab Options

[See Common Single Value Behavior Tab Options, earlier in this lesson]

The Dual Slider component does not support the Play Options.

Titles Panel Options

The Dual Slider titles panel options are shown in Figure 5-29.

Value Options

The low and high value options are used to position the low and high values on the dual slider.

LOW X Is used to shift the low value to the right or left on the slider.

HIGH X Is used to shift the high value to the right or left on the slider.

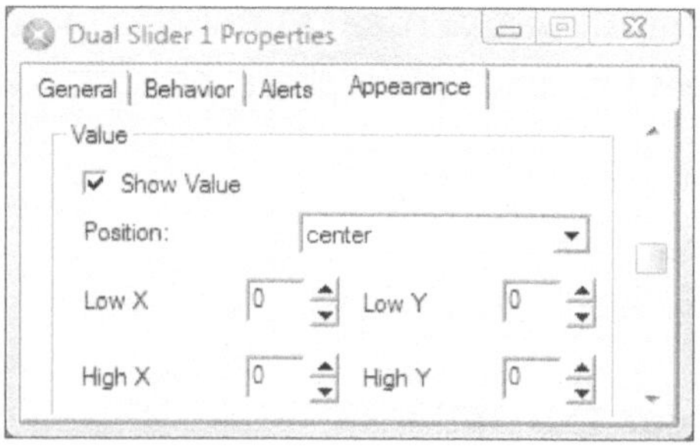

Figure 5-29 Dual Slider titles panel options

LOW Y Is used to shift the low value to the up or down on the slider.

HIGH Y Is used to shift the high value to the up or down on the slider.

Layout Panel Options

The Dual Slider layout panel options are shown in Figure 5-30.

Display Options

LOW MARKER COLOR Is used to change the color of the low value marker.

HIGH MARKER COLOR Is used to change the color of the high value marker.

GUTTER COLOR Is used to change the color of the bar that the buttons slide across.

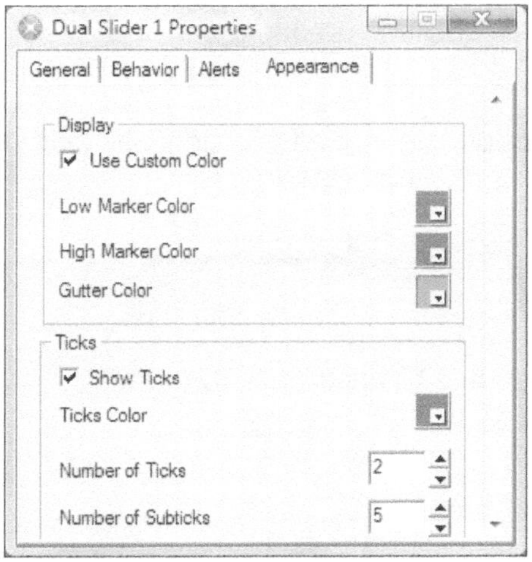

Figure 5-30 Dual Slider layout panel options

Progress Bar Components

The horizontal and vertical progress bar components have the same options on the Properties dialog box.

General Tab Options

[See Common Single Value General Tab Options, earlier in this lesson]

Behavior Tab Options

[See Common Single Value Behavior Tab Options, earlier in this lesson]

Titles Panel Options

[See Common Single Value Titles Panel Options, earlier in this lesson]

Layout Panel Options

The Progress Bar layout panel options are shown in Figure 5-31.

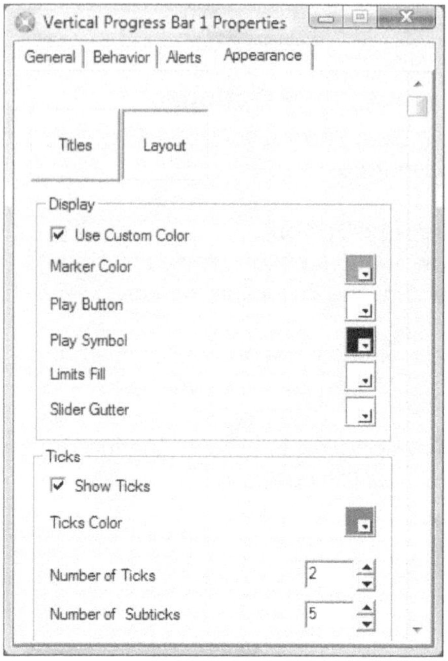

Figure 5-31 Progress bar layout panel options

Display Options

MARKER COLOR Is used to change the fill color of the progress bar, as illustrated in Figure 5-32.

SLIDER GUTTER Is used to change the background color of the progress bar.

Figure 5-32 Marker color illustrated

Gauge Component

General Tab Options

[See Common Single Value General Tab Options, earlier in this lesson]

Behavior Tab Options

The Gauge behavior tab options are shown in Figure 5-33.

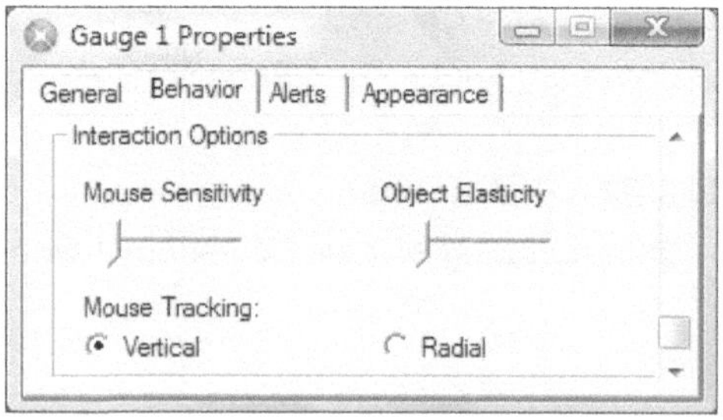

Figure 5-33 Gauge behavior tab options

Interaction Options

MOUSE SENSITIVITY [See Value Component Behavior Tab Options, earlier in this lesson]

OBJECT ELASTICITY Is used to select the elasticity of how the needle moves. After moving the bar for this option to several positions, I did not notice any difference.

MOUSE TRACKING [See Dial Component Behavior Tab Options, earlier in this lesson]

Titles Panel Options

[See Common Single Value Titles Panel Options, earlier in this lesson]

Layout Panel Options

The Gauge layout panel options are shown in Figure 5-34.

Display Options

LIMITS FILL [See Common Single Value Layout Panel Options, earlier in this lesson]

POINTER [See Dial Component Layout Panel Options, earlier in this lesson]

RIM Is used to change the color of the outer portion of the gauge.

MIDDLE Is used to change the color of the center of the gauge.

BACKING Is used to change the background color of the face of the gauge.

Figure 5-34 Gauge layout panel options

Spinner Component

General Tab Options

[See Common Single Value General Tab Options, earlier in this lesson]

Behavior Tab Options

Play Options

The Spinner component does not support the Play Options.

Titles Panel Options

[See Common Single Value Titles Panel Options, earlier in this lesson]
[See Lesson 3, Common Appearance Tab Options]

Layout Panel Options

The Spinner layout panel options are shown in Figure 5-35.

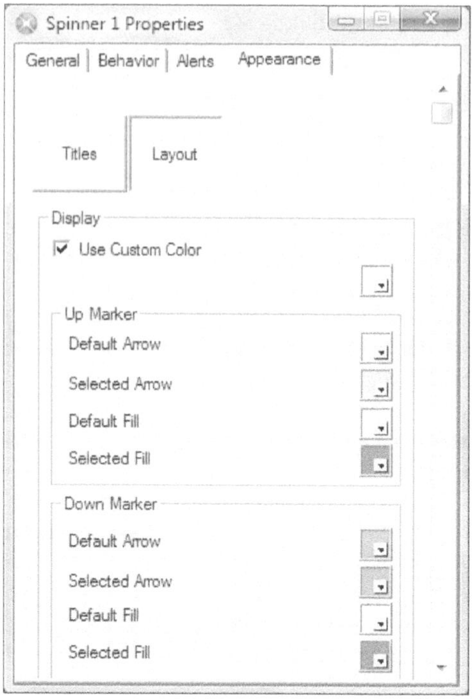

Figure 5-35 Spinner layout panel options

Up Marker Options

DEFAULT ARROW Is used to change the color of the up arrow when the dashboard is first displayed.

SELECTED ARROW Is used to change the color of the up arrow when the arrow is clicked.

DEFAULT FILL Is used to change the default background color of the up arrow section of the component.

SELECTED FILL Is used to change the background color of the up arrow section of the component when the up arrow is clicked.

Down Marker Options

DEFAULT ARROW Is used to change the color of the down arrow when the dashboard is first displayed.

SELECTED ARROW Is used to change the color of the down arrow when the arrow is clicked.

DEFAULT FILL Is used to change the default background color of the down arrow section of the component.

SELECTED FILL Is used to change the background color of the down arrow section of the component when the down arrow is clicked.

Interactive Map Component

Map components display the spreadsheet data geographically. Crystal Xcelsius has nine maps, each with regions already set up. The characteristics of map components are:

① Each region on a map can be used as a selector component to display data for that region in another component like a chart, on the dashboard.
② Maps show data for each region.
③ You can elect to have the data for each region appear when the mouse pointer is hovered over a region on the map.

How Does The Map Component Work?

Overall, the map component gathers data differently then other components, even though the same options are used on the Properties dialog box. Depending on the map being used, the term region will refer to something different. On one map a region could refer to a state and on another map a region could refer to a country.

If you have an existing spreadsheet that has data by state or country for example, that you want to use to create a map, more than likely, you will have to modify it before importing it into a model. The region names must be the first column of the spreadsheet.

One change that you may have to make is to create or edit the region codes in your spreadsheet. This could entail changing the region names or adding region codes to the spreadsheet. For example, the United States by state map uses the full state name as the region name, as shown in Figure 5-36.

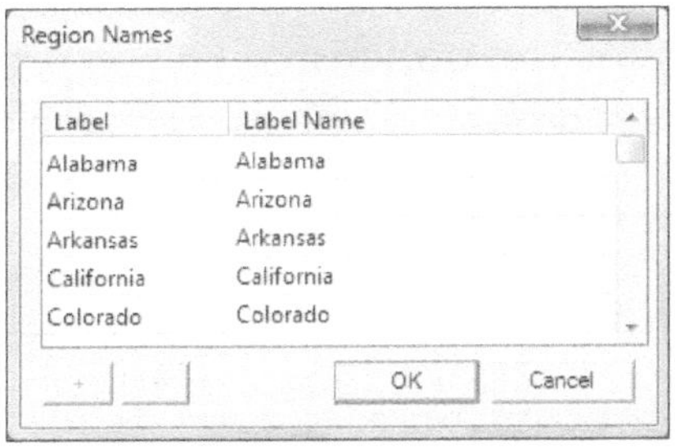

Figure 5-36 Region Names dialog box

If your spreadsheet currently uses the two character state abbreviations, you will not have to modify the spreadsheet, as long as the states are in the same order as shown in Figure 5-36.

If you import your spreadsheet, the dialog box will look like the one shown in Figure 5-37, if you are using two character state abbreviations. Keep in mind that the values in the Label Name column is what will be displayed on the map. Figure 5-38 shows one state with a two character abbreviation and one state with the full name.

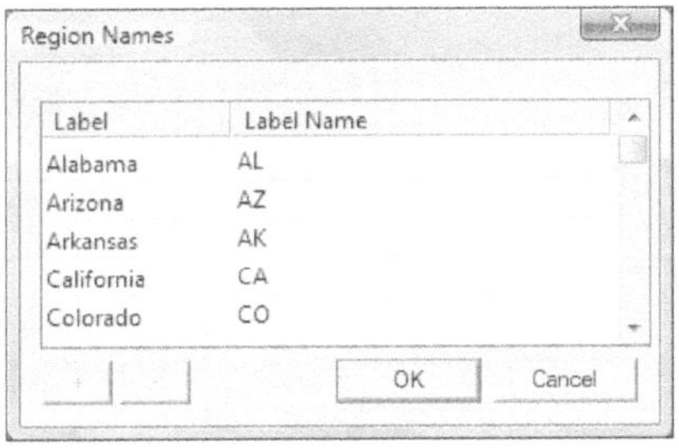

Figure 5-37 Label names with two character state abbreviations

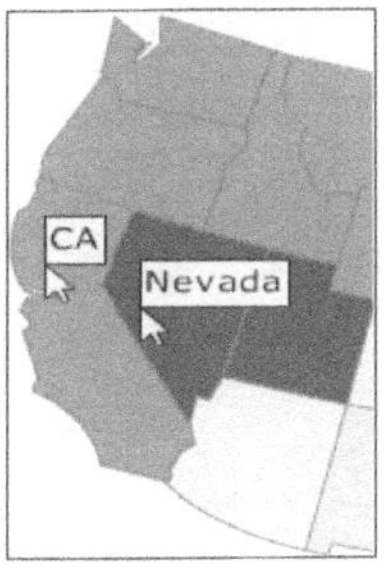

Figure 5-38 Differences in label names

The United States by state map does not include Alaska or Hawaii.

For a map to work, the region codes must be set up correctly because Crystal Xcelsius links the data in a spreadsheet to a region in the map. By correctly, I mean that your data must be in the same order as they are in the Region Names dialog box. Each region on the map has its own code. When the **SOURCE DATA**, **DISPLAY DATA** or **TARGET** field is selected, the map component searches the first row or column of the cell range that is defined in the Region Names field for the codes. When the code is found, the data in the row or column is associated with the corresponding region on the map.

It seems to me that there should be a way to let Crystal Xcelsius know that the data in the spreadsheet is not in the same order as what the map component is expecting.

Map Component

All of the map components have the options discussed below.

General Tab Options

The Map general tab options are shown in Figure 5-39.

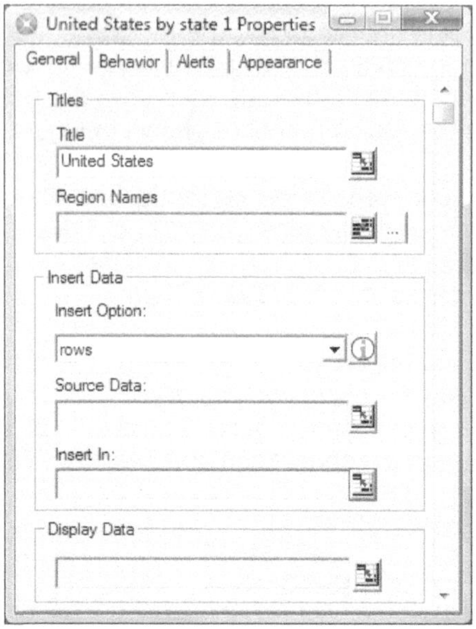

Figure 5-39 Map general tab options

Titles Options

TITLE Is used to enter the title for the map or select a cell in the spreadsheet that has the title.

REGION NAMES Is used to define the cell range for the codes for each region on the map.

There are two ways to select the region codes as discussed below.

① Select them from the imported spreadsheet.

② Click the Browse button for the Range Names option, then type in the region codes on the dialog box shown earlier in Figure 5-36.

Insert Data Options

INSERT OPTION Is used to select how the region data should be added to the empty cells.

SOURCE DATA Is used to select the cells on the spreadsheet that have the regions and data for the map. This field configures the map to be used as a selector.

INSERT IN Is used to select a range of empty cells in the spreadsheet to store the data for the region that the user clicks on, on the map. The range that you select for this option must be the same (a row or column) as what you selected for the Insert Option field.

DISPLAY DATA Is used to select the cells on the spreadsheet that have the region (on the USA map, this is the full state name) and the data for each state that should be displayed when the user clicks on a region on the map.

Behavior Tab Options

The Map behavior tab options are shown in Figure 5-40.

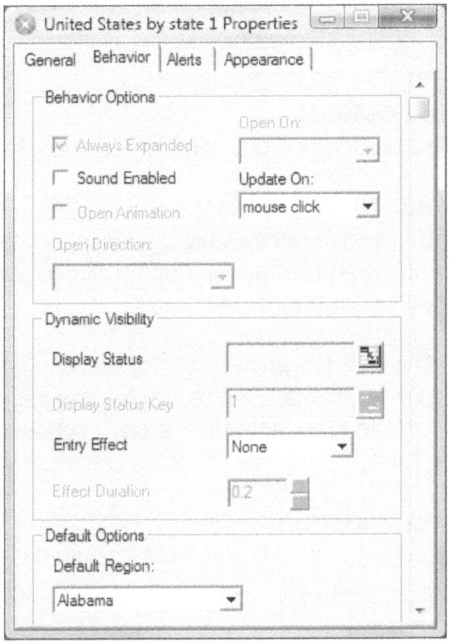

Figure 5-40 Map behavior tab options

Behavior Options

UPDATE ON Is used to select how the component should recognize that an option on the menu has been selected.

Default Options

DEFAULT REGION Select the region that you want to be automatically selected when the dashboard is opened. The selected region will usually be a different color from all of the other regions on the chart if you change the color for the Selected Fill option on the Appearance tab.

Appearance Tab Options

The Map appearance tab options are shown in Figure 5-41.

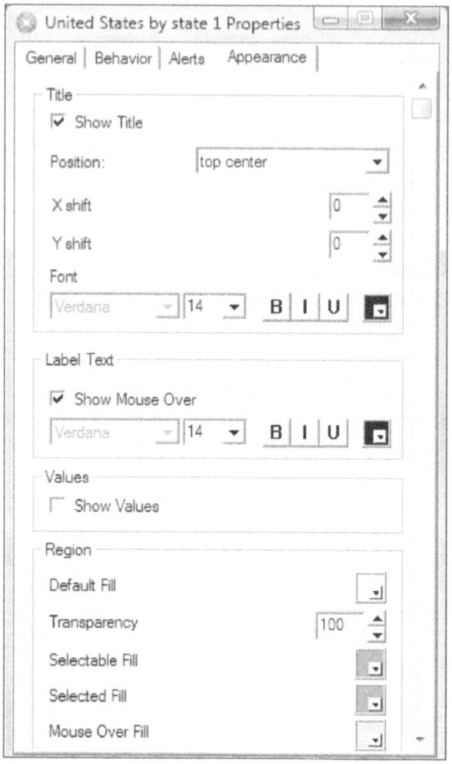

Figure 5-41 Map appearance tab options

Title Options

[See Lesson 3, Common Titles Panel Options]

Label Text Options

SHOW MOUSE OVER Is used to display the region name when the mouse pointer is hovered over a region on the map.

Values Options

SHOW VALUES Is used to display the region value when the mouse pointer is hovered over a region on the map.

Region Options

The options in this section are used to customize the region colors on the map.

DEFAULT FILL Is used to change the default color of regions that do not have source data.

SELECTABLE FILL Is used to change the default color of regions that can be selected and have source data.

SELECTED FILL Is used to change the default color of the region that is clicked on.

MOUSE OVER FILL Is used to change the color of the region that the mouse pointer is hovered over.

Exercise 5.3: Create A Revenues By State Map

In this exercise you will create a map that displays the revenue when the mouse pointer is hovered over a region on the map. The map will also be used as an input selector for a chart. When a region is clicked on the map, the corresponding data will be displayed in the chart below it. Figure 5-42 shows the data for this exercise.

	A	B	C	D	E	F	G	H	I	J	K	L
1	Revenues by State											
2												
3	**Display Data Range**			Source Data Range								
4	**State**	FY2002		**State**	FY1995	FY1996	FY1997	FY1998	FY1999	FY2000	FY2001	FY2002
5	Alabama	$ 31.66		Alabama	$ 28.23	$ 18.89	$ 21.89	$ 28.36	$ 24.85	$ 21.70	$ 20.21	$ 31.66
6	Arizona	$ 17.14		Arizona	$ 21.58	$ 17.11	$ 22.58	$ 24.11	$ 24.04	$ 19.27	$ 17.09	$ 17.14
7	Arkansas	$ 25.61		Arkansas	$ 17.64	$ 16.43	$ 22.96	$ 17.29	$ 25.74	$ 19.22	$ 19.23	$ 25.61
8	California	$ 23.92		California	$ 23.94	$ 23.93	$ 22.76	$ 26.20	$ 22.51	$ 17.74	$ 27.77	$ 23.92
9	Colorado	$ 17.69		Colorado	$ 16.45	$ 27.71	$ 28.40	$ 22.98	$ 18.13	$ 16.84	$ 26.13	$ 17.69
10	Connecticut	$ 28.93		Connecticut	$ 22.78	$ 20.08	$ 26.02	$ 28.89	$ 22.65	$ 20.15	$ 26.41	$ 28.93

Figure 5-42 State map data

1. Import the Map spreadsheet.

2. Save the model as `My USA map`.

Create The Chart

1. Add the Column Chart component near the bottom of the canvas.

2. On the General tab, make the changes in the table.

Property	Change To
Chart title	A1
Chart subtitle	D55
Value (Y) axis title	Millions US
Data Range	E55:L55
Category Axis Labels	E4:L4

3. On the Behavior tab, make the changes in the table.

Property	Change To
Manual Scale	Select this option
Y-Axis Maximum Value	500
Auto Scale	Select this option

4. On the Appearance tab, click the Series button, then change the Bar Width option to 30.

5. Save the changes.

Create The Revenues By State Map

1. Open the Maps Library category folder, then add the United States by state map above the chart.

2. On the General tab, make the changes in the table.

Property	Change To
Title	United States of America
Region Names	A5:A53
Insert Option	Rows
Source Data	D5:L53
Insert In	D55:L55
Display Data	A5:B53

3. On the Behavior tab, open the Default Region drop-down list and select Texas.

4. Save the changes.

   When you click on a state in the map, the chart will display the revenue data by fiscal year for the state, as shown in Figure 5-43.

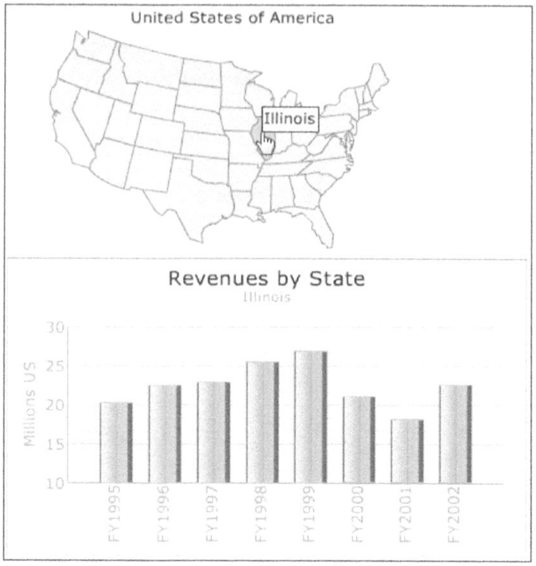

Figure 5-43 Revenues by state map

Mapping To Specific States

You do not have to provide data for all of the states on the map that you just created. The only requirement is that the states that you map to are adjoining states in the spreadsheet. Figure 5-44 shows a map with only 10 states (Delaware to Kentucky) that have data. If you click on or hold the mouse pointer over any other state, no information will be displayed.

To accomplish this, on the General tab, I changed the Source Data option to D11:L20 and the Display Data option to A11:B20.

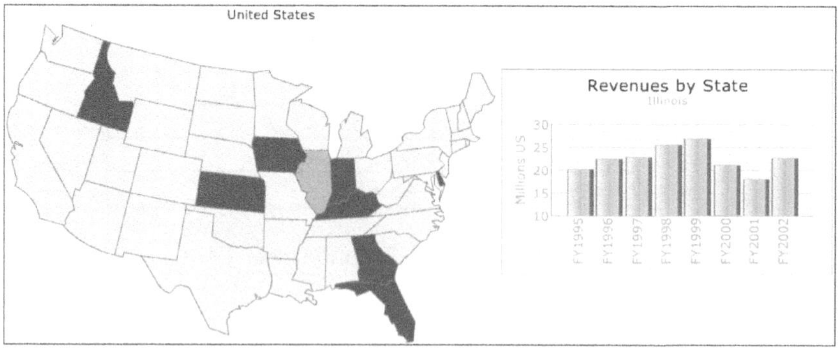

Figure 5-44 Map that only displays data for specific regions

CREATING CHARTS

In this lesson you will learn about the common chart options and options that are specific to a chart type. You will accomplish this by learning how to create the following types of charts:

- ☑ Line chart
- ☑ Pie chart
- ☑ Column chart
- ☑ Area chart
- ☑ Bubble chart
- ☑ Candlestick chart
- ☑ XY chart
- ☑ Radar chart
- ☑ Combination chart

Charts Overview

In previous lessons you saw a few charts, but there was not a lot of discussion about them. Based on the dashboards that have been presented so far in this book, hopefully it is evident that charts play a major role in dashboards. And as such, I feel that it is imperative that you understand as many of the chart options as possible. In this lesson you will learn to create a variety of charts, some of which will be used as the basis for exercises in future lessons.

Crystal Xcelsius comes with 15 chart types, as discussed in Table 6-1. If you have created charts in Crystal Reports or Excel, many of the chart types should be familiar. If you have not created charts before, Crystal Xcelsius is pretty intuitive. Between that and the step-by-step instructions, you will be able to select an appropriate chart type and create charts based on a series of data in the spreadsheet, opposed to all of the data in a spreadsheet, in no time.

Chart Type	Description
Line	Line charts show trends and changes over a period of time. The markers across the bottom of the chart represent exact values. Line charts can have a single series of data, as shown in Figure 6-1 or multiple series of data, as shown in Figure 6-2.
Pie	Pie charts display information for one point in time. Figure 6-3 shows sales by region. Each slice of the pie represents the percent for a different region. Pie charts show how the whole (100%) is divided.
OHLC & Candlestick	OHLC stands for Open High Low Close. These chart types are similar to bar charts. The difference is that the items for these charts usually do not touch the bottom of the chart because they are used to display stock data. On an OHLC chart, the values are represented by lines attached to markers, as illustrated in Figure 6-4. Figure 6-5 shows the same stock data on a Candlestick chart.
Column	Column charts are similar to bar charts because they compare one or more items that are in a specific range of values or compares items over a period of time. This is probably the most used chart type.
Stacked Column	This chart type shows each item as a percent of the total (vertically) in a specific range or over a period of time, as shown in Figure 6-6. Each item is displayed in a different color.
Bar	Bar charts show differences between items over a period of time. Bar charts can plot more than one series of data as shown in Figure 6-7.
Stacked Bar	This chart type shows each item as a percent of the total (horizontally) in a specific range or over a period of time. Each item on the bar is displayed in a different color.
Combination	This chart type displays changes and the magnitude of the change over time. This change is usually illustrated by two chart types: A line chart and column chart, as shown in Figure 6-8. This is also known as a **TREND LINE** or **VARIANCE** chart. The major difference between line charts, column charts and a combination chart is that a combination chart can use both columns and lines in the same chart and the other two chart types cannot.

Table 6-1 Chart types explained

Chart Type	Description
Bubble	Compares a series of items based on the X Axis, Y Axis and Z value (item size), as shown in Figure 6-9. Bubble charts represent three numeric values. Together, the X and Y Axis values determine the intersection on the X and Y Axis where the bubble will be placed on the chart. The Z value is used to determine what size the bubble should be, which is based on a comparison of all of the values for each item on the chart. Bubble charts allow more data to be added to a chart than XY charts.
XY	XY charts show how two values are related (like month of year and order amount) and how a change in one value effects the other value, as shown in Figure 6-10. This chart type displays the correlation between the items. The XY chart type is similar to the bubble chart type because it uses the X and Y values to determine where to place the marker on the chart. The X and Y Axis must display numeric data. If data like dates or months can be converted to numeric data, they can be used in this chart type. This chart type is also known as an **XY SCATTER** chart.
Area	Area charts show how the data has changed over a period of time, as shown in Figure 6-11. Area charts are almost identical to stacked line charts. The difference is that area charts are filled in below the trend line, which emphasizes the magnitude of change. Area charts are probably best suited for a few groups (series) of data.
Stacked Area Chart	This chart type is similar to area charts. The difference is that stacked area charts display the differences in more than one series of data, as shown in Figure 6-12.
Radar	Radar charts compare sets of data relative to a center point and shows how far the data value is from the standard (the center point value), as shown in Figure 6-13. The data from the X Axis is usually plotted in a circle and the Y Axis values are plotted from the center of the circle out.
Filled Radar	This chart type displays data the same way that a Radar chart does. The difference is that Filled Radar charts fill in each band with a different color to help illustrate the data, as shown in Figure 6-14.

Table 6-1 Chart types explained (Continued)

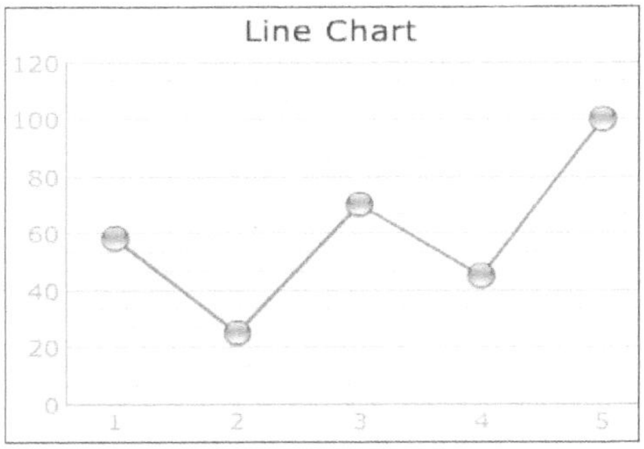

Figure 6-1 Line chart

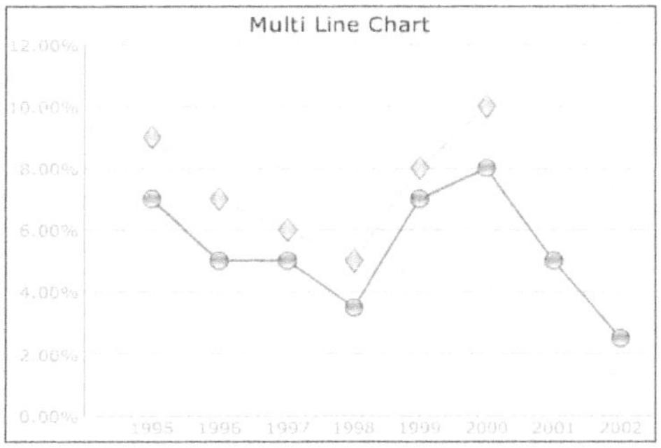

Figure 6-2 Line chart with two series of data

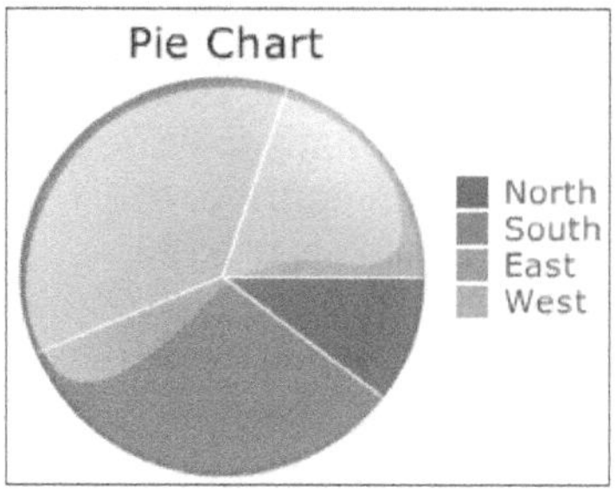

Figure 6-3 Pie chart

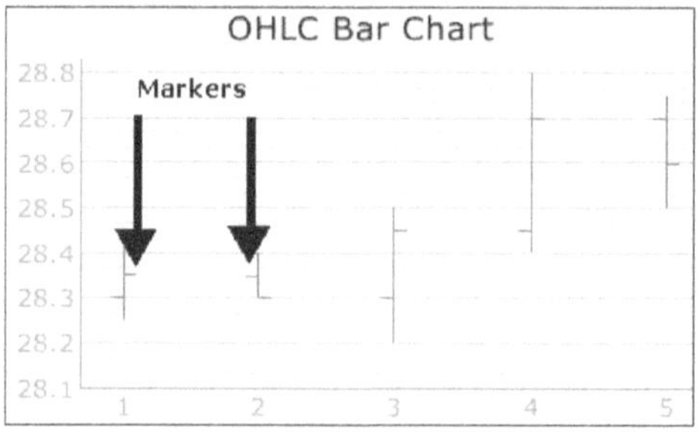

Figure 6-4 OHLC chart

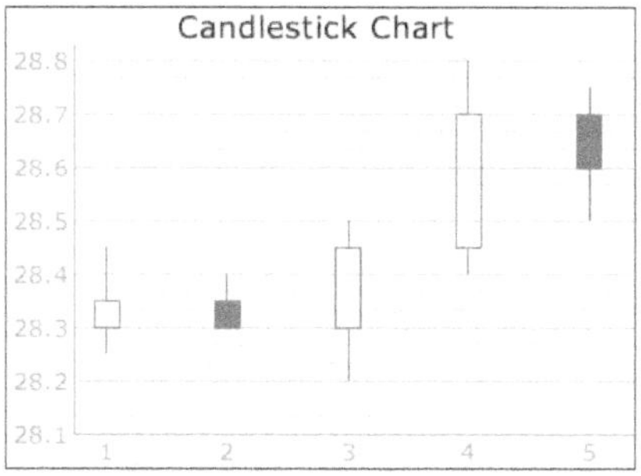

Figure 6-5 Candlestick chart

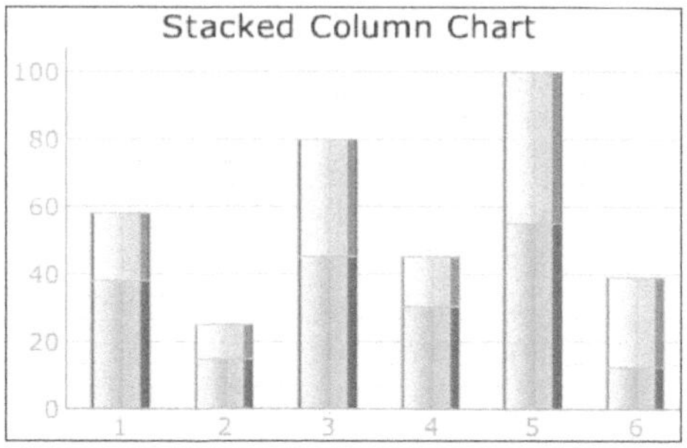

Figure 6-6 Stacked Column chart

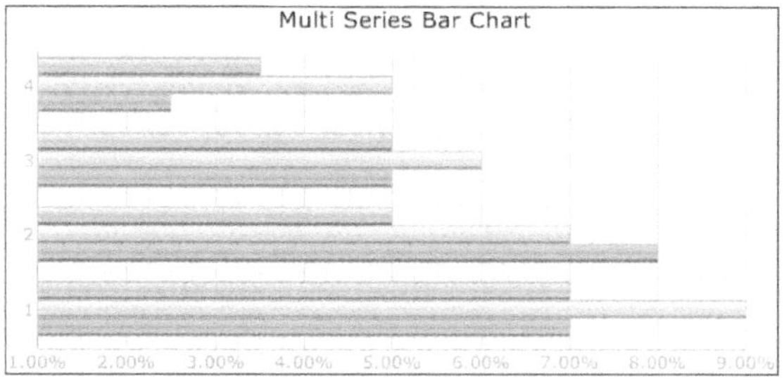

Figure 6-7 Bar chart with multiple series of data

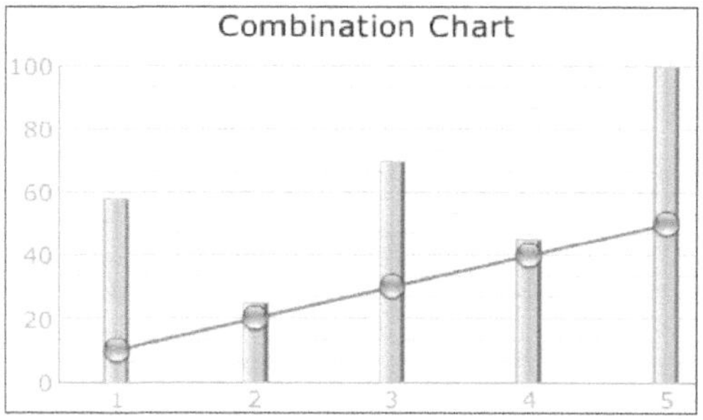

Figure 6-8 Combination chart

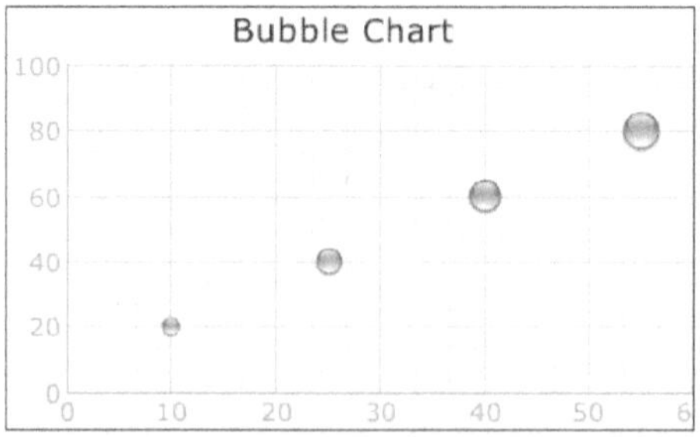

Figure 6-9 Bubble chart

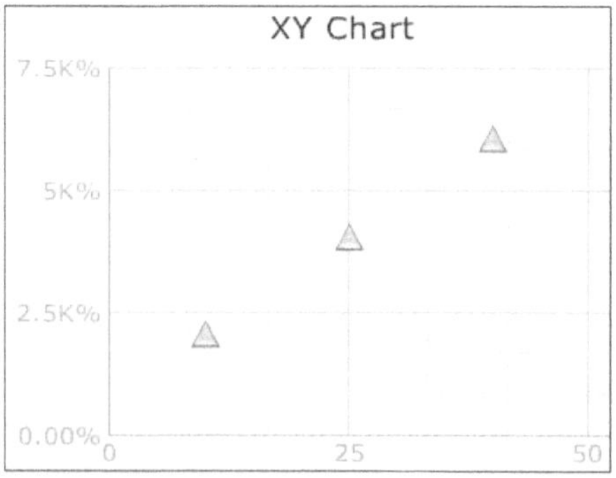

Figure 6-10 XY chart

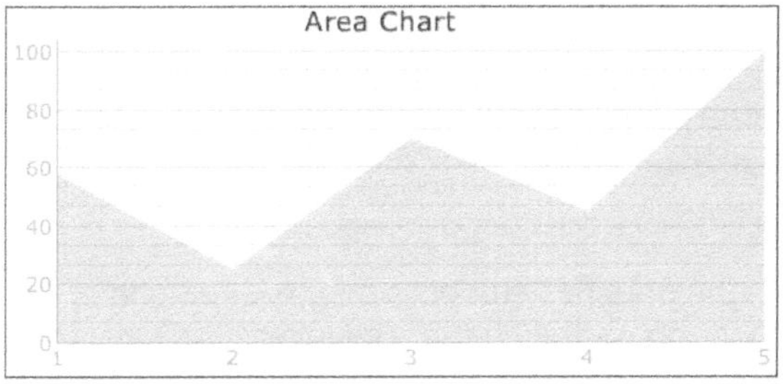

Figure 6-11 Area chart

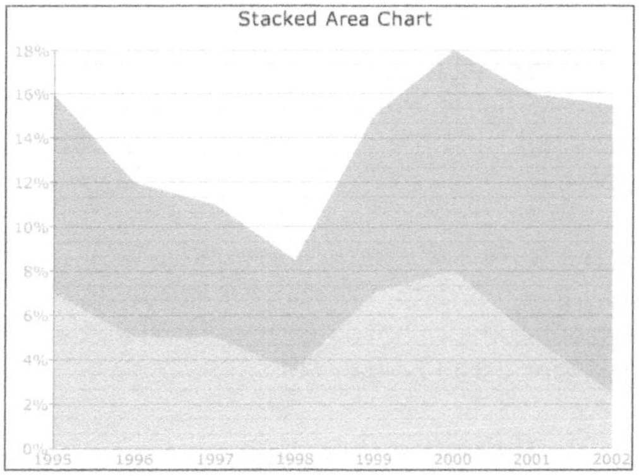

Figure 6-12 Stacked area chart

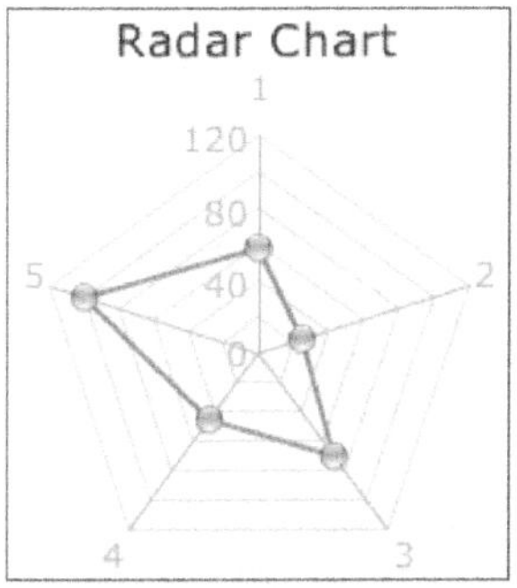

Figure 6-13 Radar chart

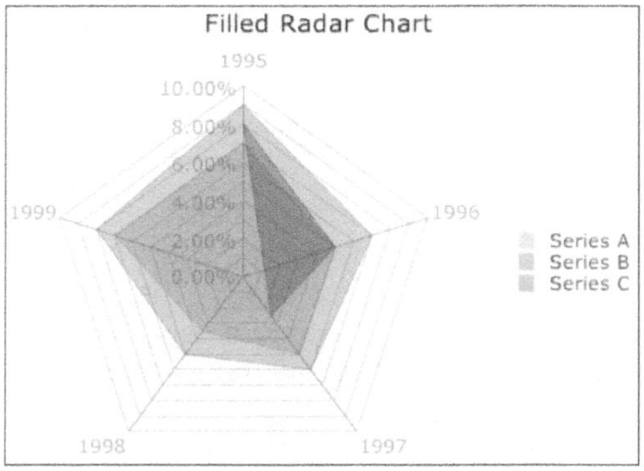

Figure 6-14 Filled Radar chart

Why Charts Are Important

In addition to being able to format data in dashboards, charts present data in a graphical format, which often makes the data easier to understand because they visually display the relationship between the data. Charts also allow data to be presented in formats that spreadsheets cannot do as well. For example, charts can show trends over time, data relationships or how one set of data compares to another set of data. Spreadsheets cannot do this.

In Lesson 3 you created a basic chart. As you saw, it is very easy to get carried away when creating charts because there are a lot of options to select from. Try to create charts that present the data in a meaningful way. Remember that sometimes, less is more.

My Brief Thoughts On Chart Design

The first thing that I want to say is that by no stretch of the imagination do I consider myself a chart design expert. I am only trying to help keep you from making some of the same poor chart design options that I made when I first started and that I have seen other people make.

As you will see in this lesson, creating a chart in Crystal Xcelsius is relatively easy. When compared to Excels chart modification options, it may not seem like Crystal Xcelsius provides as many options. That is true. Crystal Xcelsius does not have as many chart formatting options, but trust me, there are enough for you to make a chart look something terrible <smile>.

I teach a technical writing class and one of the assignments has students create three charts to visually present data. Overall, the students do a good job on the charts. However, it is easy to tell which students have never created a chart before, because the charts exhibit at least one of the reasons listed below.

① The wrong chart type was selected. Newsflash: Bar or column charts are not the best option for all types of data, especially data that shows trends or needs to show how data has changed over time.
② The values on the X and Y axes are backwards. Dollar amounts, quantity, percents, usually go on the Y Axis, while time, dates and categories usually go on the X Axis.
③ Not understanding the data that the chart is created from.

Selecting A Chart Type

There are two areas that need to be addressed before you start to create the chart: The chart type and the source of the data for the chart. You will select the chart type on the Components dialog box. There is no way to change the chart type once it is added to the canvas without deleting the chart and selecting a new chart type. If you are not sure which chart type is the most appropriate, with a few mouse clicks, you can try out a few chart types, by viewing them at the bottom of the Components dialog box. This will let you see which chart is best for the data, before linking cells to the chart. Charts should enhance the ability to understand the data and make it easy to see the differences in the data.

Like Excel, the data (a series) selected to create the chart in Crystal Xcelsius must be in adjacent cells. While it is very easy to select a chart type, the important thing to remember is that you should select the chart type that will best represent the data. For example, if the goal of the chart is to show a comparison between items, a bar chart would be a good solution. Please do not get in the bad habit of only using bar or column charts for every dashboard. If you need to display more than one data series, consider using one of the stacked chart types because they also support more than one series of data.

Chart Component Options

In Lesson 3 you learned about the common options for all components. In Lesson 5 you learned about the common options for Single Value components. In the sections that follow, you will learn about the options on the Properties dialog box that are common to charts.

Common Chart General Tab Options

Titles Options

The options in this section used for the chart title or axis titles of the chart, as shown in Figure 6-15. Using these options is optional.

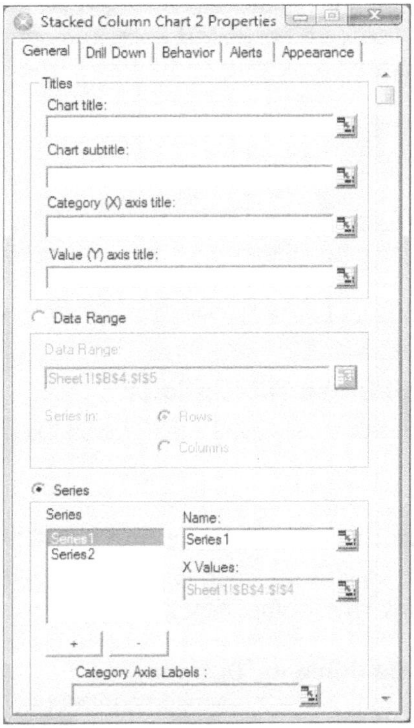

Figure 6-15 Common chart general tab options

CHART TITLE Displays text at the top of the chart. This is usually a brief description of the data on the chart. I noticed that on some chart types if this option is left blank, the plot area of a chart is displayed a little larger on the dashboard. To accommodate not using this option, I put the title in a Label component.

CHART SUBTITLE Displays the text below the chart title. This option is used to provide more information about the data displayed on the chart.

CATEGORY (X) AXIS TITLE Type in or select the cell that has the title for the horizontal axis on the chart.

VALUE (Y) AXIS TITLE Type in or select the cell that has the title for the vertical axis on the chart.

Data Range Options

The options in this section are used to select the range of data from the spreadsheet that will be displayed on the chart.

DATA RANGE The cells selected for this option have to be next to each other.

SERIES IN Based on the cells selected for the data range option, the rows or columns option will automatically be selected, based on the layout of data in the spreadsheet. If you want the data displayed on the chart in the opposite direction, select the other series option. Figure 6-16 shows a series of data in rows. Figure 6-17 shows the same series of data in columns.

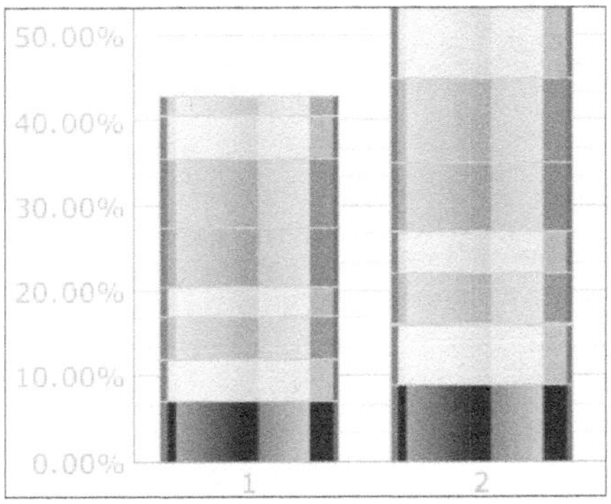

Figure 6-16 Data series displayed in rows

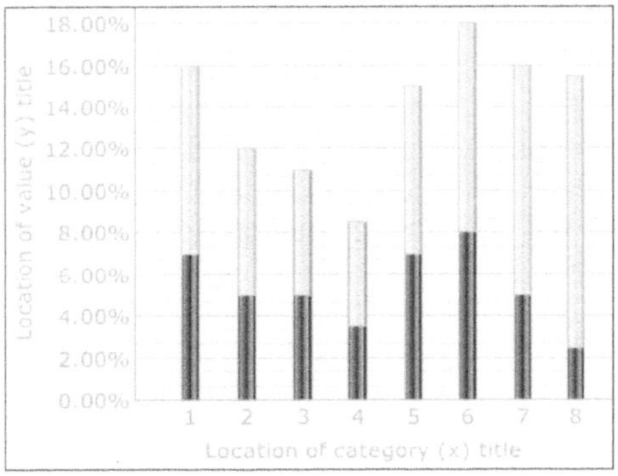

Figure 6-17 Data series displayed in columns

Series Options

The options in this section are used to modify the existing series for the chart, as well as, add new series if needed. Usually, the options in the Series section are used to select ranges of cells that are not next to each other in the spreadsheet that you want to display on the chart.

SERIES Is used to add more series to the chart, edit existing series and delete a series that is no longer needed.

NAME Is used to select a meaningful name for the series. It is not necessary to change the series name if there are only one or two series in the chart.

X VALUES Is used to select the data for the series.

Drill Down Tab Options

This tab is only available in Crystal Xcelsius Professional. [See Lesson 10, Drill Down Tab Options]

Common Chart Behavior Tab Options

The options shown in Figure 6-18 are common to many chart components.

Scale Behavior Options

The options in this section control how the axis scale changes when the data changes. A scale is the range of values that the data must be in, to appear on the chart.

AUTO ZOOM OUT Select this option to allow the axis scale to grow when the data changes. The scale will not shrink. If the chart is using animation, this option should be selected. This option enables the Zoom Out Sensitivity option.

AUTO SCALE Select this option to allow the axis scale to grow and shrink as the data changes. Selecting this option means that all values will be included on the chart. This is the default chart Scale Behavior option.

MANUAL SCALE This option is used to select the minimum and maximum values for the scale. The scale will not change when the data changes. This option enables the Y-Axis and X-Axis Minimum and Maximum Value options. They are only available for charts that have an X Axis scale.

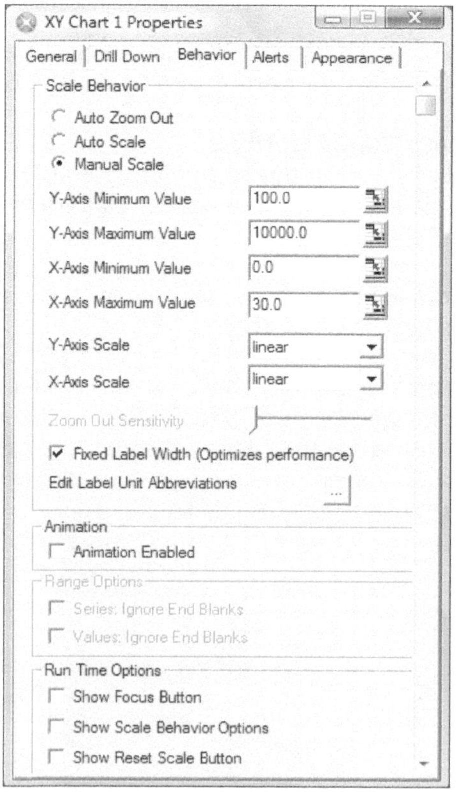

Figure 6-18 Common chart behavior tab options

Y-AXIS MINIMUM VALUE Is used to set the lowest value that will be displayed on the Y Axis on the chart.

Y-AXIS MAXIMUM VALUE Is used to set the highest value that will be displayed on the Y Axis on the chart.

X-AXIS MINIMUM VALUE Is used to set the lowest value that will be displayed on the X Axis on the chart.

X-AXIS MAXIMUM VALUE Is used to set the highest value that will be displayed on the X Axis on the chart.

The **Y-AXIS SCALE** and **X-AXIS SCALE** options are used to select the type of intervals that the scale on the chart will use. The two options in the axis scale drop-down lists are discussed below.

Linear And Logarithmic Scale Options

These options are important for charts that show trends, in particular trends that have a wide span of data. An example of a wide span of data would be the following data values: 10, 20, 5,000, 5,250, 6,125 and 7,500. If there were more high values on the chart, the low values will be difficult to see on the chart.

Figure 6-19 shows a chart that has the Y-Axis value set to linear. Figure 6-20 shows the same chart with the Y-Axis value set to logarithmic.

The **LOGARITHMIC** option provides a more accurate trend line in the chart because the spacing between the larkers on the chart does not change.

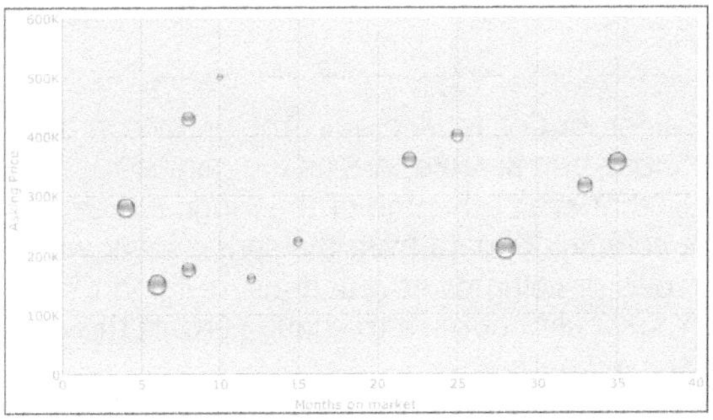

Figure 6-19 Chart using the Linear scale option

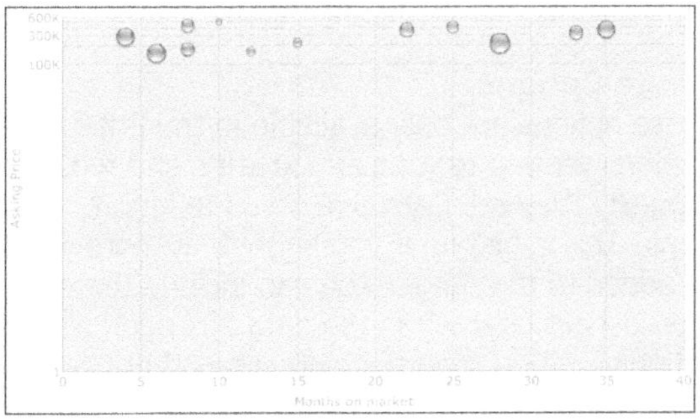

Figure 6-20 Chart using the Logarithmic scale option

① **LINEAR** uses intervals that are evenly spaced to create the scale for the axis. This option allows the scale to resize itself based on the values being charted. This is the most common option to select.

② **LOGARITHMIC** uses intervals that are unevenly spaced. Small values entered in the field force larger spaced intervals on the chart. Large values in the field force smaller spaced intervals on the chart. Select this option when the range of values displayed is large.

ZOOM OUT SENSITIVITY This option is only available if the Auto Zoom Out option is selected. This option is used to select how much a scale can grow when the data changes. Use the slider shown in Figure 6-21 to adjust how much the scale can increase. To the far right, the scale increases a lot. To the far left, the scale increases by a small amount.

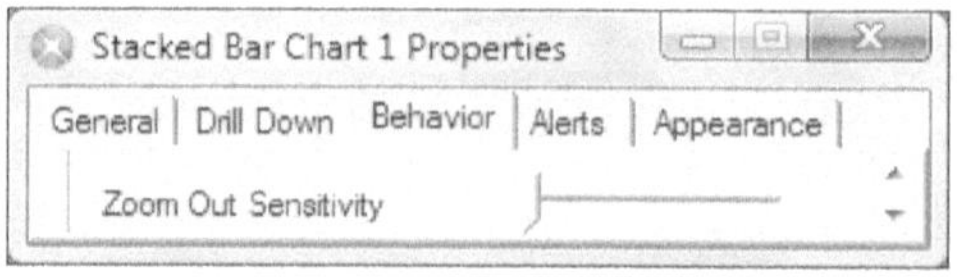

Figure 6-21 Zoom Out Sensitivity option

FIXED LABEL WIDTH Check this option if you do not want the axis labels to be resized if the scale changes.

EDIT LABEL UNIT ABBREVIATIONS This option is only available if the Fixed Label Width option is checked.

Clicking the Browse button next to the Edit Label option opens the dialog box shown in Figure 6-22. The appropriate option in the **DISPLAYED SIGN** column will appear after the numbers on the Y Axis on the chart.

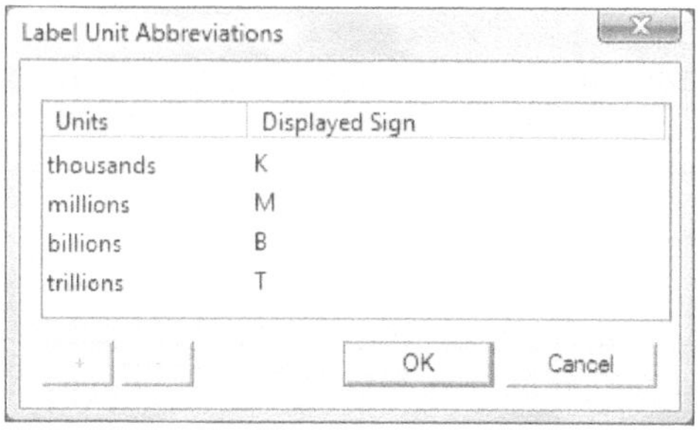

Figure 6-22 Label Unit Abbreviations dialog box

The option selected depends on the values on the scale for the axis. You can add or change the options on this dialog box as needed.

ANIMATION ENABLED Checking this option adds movement to the elements (bars, lines etc.) on the chart. The elements will grow or shrink as the data changes.

Range Options

These options are only available in the Enterprise Edition of Crystal Xcelsius. The options in this section (**SERIES: IGNORE END BLANKS** and **VALUES: IGNORE END BLANKS**) are as the names suggest. They tell Crystal Xcelsius to ignore any cells that are at the end of the range if they are blank. This is helpful if you know that more rows or columns of data from the spreadsheet will be added to the range. You can include the empty rows or columns now and just re-import the spreadsheet later when the data has been added. You would not have to change any of the options on the Properties dialog box that will use the new data.

Run Time Options

If enabled, the options in this section allow the user some control over the scale behavior of charts. The three options discussed below allow the scale of the chart to be changed by the person using the dashboard. Charts that have run time options enabled will display the icon shown in Figure 6-23.

① **SHOW FOCUS BUTTON** Allows the user to force the chart to be rescaled based on the data that is visible. This option enables the fourth button on the menu shown in Figure 6-24.

② **SHOW SCALE BEHAVIOR OPTIONS** Allows the chart to be scaled, based on which option (auto, zoom out, manual scale or auto scale) is selected after the data changes. This option enables buttons one, two and three on the menu. Selecting this option allows the user to select the following scaling options: Auto Zoom Out, Manual and Auto Scale.

③ **SHOW RESET SCALE BUTTON** Allows the user to reset the scale back to what it was when the dashboard was first opened. This option enables the fifth button on the menu.

When the mouse pointer is hovered over the icon shown in Figure 6-23, the menu shown in Figure 6-24 appears on the dashboard. Selecting the three options discussed above cause some or all of the buttons on the menu to appear in the upper left corner of the chart.

Table 6-2 explains the buttons on the menu. If you want to see how these options work, open the file cx_runtime_options.pdf.

Figure 6-23 Runtime icon

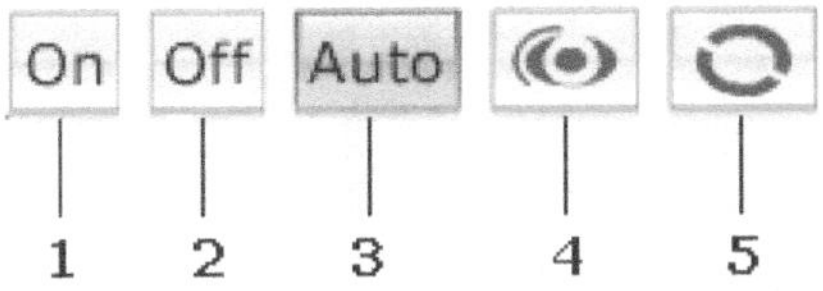

Figure 6-24 Run Time Options menu

Button	Description
1	Enables scale growth. Sets the Scale behavior to Auto Zoom Out.
2	Disables scaling. Sets the Scale behavior to Manual Scale.
3	Enables full automatic scaling. Sets the Scale behavior to Auto Scale.
4	Focus chart data. Forces the chart axes to be rescaled based on current data.
5	Resets chart scale.

Table 6-2 Run Time Options menu buttons explained

If you click the **DISABLE SCALING** button on the menu, the values on the Y-Axis will change. If you click the **ENABLE FULL AUTOMATIC SCALING** button, the values on the Y-Axis will change back to what they were when you first opened the dashboard.

Common Chart Appearance Tab Options

At the top of the Appearance tab are five buttons. Clicking on each button displays options that are used to change a specific part of the chart. I refer to these as the Series panel, Y-Axis panel, X-Axis panel, Titles panel and Layout panel. The options on these panels vary slightly, depending on the chart type.

Common Chart Series Panel Options

Figure 6-25 shows the options on the Series panel. The options on this panel are used to format the data series. The options on this panel are not available for all chart types.

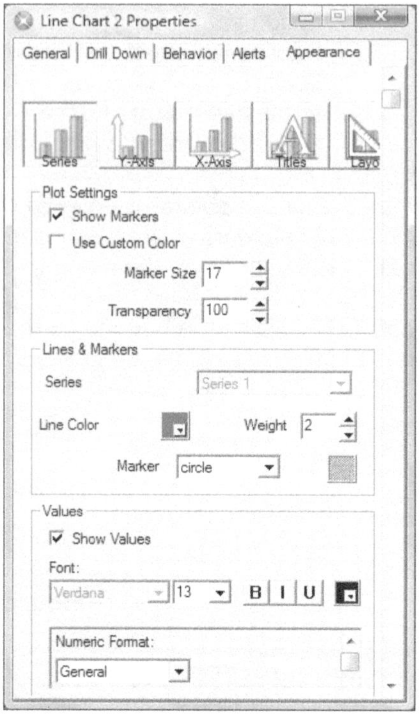

Figure 6-25 Common chart series panel options

Plot Settings Options

The options in this section are used to customize the markers on the chart.

SHOW MARKERS Is used to display markers on the chart. Figure 6-26 shows a line chart without markers. Figure 6-27 shows a line chart with markers.

MARKER SIZE Is used to change the size of the marker.

Lines & Markers Options

The options in this section are used to customize the markers for each series of data on the chart.

The **SERIES** drop-down list contains the names of the series of data that are being plotted on the chart. Select the series from the drop-down list that you want to make changes to. The names in this list come from the values that are created in the **NAME** field on the General tab.

LINE COLOR Is used to change the color of the line for each series of data in the chart.

The options in the **MARKER** drop-down list are used to select the shape for the data points for the series on the chart. In Figure 6-27, the diamond marker is selected.

Values Options

The options in this section are used to display the label values and select the formatting for the values.

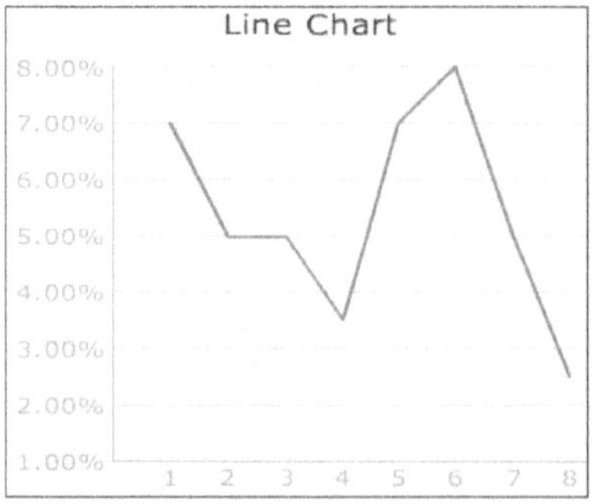

Figure 6-26 Line chart without markers

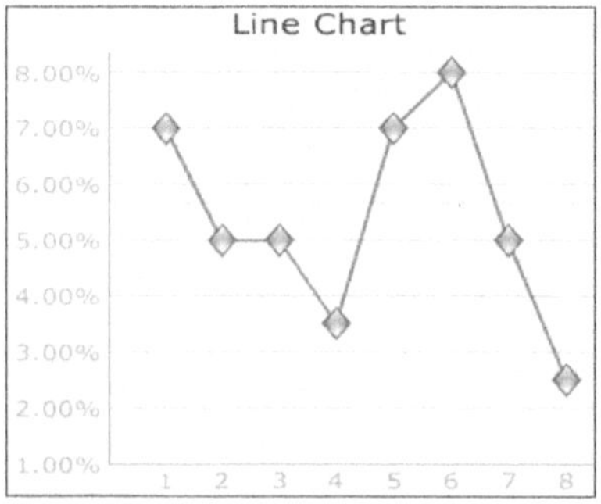

Figure 6-27 Line chart with markers

Common Chart Y-Axis Panel Options

The options on the Y-Axis panel shown in Figure 6-28 are used to customize the values on the vertical axis on the chart.

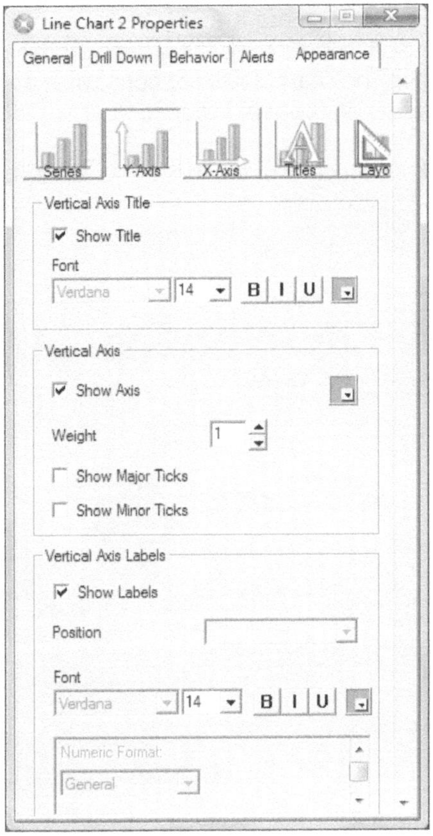

Figure 6-28 Common chart Y-Axis panel options

Vertical Axis Title Options

The options in this section are used to format the title on the Y-Axis. The title entered in the Value (Y) Axis title field on the General tab is what the option in this section will modify.

Vertical Axis Options

The options in this section are used to modify the color, weight and tick marks on the axis.

SHOW AXIS If checked, values on the Y-Axis will be displayed on the chart. The color of the values on the Y-Axis can be changed by clicking on the color button across from this option.

WEIGHT It may be helpful to enable this option if the chart will display tick marks on this axis, so that the tick marks are easier to see on the chart.

SHOW MAJOR TICKS Check this option if you want the chart to display (the large) tick marks on the Y-Axis of the chart.

SHOW MINOR TICKS Check this option if you want the chart to display (the smaller) tick marks that are between the larger tick marks.

Vertical Axis Labels Options

The options in this section are used to modify the values on the Y-Axis of the chart.

Common Chart X-Axis Panel Options

The options on the X-Axis panel shown in Figure 6-29 are used to customize the values on the horizontal axis on the chart. These options work the same as the ones on the Y-Axis panel.

[See Common Chart Y-Axis Panel Options, in the previous section]

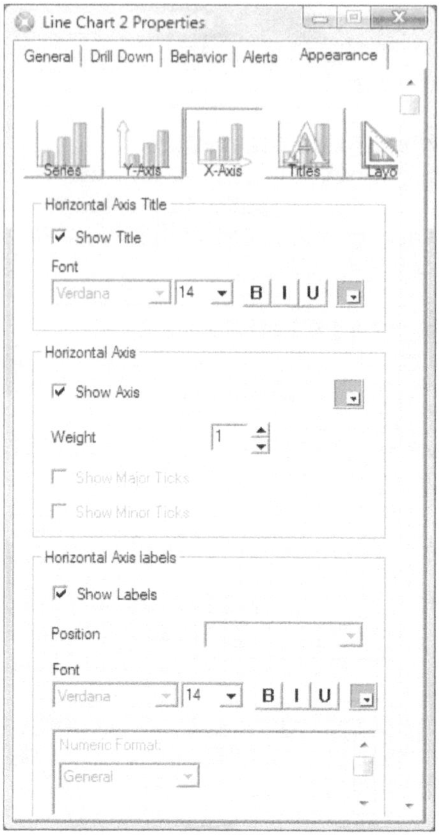

Figure 6-29 Common chart X-Axis panel options

Common Chart Titles Panel Options

The options on this panel are used to format the chart title and subtitle, by changing the font size, border and alignment options, as shown in Figure 6-30. The legend can also be customized.

Figure 6-30 Common chart titles panel options

Chart Title Options

SUBTITLE FONT If available, you can select a different font for the Chart subtitle. This option is only available if the Use Non-Embedded Fonts option is selected on the Unicode Font Options dialog box. [See Lesson 2, Figure 2-7]

SHOW BORDER Is used to add a border around the chart title and subtitle.

SHOW FILL Is used to change a background color for the chart title and subtitle.

Legend Options

The legend explains each series of data on the chart, as shown earlier in Figure 6-14.

SHOW LEGEND Check this option if you want to display a legend with the chart.

SHOW BORDER Is used to change the border color of the legend.

SHOW FILL Is used to change the background color of the legend.

Common Chart Layout Panel Options

The options on this panel are used to select backgrounds, borders, horizontal and vertical gridlines for the chart, as shown in Figure 6-31.

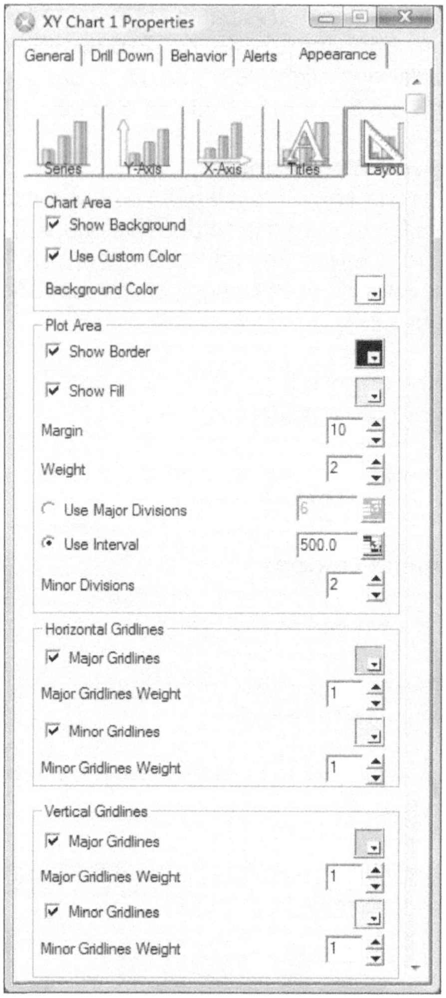

Figure 6-31 Common chart layout panel options

Chart Area Options

SHOW BACKGROUND Check this option if you want to add a background color to the chart. Because the default background color is white, if this option is checked, it will appear as a gray border instead of a color.

BACKGROUND COLOR Is used to change the background color of the chart.

Plot Area Options

The options in this section are for the center of the chart where the data is displayed. Figure 6-30 shows a line chart with the **SHOW BORDER** and **SHOW FILL** options selected.

MARGIN Is used to select the space between the outside of the plot area and the outer edges of the chart area. The smaller the number selected, the closer to the outer edge of the plot area the chart will be. The chart expands the larger the margin number is.

WEIGHT Is used to select how thick the border around the plot area is. The smaller the number, the thinner the border is.

The chart shown in Figure 6-32 has a weight of two. The chart shown in Figure 6-33 has a weight of five.

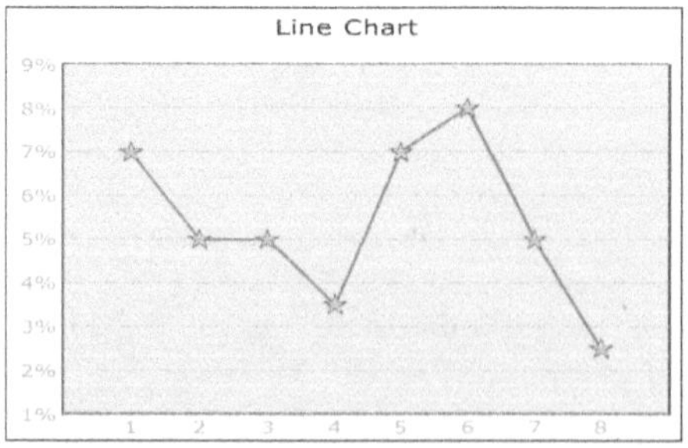

Figure 6-32 Chart with Show Border and Show Fill options selected

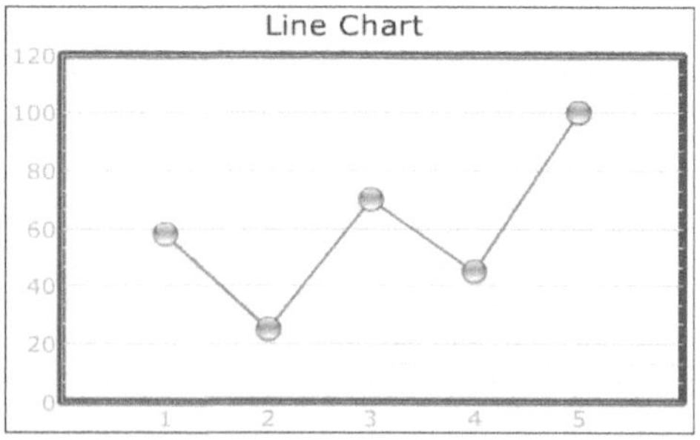

Figure 6-33 Chart with Weight option increased

USE MAJOR DIVISIONS Is used to control the number of the labels on the X axis. (1)

USE INTERVAL Is used to change the range of values on the Y Axis. (1)

For example, if the range of values on the Y Axis is $500 to $10,000 and the current Use Interval option is $5,000, you would probably want to change the option to $1,000, so that the values would be more spread out on the chart, which would make the chart easier to read.

MINOR DIVISIONS Is used to select the number of lines that are between the major gridlines in the chart.

(1) The **MANUAL SCALE** option on the Behavior tab must be selected to enable this option.

Horizontal And Vertical Gridlines Options

The options in these sections are used to change the size of the lines for the values on the X and Y Axis.

MAJOR GRIDLINES If checked, gridlines on the axis will be displayed and the color of the gridlines can be changed. Figure 6-34 shows a chart with the horizontal **MAJOR GRIDLINES** weight option set to five.

MAJOR GRIDLINES WEIGHT Is used to change the size of the major gridlines.

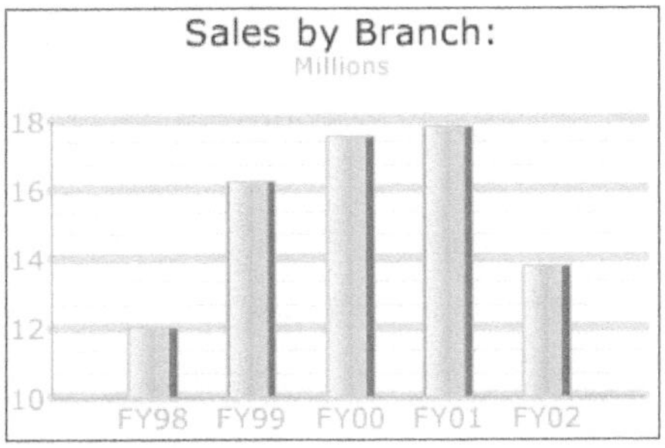

Figure 6-34 Chart with major gridlines value increased

MINOR GRIDLINES If checked, smaller gridlines will be placed between the major gridlines and the color of the minor gridlines can be changed.

MINOR GRIDLINES WEIGHT Is used to change the size of the minor gridlines.

Line Chart Component

General Tab Options

[See Common Chart General Tab Options, earlier in this lesson]

Behavior Tab Options

[See Common Chart Behavior Tab Options, earlier in this lesson]

Series Panel Options

[See Common Chart Series Panel Options, earlier in this lesson]

Y-Axis Panel Options

[See Common Chart Y-Axis Panel Options, earlier in this lesson]

X-Axis Panel Options

[See Common Chart X-Axis Panel Options, earlier in this lesson]

Titles Panel Options

[See Common Chart Titles Panel Options, earlier in this lesson]

Layout Panel Options

[See Common Chart Layout Panel Options, earlier in this lesson]

Exercise 6.1: Create A Line Chart

Line charts are similar to bar charts. The charts that you have created so far have only displayed one series of data. In this exercise you will create a chart that displays two series of data: Market growth and sales growth. Figure 6-35 shows the data for the chart.

	A	B	C	D	E	F	G	H	I
1	Sales Growth vs Market Growth								
2									
3		1995	1996	1997	1998	1999	2000	2001	2002
4	Market Growth	7.00%	5.00%	5.00%	3.50%	7.00%	8.00%	5.00%	2.50%
5	Sales Growth	9.00%	7.00%	6.00%	5.00%	8.00%	10.00%	11.00%	13.00%

Figure 6-35 Line chart data

1. Click the Import Model button.
2. Double-click on the Line Chart spreadsheet file in your folder, then click OK.
3. Add the Line Chart component, then make the chart larger.
4. On the General tab, make the changes in the table.

   When you are finished, two series of data should have been added to the chart, as shown in Figure 6-36.

Property	Change To
Chart title	A1
Chart subtitle	Historic Trend
Category X axis title	Years
Data Range	A4:I5
Category Axis Labels	B3:I3

Figure 6-37 shows the series data options on the General tab. If you clicked the **PLUS** button under the Series list box, you could add another series of data to the chart.

If you click on an option in the Series list (ie. Market Growth, Sales Growth), the data in the **NAME** and **X VALUES** fields will change to display the values for the series that you selected.

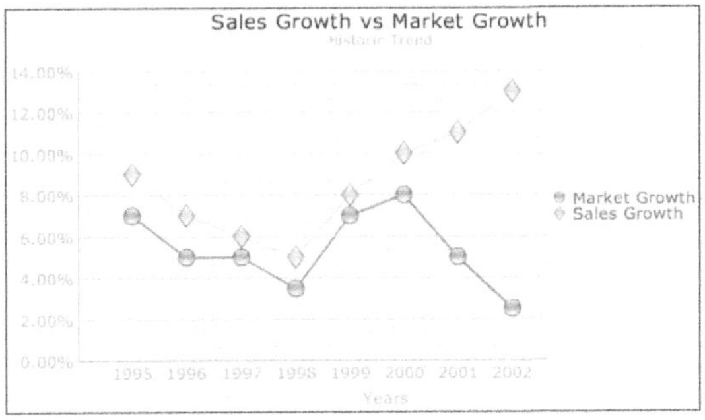

Figure 6-36 Two series of data added to the chart

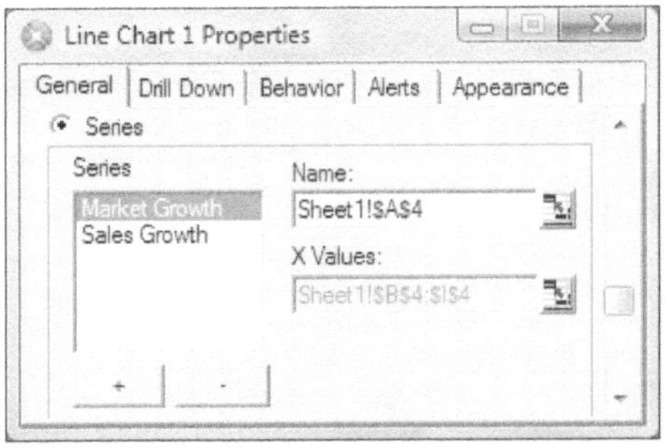

Figure 6-37 Series data

5. On the Behavior tab, make the changes in the table.

Property	Change To
Manual Scale	Select this option
Y-Axis Maximum Value	.40
Fixed Label Width	Select this option
Auto Scale	Select this option

6. On the Appearance tab, click the Series button, then change the **MARKER SIZE** option to 14.

7. If the Category Axis Labels across the bottom of the chart are sideways, make the chart larger.

   The chart should look like the one shown in Figure 6-38.

   If you did not want decimal places on the Y-Axis, you would have to remove them from the cell range B4:I5 in the spreadsheet shown earlier in Figure 6-35.

Figure 6-38 Line chart model

8. Click the Save button. Type `My line chart` as the model name.

Modify The Chart

As you can see, the Sales Growth series is yellow and does not stand out. In this part of the exercise, you will change the series color and make the markers for the Sales Growth series larger.

1. On the Appearance tab, click the Series button, then make the changes in the table.

Property	Change To
Use Custom Color	Select this option
Marker Size	18
Series	Sales Growth
Line Color	Red
Weight	5
Marker Color	Red

2. Save the changes.

   The chart should look like the one shown in Figure 6-39.

Figure 6-39 Modified chart

Pie Chart Component

General Tab Options

[See Common Chart General Tab Options, earlier in this lesson]

Behavior Tab Options

[See Common Chart Behavior Tab Options, earlier in this lesson]

Series Panel Options

The options shown in Figure 6-40 that are specific to pie charts are explained below.

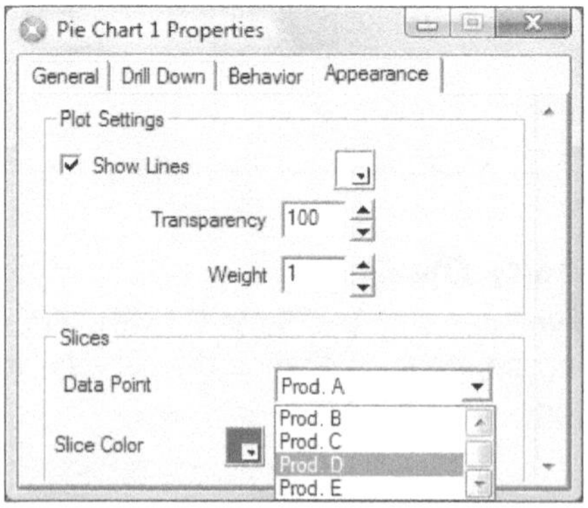

Figure 6-40 Pie chart slice options

Plot Settings Options

SHOW LINES If checked, dividing lines will be placed between the slices on the chart. You can change the color and weight of the dividing line.

WEIGHT Is used to select the size of the dividing line between the slices in the chart.

Slices Options

Clicking the **SERIES** button on the Appearance tab displays the pie chart slice options shown in Figure 6-40.

The **DATA POINT** drop-down list contains all of the slices of the pie. Select the slice that you want to modify.

SLICE COLOR Is used to change the color of a slice of the pie.

Y-Axis Panel Options

[See Common Chart Y-Axis Panel Options, earlier in this lesson]

X-Axis Panel Options

[See Common Chart X-Axis Panel Options, earlier in this lesson]

Titles Panel Options

[See Common Chart Titles Panel Options, earlier in this lesson]

Layout Panel Options

[See Common Chart Layout Panel Options, earlier in this lesson]

Exercise 6.2: Create The Revenues By Product Pie Chart

In this exercise you will create a pie chart that shows the revenue for several products in North America. Figure 6-41 shows the data for the chart.

	A	B	C	D	E	F	G
1	Revenues By Product		Rev				
2							
3		Status List	Prod. A	Prod. B	Prod. C	Prod. D	Prod. E
4	North America		$ 14.22	$ 20.12	$ 12.18	$ 25.49	$ 15.64
5	Latin America		$ 21.05	$ 19.54	$ 15.88	$ 18.73	$ 15.02
6	Europe		$ 21.06	$ 20.45	$ 14.49	$ 16.78	$ 13.61
7	Asia		$ 12.25	$ 17.12	$ 20.99	$ 16.79	$ 12.07
8	Australia & Pacific		$ 15.36	$ 25.74	$ 13.17	$ 19.42	$ 12.70

Figure 6-41 Pie chart data

1. Click the Import Model button. Double-click on the Status list spreadsheet file, then click OK.

2. Add the Pie Chart component.

3. On the General tab, make the changes in the table.

Property	Change To
Chart title	A1
Chart subtitle	In North America
Data Range	C4:G4
Category Axis Labels	C3:G3

4. On the Appearance tab, click the Series button, then make the Data Point changes in the table.

Data Point	Change To
Prod. C	Red
Prod. E	Yellow

5. On the Appearance tab, click the Titles button, then change the **PLACEMENT** of the legend to Bottom.

6. Save the model as `My pie chart.`

   If you hold the mouse pointer over a slice of the chart, as shown in Figure 6-42, you will see the amount of sales for the product and the percent that the product represents of the total sales.

   If the **SHOW LINES** option on the Series panel shown earlier in Figure 6-40 is checked and the Weight is changed to 6, the pie chart would look like the one shown in Figure 6-43.

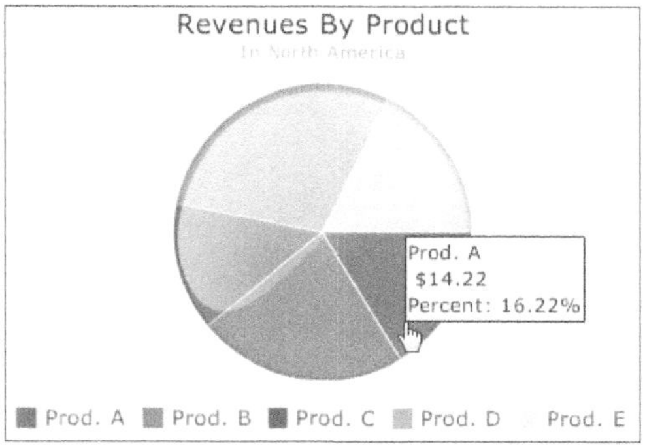

Figure 6-42 Pie chart model

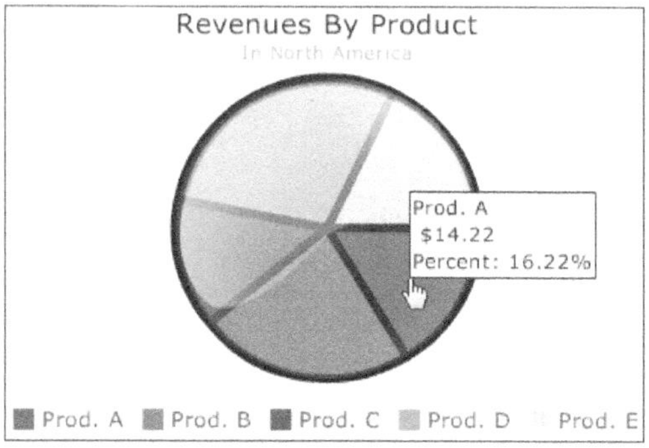

Figure 6-43 Pie chart with modified plot settings options

Bar And Column Chart Components

The only differences between bar and column charts is the direction that the bars are placed on the chart. Bar charts use vertical bars and Column charts use horizontal columns. The data on the X and Y Axis is also switched. You will learn how to create a bar chart in Exercise 10.3.

General Tab Options

[See Common Chart General Tab Options, earlier in this lesson]

Behavior Tab Options

[See Common Chart Behavior Tab Options, earlier in this lesson]

Series Panel Options

The options shown in Figure 6-44 that are specific to bar and column charts are explained below.

Plot Settings Options

BAR WIDTH Is used to change the size of the bars or columns on the chart. The range of values for this option is 1 to 100.

Bars Options

BAR COLOR Is used to change the color of the bars or columns in the selected series.

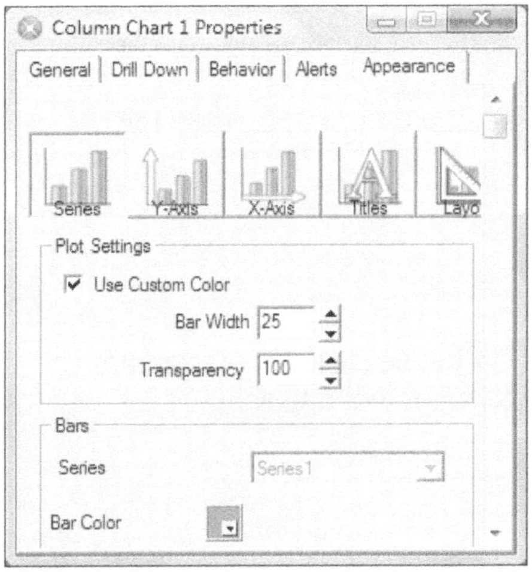

Figure 6-44 Bar and Column chart series panel options

Y-Axis Panel Options

[See Common Chart Y-Axis Panel Options, earlier in this lesson]

X-Axis Panel Options

[See Common Chart X-Axis Panel Options, earlier in this lesson]

Titles Panel Options

[See Common Chart Titles Panel Options, earlier in this lesson]

Layout Panel Options

[See Common Chart Layout Panel Options, earlier in this lesson]

Exercise 6.3: Create The Sales By Branch Column Chart

In this exercise you will create a column chart. In the next lesson, this chart will be connected to a List Box component.

The chart will display the sales for five fiscal years. Figure 6-45 shows the data for the chart.

	A	B	C	D	E	F
1	Sales by Branch:					
2						
3		FY98	FY99	FY00	FY01	FY02
4	Atherton	$ 19.7	$ 17.1	$ 18.3	$ 14.8	$ 19.8
5	Berkeley	$ 14.4	$ 18.0	$ 16.4	$ 16.7	$ 19.3
6	Carmel	$ 18.8	$ 13.5	$ 18.7	$ 13.9	$ 15.7
7	Cupertino	$ 12.0	$ 16.2	$ 17.5	$ 17.8	$ 13.8
8	Freemont	$ 19.2	$ 15.6	$ 19.6	$ 15.9	$ 14.4
9	Irvine	$ 18.9	$ 14.6	$ 16.7	$ 12.1	$ 13.9
10	Milpitas	$ 18.7	$ 17.8	$ 14.0	$ 18.5	$ 13.7
11	Orange County	$ 17.0	$ 19.4	$ 17.1	$ 17.3	$ 17.3
12	San Francisco	$ 14.4	$ 14.0	$ 13.9	$ 15.4	$ 18.3
13						
14	Insert In Row:					

Figure 6-45 Column chart data

1. Click the Import Model button. Double-click on the List Box spreadsheet file, then click OK.

2. Add the Column Chart component.

3. On the General tab, make the changes in the table.

Property	Change To
Chart title	A1
Chart subtitle	Millions
Data Range	B14:F14
Category Axis Labels	B3:F3

4. On the Behavior tab, make the changes in the table.

Property	Change To
Manual Scale	Select this option
Y-Axis Maximum Value	500
Auto Scale	Select this option

5. On the Appearance tab, click the Series button, then change the **BAR WIDTH** option to 25.

6. The chart should look like the one shown in Figure 6-46.

   Save the model as `My list box selector.`

   Yes, the chart does not display any data. There is nothing wrong with the chart. The List Box component that you add to this model will be used to select the data that will be displayed in the column chart.

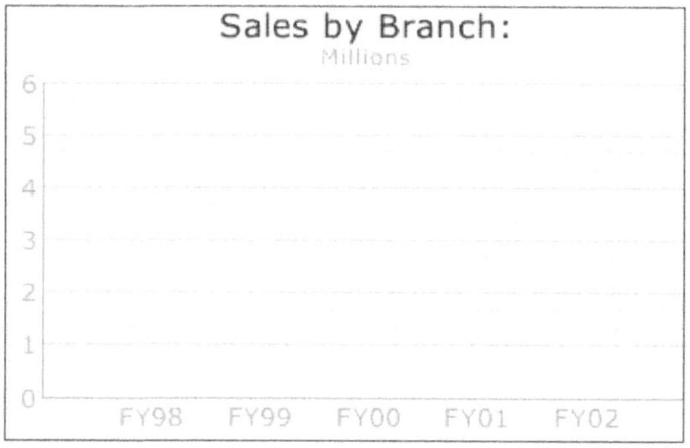

Figure 6-46 Column chart model

Exercise 6.4: Create A Revenues By Product Column Chart

In this exercise you will create a column chart that will be connected to the Play Selector component in Exercise 7.3.

The chart will display the Product revenue for four quarters.

Figure 6-47 shows the data for the chart.

	A	B	C	D	E	F
1		Revenues by Product				
2						
3			Q1	Q2	Q3	Q4
4		Product 1	$ 27.0	$ 34.6	$ 48.7	$ 54.8
5		Product 2	$ 43.3	$ 52.5	$ 33.5	$ 30.7
6		Product 3	$ 46.8	$ 23.1	$ 41.8	$ 50.9
				• • •		
24		Product 21	$ 37.6	$ 52.5	$ 44.3	$ 29.8
25		Product 22	$ 45.2	$ 50.8	$ 46.4	$ 43.5
26						
27	Insert In Row					

Figure 6-47 Column chart data

1. Import the Player Selector spreadsheet.

2. Add the Column Chart component.

3. On the General tab, make the changes in the table.

   Selecting cell B27 for the chart subtitle will display the product name for the current row of data. This means that the subtitle will change each time a different product is selected.

Property	Change To
Chart title	B1
Chart subtitle	B27
Data Range	C27:F27
Category Axis Labels	C3:F3

4. On the Behavior tab, make the changes in the table.

Property	Change To
Manual Scale	Select this option
Y-Axis Maximum Value	500
Auto Scale	Select this option

5. On the Appearance tab, click the Series button, then change the Bar Width option to 40.

6. The chart should look like the one shown in Figure 6-48.

   Save it as `My play selector`.

   The chart does not display any values because no data has been added to cells C27:F27. The values will be added to these cells from the Play Selector component.

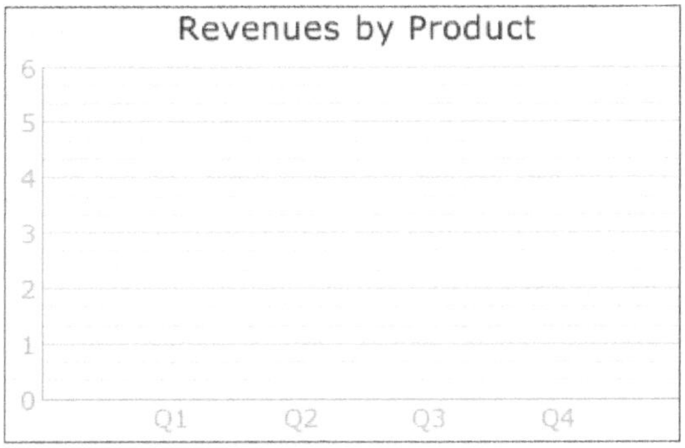

Figure 6-48 Column chart model

Exercise 6.5: Create A Chart For Historic Income

In this exercise you will create a chart that will display the historic data for a line item on the Income Statement. This chart will be used with a Table component in Exercise 7.4. Figure 6-49 shows the data for the chart.

	A	B	C	D	E	F	G	H	I	J	K	L
1	Income Statement				Historic Data							
2												
3												
4	Revenues	FY2003			FY1995	FY1996	FY1997	FY1998	FY1999	FY2000	FY2001	FY2002
5	Gross Sales	$ 12,000			12,600.00	13,104.00	13,628.16	14,173.29	14,740.22	15,329.83	15,943.02	16,580.74
6	Sales Return & Allowances	$ 125			131.25	136.50	141.96	147.64	153.54	159.69	166.07	172.72
7	Net Sales	$ 11,875			12,468.75	12,967.50	13,486.20	14,025.65	14,586.67	15,170.14	15,776.95	15,408.02
8	Cost of Good Sold	$ 5,666			5,949.30	6,187.27	6,434.76	6,692.15	6,959.84	7,238.23	7,527.76	7,828.87
9	Gross Profit	$ 6,209			6,519.45	6,780.23	7,051.44	7,333.49	7,626.83	7,931.91	8,249.18	8,579.15
10	Selling Expenses	$ 2,345			2,462.25	2,560.74	2,663.17	2,769.70	2,880.48	2,995.70	3,115.53	3,240.15
11	General & Admin.	$ 1,546			1,623.30	1,688.23	1,755.76	1,825.99	1,899.03	1,974.99	2,053.99	2,136.15
12	Operating Income	$ 2,318			2,433.90	2,531.26	2,632.51	2,737.81	2,847.32	2,961.21	3,079.66	3,202.85
13	Other Income / Expenses	$ 988			1,037.40	1,078.90	1,122.05	1,166.93	1,213.61	1,262.16	1,312.64	1,365.15
14	Income Before Interest & Taxes	$ 3,306			3,471.30	3,610.15	3,754.56	3,904.74	4,060.93	4,223.37	4,392.30	4,567.99
15	Interest Expenses & Taxes	$ 2,333			2,449.65	2,547.64	2,649.54	2,755.52	2,865.74	2,980.37	3,099.59	3,223.57
16	**Net Income**	**$ 973**			1,021.65	1,062.52	1,105.02	1,149.22	1,195.19	1,242.99	1,292.71	1,344.42
17												
18				Insert In								

Figure 6-49 Historic Income data

1. Import the Table spreadsheet.

2. Add the Column Chart component.

3. On the General tab, make the changes in the table.

Property	Change To
Chart title	A1
Chart subtitle	E1
Data Range	E18:L18
Category Axis Labels	E4:L4

4. On the Behavior tab, make the changes in the table.

Property	Change To
Manual Scale	Select this option
Y-Axis Maximum Value	500
Fixed Label Width	Select this option
Auto Scale	Select this option

5. On the Appearance tab, click the Series button, then change the Bar Width option to 25.

6. The chart should look like the one shown in Figure 6-50.

   Save the model as `My table`.

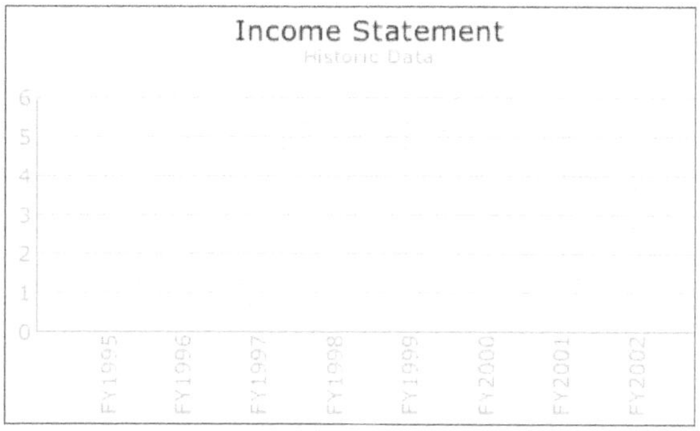

Figure 6-50 Column chart model

Stacked Bar And Stacked Column Chart Components

The Stacked Bar and Stacked Column chart components have the same options.

General Tab Options

[See Common Chart General Tab Options, earlier in this lesson]

Behavior Tab Options

[See Common Chart Behavior Tab Options, earlier in this lesson]

Series Panel Options

The options shown in Figure 6-51 that are specific to stacked bar and stacked column charts are explained below.

Plot Settings Options

BAR GAP Is used to set the space between the bars or columns on the chart. Figure 6-52 shows this option set to 10. Figure 6-53 shows this option set to 100. (2)

BAR OVERLAP Is used to set how much each series on the bar or column are lined up. Figure 6-53 shows this option set to 100. Figure 6-54 shows this option set to 10. Notice that the series for the column barely overlaps. Figure 6-55 shows this option set to 50. (2)

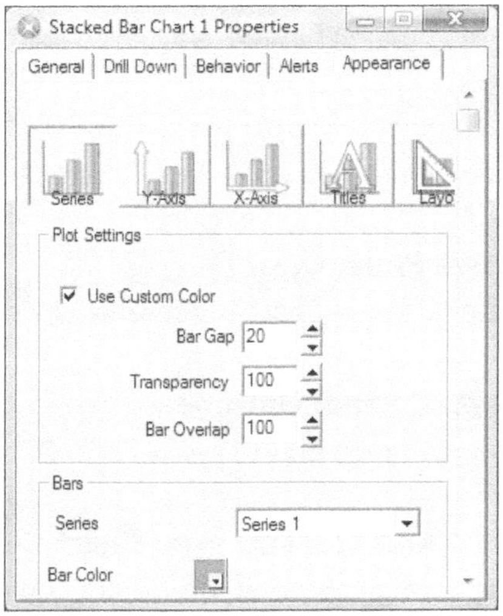

Figure 6-51 Stacked Bar and Stacked Column chart series panel options

(2) The acceptable range for this option is 1 to 100.

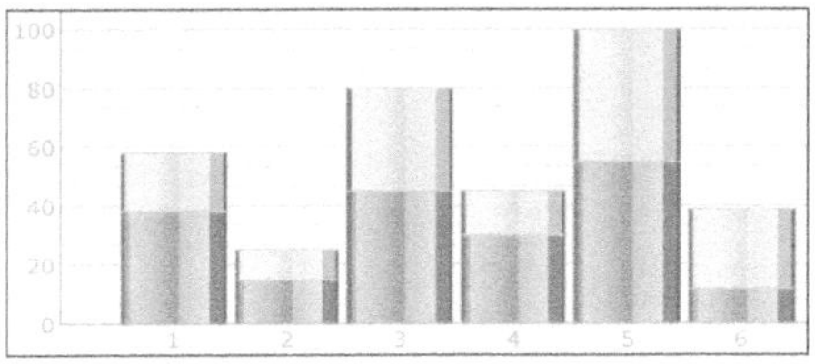

Figure 6-52 Bar Gap option set to 10

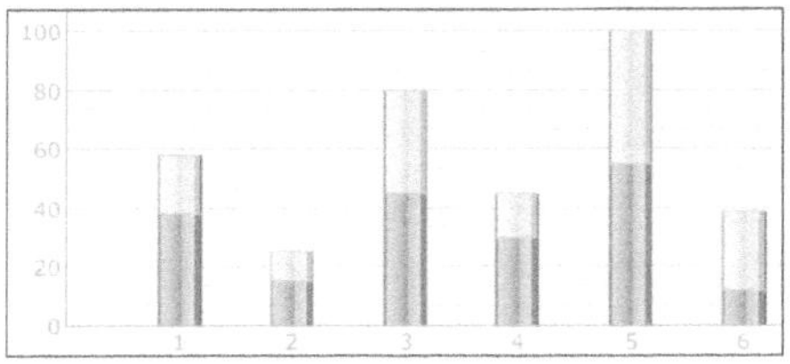

Figure 6-53 Bar Gap option set to 100 and Bar Overlap option set to 100

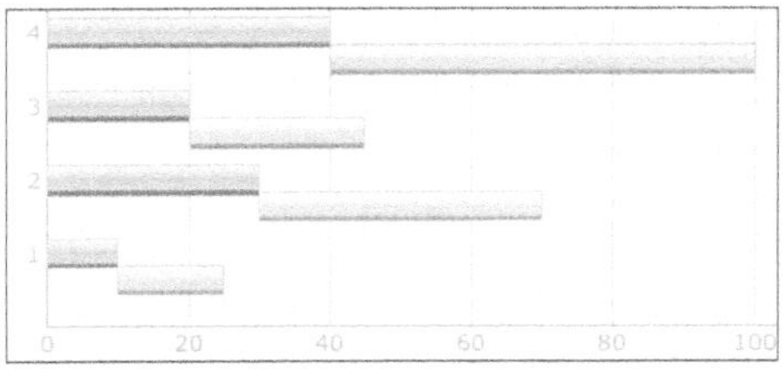

Figure 6-54 Bar Overlap option set to 10

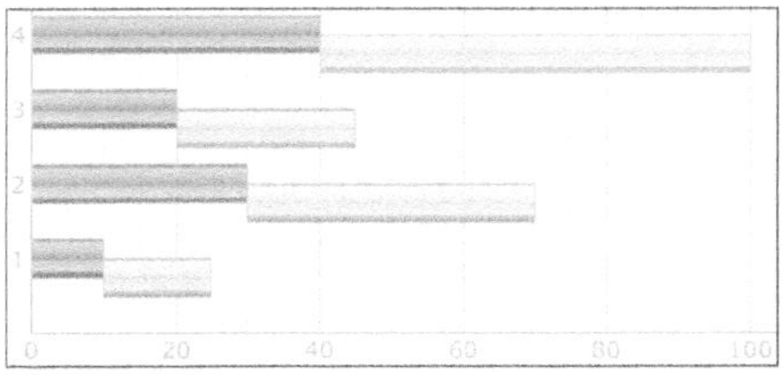

Figure 6-55 Bar Overlap option set to 50

Bars Options

[See Bar And Column Chart Component Options, earlier in this lesson]

Y-Axis Panel Options

[See Common Chart Y-Axis Panel Options, earlier in this lesson]

X-Axis Panel Options

[See Common Chart X-Axis Panel Options, earlier in this lesson]

Titles Panel Options

[See Common Chart Titles Panel Options, earlier in this lesson]

Layout Panel Options

[See Common Chart Layout Panel Options, earlier in this lesson]

Area And Stacked Area Chart Components

The Area and Stacked Area chart components have the same options.

General Tab Options

[See Common Chart General Tab Options, earlier in this lesson]

Behavior Tab Options

[See Common Chart Behavior Tab Options, earlier in this lesson]

Series Panel Options

The options shown in Figure 6-56 are used to customize each series of data on the Area chart.

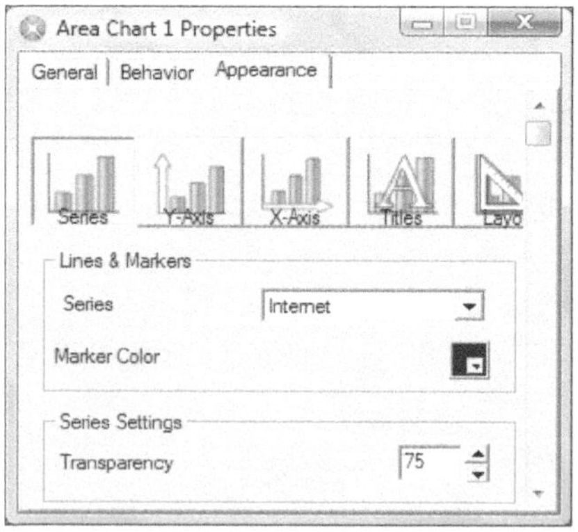

Figure 6-56 Area and Stacked Area chart series panel options

Lines & Markers Options

MARKER COLOR Is used to change the color of the series.

Y-Axis Panel Options

[See Common Chart Y-Axis Panel Options, earlier in this lesson]

X-Axis Panel Options

[See Common Chart X-Axis Panel Options, earlier in this lesson]

Titles Panel Options

[See Common Chart Titles Panel Options, earlier in this lesson]

Layout Panel Options

[See Common Chart Layout Panel Options, earlier in this lesson]

Exercise 6.6: Create An Area Chart

The area chart that you will create will display two series of data from the spreadsheet: Internet and Mail Order, as shown in Figure 6-57.

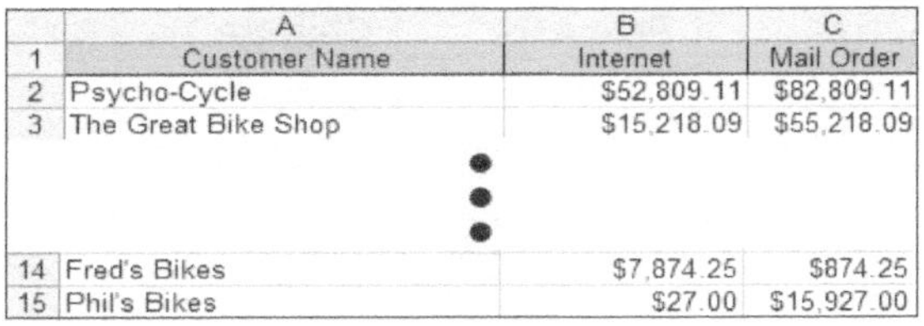

	A	B	C
1	Customer Name	Internet	Mail Order
2	Psycho-Cycle	$52,809.11	$82,809.11
3	The Great Bike Shop	$15,218.09	$55,218.09
	• • •		
14	Fred's Bikes	$7,874.25	$874.25
15	Phil's Bikes	$27.00	$15,927.00

Figure 6-57 Area chart data

1. Import the cx_area_chart spreadsheet.

2. Add the Area Chart component.

3. On the General tab, make the changes in the table.

   You should have the options shown in Figure 6-58.

Property	Change To
Chart title	Sales Area Chart
Chart subtitle	Sources of Income
Data Range	B2:C15
Series 1 Name	Internet
Series 2 Name	Mail Order
Category Axis Labels	A2:A15

Figure 6-58 Area chart general tab options

4. On the Behavior tab, make the changes in the table.

Property	Change To
Manual Scale	Select this option
Y-Axis Minimum Value	500
Y-Axis Maximum Value	100000
Fixed Label Width	Select this option
Auto Scale	Select this option

5. On the Appearance tab, click the Series button, then make the changes in the table. You should have the options shown in Figure 6-59.

Series	Property	Change To
Internet	Marker color	Navy blue
Mail Order	Marker color	Orange
Mail Order	Transparency	75

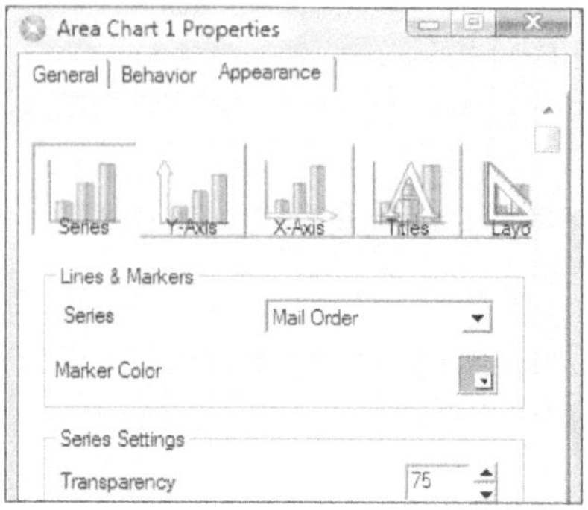

Figure 6-59 Area chart series panel options

6. On the Appearance tab, click the Titles button, then select the **SHOW LEGEND** option.

7. On the Appearance tab, click the Layout button, then clear the **MINOR GRIDLINES** option.

8. The chart should look like the one shown in Figure 6-60.

   Save the model as `My area chart.`

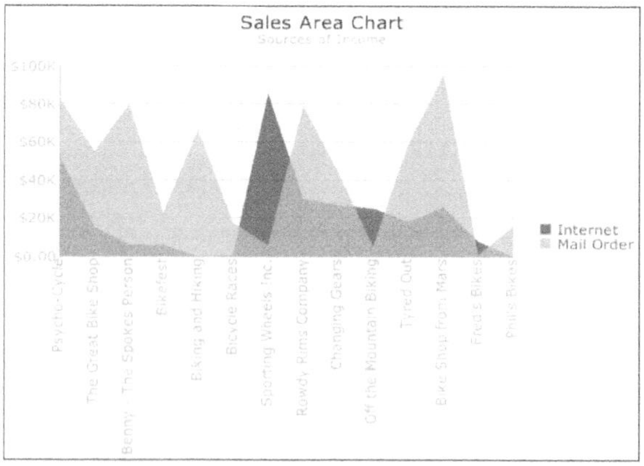

Figure 6-60 Area chart model

Bubble Chart Component

General Tab Options

The options shown in Figure 6-61 that are specific to the Bubble chart are explained below.

Y VALUES Is used to select the values for the Y Axis.

SIZES Is used to select the values that determine the size of the bubble.

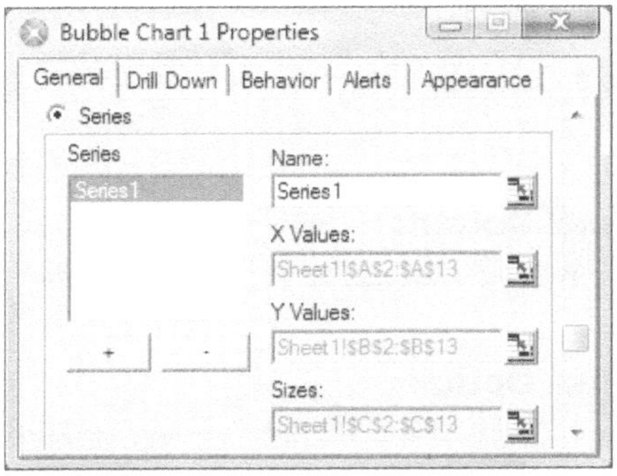

Figure 6-61 Bubble chart general tab options

Behavior Tab Options

[See Common Chart Behavior Tab Options, earlier in this lesson]

Series Panel Options

The options shown in Figure 6-62 that are specific to bubble charts are explained below.

Plot Settings Options

The options in this section are used to configure custom colors and the bubble size.

BUBBLE SIZE Is used to change the size of the bubble.

Bubble Options

The options in this section are used to change the color of a series of data in the chart.

Values Options

[See Common Chart Appearance Tab Options, earlier in this lesson]

CURRENT VALUE Is used to select the label value (The X or Y Axis), that you want to change the font or numeric format of, as shown in Figure 6-63.

SIZES Is used to change the font size of text that is displayed when the mouse pointer is hovered over a bubble on the chart, as shown in Figure 6-64.

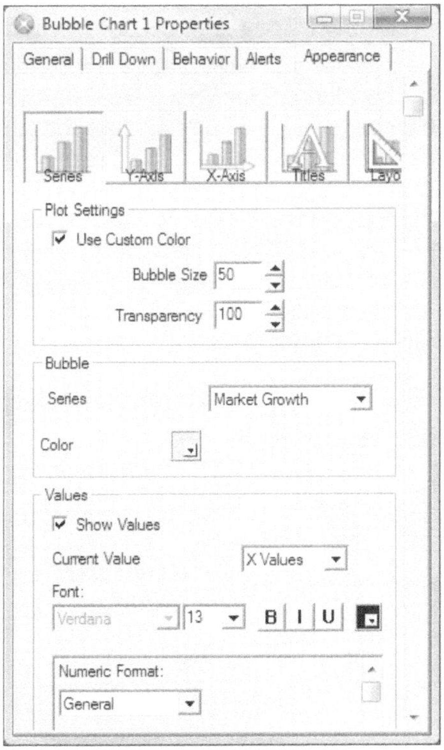

Figure 6-62 Bubble chart series panel options

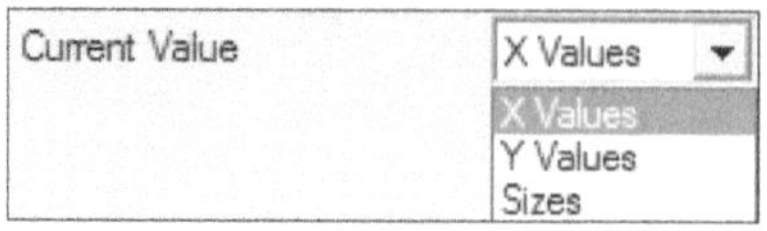

Figure 6-63 Current value options

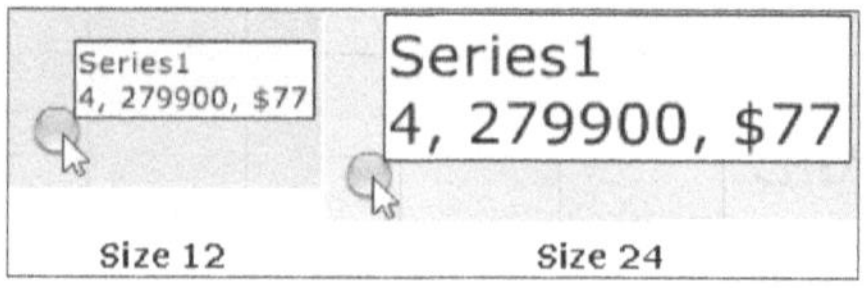

Figure 6-64 Current value font size set to 12 and 24

Y-Axis Panel Options

[See Common Chart Y-Axis Panel Options, earlier in this lesson]

X-Axis Panel Options

[See Common Chart X-Axis Panel Options, earlier in this lesson]

Titles Panel Options

[See Common Chart Titles Panel Options, earlier in this lesson]

Layout Panel Options

[See Common Chart Layout Panel Options, earlier in this lesson]

Exercise 6.7: Create A Bubble Chart

In this exercise you will create a bubble chart that will display how long homes have been on the market. Bubble charts require numeric data for three axis. Figure 6-65 shows the data for this exercise.

In this exercise the **X AXIS** will display the number of months the homes have been on the market.
The **Y AXIS** will display the asking price of the home.
The **Z AXIS** is used to calculate the size of the bubble for each column of data.

The Qty column will be used for the Z Axis. The larger the quantity, the larger the bubble size will be.

	A	B	C
1	Months on market	Asking Price	Qty
2	35	$355,000	78
3	12	$160,000	19
4	6	$150,000	89
5	25	$400,000	36
6	28	$210,000	100
7	8	$175,000	47
8	22	$360,000	51
9	15	$223,000	22
10	33	$316,000	53
11	10	$500,000	10
12	8	$429,000	44
13	4	$279,900	77

Figure 6-65 Bubble chart data

1. Import the cx_bubble_chart spreadsheet.

2. Add the Bubble Chart component.

3. On the General tab, make the changes in the table.

   You should have the options shown in Figure 6-66.

Property	Change To
Chart subtitle	Homes For Sale
Value (X) Axis	A1
Value (Y) Axis	B1
Data Range	A2:C13

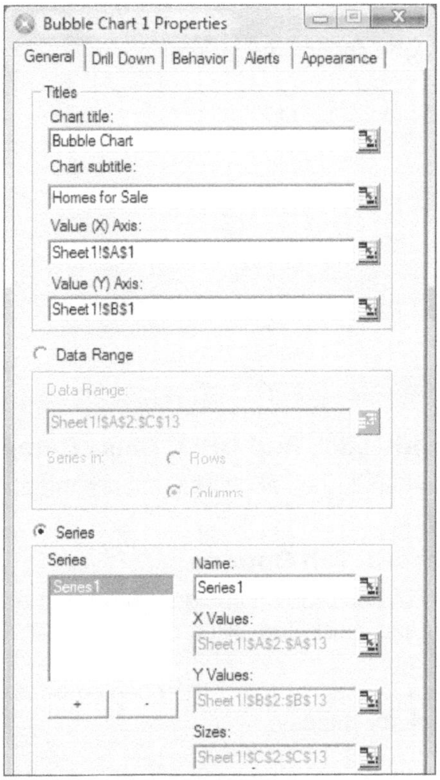

Figure 6-66 Bubble chart general tab options

4. On the Behavior tab, make the changes in the table.

Property	Change To
Manual Scale	Select this option
Y-Axis Minimum Value	100000
Y-Axis Maximum Value	600000
X-Axis Maximum Value	40
Fixed Label Width	Select this option
Auto Scale	Select this option

5. On the Appearance tab, click the Titles button, then check the Show Border option.

6. On the Appearance tab, click the Layout button, then make the changes in the table.

Property	Change To
Show Fill	Select this option
Horizontal Minor Gridlines	Clear this option
Vertical Minor Gridlines	Clear this option

7. The chart should look like the one shown in Figure 6-67.

   Save the model as `My bubble chart.`

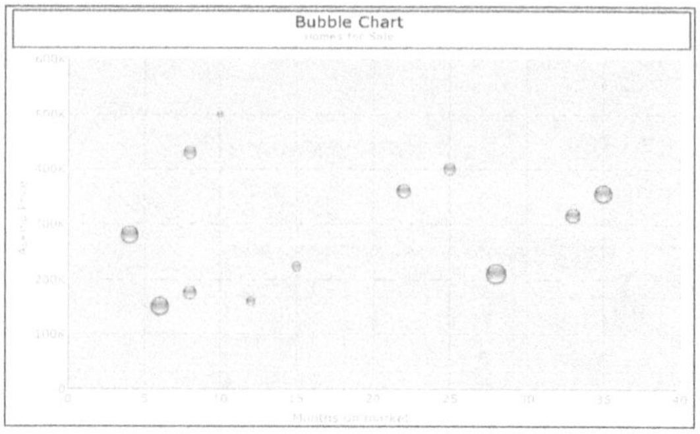

Figure 6-67 Bubble chart model

Candlestick And OHLC Chart Components

The Candlestick and OHLC chart components have the same options.

General Tab Options

The options shown in Figure 6-68 that are specific to Candlestick and OHLC charts are explained below.

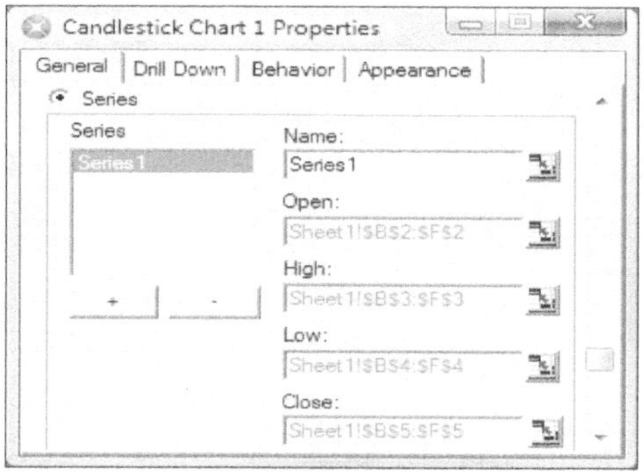

Figure 6-68 Candlestick and OHLC chart general tab options

OPEN Is used to select the opening price of the stock for the day.

HIGH Is used to select the highest price of the stock for the day.

LOW Is used to select the lowest price of the stock for the day.

CLOSE Is used to select the closing price of the stock for the day.

Behavior Tab Options

[See Common Chart Behavior Tab Options, earlier in this lesson]

Series Panel Options

The options shown in Figure 6-69 that are specific to Candlestick and OHLC charts are explained below.

Markers Options

POSITIVE COLOR Is used to change the color that positive stock prices will be displayed in.

NEGATIVE COLOR Is used to change the color that negative stock prices will be displayed in.

Values Options

[See Chart Appearance Tab Common Options, earlier in this lesson]

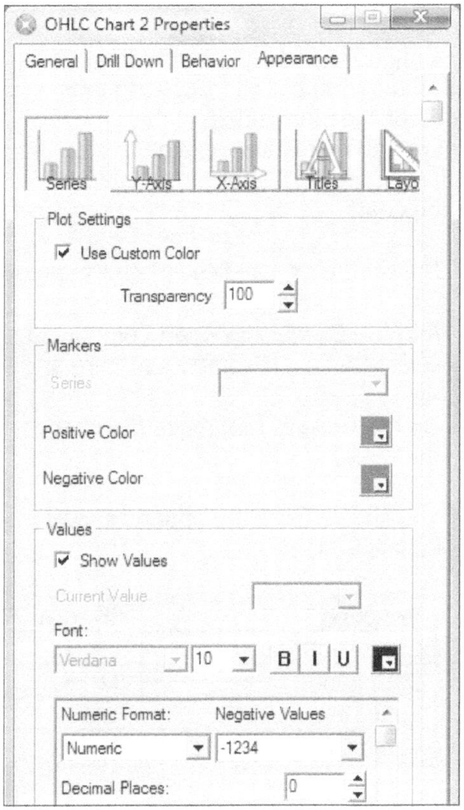

Figure 6-69 Candlestick and OHLC chart series panel options

Y-Axis Panel Options

[See Common Chart Y-Axis Panel Options, earlier in this lesson]

X-Axis Panel Options

[See Common Chart X-Axis Panel Options, earlier in this lesson]

Titles Panel Options

[See Common Chart Titles Panel Options, earlier in this lesson]

Layout Panel Options

[See Common Chart Layout Panel Options, earlier in this lesson]

Exercise 6.8: Create A Candlestick Chart

Candlestick and OHLC charts are primarily used to display stock data. Each marker on the chart corresponds to one of the four values on the General tab that were explained earlier. Figure 6-70 shows the data for the chart.

	A	B	C	D	E	F
1		Stock 1	Stock 2	Stock 3	Stock 4	Stock 5
2	Open	$11	$55	$23	$44	$30
3	High	$20	$55	$60	$44	$68
4	Low	$5	$50	$23	$44	$45
5	Close	$18	$50	$60	$44	$65

Figure 6-70 Candlestick chart data

1. Import the cx_candlestick_chart spreadsheet.

2. Add the Candlestick chart component. If you wanted to create an OHLC chart, you would select that chart component here and follow the rest of the instructions.

3. On the General tab, make the changes in the table.

   You should have the options shown in Figure 6-71.

Property	Change To
Chart subtitle	5 Stocks
Data Range	B2:F5
Series in	Rows
Category Axis Labels (3)	B1:F1

(3) Select the Series option to enable this option.

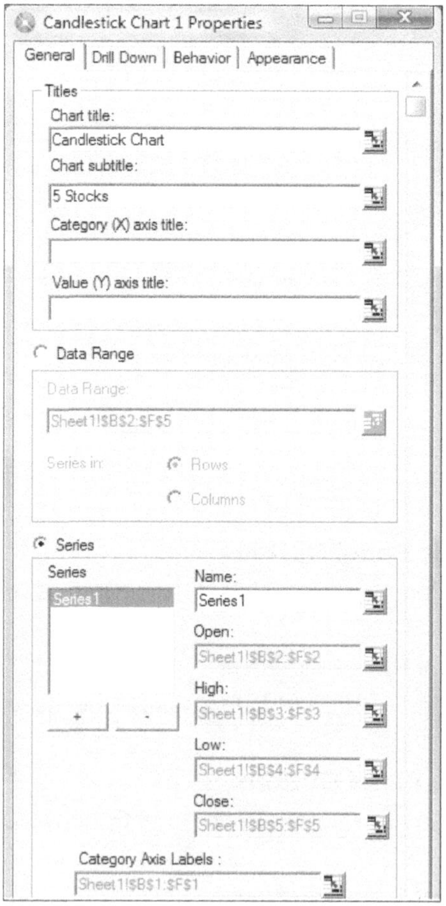

Figure 6-71 Candlestick chart general tab options

4. On the Behavior tab, make the changes in the table.

Property	Change To
Manual Scale	Select this option
Y-Axis Maximum Value	70
Auto Scale	Select this option

5. On the Appearance tab, click the Layout button, then make the changes in the table.

Property	Change To
Use Major Divisions	5
Use Interval	10
Horizontal Minor Gridlines	Clear this option

6. The chart should look like the one shown in Figure 6-72.

   Save the model as `My candlestick chart.`

   The reason that Stock 2 is orange (a negative number) is because the closing price is lower than the opening price.

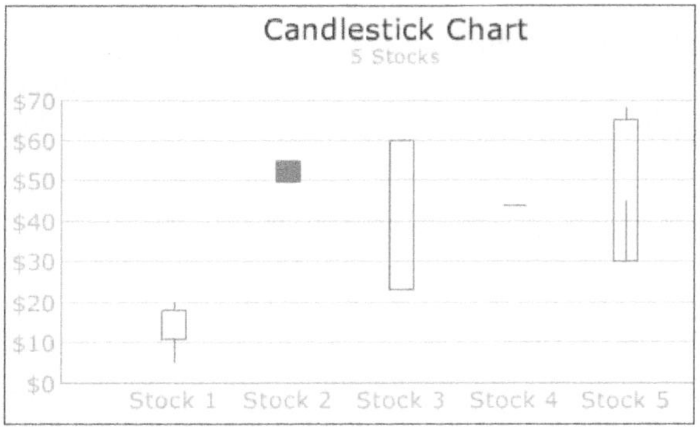

Figure 6-72 Candlestick chart model

The reason that Stock 4 is a line is because the closing price is the same as the other prices, as if there was no activity for the stock that day.

XY Chart Component

General Tab Options

The options shown in Figure 6-73 are the same as the Bubble chart options.

[See Bubble Chart Component General Tab Options, earlier in this lesson]

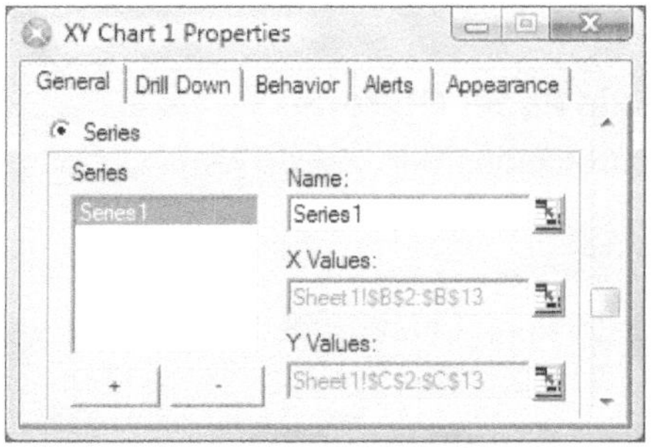

Figure 6-73 XY chart general tab options

Behavior Tab Options

[See Common Chart Behavior Tab Options, earlier in this lesson]

Series Panel Options

The options shown in Figure 6-74 that are specific to XY charts are explained below.

Plot Settings Options

The options in this section are used to configure markers, custom colors and the size of the symbol.

SYMBOL SIZE Is used to change the size of the symbol (marker) on the chart.

Symbols Options

The options in this section are used to configure the appearance of the series markers, including selecting a different symbol.

The options in the **SYMBOLS** drop-down list are used to select a different shape.

Values Options

[See Common Chart Appearance Tab Options, earlier in this lesson]

CURRENT VALUE [See Bubble Chart Series Panel Options, earlier in this lesson]

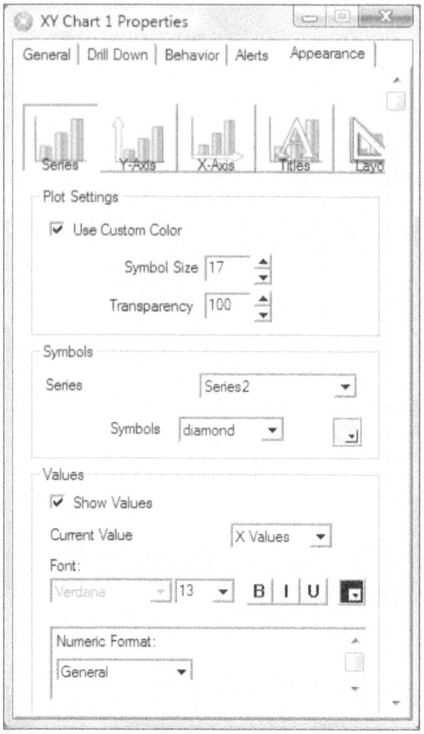

Figure 6-74 XY chart series panel options

Y-Axis Panel Options

[See Common Chart Y-Axis Panel Options, earlier in this lesson]

X-Axis Panel Options

[See Common Chart X-Axis Panel Options, earlier in this lesson]

Titles Panel Options

[See Common Chart Titles Panel Options, earlier in this lesson]

Layout Panel Options

[See Common Chart Layout Panel Options, earlier in this lesson]

Exercise 6.9: Create An XY Chart

The XY chart that you will create in this exercise will display the sales amount and the number of orders per month. Figure 6-75 shows the data for the chart.

Like the Bubble chart, the XY and Radar chart can use three rows or columns of data.

The difference is that only Bubble charts require all of the data to be numeric. Compare the data shown earlier in Figure 6-65 to the data shown in Figure 6-75.

	A	B	C
1	Month	Orders	Total Amount
2	Jan	4	$1,276.74
3	Feb	7	$1,784.75
4	Mar	20	$7,981.41
5	April	17	$5,879.70
6	May	15	$4,751.27
7	June	13	$12,546.12
8	July	25	$21,264.30
9	Aug	31	$31,019.40
10	Sept	26	$8,823.65
11	Oct	1	$819.55
12	Nov	24	$5,879.70
13	Dec	20	$2,378.35

Figure 6-75 XY chart data

1. Import the cx_xy_and_radar_chart spreadsheet.
2. Add the XY Chart component.
3. On the General tab, make the changes in the table.

Property	Change To
Chart subtitle	Monthly Sales
Value (X) Axis	Number of sales
Value (Y) Axis	Total monthly sales amount
Data Range	A2:C13

4. On the Behavior tab, make the changes in the table.

Property	Change To
Manual Scale	Select this option
Y-Axis Minimum Value	100
Y-Axis Maximum Value	40000
X-Axis Maximum Value	30
Fixed Label Width	Select this option
Auto Scale	Select this option

5. On the Appearance tab, click the Series button. Open the **SYMBOLS** drop-down list and select Diamond.
6. On the Appearance tab, click the Layout button, then clear the horizontal and vertical **MINOR GRIDLINES** options.

7. The chart should look like the one shown in Figure 6-76.

   Save the model as `My XY chart.`

   As you can see, it is difficult to know which diamond value is for which month of sales.

   In Lesson 11 you will modify this chart so that it will be easier to tell which marker is for which month.

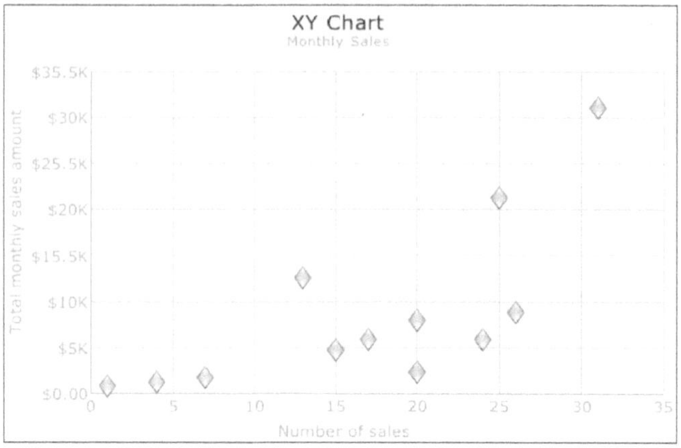

Figure 6-76 XY chart model

Radar And Filled Radar Chart Components

The majority of options for Radar and Filled Radar chart components are the same.

General Tab Options

[See Common Chart General Tab Options, earlier in this lesson]

Behavior Tab Options

[See Common Chart Behavior Tab Options, earlier in this lesson]

Radar Chart Series Panel Options

The options shown in Figure 6-77 that are specific to Radar charts are explained below.

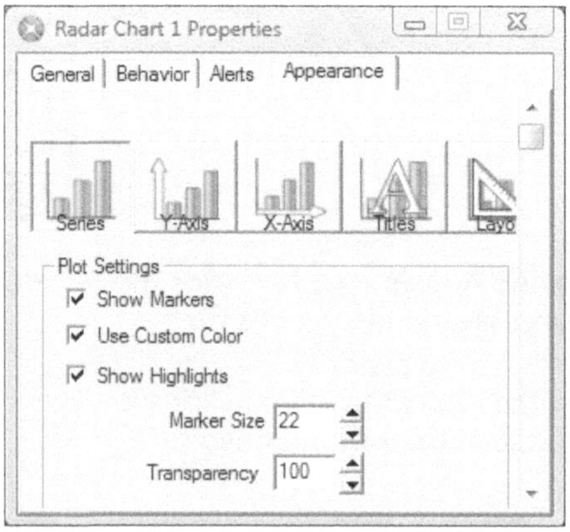

Figure 6-77 Radar chart series panel options

Plot Settings Options

SHOW HIGHLIGHTS Is used to display a highlight color behind the marker symbol. It could be my laptop, but I did not see any difference in the markers when this option is selected. The **SHOW MARKERS** and use **CUSTOM COLORS OPTIONS** must be selected to use this option.

Filled Radar Chart Series Panel Options

The options shown in Figure 6-78 that are specific to Filled Radar charts are explained below.

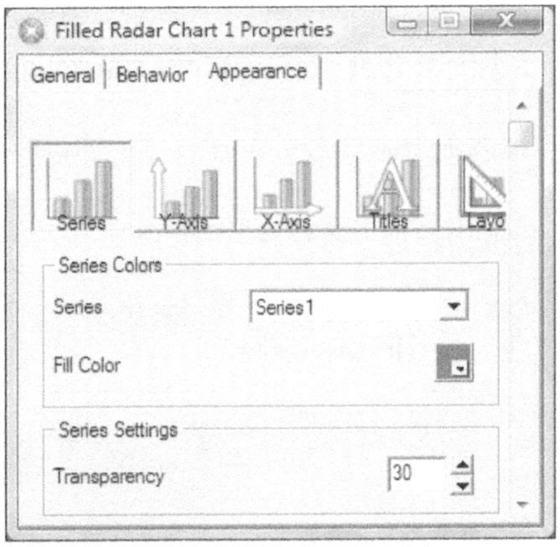

Figure 6-78 Filled Radar chart series panel options

Series Colors Options

The options in this section are used to select the fill color for the series that is selected in the **SERIES** drop-down list.

FILL COLOR Is used to change the color of the data series selected in the Series drop-down list.

Y-Axis Panel Options

[See Common Chart Y-Axis Panel Options, earlier in this lesson]

X-Axis Panel Options

The options shown in Figure 6-79 are used to change the labels across the bottom of the chart.

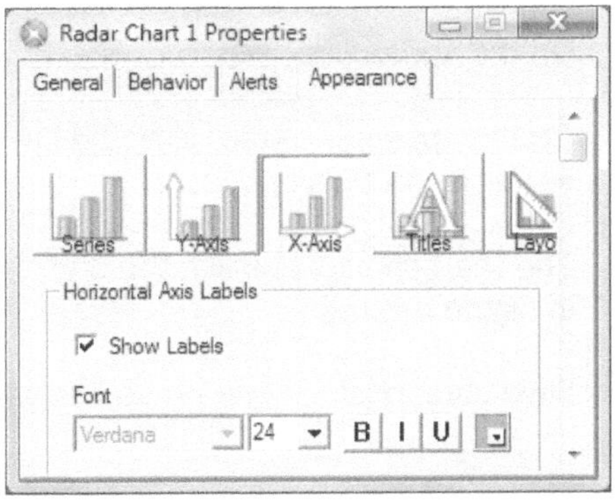

Figure 6-79 Radar and Filled Radar X-Axis chart panel options

Horizontal Axis Labels Options

SHOW LABELS Is used to display the values in the Category Axis Labels option on the General tab.

Titles Panel Options

[See Common Chart Titles Panel Options, earlier in this lesson]

Layout Panel Options

[See Common Chart Layout Panel Options, earlier in this lesson]

Exercise 6.10: Create A Radar Chart

Radar charts function very similar to XY charts. In this exercise you will use the same spreadsheet that you used for the XY chart. [See Figure 6-75]

1. Import the cx_xy_and_radar_chart spreadsheet.

2. Add the Radar Chart component.

3. On the General tab, make the changes in the table.

Property	Change To
Chart subtitle	Monthly Sales
Data Range	A2:C13
Series 1	Delete this series

4. On the Behavior tab, make the changes in the table.

Property	Change To
Manual Scale	Select this option
Y-Axis Minimum Value	100
Y-Axis Maximum Value	40000
Fixed Label Width	Select this option
Auto Scale	Select this option

5. On the Appearance tab, click the Series button. Open the **MARKER** drop-down list and select Diamond.

6. On the Appearance tab, click the Titles button, then clear the **SHOW LEGEND** option.

7. On the Appearance tab, click the Layout button, then clear the horizontal and vertical **MINOR GRIDLINES** options.

8. The chart should look like the one shown in Figure 6-80.

   Save the model as `My Radar chart`.

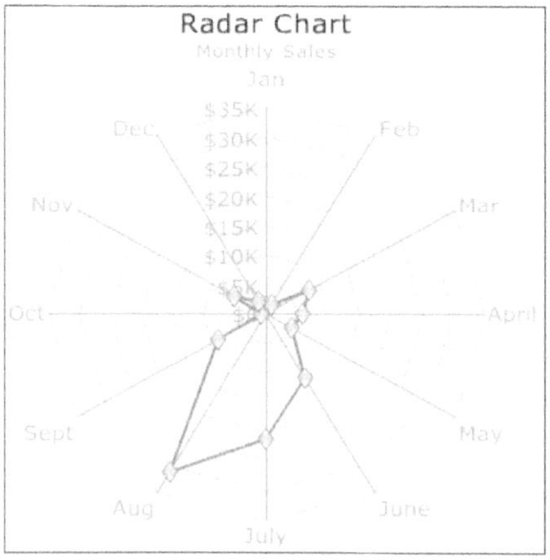

Figure 6-80 Radar chart model

Combination Chart Component

As you read earlier in Table 6-1, Combination charts allow you to plot two or more series of data, using different chart types in the same chart. There are some automatic default chart type selections that you should be aware of, as discussed below. You can change the chart types of any series on the chart.

① The first series defaults to a column chart.
② The second series defaults to a line chart.
③ The third series and above defaults to a column chart.
④ If the second series is deleted in a chart that has at least three data series, the third data series becomes the second data series and defaults to a line chart.

General Tab Options

[See Common Chart General Tab Options, earlier in this lesson]

Behavior Tab Options

[See Common Chart Behavior Tab Options, earlier in this lesson]

Series Panel Options

The options shown in Figure 6-81 that are specific to Combination charts are explained below.

The Combination chart type options shown in Figure 6-81 are for a Line Series. Figure 6-82 shows the options for a Column Series type Combination chart.

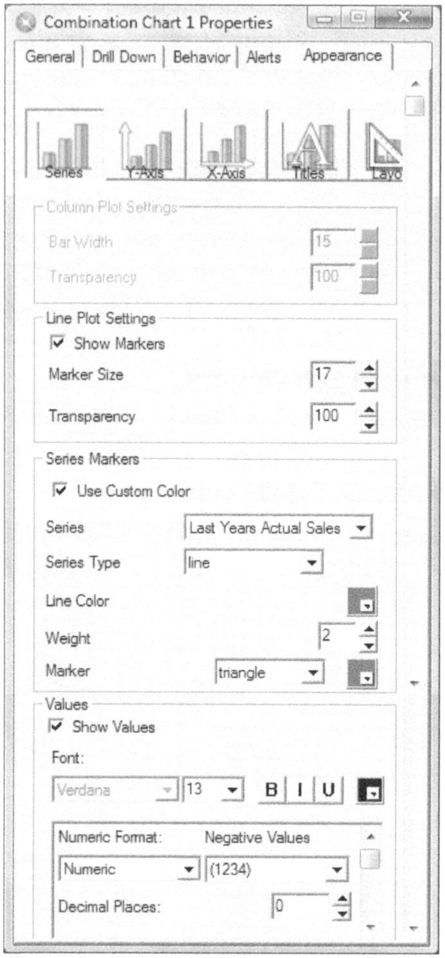

Figure 6-81 Combination chart series panel options for a line series type

Line Plot Settings Options

The options in this section are used to display and configure the size of the markers.

SHOW MARKERS Displays or hides the markers on the chart.

Series Markers Options

The options in this section are used to customize the markers for the series of data that is selected in the Series drop-down list.

The **SERIES TYPE** drop-down list is used to select how the series of data should be represented on the chart, as a line or column. I think that this is a pretty cool feature to use.

MARKER Is used to select the symbol that is used to plot each value in the series.

MARKER COLOR Is used to change the color of the marker.

Values Options

[See Common Chart Appearance Tab Options, earlier in this lesson]

Column Plot Settings Options

The options in this section are used to configure the bar width for markers.

[See Combination Chart Series Panel Options, earlier in this lesson]

BAR WIDTH [See Bar And Column Chart Components Options, earlier in this lesson]

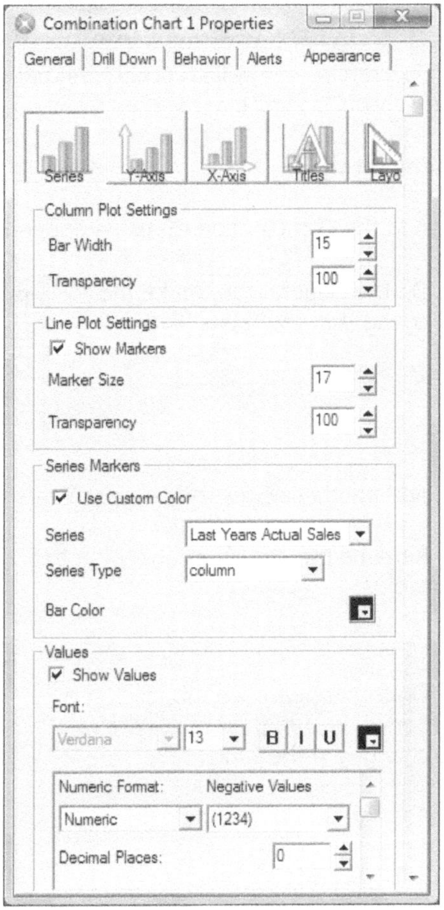

Figure 6-82 Combination chart series panel options for a column series type

Y-Axis Panel Options

[See Common Chart Y-Axis Panel Options, earlier in this lesson]

X-Axis Panel Options

[See Common Chart X-Axis Panel Options, earlier in this lesson]

Titles Panel Options

[See Common Chart Titles Panel Options, earlier in this lesson]

Layout Panel Options

[See Common Chart Layout Panel Options, earlier in this lesson]

Exercise 6.11: Create A Combination Chart

In this exercise you will create the Actual vs Projected chart that you saw in Lesson 1. [See Lesson 1, Figure 1-13]

1. Import the cx_actual_vs_projected spreadsheet.

2. Add the Combination Chart component.

3. On the General tab, make the changes in the table.

Property	Change To
Chart title	A1
Chart subtitle	B3
Data Range	B5:B8
Category Axis Labels	A5:A8

4. Add another series for the Last Years projected sales data.

5. Rename the series, as shown in the table.

Series	New Name
Series 1	Last Years Actual Sales
Series 2	Projected Sales

6. On the Appearance tab, click the Series button, then make the changes in the table.

Property	Change To
Use Custom Color	Select this option
Series	Last Years Actual Sales
Bar color	Red
Series	Projected Sales
Series Type	Line
Marker	Triangle

7. On the Appearance tab, click the Layout button, then clear the **MINOR GRIDLINES** option.

8. The chart should look like the one shown in Figure 6-83.

   Save the model as `My combination chart.`

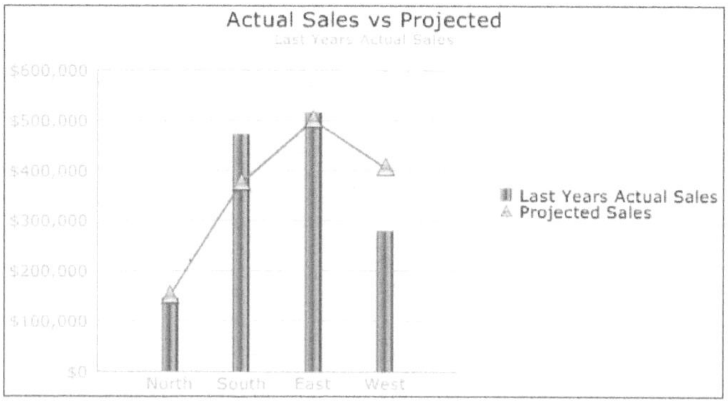

Figure 6-83 Actual Sales vs Projected chart

CREATING MENU BASED DASHBOARDS

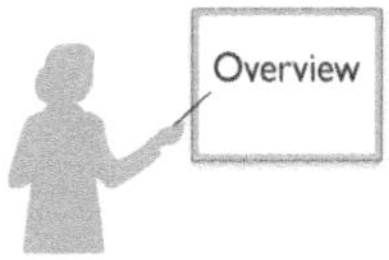

In this lesson you will learn how to create the following types of menu based dashboards.

- ☑ List Box
- ☑ Play Selector
- ☑ Table Selector
- ☑ Radio Button
- ☑ Combo Box
- ☑ Filter
- ☑ Label Based

Menu Component Overview

Menus add another level of functionality to dashboards. Like the menus in the Crystal Xcelsius applications and other applications, the menus that you can add to a dashboard allow the user to select an option on the menu, which causes an action to happen. The action that usually happens in a dashboard is data being displayed. Each option on the menu will display the data differently. Different data will be displayed for each menu option or the same data is displayed in a different format, like a different chart type. The choices for each menu item come from one of two sources: From cells in the spreadsheet or you can type the menu items in.

Menus are selector components. Each item on the menu is linked to a cell or range of cells. This link is what controls the data that is displayed in another component in the dashboard.

Filter Data Using Selectors

Filtering data is a way to manage large amounts of data in a dashboard. Filtered data is a subset of all of the data that is selected for the dashboard. If you have a dashboard that displays data for all sales reps in a chart and you wanted to be able to display the data for one sales rep at a time, you could create a filter, by using a selector component and link it to the chart component.

In Lesson 6 you created charts that did not display any data. In this lesson, you will add a menu selector component to these models, so that the charts will display data.

Selector Components

You have seen some of the menu layouts that can be created in Crystal Xcelsius or have used them in other software. Other selector component types that you will learn about will be brand new. The selectors are shown in Figure 7-1 and are explained below. The selectors that have arrows are not available in the Standard version of Crystal Xcelsius. Table 7-2 lists each component and the lesson that it is covered in, in detail.

In Lesson 4 you learned that the form controls in Excel are not available in Crystal Xcelsius, but that some of the functionality of the form controls can be reproduced. The Selector components can be used to replicate form control functionality.

In Lesson 5 you learned about Single Value components, which only allow the component to be linked to one cell in the spreadsheet.

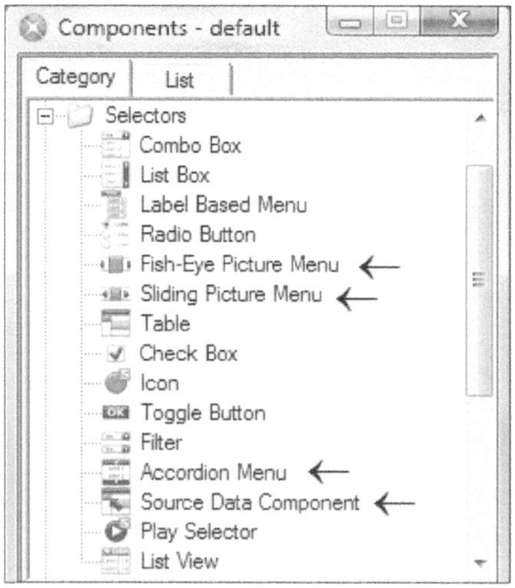

Figure 7-1 Selector components

You also learned that in that regard they are somewhat static, when compared to the functionality of selector components.

Selector components are used to link the component to several cells in the spreadsheet, which will give the dashboard a more dynamic effect. This is how selector components can be used to create a variety of menus.

Combo Box

Creates a single level filter as shown in Figure 7-2. This component ensures that duplicate records from the range of data that is selected is not displayed in the drop-down list. When the arrow shown in Figure 7-2 is clicked, a drop-down list appears. An option from the list is selected and the corresponding data is displayed in another component on the dashboard.

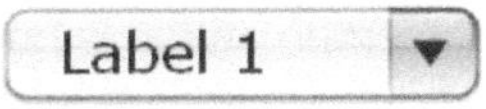

Figure 7-2 Combo Box component

List Box

Is similar to a Combo Box. The biggest difference is that the menu options are visible on the dashboard, as shown in Figure 7-3.

The slider on the right side of the figure indicates that there are more options that are currently not visible, that can be selected.

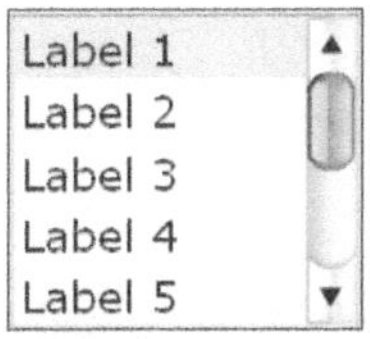

Figure 7-3 List Box component

Label Based Menu

This menu type can be vertical, as shown in Figure 7-4, or horizontal, as shown in Figure 7-5.

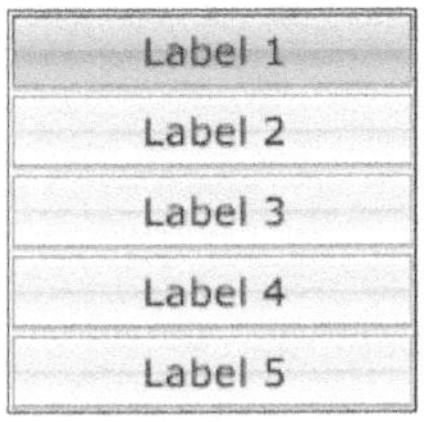

Figure 7-4 Vertical Label Based menu component

Figure 7-5 Horizontal Label Based component

Radio Button

Allows one option to be selected from a group of options, as shown in Figure 7-6. This menu type can also be placed horizontally.

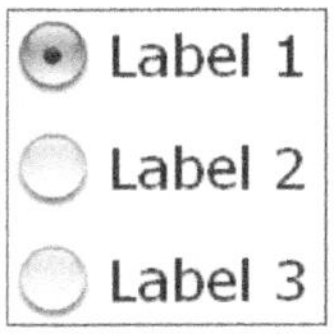

Figure 7-6 Radio Button component

Fish-Eye Picture Menu

(Only available in the Professional Edition)
Uses pictures or icons instead of text for the menu options, as shown in Figure 7-7.
While the menu can support more than five images, keep in mind that all of the images will be displayed on the dashboard all the time.

Figure 7-7 Fish-Eye Picture Menu component

There is no option to make the menu smaller, in terms of the number of images that are displayed. This menu type may require more space than you have allocated for a menu.

Clicking on an image is how an option is selected. When an option on the menu is clicked, the data that is linked to the picture or icon is displayed in another component on the dashboard. The term Fish-Eye comes from a type of camera lens.

Sliding Picture Menu
(Only available in the Professional Edition)
Is similar to a Fish-Eye Picture Menu because pictures or icons are used instead of text for the items on the menu.

Figure 7-8 Sliding Picture Menu component

This menu has arrows on the left and right that are used to scroll through the menu options, as shown above in Figure 7-8. This allows the menu to have more options while not taking up additional space on the dashboard. There is also an option to scroll through the pictures by holding the mouse pointer over them, like the Fish-Eye Picture Menu has.

Table
The Table component is similar to the List View component (discussed later).

As shown in Figure 7-9, the Table component displays the data from cells in a spreadsheet, just as they are. This component will remind you of a spreadsheet.

Stores	State
# 210	CA
# 45	FL
# 88	NY
# 105	MD

Figure 7-9 Table component

Check Box
Toggles between two states: Checked (On), as shown in Figure 7-10 and Not Checked (Off). (1)

Figure 7-10 Check Box component

Icon
This component, as shown in Figure 7-11, has the same functionality as the Check box. The icon component has the following uses. (1)

Figure 7-11 Icon component

① It can represent the value in one cell and be compared to a target value.
② It can be used as an object or selector.

Toggle Button
The Toggle button component shown in Figure 7-12 has the on and off states like the Check Box has. (1)

Figure 7-12 Toggle component

(1) The component is most often used to display and hide another component on the dashboard.

Filter

This component is similar to the Combo Box component. Select this component when you need to filter on more than one value (column of data). The values displayed in the second filter are based on the value selected in the first filter.

Figure 7-13 Filter component

Accordion Menu

(Only available in the Professional Edition)
Creates a two level filter based on the relationship of data in two fields, as shown in Figure 7-14.

The item selected in the top level menu (Category 1, Category 2, etc.) controls (filters) the options that are displayed in the second level of the menu (the items for the selected category).

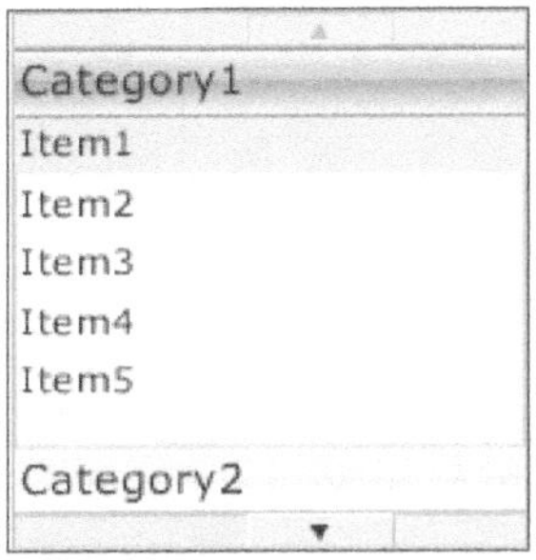

Figure 7-14 Accordion Menu component

For example, if you need to display sales for a sales rep in a region. The top level menu would contain the regions. Once a region is selected, the second level menu would be filtered to only display sales reps for the selected region.

Source Data Component

(Only available in the Professional Edition)
Unlike the other selector components, you cannot see this component on the dashboard.
It is used to put data in other cells of the spreadsheet.

Play Selector

This component adds automation to the dashboard. Clicking the play button causes the data to be displayed automatically. The controls on this component allow the user to pause or continue to the end of the animation.

The VCR style buttons shown in Figure 7-15 allow the data to be viewed one row or column at a time by clicking the Forward button or automatically, by clicking the Play button. Table 7-1 explains the buttons.

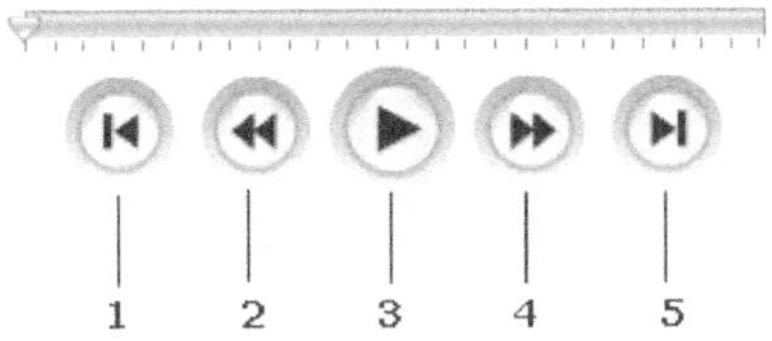

Figure 7-15 Play Selector component

Button	Description
1	Previous
2	Rewind
3	Play/Pause
4	Forward
5	Next

Table 7-1 Play Selector component buttons explained

The difference between the Play Options that you learned about in Lesson 5 and the Play Selector is that the play options are functionality that you can add to a component. The Play Selector is a component.

List View

The List View component shown in Figure 7-16 works the same as the Table component, that was discussed earlier. The benefit that the List View component has over the Table component is that it also allows the data to be sorted by the columns and the width of the columns can be adjusted by the user.

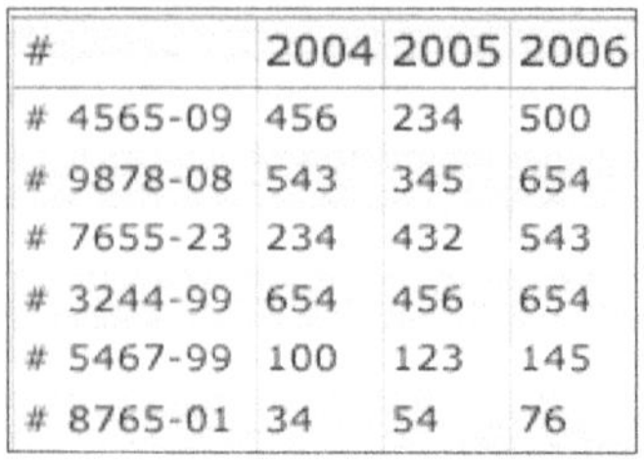

#	2004	2005	2006
# 4565-09	456	234	500
# 9878-08	543	345	654
# 7655-23	234	432	543
# 3244-99	654	456	654
# 5467-99	100	123	145
# 8765-01	34	54	76

Figure 7-16 List View component

To sort by a column, click on the column heading. You will see an arrow, as illustrated in Figure 7-17.

The arrow lets you know if the data in the column is sorted in ascending ▲ or descending ▼order.

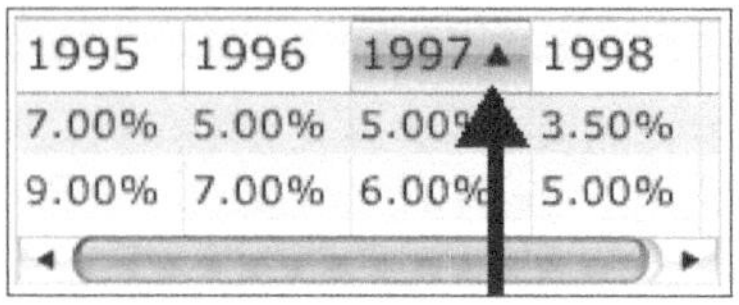

Figure 7-17 Column sorted

To change the column width, place the mouse pointer to the right of the column that you want to resize. You will see a double headed arrow. Drag the mouse in the direction that you want to resize the column to.

Menu Selector	Covered In
Accordion Menu	Lesson 10
Check Box	Lesson 11
Combo Box	Lesson 7
Filter	Lesson 7
Fish-Eye Picture Menu	Lesson 10
Icon	Lesson 11
Label Based Menu	Lesson 7
List Box	Lesson 7
List View	Lesson 7
Play Selector	Lesson 7
Radio Button	Lesson 7
Sliding Picture Menu	Lesson 10
Source Data Component	Lesson 10
Table	Lesson 7
Toggle Button	Lesson 11

Table 7-2 Lesson that menus are covered in detail

Selector Component Options

Selector components, like Single Value components, allow the user to interact with the dashboard to create what-if scenarios and other types of analysis. Selector components provide a lot of flexibility. Initially, selector components may appear to have limited functionality because only one item on the menu can be selected at a time, but they do a lot. They keep you from hard coding values. The values that the selector component capture are usually used by another component on the dashboard.

For example, in the first dashboard that you created in this book, the slider component that you configured controls the values that are displayed on the chart [See Exercise 3.1]. That is a Single Value component, which can only control one value. Selector components let the user select an item from a list. This causes the corresponding data for the selected item to be displayed in another component. In a way, selector components allow you to put multiple dashboards into one dashboard. The next few sections explain the common options that selectors have.

Common Selector General Tab Options

The common general tab options for selector components are shown in Figure 7-18.

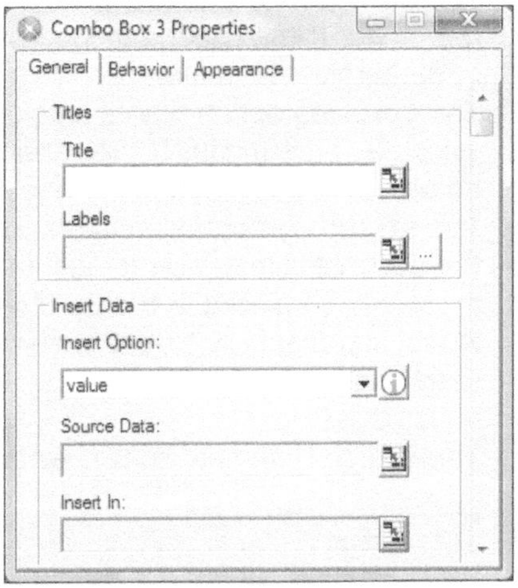

Figure 7-18 Common selector general tab options

Titles Options

The options in this section are used to create the title or labels for the selector. Like the Chart title option that you learned about and used in Lesson 6, you can type in the title for a selector. By default, the title will appear at the top of the menu. If you want to change the location of the title, you can change it on the Appearance tab.

The **LABELS** option contains the cell range for the row or column that has the name for each item in the menu. For example, in Figure 7-19, the names for the menu items would come from the range A4:A12.

Insert Data Options

The options in this section are used to select the data for the Selector component. This section is the equivalent to the Data Range section for charts.

The options in the **INSERT OPTION** drop-down list shown in Figure 7-20 are used to define the type of data or value that is delivered to the target destination (the Insert In option). The six options are explained below.

	A	B	C	D	E	F
1	Sales by Branch:					
2						
3		FY98	FY99	FY00	FY01	FY02
4	Atherton	$ 19.7	$ 17.1	$ 18.3	$ 14.8	$ 19.8
5	Berkeley	$ 14.4	$ 18.0	$ 16.4	$ 16.7	$ 19.3
6	Carmel	$ 18.8	$ 13.5	$ 18.7	$ 13.9	$ 15.7
7	Cupertino	$ 12.0	$ 16.2	$ 17.5	$ 17.8	$ 13.8
8	Freemont	$ 19.2	$ 15.6	$ 19.6	$ 15.9	$ 14.4
9	Irvine	$ 18.9	$ 14.6	$ 16.7	$ 12.1	$ 13.9
10	Milpitas	$ 18.7	$ 17.8	$ 14.0	$ 18.5	$ 13.7
11	Orange County	$ 17.0	$ 19.4	$ 17.1	$ 17.3	$ 17.3
12	San Francisco	$ 14.4	$ 14.0	$ 13.9	$ 15.4	$ 18.3
13						
14	Insert In Row:					

Figure 7-19 Data for menu labels

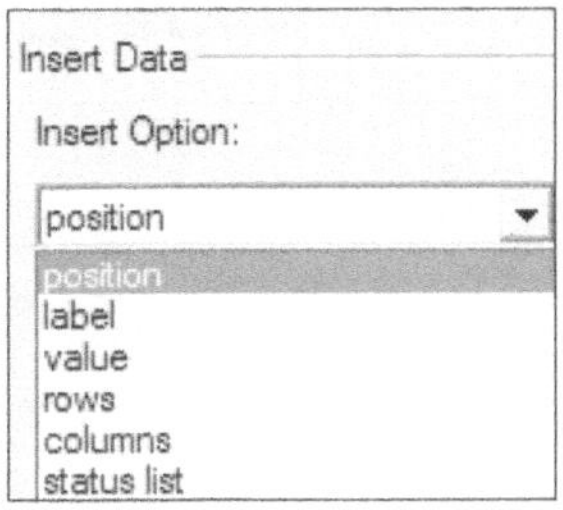

Figure 7-20 Insert Option drop-down list options

① The **POSITION** option stores the location of the item selected. For example, Figure 7-21 shows a menu component on the left with five buttons. The table on the right is the data. If you selected the Label 3 menu option and the target cell is C5, a three would be placed in cell C5, the target cell because Label 3 is in the third position on the menu. (2)

② The **LABEL** option stores the selected menu label name in the target field. If the Label 1 menu option shown in Figure 7-21 is selected and the target cell is C5, "Label 1" would be placed in cell C5. (2)

③ The **VALUE** option stores the actual value that the menu item points to. If the Label 2 menu option is selected, and the menu range is B1:B5, the value 11 would be placed in cell C5.

④ The **ROWS** option places a row of data in the target cells, based on the option selected in the menu. If the Label 4 menu option was selected, the data in cells A4:B4 would be placed in the target cell range.

⑤ The **COLUMNS** option places a column of data in the target cells, based on the option selected in the menu. If the Label 2 menu option was selected, the values in B1:B5 would be placed in the target cell range.

⑥ The **STATUS LIST** option sets one of the cells in the target cell range to one and sets all of the other cells in the target cell range to zero. If the Label 3 menu option was selected, a 1 would be placed in the third cell of the target cell range and all of the other target cells would automatically be set to zero. The Status List option is primarily used with dynamic functionality. (2)

(2) The Source Data field shown earlier in Figure 7-18 is not available if this option is selected.

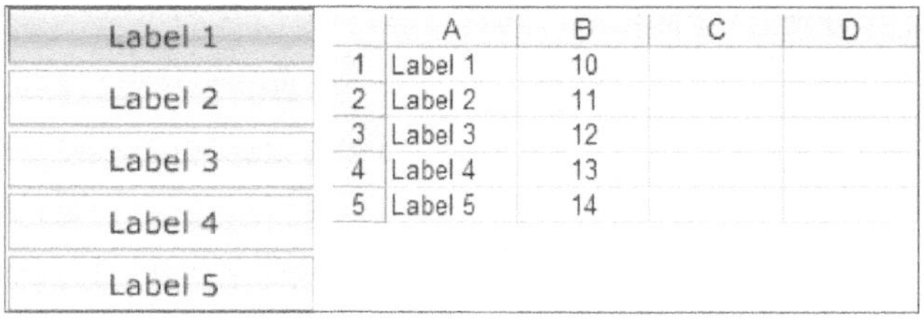

	A	B	C	D
1	Label 1	10		
2	Label 2	11		
3	Label 3	12		
4	Label 4	13		
5	Label 5	14		

Figure 7-21 Sample data for the Insert Option property

SOURCE DATA Is used to select the data for the selector component.

INSERT IN Is used to store the destination of the data. This is the target cell(s). The cell(s) selected for this option should be empty.

Common Selector Behavior Tab Options

The common behavior tab options for selector components are shown in Figure 7-22.

Behavior Options

ALWAYS EXPANDED If checked, this option forces all of the labels on the menu to be displayed. If checked, it also disables other options on the Behavior tab.

SOUND ENABLED If checked, the component will make a sound when it is clicked on.

OPEN ANIMATION If checked, a brief animation will appear when the menu is opened or closed.

OPEN DIRECTION Is used to select the direction that the menu will expand when it is opened. The options in this drop-down list change, based on the orientation of the menu. The options that appear for Label Based and Radio Button menus depend on the option selected in the **ORIENTATION** option on the General tab.

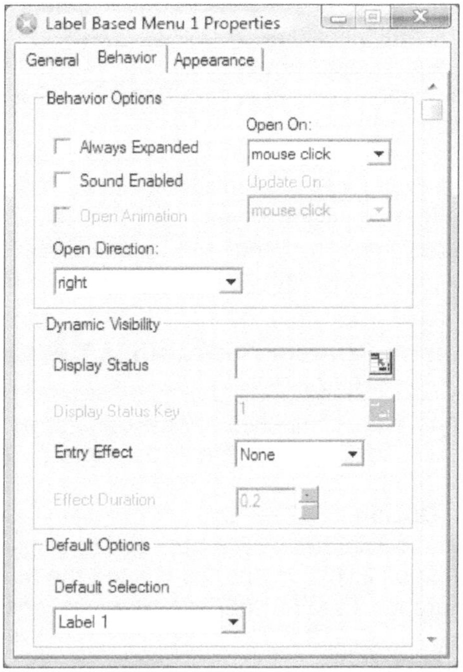

Figure 7-22 Common selector behavior tab options

Figure 7-23 shows the Open Direction options for a Label Based menu component with vertical orientation.

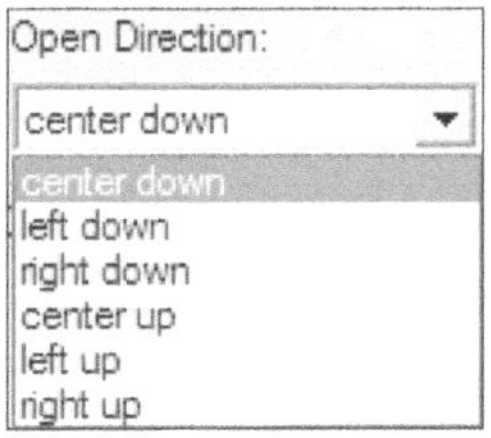

Figure 7-23 Open Direction drop-down list options

OPEN ON Is used to select how the component should recognize that an option on the menu has been selected that requires data to be displayed on another component. (3)

UPDATE ON Is used to select how the component should recognize that an option on the menu has been selected. (3)

(3) This option is not available for the Fish-Eye and Sliding Picture Menu components.

Default Options

The options in this section are used to select the default options for the component when the dashboard is first opened.

DEFAULT SELECTION This option is used to select the default behavior of the component. You can select whether or not an item on the component is selected when the dashboard is first opened. For example, in Figure 7-21 shown earlier, the Label 1 menu option is selected. If you wanted the menu component to open and have the Label 4 option selected, you would select the Label 4 option from this drop-down list. The options in this drop-down list vary depending on the component.

The default for the Default Selection option is the first entry in the list, but you can select any entry that you want. If you know that the users will select a certain option in the menu most of the time, you can change the Default Selection to that option. That way, when the dashboard is first opened, the data for the option that they use most will automatically be displayed.

Common Selector Appearance Tab Options

The options shown in Figure 7-24 are used to customize the component. Some options vary from one selector component to another.

Title Options

The options in this section are used to display the title on a component and change the titles appearance. [See Lesson 3, Position Options]

Labels Options

MOUSE OVER TEXT Is used to change the background color of the menu item that the mouse pointer is hovered over.

SELECTED TEXT Is used to change the background color for the menu item that was clicked on or selected.

Markers & Backgrounds Options

The options in this section are used to customize the menu background and colors for different parts of the menu and scroll bar.

DEFAULT FILL Is used to change the background color of the selector.

ARROW COLOR Is used to change the color of the arrows on the scroll bar.

GUTTER COLOR Is used to change the background color of the scroll bar area on the component.

SELECTED FILL Is used to change the background color of the menu option that is clicked on (selected).

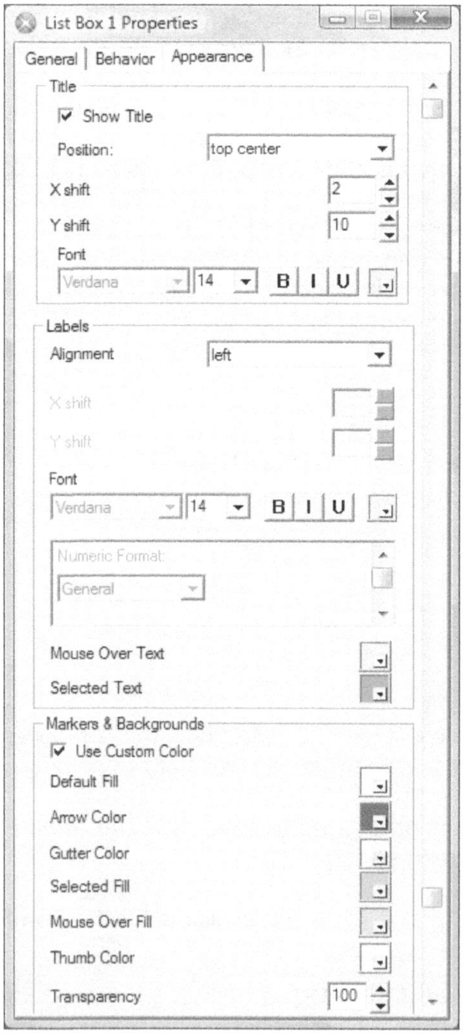

Figure 7-24 Common selector appearance tab options

MOUSE OVER FILL Is used to change the background color when the mouse pointer is hovered over an option on the menu.

THUMB COLOR Is used to change the color of the scroll bar.

List Box Component

General Tab Options

[See Common Selector General Tab Options, earlier in this lesson]

Behavior Tab Options

[See Common Selector Behavior Tab Options, earlier in this lesson]

Appearance Tab Options

[See Common Selector Appearance Tab Options, earlier in this lesson]

Exercise 7.1: Add A List Box To The Model

In this exercise you will add a List Box component to the model that you created in Exercise 6.3. The List Box will allow the user select the branch that they want to see the sales data for.

1. Open the My list box selector model.
2. Add the List Box component to the left of the chart.
3. On the General tab, make the changes in the table.

   The data that will be added to the cells in the Insert In option will be displayed on the chart. The data in the chart will change, based on the option that is selected in the List Box menu.

Property	Change To
Labels	A4:A12
Insert Option	Rows
Source Data	B4:F12
Insert In	B14:F14

4. Save the changes.

   Preview the model.
   Select the Carmel branch in the List Box. The model should look like the one shown in Figure 7-25.

   When you first preview the model, you see the data for the Atherton branch. That is because the **DEFAULT SELECTION** option, shown earlier in Figure 7-22 is set to Label 1.

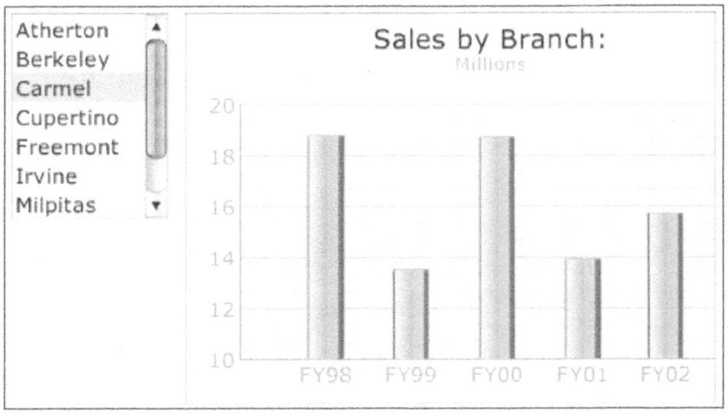

Figure 7-25 List Box model

Exercise 7.2: Adding Animation To A Model

When used appropriately, animation can visually enhance charts in a dashboard. In my opinion, bar, column and combination charts are better suited for animation then other chart types.
In this exercise you will add animation to the List Box model that you created in the previous exercise.

1. Save the My list box selector model as `My animation chart`.

2. On the Behavior tab for the chart, check the **ANIMATION ENABLED** option.

3. Save the changes. Each time that a city is selected in the menu, the animation effect will be used on the chart.

Play Selector Component

General Tab Options

[See Common Selector General Tab Options, earlier in this lesson]

Behavior Tab Options

The options shown in Figure 7-26 that are specific to the Play Selector are explained below. The options shown provide the functionality for the Play Selector component.

Figure 7-26 Play Selector behavior tab options

SHOW SLIDER If checked, a slider will be added to the Play Selector, as shown earlier at the top of Figure 7-15.

SOUND ENABLED This option is not available for the Play Selector component in Crystal Xcelsius version 4.5.

SHOW REW/FWD If checked, this option adds the rewind and fast forward buttons to the Play Selector.

SHOW PREV/NEXT If checked, this option adds the previous and next buttons to the Play Selector.

Appearance Tab Options

Display Options

The options shown in Figure 7-27 are used to change the colors of different parts of the Play Selector.

Figure 7-27 Play Selector appearance tab options

SHOW BACKGROUND This option must be selected if you want to display or change the background color of the Play Selector.

BUTTON BACKGROUND COLOR Is used to change the background color of the button on the Play Selector.

BUTTON FOREGROUND COLOR Is used to change the color of the arrow on the Play Selector button.

GUTTER COLOR Is used to change the color of the bar and tick marks for the slider.

SLIDE COLOR Is used to change the color of the triangle that moves across the bar on the slider.

Exercise 7.3: Add A Play Selector To A Model

In this exercise you will add the Play Selector component to the My play selector model that you created in Exercise 6.4.

1. Open the My play selector model, then add the Play Selector component below the chart.
2. On the General tab, make the changes in the table.

Property	Change To
Insert Option	Row
Source Data	B4:F25
Insert In	B27:F27

3. On the Behavior tab, make the changes in the table.

Property	Change To
Show Slider	Select this option
Show Rew/Fwd	Select this option
Show Prev/Next	Select this option
Play Time	4
Default Selection	Row 2

4. On the Appearance tab, clear the **SHOW BACKGROUND** option.

5. Save the changes.

   When you first open the model, the data for Product 2 is automatically displayed.

   Click the Forward button until you see Product 5.

   You should see the data shown in Figure 7-28.

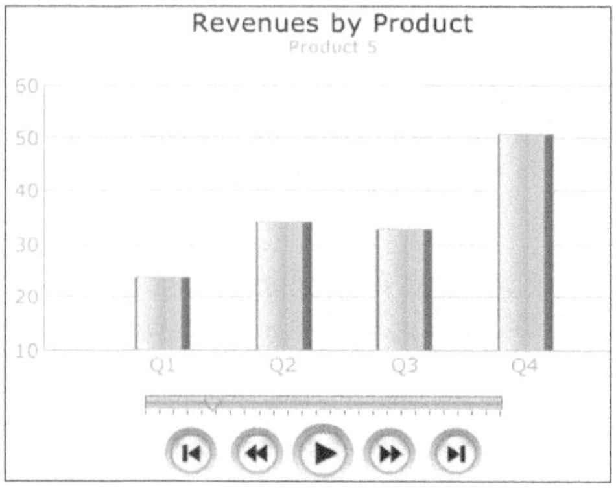

Figure 7-28 Player Selector model

Table Component

General Tab Options

The options shown in Figure 7-29 are used to select the data for the Table component. To use the Table selector as a display component, on the General tab, click the **DISPLAY DATA** cell selector, then select the range of cells that should be used as the menu options, then set the **INSERT OPTION** to row.

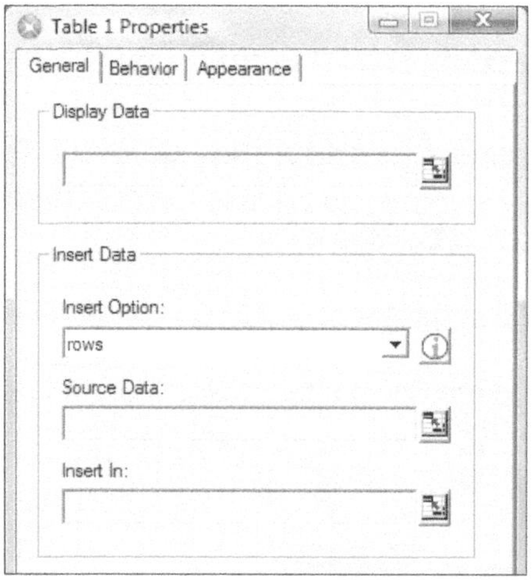

Figure 7-29 Table general tab options

To use the Table component as a display component, select the range of cells that you want to display in the Display Data option.

DISPLAY DATA Is used to store the cells for the data that will be displayed in the table.

Behavior Tab Options

The options shown in Figure 7-30 that are specific to the Table component are explained below. The options are used to select whether or not a row in the Table component can be selected.

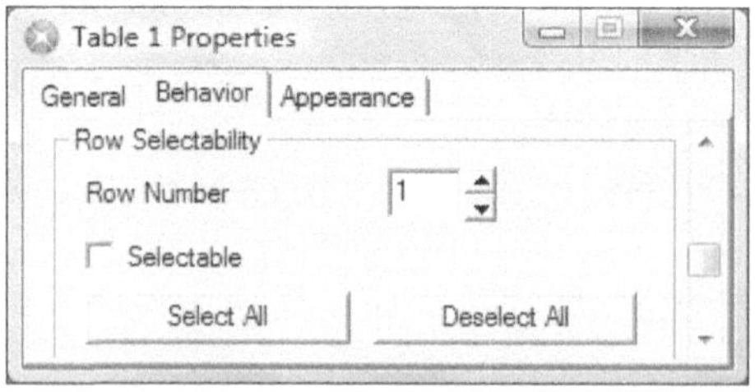

Figure 7-30 Table behavior tab options

Row Selectability Options

ROW NUMBER This option is tied to the Selectable check box option.

SELECTABLE Is used to enable or disable the row in the Row Number field. If checked, the row number displayed will not be able to be selected in the dashboard.

SELECT ALL If clicked, allows all rows in the table to be selected.

DESELECT ALL If clicked, prevents all of the rows in the table from being selected.

Appearance Tab Options

The options shown in Figure 7-31 that are specific to the Table component are explained below. They are used to customize the grid.

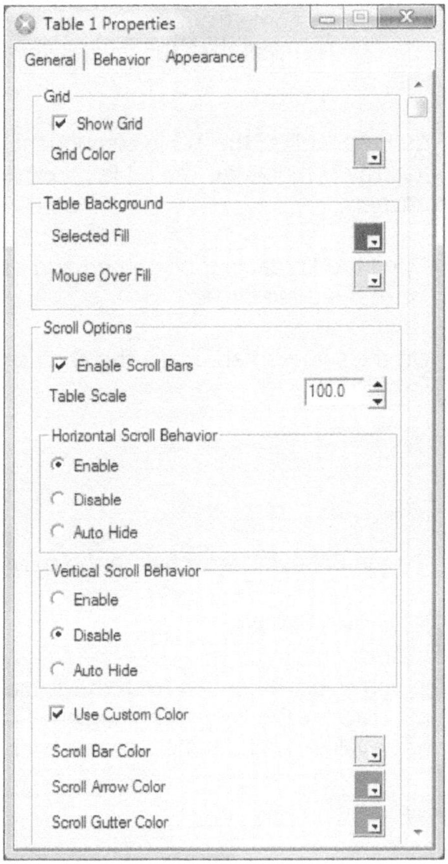

Figure 7-31 Table appearance tab options

Grid Options

SHOW GRID This option enables the grid to be displayed in the Table component.

GRID COLOR Is used to change the color of the gridlines (from the spreadsheet).

Table Background Options

The options in this section are used to select the colors that will be displayed when a part of the table is selected.

SELECTED FILL Is used to change the color that will be displayed when a row in the table is selected.

MOUSE OVER FILL Is used to change the color that will be displayed when the mouse pointer is hovered over a row.

Scroll Options

The options in this section are used to modify the scroll bars and labels on the component.

ENABLE SCROLL BARS If checked, this option will add scroll bars to the table component.

TABLE SCALE Is used to set the size of the labels in the table.

Horizontal And Vertical Scroll Behavior Options

The options in these sections are used to display, disable or automatically hide the scroll bars.

AUTOHIDE If selected, the scrollbar is only enabled when the length or height of the table is larger than the text area.

SCROLL BAR COLOR Is used to change the color of the scroll bar.

SCROLL ARROW COLOR Is used to change the color of the arrows on both (horizontal and vertical) scroll bars.

SCROLL GUTTER COLOR Is used to change the background color of the scroll bar.

Exercise 7.4: Add A Table Component To A Model

In this exercise you will add the Table component to a model. The data in the table menu will be used to select the data that will be displayed in the chart. In this exercise, the data in the table component will come from the Income statement line items. The data that will be displayed in the chart is the fiscal data for several years. [See Exercise 6.5, Create A Chart For Historic Income]

As you read earlier, the Table component can also be used as a display component. When used as a display component, the table becomes a graphic that displays a range of cells in the spreadsheet.

1. Open the My table model, then add the Table component to the left of the chart. Make the table larger.

2. On the General tab, make the changes in the table.

Property	Change To
Display Data	A4:B16
Insert Option	Rows
Source Data	E4:L16
Insert In	E18:L18

3. On the Behavior tab, change the **DEFAULT SELECTION** option to Row 3.

4. Save the changes.

When you select an option from the Table menu shown on the left of Figure 7-32, the historic income data for the item that you select is displayed in the chart. Notice that the Y Axis (vertical) values on the chart change each time that you select a different item in the menu.

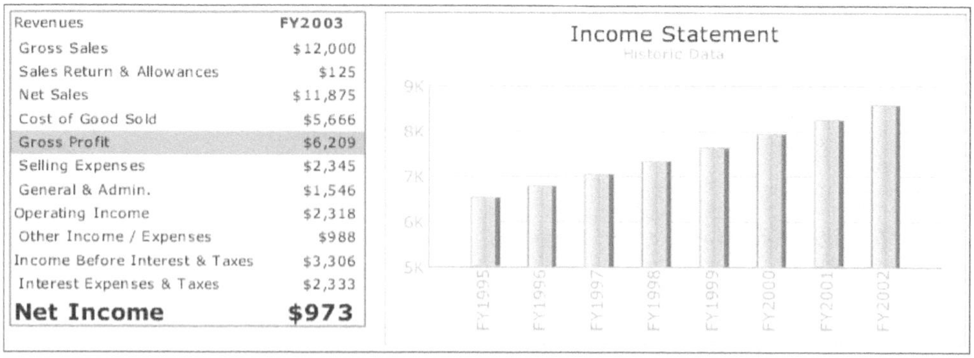

Figure 7-32 Table menu model

If you wanted to change the mouse pointer rollover colors and add a scroll bar to the Table component, as shown in Figure 7-33, you would select the options shown in Figure 7-34.

These changes are in the cx_table_model file. The scroll bar would be helpful if there were a lot of items in the table and you needed to save space on the dashboard by making the menu smaller.

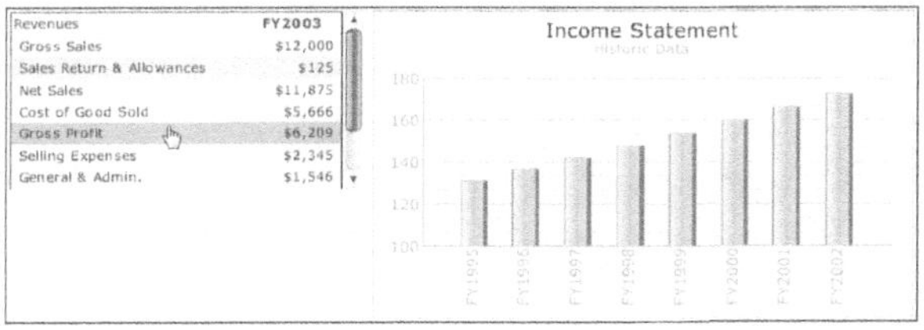

Figure 7-33 Table component with a scroll bar

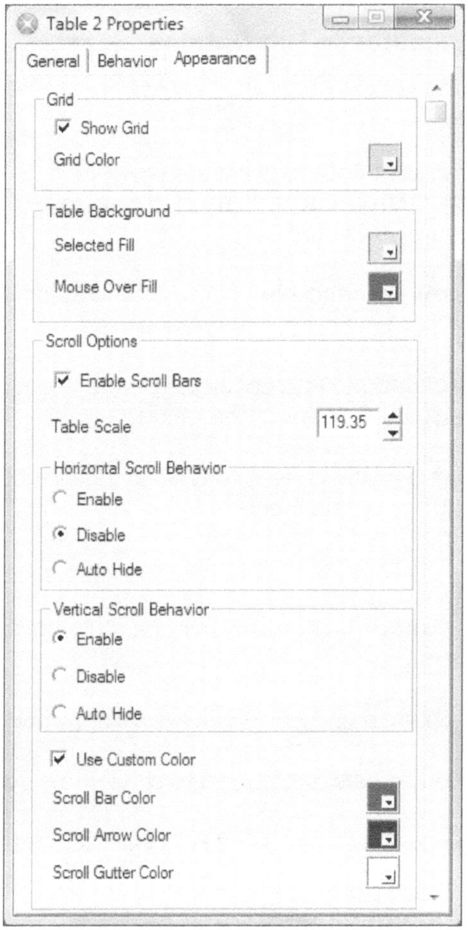

Figure 7-34 Table scroll bar options

Radio Button Component

General Tab Options

All of the options except for the ones shown in Figure 7-35 for the Radio Button component are the same as the Table General tab options, shown earlier in Figure 7-29.

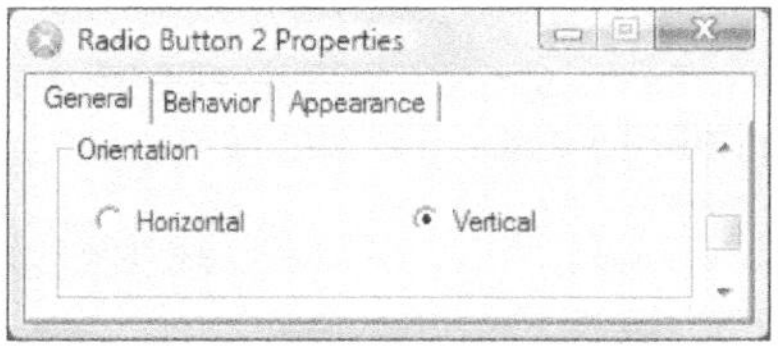

Figure 7-35 Radio Button general tab options

Orientation Options

These options are used to select how the Radio Button menu will be displayed. They also control the items that are available in the **OPEN DIRECTION** drop-down list on the Behavior tab.

Behavior Tab Options

[See Common Selector Behavior Tab Options, earlier in this lesson earlier]

Appearance Tab Options

The options shown in Figure 7-36 are used to customize the radio buttons.

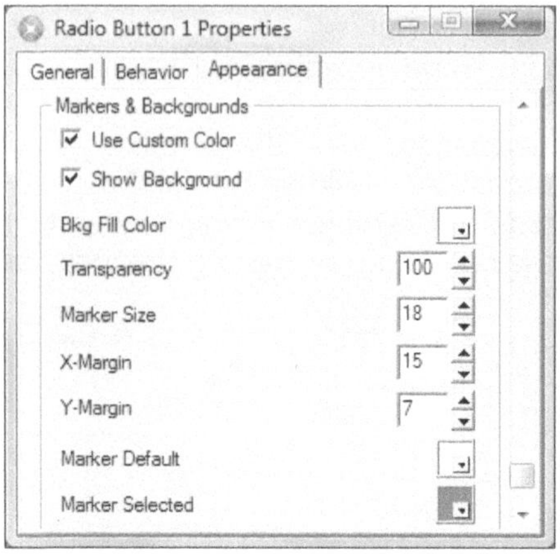

Figure 7-36 Radio Button appearance tab options

Markers & Backgrounds Options

USE CUSTOM COLOR Is used to customize the colors of the scroll bars.

SHOW BACKGROUND Is used to display or hide the background color of the menu.

BACKGROUND FILL COLOR Is used to change the background color of the menu.

MARKER SIZE Is used to change the size of the radio buttons on the menu.

X-MARGIN Is used to move the radio buttons closer or further away from the left side of the menu.

Y-MARGIN Is used to move, add or remove space from the top and bottom of the menu.

MARKER DEFAULT Is used to change the border color of the radio buttons that are not selected.

MARKER SELECTED Is used to change the border color of the radio button that is selected.

Grid Component

The Grid component can be used as an input or output component. It is used as an output component when you want to display the underlying data for another component on the dashboard in a traditional table layout. The values displayed in the grid component are a group of linked value components.

General Tab Options

The options shown in Figure 7-37 are used to select the data to display in the grid.

LINK TO CELL Type in or select the cell in the spreadsheet that the component should be linked to.

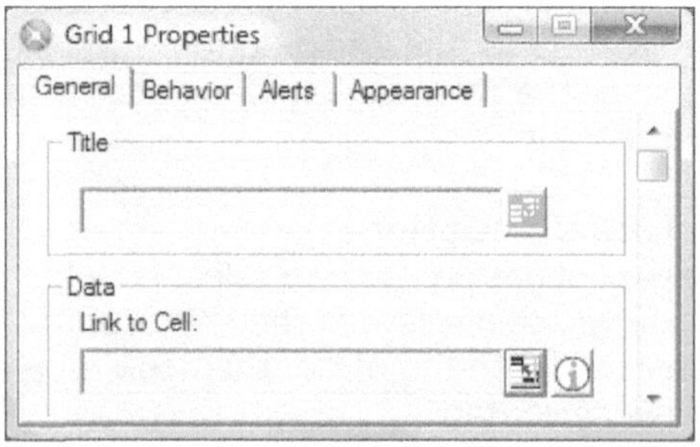

Figure 7-37 Grid general tab options

Behavior Tab Options

The Grid behavior tab options are shown in Figure 7-38.

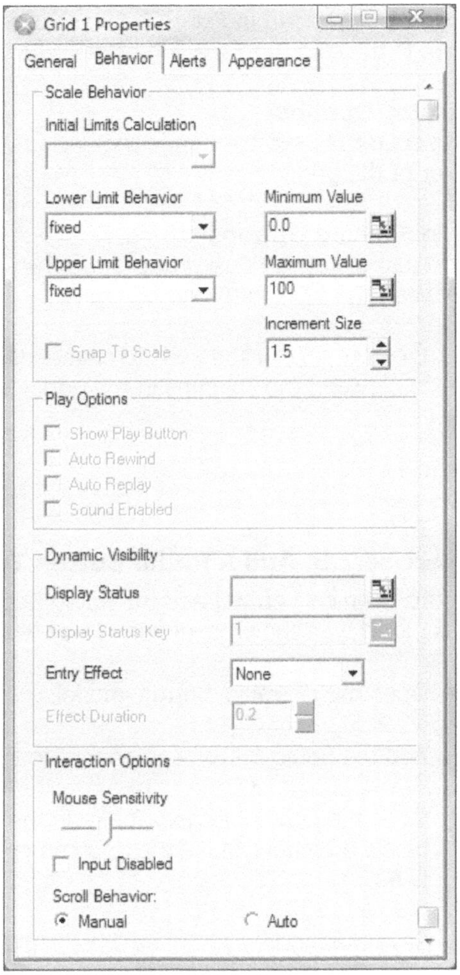

Figure 7-38 Grid behavior tab options

Scale Behavior Options

The options in this section are used to select the lower and upper limits for the grid.

[See Lesson 5, Common Behavior Tab Options]

Interaction Options

The options in this section are used to select the Run time mouse and scroll behavior options for the grid component.

MOUSE SENSITIVITY [See Lesson 5, Value Component Behavior Tab Options]

INPUT DISABLED Is used to prevent the user from selecting an option on the dashboard.

Titles Panel Options

[See Lesson 5, Common Single Value Titles Panel Options]

Layout Panel Options

The options shown in Figure 7-39 are used to change the color and spacing of the grid.

Display Options

FILL COLOR Is used to change the background color of the grid.

Grid Spacing Options

VERTICAL SPACING Is used to change the space between the rows in the grid.

HORIZONTAL SPACING Is used to change the space between the columns in the grid.

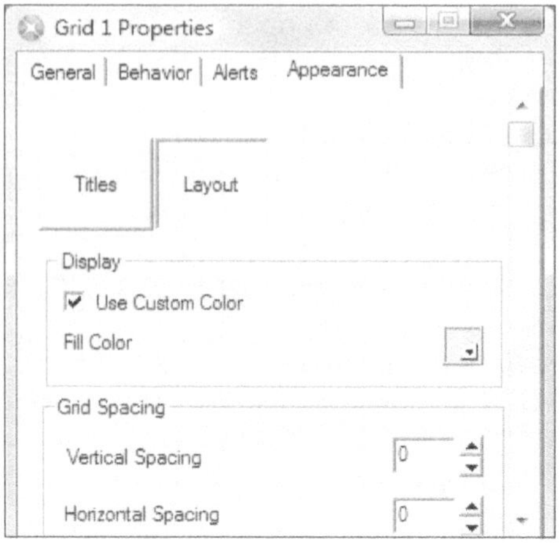

Figure 7-39 Grid layout panel options

Exercise 7.5: Add A Radio Button To A Model

In this exercise you will add the Radio Button and Grid components to the model. The data for this model was shown earlier in Figure 7-19.

1. Open the cx_radio_button_model.
2. Add the Radio Button component to the left of the chart.
3. Open the Other category folder in the Components dialog box, then add the Grid component below the chart. Make the grid component as wide as the titles on the horizontal axis on the chart.
4. Save the model as `My radio button menu`.

Select The Radio Button Options

1. On the General tab, make the changes in the table.

Property	Change To
Labels	A4:A12
Insert Option	Rows
Source Data	B4:F12
Insert In	B14:F14

2. On the Appearance tab, change the following options in the Markers & Backgrounds section.

Property	Change To
Marker Size	17
X-Margin	20
Y-Margin	10

3. Resize the Radio Button component so that all of the options are visible.

Select The Grid Component Options

1. On the General tab, change the **LINK TO CELL** option to B13:F14.

2. Save the changes.

   When you click on a city in the menu, the sales for the city will be displayed on the chart and in the grid below the chart.

   The model should look like the one shown in Figure 7-40.

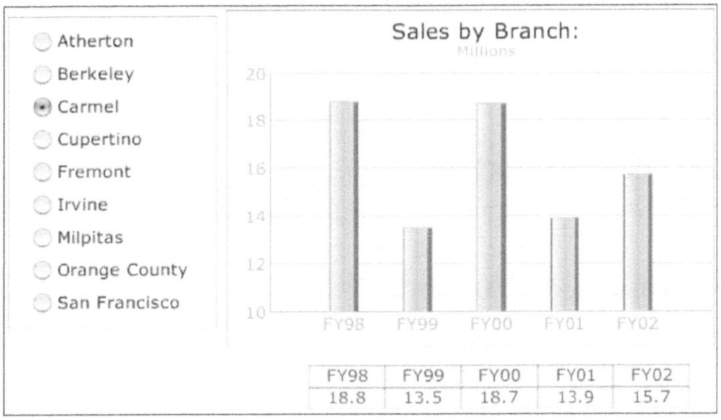

Figure 7-40 Radio Button model

If you wanted to add a background color to the grid, as shown in Figure 7-41, select the options shown in Figure 7-42. You have to select a Fill Color.

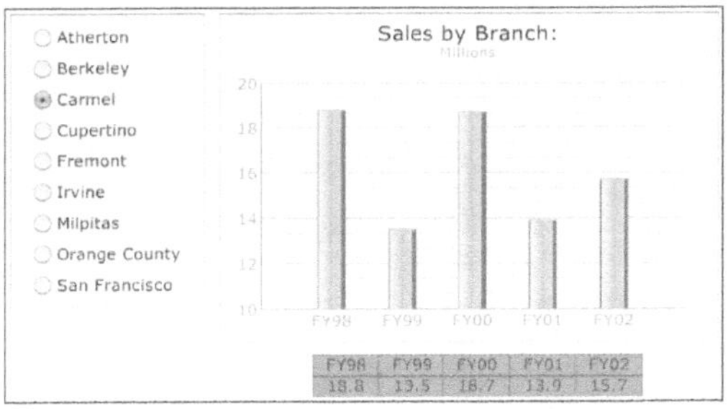

Figure 7-41 Grid with a background color

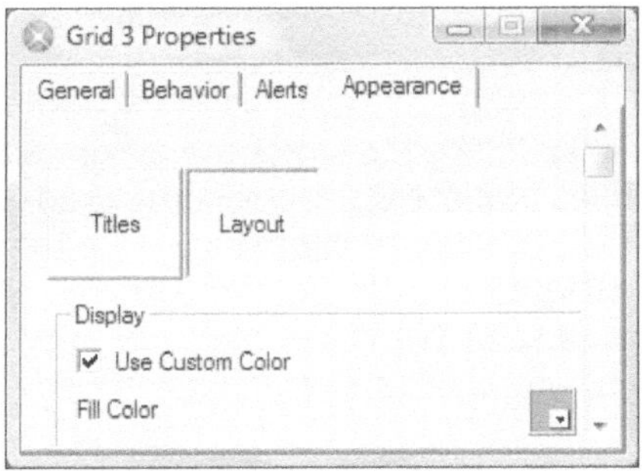

Figure 7-42 Grid options to add a background color

Combo Box Component

This component has the same functionality as the List Box component that you learned how to use in Exercise 7.1. The Combo Box component creates the drop-down list shown in Figure 7-43.

When an option in the drop-down list is selected, the corresponding data is displayed in another component like a chart or grid. The benefit that the Combo Box has over a List box is that it does not have to be expanded to accommodate a lot of options.

Figure 7-43 Combo Box drop-down list

If the list has 10,000 items, it does not need any more space on the dashboard, then a Combo Box that has 10 items. To demonstrate that List Box and Combo Box components have the same functionality, you will use the same model.

General Tab Options

[See Common Selector General Tab Options, earlier in this lesson]

Behavior Tab Options

[See Common Selector Behavior Tab Options, earlier in this lesson]

Appearance Tab Options

The options shown in Figure 7-44 are used to customize the Combo Box component.

Labels Options

MOUSE OVER TEXT Is used to change the color of the text of the item on the drop-down list that the mouse pointer is hovered over.

SELECTED TEXT Is used to change the color of the text of the item in the drop-down list that is currently selected.

ROWS DISPLAYED Is used to select the maximum number of rows that are displayed in the drop-down list. If the number of rows selected in the spreadsheet is greater than the number selected in this option, a scroll bar is automatically added to the drop-down list, as shown in Figure 7-45.

Label Background Options

DEFAULT FILL Is used to change the background color of the label and drop-down list. The Use Custom Color option must be selected to use this option.

SELECTED FILL Is used to change the background color that will be displayed when a row in the drop-down is selected.

MOUSE OVER FILL Is used to change the color that will be displayed when the mouse pointer is hovered over an option in the drop-down list.

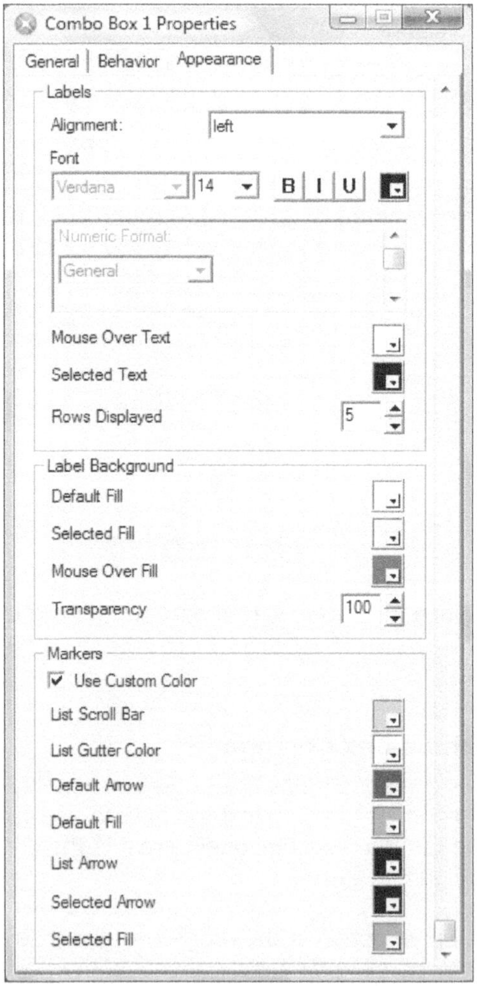

Figure 7-44 Combo Box appearance tab options

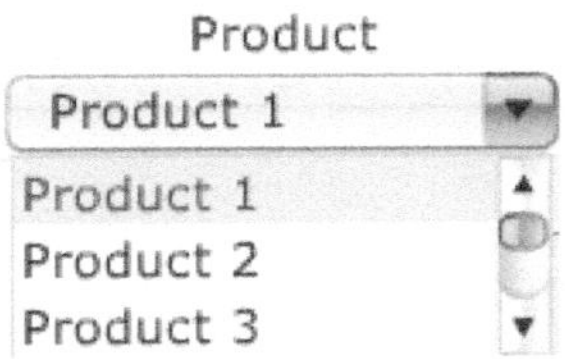

Figure 7-45 Scroll bar added to the Combo Box drop-down list

Markers Options

The options in this section are used to change the color of the options on the Combo Box and drop-down list.

LIST SCROLL BAR Is used to change the color of the slider on the scroll bar on the drop-down list.

LIST GUTTER COLOR Is used to change the background color of the scroll bar on the drop-down list.

DEFAULT ARROW Is used to change the color of the arrow on the Combo Box.

DEFAULT FILL Is used to change the background color of the arrow on the Combo Box.

LIST ARROW Is used to change the color of the scroll bar arrows on the drop-down list.

SELECTED ARROW Is used to change the color of the arrow on the label.

SELECTED FILL Is used to change the background color of the arrow on the label when it is selected.

Exercise 7.6: Add A Combo Box To A Model

In this exercise you will add the Combo Box component to the model that you created in Exercise 6.3. The combo box will allow the user to select the branch that they want to see the sales data for.

Modify The Model

1. Save the My list box selector model as `My combo box`.
2. Delete the List Box component.
3. On the Behavior tab of the Column chart, check the Animation Enabled option.
4. On the Appearance tab, click the Series button, then make the changes in the table.

Property	Change To
Use Custom Color	Select this option
Bar Width	10
Bar Color	Red

5. Make the chart larger and save the changes.

Add The Combo Box Component

1. Add the Combo Box component to the upper left corner of the chart.

2. On the General tab, make the changes in the table.

Property	Change To
Labels	A4:A12
Insert Option	Rows
Source Data	B4:F12
Insert In	B14:F14

3. On the Behavior tab, make the changes in the table.

Property	Change To
Sound Enabled	Select this option
Default Selection	Label 4

4. On the Appearance tab, make the changes in the table.

Property	Change To
Rows Displayed	4
Selected Fill (4)	Light yellow
Use Custom Color	Select this option
List Scroll Bar	Light green
Default Arrow	Red
Default Fill (5)	Light red

(4) This option is in the Label Background section.
(5) This option is in the Markers section.

5. Save the changes. Compare the model shown in Figure 7-46 to the model shown earlier in Figure 7-25. As you can see, the Combo Box takes up less space.

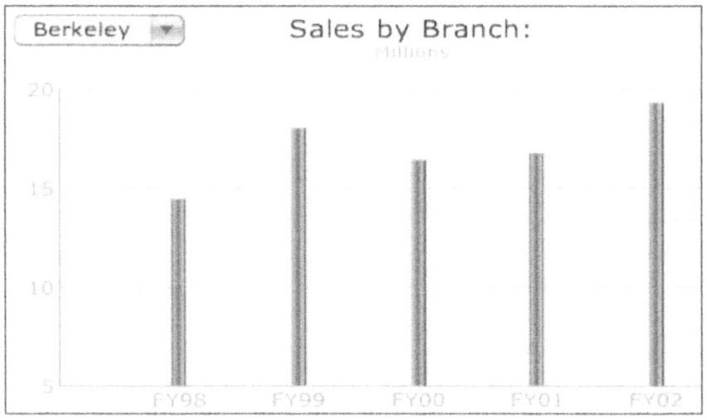

Figure 7-46 Combo Box model

Filter Component

Many of the Filter component options are the same as the Combo Box options.

General Tab Options

The option shown in Figure 7-47 is specific to the Filter component.

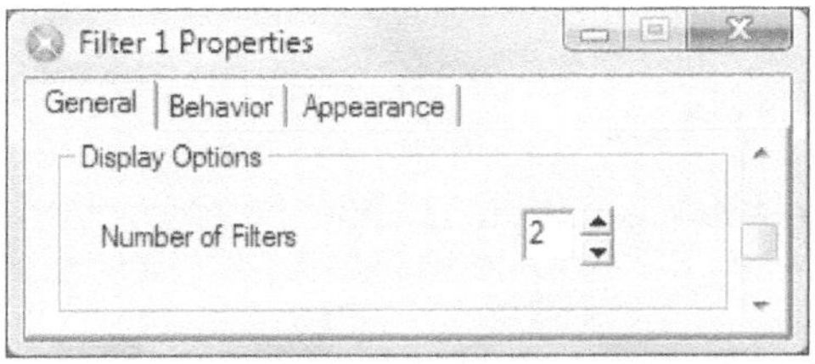

Figure 7-47 Number of Filters option

NUMBER OF FILTERS Is used to select the number of drop-down lists that the menu will have.

Behavior Tab Options

[See Common Selector Behavior Tab Options, earlier in this lesson]

Appearance Tab Options

The options shown in Figure 7-48 are used to customize the filter component.

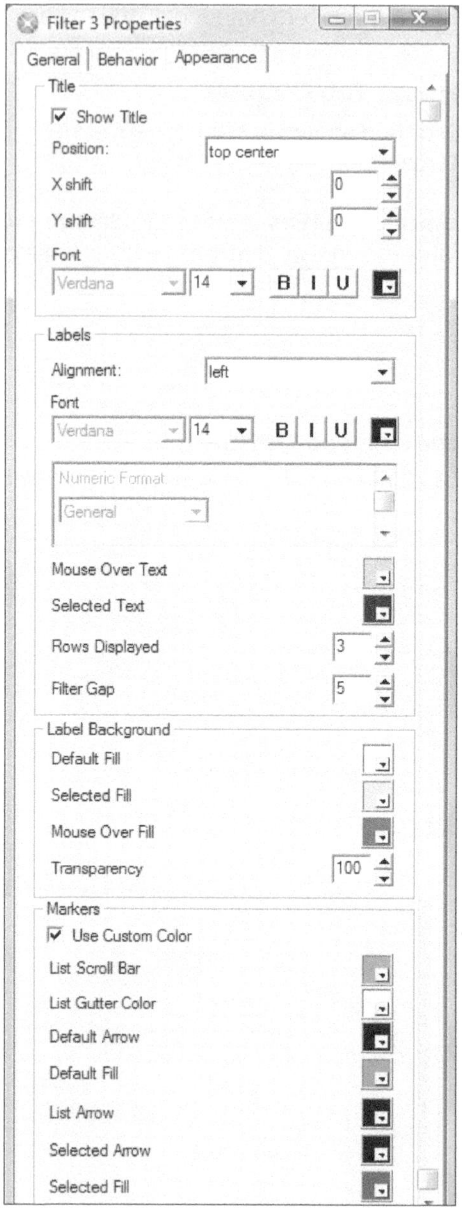

Figure 7-48 Filter appearance tab options

Labels Options

[See Combo Box Appearance Tab Options, earlier in this lesson]

FILTER GAP Is used to change the amount of space between the drop-down lists on the Filter component.

Label Background Options

The options in this section are used to change the background colors on the filter.

DEFAULT FILL Is used to change the default background color of the filters.

SELECTED FILL Is used to change the background color of the item in the drop-down list that is currently selected.

MOUSE OVER FILL Is used to change the background color of the item in the drop-down list that the mouse pointer is hovered over.

Markers Options

The options in this section are used to change the color of options on the filter and drop-down list.

DEFAULT ARROW Is used to change the color of the arrow on the filter.

DEFAULT FILL Is used to change the background color of the arrow on the filter.

LIST ARROW Is used to change the color of the scroll bar arrows on the drop-down list.

SELECTED ARROW Is used to change the color of the arrow on the filter that is selected.

SELECTED FILL Is used to change the background color of the arrow on the filter that is selected.

Exercise 7.7: Add A Filter Drop-Down List To A Model

In this exercise you will add a Filter component that has three drop-down lists (for the product, sales rep and account type) to the model. Each list will allow the user to select options which control the data that is displayed in the chart. The option selected in the first filter will control the value in the second filter. The Filter component looks like the Combo Box component that you created in the previous exercise. Figure 7-49 shows the data for this exercise.

	A	B	C	D	E	F	G
1	Sales by Sales Representative						
2							
3	*Product*	*Sales Rep*	*Account Type*	Q1	Q2	Q3	Q4
4	Product 1	Sales Rep. 1	New Customer	$ 44.2	$ 64.4	$ 55.3	$ 50.7
5	Product 2	Sales Rep. 1	New Customer	$ 39.6	$ 38.3	$ 34.7	$ 47.2
6	Product 3	Sales Rep. 1	New Customer	$ 41.9	$ 66.8	$ 55.5	$ 54.2
7	Product 4	Sales Rep. 1	New Customer	$ 41.5	$ 66.9	$ 40.8	$ 59.4
8	Product 5	Sales Rep. 1	New Customer	$ 63.2	$ 40.2	$ 58.1	$ 46.7
9	Product 6	Sales Rep. 1	New Customer	$ 50.9	$ 44.3	$ 50.1	$ 51.9
10	Product 7	Sales Rep. 1	New Customer	$ 53.7	$ 54.8	$ 39.1	$ 54.7
11	Product 8	Sales Rep. 1	New Customer	$ 62.0	$ 58.7	$ 56.6	$ 62.6
12	Product 9	Sales Rep. 1	New Customer	$ 63.8	$ 37.6	$ 48.1	$ 53.3
13	Product 1	Sales Rep. 1	Existing Customer	$ 52.8	$ 43.5	$ 44.0	$ 63.6
14	Product 2	Sales Rep. 1	Existing Customer	$ 63.7	$ 41.0	$ 45.3	$ 40.4

Figure 7-49 Filter drop-down list data

1. Save the cx_filter_model file as `My filter drop-down list.`

2. Add the Filter component above the chart.

3. On the General tab, make the changes in the table.

Property	Change To
Titles	A3:C3
Insert Option	Rows
Source Data	A4:G26
Insert In	D27:G27
Number of Filters	3

The **TITLES** option will display the name for each of the drop-down lists above the option. Each drop-down list created by the **NUMBER OF FILTERS** option will store the values for a different field, which is usually a column of data.

4. On the Appearance tab in the Labels section, make the changes in the table.

Property	Change To
Rows Displayed	4
Filter Gap	5

5. Make the Filter component as wide as the chart, then save the changes.

6. Open the Product drop-down list and select Product 2.

   Open the Account Type drop-down list and select New Customer.

   The model should look like the one shown in Figure 7-50.

   It appears that each drop-down list is a separate object, but that is not the case. It would be nice if each drop-down list could be sized individually so that the items in the list would not get cut off, like the New Customer option does in the figure.

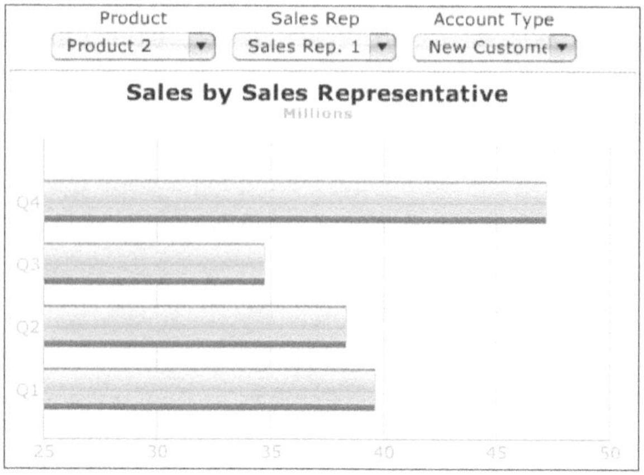

Figure 7-50 Filter model

List View Component

This component is used to view rows of data from the spreadsheet. The columns can be sorted and the column width can be adjusted.

General Tab Options

[See Common Selector General Tab Options, earlier in this lesson]
[See Table Component General Tab Options, earlier in this lesson]

Behavior Tab Options

[See Common Selector Behavior Tab Options, earlier in this lesson]

Titles Panel Options

Header Options

The options in this section are used to change the color and font size of the header section of the component, as shown in Figure 7-51.

MOUSE OVER TEXT Is used to change the text color of the column heading that the mouse pointer is hovered over.

SELECTED TEXT Is used to change the text color of the column that was clicked on.

Value Options

The options in this section are used to change the color and font size of the values displayed on the component.

MOUSE OVER TEXT Is used to change the color of the text in the table that the mouse pointer is hovered over.

SELECTED TEXT Is used to change the color of the text in the row that is selected.

Figure 7-51 List View titles panel options

Layout Panel Options

The options shown in Figure 7-52 are used to customize the List View component.

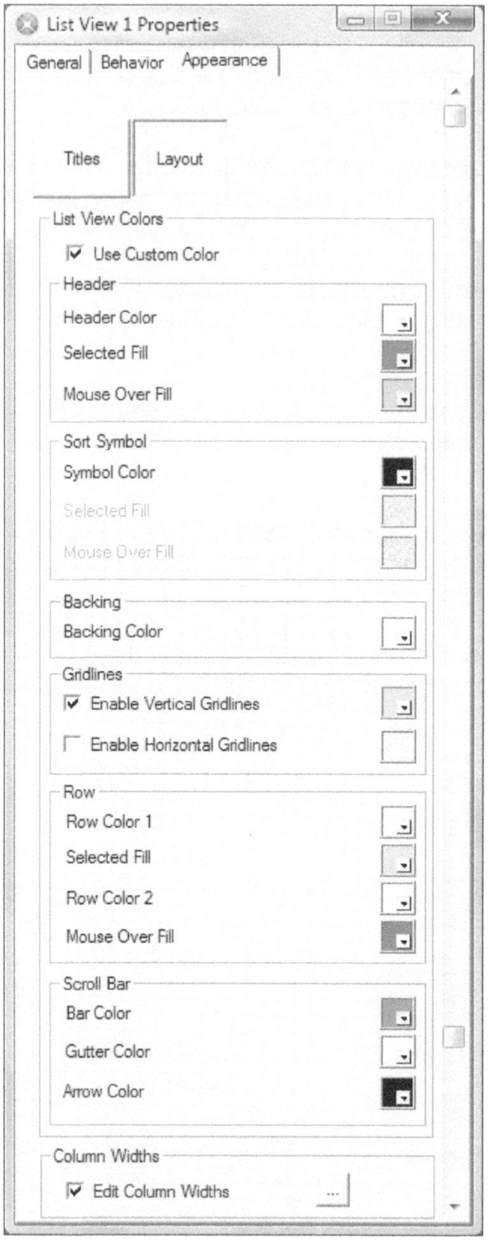

Figure 7-52 List View layout panel options

Header Options

HEADER COLOR Is used to change the background color of the header section of the component.

SELECTED FILL Is used to change the background color of the text of the column that is clicked on.

MOUSE OVER FILL Is used to change the background color of the column that the mouse pointer is hovered over.

Sort Symbol Options

SYMBOL COLOR Is used to change the color of the arrow on the column that was used to change the sort order, as shown earlier in Figure 7-17.

Backing Option

BACKING COLOR Is used to change the border color of the table.

Gridlines Options

ENABLE VERTICAL GRIDLINES Is used to add vertical gridlines to the table.

ENABLE HORIZONTAL GRIDLINES Is used to add horizontal gridlines to the table.

Row Options

ROW COLOR 1 Is used to change the default background color of the even numbered rows in the table.

SELECTED FILL Is used to change the background color of the selected row in the table.

ROW COLOR 2 Is used to change the default background color of the odd numbered rows in the table.

MOUSE OVER FILL Is used to change the background color of the row that the mouse pointer is hovered over.

Scroll Bar Options

Vertical or horizontal scroll bars are automatically added when the number of rows or columns exceeds the size of the table.

BAR COLOR Is used to change the color of the slider on the scroll bar.

GUTTER COLOR Is used to change the background color of the scroll bar.

Column Widths Options

EDIT COLUMN WIDTHS If checked, the column width cannot be changed. Instead, a scroll bar is automatically added to the bottom of the table.

The Browse button is only enabled when the Edit Column Widths option is selected. The button opens the dialog box shown in Figure 7-53, which is used to enter a specific width for the columns.

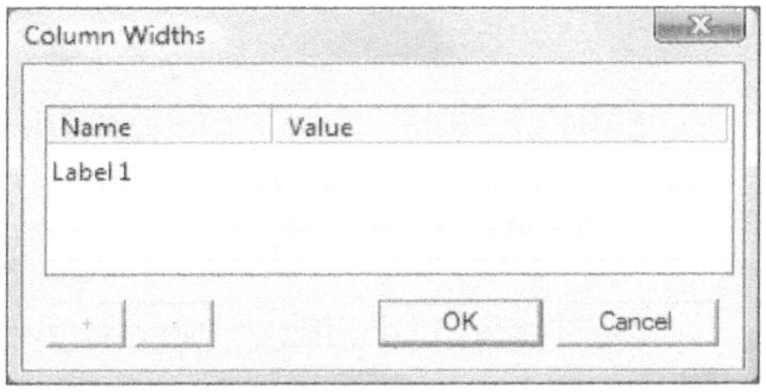

Figure 7-53 Column Widths dialog box

Label Based Menu Component

This component is used to display and hide other components on the dashboard. If you need to display several charts in a small space, with easy access to all of the charts, using the Label Based Menu component is a good option. In terms of functionality, it will remind you of the Radio Button menu that you created in Exercise 7.5.

General Tab Options

[See Radio Button General Tab Options, earlier in this lesson]

Behavior Tab Options

[See Common Selector Behavior Tab Options, earlier in this lesson]

Appearance Tab Options

The options shown in Figure 7-54 are used to customize the Label Based Menu component.

Figure 7-54 Label Based Menu appearance tab options

Label Background Options

SEPARATION Is used to select how much space is between each button on the menu.

DEFAULT FILL Is used to change the initial background color of the buttons.

SELECTED FILL Is used to change the background color of the button that was last clicked on.

MOUSE OVER FILL Is used to change the background color of the button when the mouse pointer is hovered over a button.

Exercise 7.8: Use The Label Based Menu Component

In this exercise you will add this component to a model that has five charts. When you open the model, you will only see one chart. The other four charts are behind the one that you see. In Lesson 11, you will learn how to layer several objects. Each chart will be linked to a different button on the menu.

1. Save the cx_label_based_menu model as `My label based menu`.

2. Add the Label Based Menu component above the chart.

3. On the General tab, make the changes in the table.

Property	Change To
Title	Clear this option
Insert Option	Status list
Insert In	B4:B8

4. On the General tab, click the Browse button, then make the changes shown in Figure 7-55.

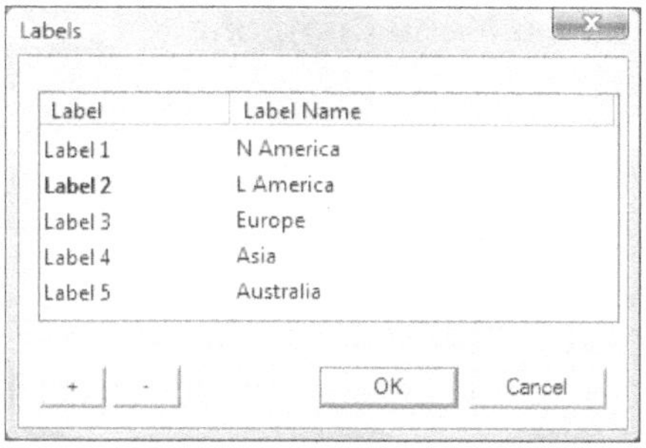

Figure 7-55 Label name changes

5. On the Behavior tab, make the changes in the table.

Property	Change To
Sound Enabled	Select this option
Default Selection	Label 3

6. On the Appearance tab, make the changes in the table.

Property	Change To
Font Size	12
Use Custom Color	Select this option
Default Fill	Light yellow
Selected Fill	Orange
Mouse Over Fill	Light green

7. Make the label long enough so that you can see all of the names, then save the changes.

As you click on each button, you will see a different chart.

The charts would look better if they had the region in the subtitle instead of the word millions.

To change the subtitle, click on the chart in the Object Browser, then change the Chart subtitle option to the corresponding cell in the spreadsheet.

The Latin America chart should look like the one shown in Figure 7-56.

Figure 7-56 Label Based menu

How To Make The Label Based Menu Smaller

As shown above in Figure 7-56, the menu takes up a lot of space because it stays expanded. You can shrink the menu so that only one button is displayed by default. If the dashboard has a lot of components, only displaying one button will save space. Make the changes below to have the menu display like the one shown in Figure 7-57 when the dashboard is first opened. When you click the menu button shown in Figure 7-57, the rest of the menu will be displayed, as shown in Figure 7-58. Once you select an option on the menu, the menu will automatically go back to only displaying one button.

1. On the General tab, enter a brief description of the menu in the **TITLE** option.
2. On the Behavior tab, clear the **ALWAYS EXPANDED** option. If necessary, change the **OPEN DIRECTION** option.

Figure 7-57 Menu when the dashboard is first opened

Figure 7-58 Menu after a button is clicked

CREATING DASHBOARDS WITH ALERTS

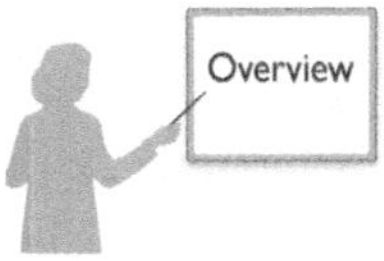

In this lesson you will learn how to create dashboards that have the following types of alerts:

- ☑ Percent alert chart
- ☑ Singe Value alerts
- ☑ Alerts map

Alerts Overview

Alerts are created to let the person using the dashboard know that a value has been reached in a field that they should be aware of. Alerts can be informational, like 50 or more customers ordered a specific product. Alerts can also be used as a reminder. For example, an inventory dashboard could have an alert to let the person know which products need to be reordered, based on the quantity on hand.

Alerts are not available for all components. Alerts are created with formulas that evaluate the conditions that you specify. A dashboard can have more than one alert. Alerts are only activated when the data is refreshed in the dashboard. If the dashboard is located on a server or in the Business Objects Enterprise and is scheduled, an email can be sent to a user when an alert is triggered. There are two types of alerts that can be created: Value alerts and Percent alerts.

Alerts Tab Options

The options on the Alerts tab shown in Figure 8-1 are used to create a percent alert. They are discussed below. Figure 8-2 shows the options used to create a value alert.

ENABLE ALERTS To create an alert, this option has to be selected.

Alert Method Options

The options in this section specify how the alert value will be processed.

VALUE ALERTS Select this option when the alert value is a number. You can select a value from the spreadsheet or you can enter the value manually.

PERCENT ALERTS Select this option when the alert value is a percent. The alert range is determined by percent ranges and the target.

Alert Definition Options

The options in this section determine which values will trigger the alert. The spreadsheet data is compared to the target values. Data that does not meet the target values selected here can trigger the alert, depending on which of the three options discussed below are selected. This is also how the range for each color on the component for the alert values is determined. By default, the data that is in the low, high or middle value range should be in the green section of the component, because it is the data that you are expecting to see.

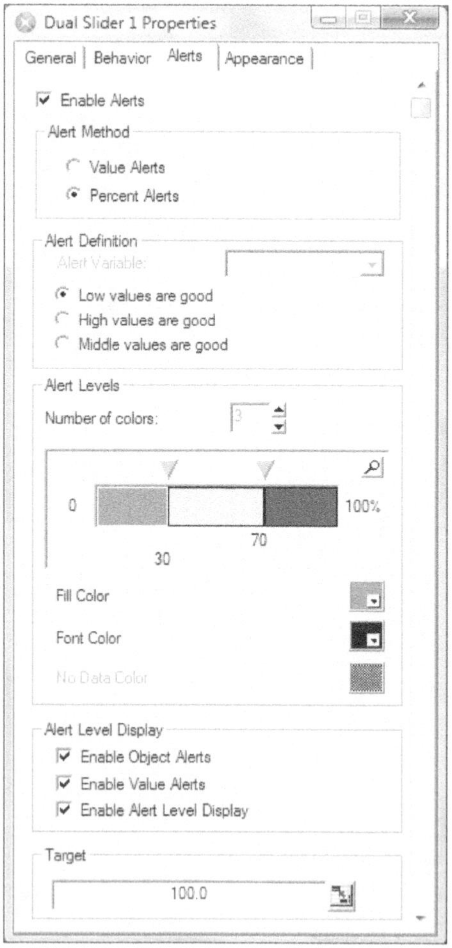

Figure 8-1 Alerts tab percent alerts options

ALERT VARIABLE Is used to select the X or Y-Axis values to trigger an alert. This option is only available for multi variable charts. Bubble and XY charts have multi variable functionality, because bubble charts require three variables, (Size, X values and Y values) as illustrated in Figure 8-2 and XY charts require two variables to plot a point on the chart.

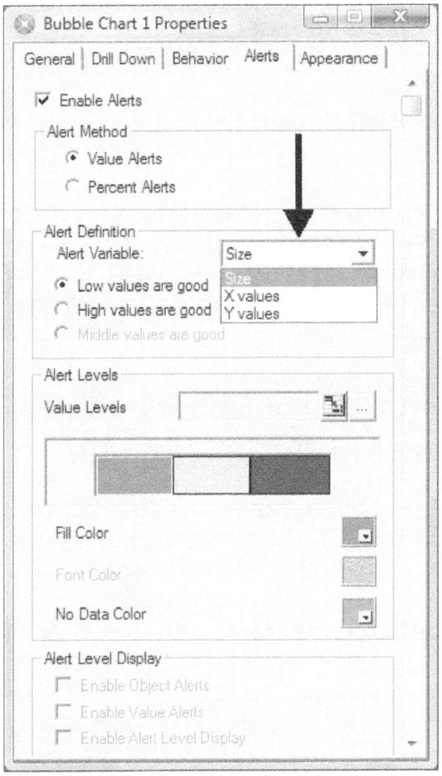

Figure 8-2 Alerts tab value alerts options

Alert Options

The options discussed below are used to select the criteria for the alert.

① **LOW VALUES ARE GOOD** Selecting this option means that data (from the spreadsheet) that is below the target value will not trigger the alert.

② **HIGH VALUES ARE GOOD** Selecting this option means that data that is greater than the target value will not trigger the alert.

③ **MIDDLE VALUES ARE GOOD** Selecting this option means that values that are close to the target will not trigger the alert. This option is only available for percent alerts.

Alert Levels Options

The options in this section are used to select specifics about the alert values. The properties in this section are used to select the colors for the alert, the number of alerts and the values that will trigger the alerts. The options change depending on which alert method, value or percent, is selected.

Alert Level Options For Value Alerts

The options discussed in this section are only available for Value alerts, as shown in Figure 8-3.

Figure 8-3 Value Alerts options

VALUE LEVELS As shown above in Figure 8-3, this field is used to select the number of alerts. Clicking the Cell Selector button is used to select a value from the spreadsheet. Clicking the Browse button will open the dialog box shown in Figure 8-4. The options are explained below. You can create as many alert values as you need.

The **VALUE NUMBER** determines the order of the alert values. This number cannot be changed.

The **ALERT VALUE** is the beginning number of the trigger.

To **ADD AN ALERT LEVEL VALUE**, click the plus button at the bottom of the Alert Numbers dialog box. To **DELETE AN ALERT LEVEL VALUE**, click on it, then click the minus button at the bottom of the Alert Numbers dialog box.

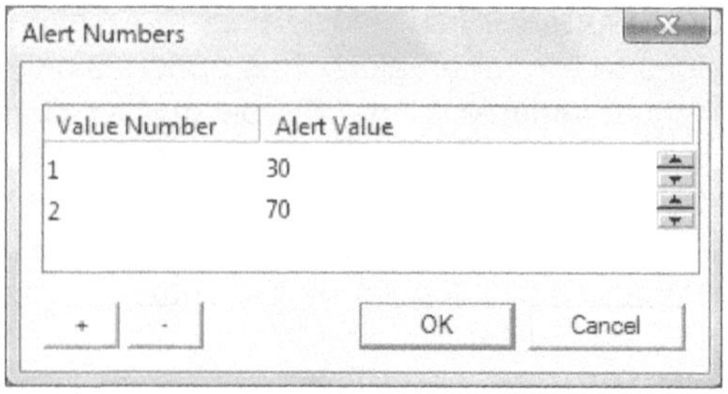

Figure 8-4 Alert Numbers dialog box

Alert Level Options For Percent Alerts

The options discussed in this section are only for Percent alerts, as shown earlier in Figure 8-1.

NUMBER OF COLORS Is used to select the number of colors for the alert, as shown earlier in Figure 8-1. The minimum number is two and the maximum number of colors is 10. The number that you select should correspond to the number of triggers that the component needs.

Control Panel Limits Dialog Box

Clicking the Control Panel Limits button (The magnifying glass button shown earlier in Figure 8-1.) opens the dialog box shown in Figure 8-5. The options shown are the defaults.

These options are used to select the minimum and maximum percent values for the alert.

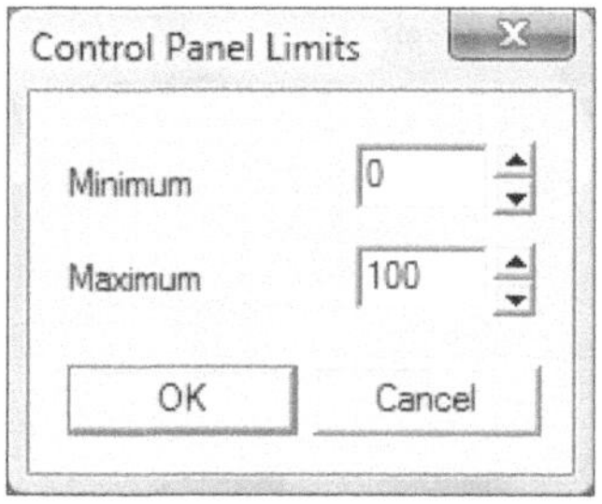

Figure 8-5 Control Panel Limits dialog box

Common Alert Levels Options

These options are available for value and percent alerts.

ALERT LEVELS COLOR SCALE Is used to select the percents that will trigger the alert colors, as shown in Figure 8-6. For a value alert, the color scale represents the values in the Value Levels field.

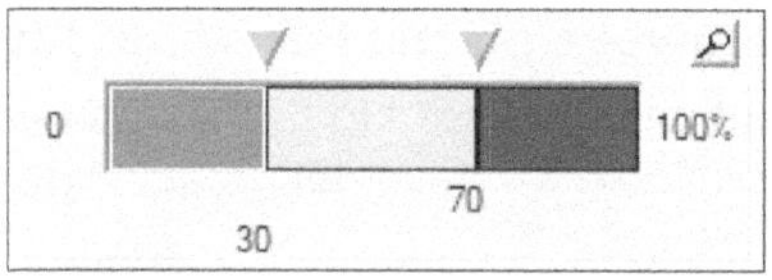

Figure 8-6 Alert Levels Color Scale

Default Alert Level Colors

By default, Crystal Xcelsius creates three levels of alerts. Each level has a different color: Green for good, Yellow for satisfactory and Red for poor. The range of values that you select for each alert level are arbitrary, but should correspond to the data. For example, the range levels could be 0-60 red, 61-75 yellow and 76-100 green. You could select the following range levels: 0-62 red, 63-79 yellow, 80-100 green for the same data and still achieve the same results.

In both examples, if the range of values that you are expecting to see is greater than 75, the **HIGH VALUES IS GOOD** option has to be selected to have the alert options display the data correctly. This is because by default, values that are in the green represent the good values. You can change the colors as needed.

Depending on which of the three alert definition methods discussed above (low values, high values or middle values) that you select, the colors will be in a different location on the component, as illustrated in Figures 8-7 to 8-9.

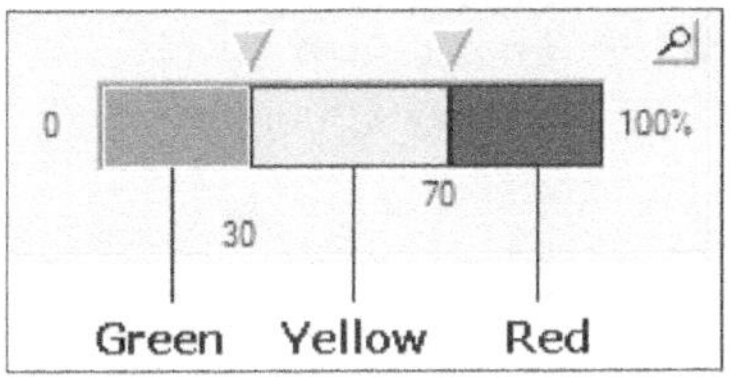

Figure 8-7 Low values are good default color order

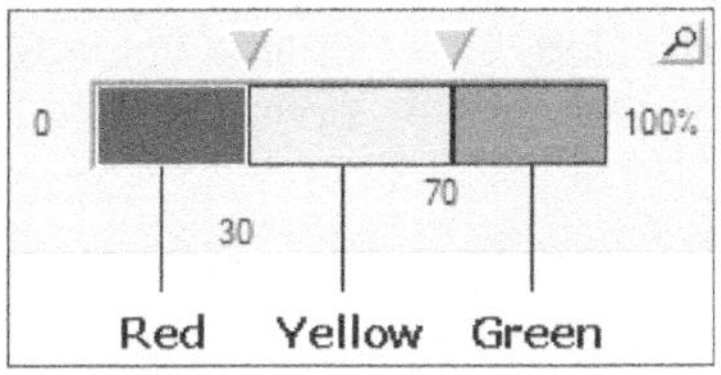

Figure 8-8 High values are good default color order

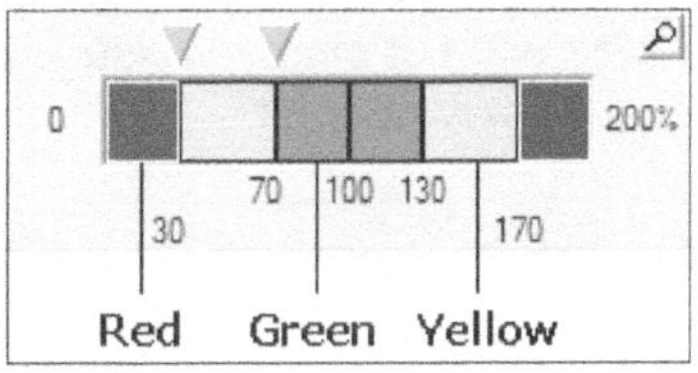

Figure 8-9 Middle values are good default color order

FILL COLOR Is used to change the fill colors for the alert levels.

FONT COLOR Is used to change the color for the value displayed on the alert. The **ENABLE VALUE ALERTS** option in the Alert Level Display section must be selected to use the Font Color option.

NO DATA COLOR Is used to change the alert color for any part of the component that does not have data. This option is not available for Single Value components.

To change a color, click on the color that you want to change in the Alert Levels Color Scale, shown earlier in Figure 8-6, then select the Fill Color or No Data Color option to change the color.

Alert Level Display Options

(Single Value components only) The options in this section are used to customize how alerts are displayed, as shown earlier in Figure 8-1.

ENABLE OBJECT ALERTS Is used to select whether or not the alert colors will be displayed. This option is what allows the slider to change colors or the needle on a gauge to change colors. Figure 8-10 shows the gauge without any alert level display options selected. Figure 8-11 is the same gauge with the Enable Object Alerts option selected.

ENABLE VALUE ALERTS Is used to select whether or not the value is enclosed in a box. This option adds a background to the value that changes colors, as illustrated in Figure 8-12.

ENABLE ALERT LEVEL DISPLAY Is used to select whether or not the component displays all of the alert colors or just the value ranges. This option turns on all of the alert level options, as shown in Figure 8-13.

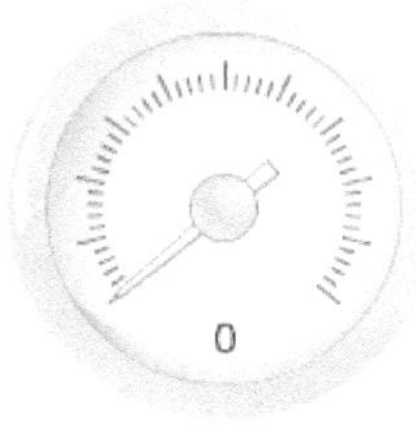

Figure 8-10 Gauge without alert level display options

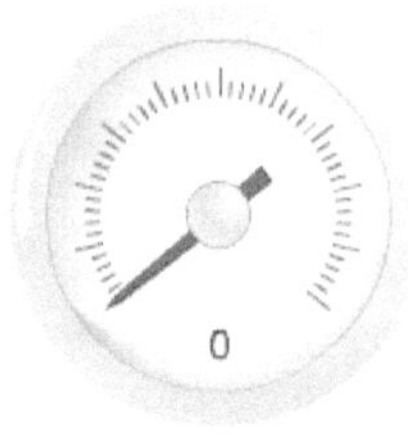

Figure 8-11 Gauge with alert level display options

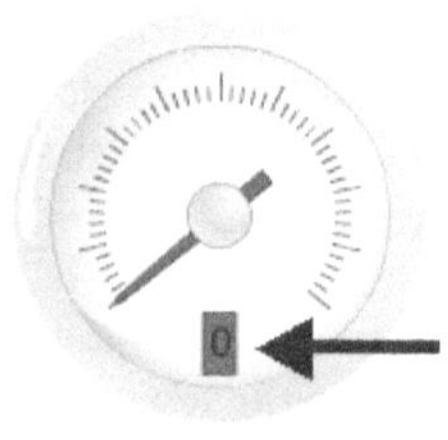

Figure 8-12 Enable Value Alerts option selected

Figure 8-13 Enable Alert Level display option selected

Target Option

(Not available for Single Value components when the Values method is selected.) The Target option is used to type in or select the target value, as shown in Figure 8-14 for the percent levels.

The Cell Selector button is used to select the target range. Usually this value is 100. When creating a percent alert, you would enter a one in this field to represent 100%. Clicking the Browse button will open the dialog box shown in Figure 8-15. This is how you enter the target values for the low, middle and high value ranges that are needed for the alert.

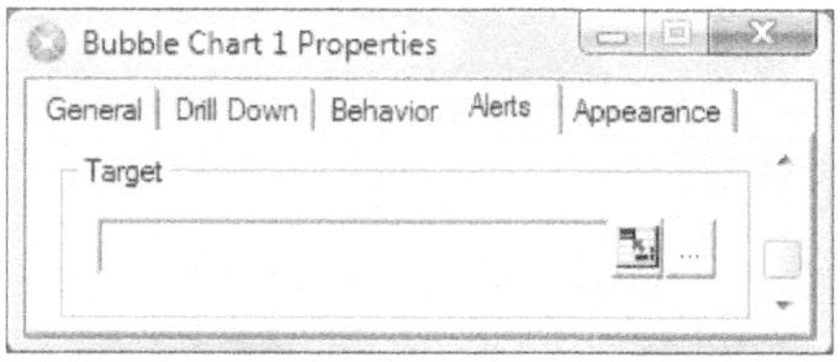

Figure 8-14 Target field options

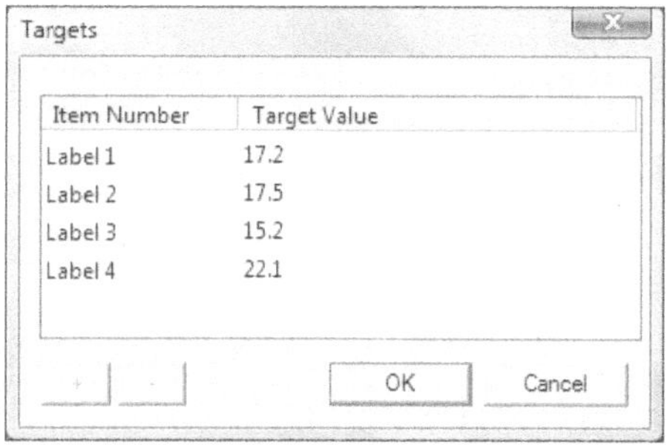

Figure 8-15 Targets dialog box

Exercise 8.1: Create A Percent Alert Chart

In this exercise you will create a chart that has percent alerts for quarterly revenues.

Figure 8-16 shows the data for this exercise.

	A	B	C	D	E
1	North America Revenues				
2				Actual Data	
3		Q1	Q2	Q3	Q4
4	Actual Values	$ 14.22	$ 20.12	$ 12.18	$ 25.49
5	Target	$ 17.20	$ 17.50	$ 15.20	$ 22.10

Figure 8-16 Alerts chart data

The Target amounts are the amount of revenue that a company wants to make in North America. As you can see, some of the target values are less than the actual values (which would be good if the targets are realistic) and other target values are greater than the actual value. In most cases, this means that for the quarter, the company did not meet the projected target amount. On a chart that has alerts, quarters that fall into this category would be displayed in red, if the default alert colors are used.

1. Import the Alerts Charts spreadsheet.

2. Add the Column Chart component.

Select The Chart Options

1. On the General tab, make the changes in the table.

Property	Change To
Chart title	A1
Chart subtitle	Millions $
Data Range	B4:E4
Category Axis Labels	B3:E3

2. On the Behavior tab, make the changes in the table.

Property	Change To
Manual Scale	Select this option
Y-Axis Minimum Value	10
Y-Axis Maximum Value	30

3. On the Appearance tab, click the Series button, then change the Bar Width option to 30.

4. On the Appearance tab, click the Layout button, then make the changes in the table.

Property	Change To
Use Major Divisions	4
Minor Divisions	2

Select The Alert Options

1. On the Alerts tab, make the changes in the table.

Property	Change To
Enable Alerts	Select this option
Alert Method	Percent Alerts
High values are good	Select this option
Number of colors	3
Target	B5:E5

2. If you open the Targets dialog box you will see the options shown earlier in Figure 8-15. If you look on the spreadsheet for this model, shown above in Figure 8-16, you will see that the values in the Target row are the same values as the Target Value column on the Targets dialog box.

How To Select The Colors For The Alert

Alert values need a range. The creator of this dashboard determined that the range values are as follows:

Red 0-90, means that the actual revenue is less than the target.
Yellow 91-110, means that the actual revenue is in the target range.
Green 111 +, means that the actual revenue is more than the target.

Based on the default values on the Control Panel Limits dialog box, shown earlier in Figure 8-5, the maximum value has to be raised to accommodate the values in green.

1. Click the magnifying glass button in the Alerts Levels section and change the **MAXIMUM VALUE** to 120.

2. Click on the triangle after the color yellow on the Alert Levels Color Scale and slide it to the right until it is on the number 110.

3. Click on the triangle after the color red and slide it to the right until it is on the number 90, as shown in Figure 8-17.

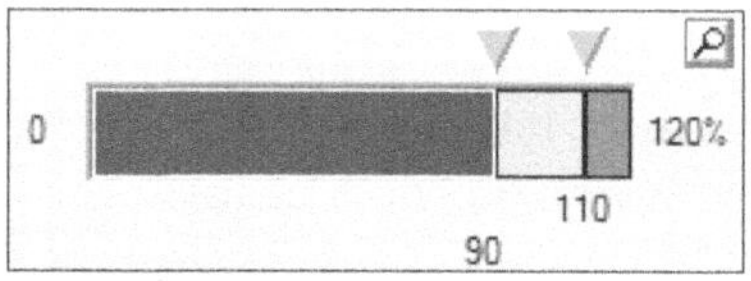

Figure 8-17 Alert Levels colors set

4. Save the model as `My alerts chart.`

   The model should look like the one shown in Figure 8-18.

   The alert colors let you know visually that in the first and third quarters, the actual revenue is less than the target revenue.

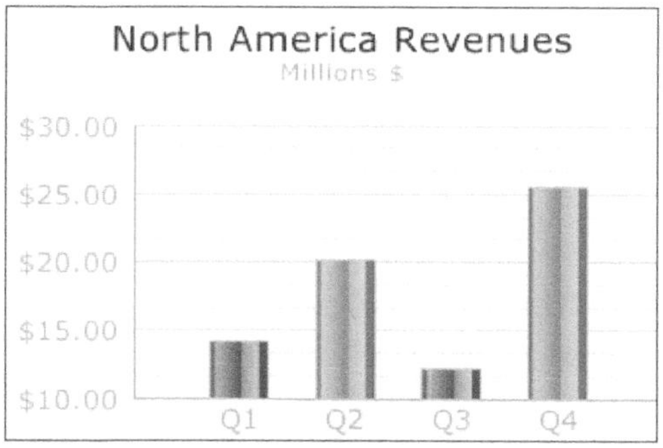

Figure 8-18 Alert chart model

The reason that you and I know what the colors represent is because we created the model. Users may not know this, which is why I think that it is a good idea to include what the colors represent on the dashboard. I can't imagine how confusing it would be for a user to understand a different set of alert colors on the next dashboard that you create, without including something to indicate what the colors represent.

Exercise 8.2: Create A Single Value Alert

The alert that you will create in this exercise will use three gauges to display actual balances versus the target balance.

Figure 8-19 shows the data for this exercise.

	A	B	C	D
1	Summary Report			
2	Corporate Health Measures			
3				
4		Sales	Inventories	Cost of Goods Sold
5	Actual Value	$ 456.00	$ 78.00	$ 256.00
6	Target	$ 435.00	$ 54.00	$ 220.00

Figure 8-19 Single Value alert data

1. Import the Alert Single Values spreadsheet.
2. Add the Gauge-0 component.
3. Add the Horizontal Slider-0 component. Put it below the gauge component.
4. Save the model as `My single value alerts`.

Select The Sales Gauge Options

In this part of the exercise you will set up three gauge components for sales, inventory and cost of goods sold. There is a column of data in the table for each gauge in each step. It will be easier to copy the first gauge after all of the options have been selected and use it as the basis for the other two gauges, rather than create each gauge from scratch. As you go through each step, you only have to change what is different for the second and third gauge.

1. On the General tab, make the changes in the table.

Property	Sales	Inventory	Cost of Goods
Title	B4	C4	D4
Link to Cell	B5	C5	D5

2. On the Behavior tab, make the changes in the table.

Property	Sales	Inventory	Cost of Goods
Initial Limits Calculation	Manual	Manual	Manual
Lower Limit Behavior	Fixed	Fixed	Fixed
Upper Limit Behavior	Fixed	Fixed	Fixed
Minimum Value	99	0.0	0.0
Maximum Value	500	108.0	440.0
Mouse Tracking	Radial	Radial	Radial

3. On the Appearance tab, click the Titles button, then make the changes in the table. You only have to select these options for the first gauge.

Property	Sales	Inventory	Cost of Goods
Show Value	Select this option	Select this option	Select this option
Value X Shift	0	0	0
Value Y Shift	35	35	35

4. On the Appearance tab, click the Layout button, then make the changes in the table. You only have to select these options for the first gauge.

Property	Sales	Inventory	Cost of Goods
Show Ticks	Select this option	Select this option	Select this option
Number of Ticks	11	11	11
Number of Subticks	4	4	4
Minimum Angle	-130	-130	-130
Maximum Angle	130	130	130

5. Make a copy of the Sales gauge component and place the copy to the right of the Sales gauge.

6. Repeat steps 1-4 above to set up the Inventory gauge by using the values in the Inventory column in each table.

7. Make a copy of the Inventory gauge and place it to the right of the Inventory gauge.

8. Repeat steps 1-4 above to set up the Cost of Goods Sold gauge by using the values in the Cost of Goods column in each table.

9. Save the changes.

Add The Alert Options

In this part of the exercise you will set up the alert functionality for the three gauge components that you just created.

Select The Alert Tab Options For The Sales Gauge

1. On the Alerts tab, select the following options for the Sales gauge: Enable Alerts, Percent Alerts and High values are good.

2. Adjust the triangles on the Alert Levels Color Scale for the following ranges: 0-80 red, 81-100 yellow, 100 green.

3. Select the following options: Enable Object Alerts and Enable Alert Level Display.

4. Change the Target option to B6.

   The Alert Levels section should look like the one shown in Figure 8-20.

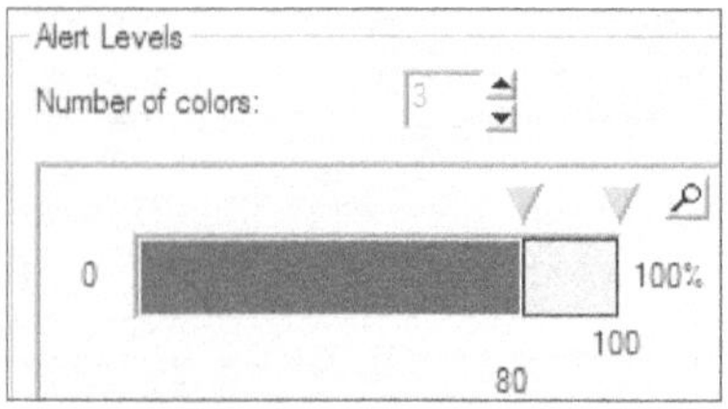

Figure 8-20 Sales Alert Level options

Select The Alert Tab Options For The Inventory Gauge

1. On the Alerts tab, select the following options for the Inventory gauge: Enable Alerts, Percent Alerts and Middle values are good.
2. Adjust the triangles on the Alert Levels Color Scale for the following ranges: 0-30 red, 31-70 yellow, 71-130 green, 131-169 yellow, 170+ red.
3. Select the following options: Enable Object Alerts and Enable Alert Level Display.
4. Change the Target option to C6.

   The Alert Levels section should look like the one shown in Figure 8-21.

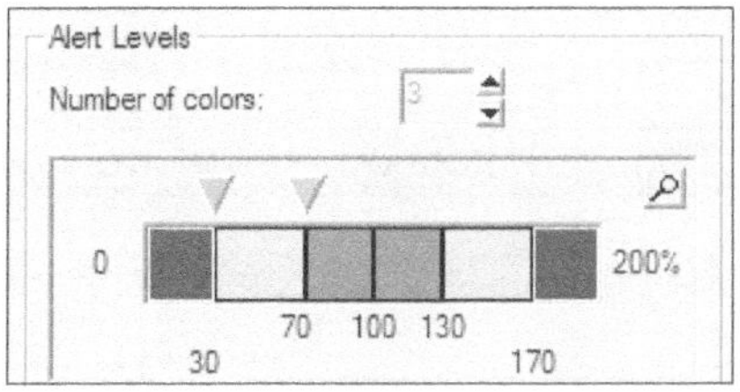

Figure 8-21 Inventory Alert Level options

Select The Alert Tab Options For The Cost Of Goods Sold Gauge

1. On the Alerts tab, select the following options for the Cost of Good Sold gauge: Enable Alerts, Percent Alerts and Low values are good.
2. Adjust the triangles on the Alert Levels Color Scale for the following ranges: 0-74 green, 75-106 yellow, 107+ red.
3. Select the following options: Enable Object Alerts and Enable Alert Level Display.
4. Change the Target option to D6.

   The Alert Levels section should look like the one shown in Figure 8-22.

   Save the changes.

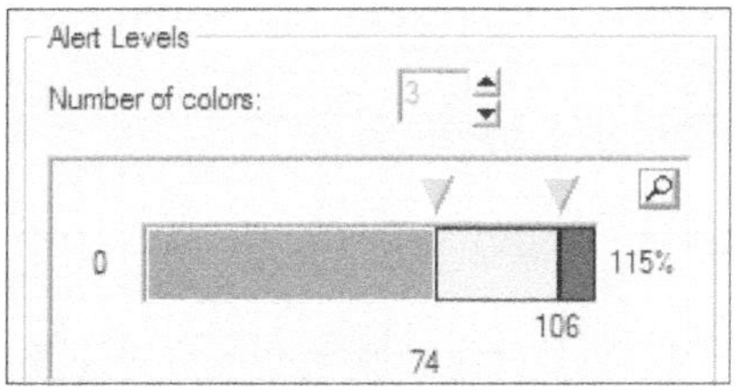

Figure 8-22 Cost of Goods Sold Alert Level options

Set Up The Slider Component Options

In this part of the exercise you will set up three sliders, one for each gauge.

1. On the General tab, make the changes in the table.

Property	Sales	Inventory	Cost of Goods
Link to cells	B5	C5	D5

2. On the Behavior tab, make the changes in the table.

Property	Sales	Inventory	Cost of Goods
Minimum Value	99	0	0
Maximum Value	900	100	512
Show Play Button	Select this option	Select this option	Select this option

3. On the Appearance tab, click the Titles button, then make the changes in the table. You only have to select these options for the Sales slider.

Property	Sales	Inventory	Cost of Goods
Value Position	Bottom center	Bottom center	Bottom center

4. Make a copy of the Sales slider component and place the copy to the right of the Sales slider.

5. Repeat steps 1-3 above to set up the Inventory slider by using the values in the Inventory column in each table.

6. Make a copy of the Inventory slider and place it to the right of the Inventory slider.

7. Repeat steps 1-3 above to set up the Cost of Goods slider by using the values in the Cost of Goods column in each table.

8. Save the changes.

Finish And Test The Model

1. Add a Label (Text) component above the Inventory slider.

2. On the General tab, type `Forecast` in the **ENTER TEXT** field.

3. On the Appearance tab, select the Center alignment option, then click the Bold button.

4. Save the changes. The model should look like the one shown in Figure 8-23. Notice that the needle on each gauge changes color to match the section of the gauge that its in. You can use the gauge as a selection tool just like you can use the slider.

This means that you can move the needle on the gauge without using the slider.

The play button on each slider can be started and stopped as needed.

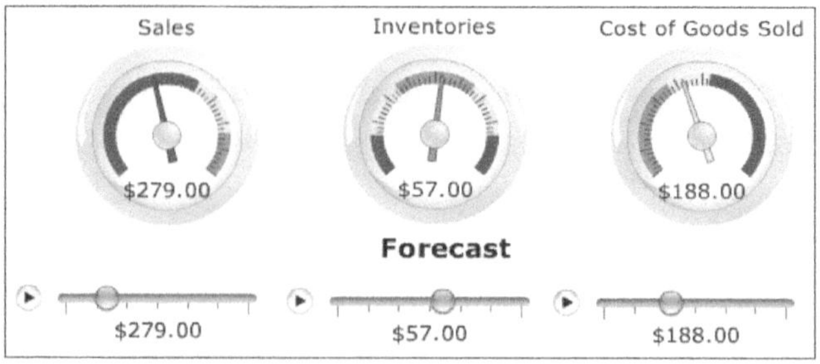

Figure 8-23 Single Value Alerts model

Exercise 8.3: Create A Map That Has Alerts

In this exercise you will create a map similar to the Revenues by State map that you created earlier in Exercise 5.3.

The map that you will create will change the color of states on the map based on whether or not the annual fiscal year amount is below, above or within the target amount.

Figure 8-24 shows the data for this exercise.

	A	B	C	D
1	Revenues by State			
2				
3	Display Data Range			
4		Actual		Target
5	State	FY2002	State	FY2002
6	Alabama	$ 31.66	Alabama	$ 28.00
7	Arizona	$ 17.14	Arizona	$ 27.90
8	Arkansas	$ 25.61	Arkansas	$ 19.88
9	California	$ 23.92	California	$ 19.85
10	Colorado	$ 17.69	Colorado	$ 21.30
11	Connecticut	$ 28.93	Connecticut	$ 23.14
12	Delaware	$ 25.67	Delaware	$ 28.99
13	District of Columbia	$ 18.69	District of Columbia	$ 18.09
14	Florida	$ 17.96	Florida	$ 22.42
15	Georgia	$ 17.49	Georgia	$ 20.70
16	Idaho	$ 19.95	Idaho	$ 17.30
17	Illinois	$ 22.60	Illinois	$ 34.15

Figure 8-24 Map with alerts data

1. Import the Alerts Map spreadsheet, then add the United States by state map component.

2. Save the model as `My map with an alert.`

3. On the General tab, make the changes in the table.

Property	Change To
Title	Revenues by State FY2002
Region Names	A6:A54
Insert Option	Rows
Display Data	A6:B54

4. On the Appearance tab, change the Title font size to 18.

5. On the Alerts tab, select the following options: Enable Alerts, Percent Alerts and High values are good. Change the Target option to C6:D54.

6. Adjust the triangles on the Alert Levels Color Scale for the following ranges: 0-50 red, 51-95 yellow, 96-100 green

   The Alert Levels section should look like the one shown in Figure 8-25.

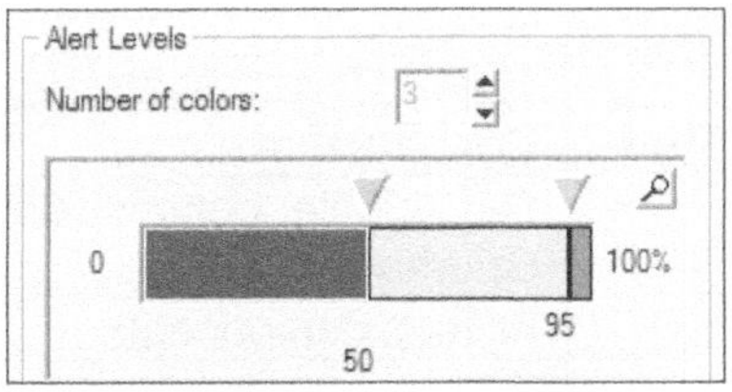

Figure 8-25 Alert Levels options

7. Save the changes.

   Your model should look like the one shown in Figure 8-26.

   Red represents states that the actual fiscal year revenue is below the target.

   Yellow represents states that the actual fiscal year revenue is in the acceptable target range.

   Green represents states that the actual fiscal year revenue is above the target range.

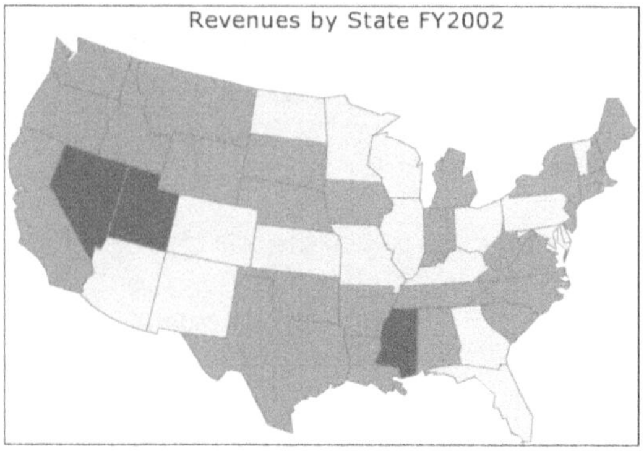

Figure 8-26 United States map with alerts

If the alert levels were the following;
0-80 red, 81-98 yellow, 99-100 green, the map would look like the one shown in Figure 8-27.

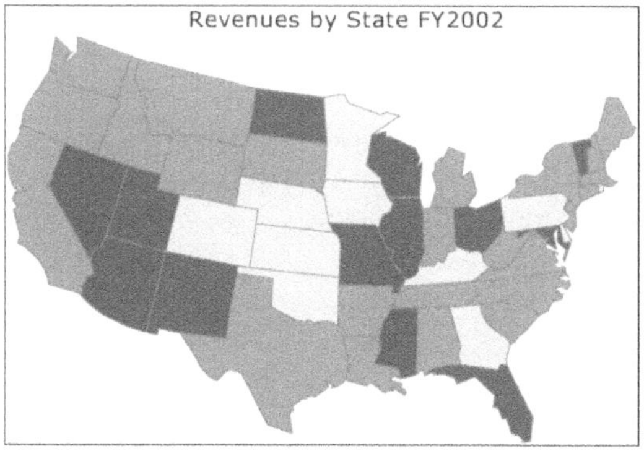

Figure 8-27 United States map with different alert ranges

Components That Have Alerts

As you read earlier, not all components have alerts. Table 8-1 lists the components that have alerts.

Component Type	Components
Charts	Bar, Bubble, Column, Combo, Line, Radar, Stacked Bar, Stacked Column and XY.
Map	All map components.
Other	Grid
Selectors	Combo Box, Icon, Label Based Menu and List Box.
Single Value	Dial, Dual Slider, Gauge, Horizontal Progress Bar, Horizontal Slider, Spinner, Value, Vertical Progress Bar and Vertical Slider.

Table 8-1 Components that have alerts

ENHANCING DASHBOARDS

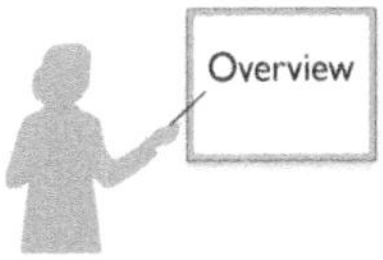

In this lesson you will learn the following ways to enhance the appearance of dashboards.

- ☑ Resize the canvas
- ☑ Refresh data
- ☑ Use the Replace Data Selection options
- ☑ Use the Art and Background components
- ☑ Create Scenarios
- ☑ Use the Web Connectivity components

Enhancing Dashboards Overview

You have created and edited a lot of models in this book. While they are effective and will get the job done, they could be enhanced to have a more professional look. That is the goal of this lesson, to discuss enhancement options and show you how to implement them. The options discussed in this lesson are not a definitive list of enhancements. Hopefully though, they will be enough to bring out your creative side. The two things that I hope that you keep in mind are:

① More than likely you will not be the only person that will use or see the dashboard. That means that you should listen to what other people say about the functionality of the dashboard. Make sure that you have incorporated all of the requirements.

② While it is very easy to add every bell and whistle, it is a better idea to have as much consistency as possible from one dashboard to the next, especially if you are designing a series of dashboards for the same users. This includes tasks like putting the corporate logo in the same place on each dashboard or using the same color scheme for all of the dashboards in the series. If several dashboards contain alerts, I believe that it will be more helpful if they use the same colors to indicate low, middle and high values in each dashboard, unless users request different colors for a reason. That way, users will know what each color represents.

Resize The Canvas

In Lesson 2, you learned two ways (Fit canvas to components and Fit canvas to the window) to resize the canvas. [See Lesson 2, Crystal Xcelsius Toolbar] When you read about the options, you learned about the Document Properties dialog box. It can be used to change the canvas size, either by selecting a preset size, modifying a preset size or selecting a width and height, which also lets you create a custom size for the dashboard.

While you are creating and editing a model, the amount of space that it takes up on the canvas is not a problem because the larger it is, the easier it is to work with. Without giving it much thought, you would probably export it at the size that it currently is. I know that you do not know me, but with dashboards, size does matter! <smile>

When exporting a model, the entire canvas is exported, whether the components are using all of the space on the canvas or not. Usually, this is not what you want or need to happen. Primarily because it is more difficult to position and resize the SWF file inside of another file, like in a PowerPoint slide. In some cases, you cannot resize the SWF file, like in a PDF file.

If you exported any of the models that you created in this book to Word or PowerPoint, you will see what I am talking about. Often, you will find that the size of the final product is too small and when you try to resize the dashboard, you will see that the frame around it is an inch or more away from the dashboard. That is why it is very difficult to resize it the way that you need to. I have found it easier to always include the steps below for every model right before it is exported as the final dashboard.

1. Make sure that all components are the correct size and in the right location in the model.
2. With the model open, click the **FIT CANVAS TO COMPONENTS** button on the toolbar.
3. Save the changes.

Figure 9-1 shows a dashboard that has been exported to Word without resizing the canvas. As you can see, it is small. Figure 9-2 shows the same dashboard exported to Word after the Fit canvas to components option was applied. The dashboard in Figure 9-2 is easier to read.

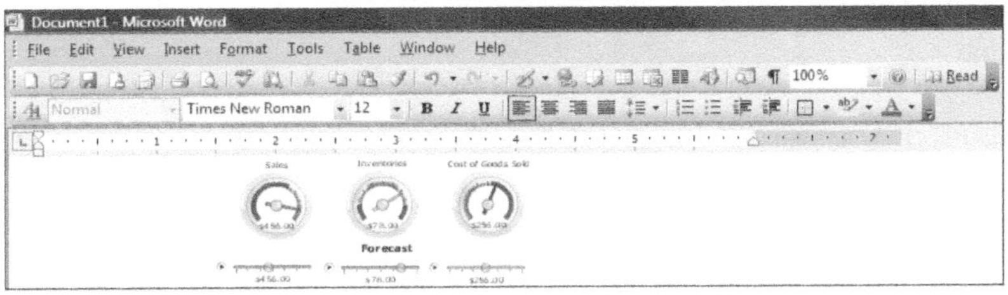

Figure 9-1 Canvas not resized

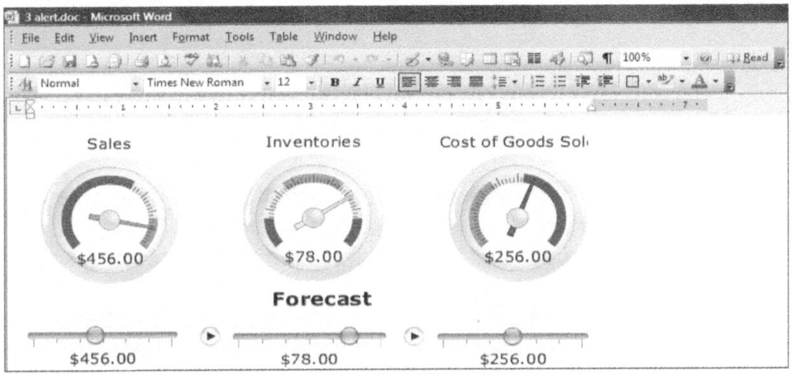

Figure 9-2 Canvas resized

Specific Size Dashboards

If the dashboard has to be a specific size for any reason, like having to accommodate a specific screen size like 14 inches, instead of 21 inches, the Fit canvas to components option may not work. Instead, use the **FIT CANVAS TO WINDOW** option or one of the options on the Document Properties dialog box.

Refreshing The Data

Earlier in this book you learned that once you import that data from the spreadsheet, any changes made to the layout of the spreadsheet or data changes are not automatically added to the model. More than likely, the majority of dashboards that are created need to have the data refreshed from time to time. As you will see, there are several options for refreshing data.

Refresh Data Options

You will learn the following ways to refresh the data in a model.

① Only refresh the data.

② Refresh the data because the layout has changed, meaning that at least some data in the spreadsheet is in different cells, or rows or columns of data have been added or deleted.

③ Refresh the data because the formatting of at least some of the data has changed that can't be duplicated in Crystal Xcelsius.

View The Refresh Data Options

1. Open the My slider model.

2. Click the Import Model button. You will see the dialog box shown in Figure 9-3.

   Notice that the dialog box has more options then when a spreadsheet is imported for the first time. [See Lesson 3, Figure 3-41] The options are explained below.

Figure 9-3 Import Model dialog box for an existing model

① **REFRESH DATA SOURCES** Select this option when only the data in the spreadsheet has changed, opposed to the structure (new or deleted rows or formatting). This option keeps all of the existing links between the spreadsheet and the components in the model intact.

② **CLEAR DATA SOURCES** Select this option when the structure of the spreadsheet has changed. The links between the spreadsheet and the components in the model will be deleted.

③ **REFRESH SPREADSHEET FORMAT** Select this option if the changes that will be imported are formatting changes. For example, the format of some numbers have changed from no formatting to currency or negative number formatting. This option keeps all of the existing links between the spreadsheet and the components in the model intact.

What may not be obvious is that you can also select a different spreadsheet. If I am not sure how the changes made to the spreadsheet will look in the model, I save the spreadsheet changes to a new file name and select the new spreadsheet on this dialog box.

To demonstrate the different options, you will have to select different spreadsheets for each exercise.

Figure 9-4 shows the spreadsheet used for the My slider model.

	A	B	C	D	E
1	Car Sales by Location				
2	Model XXL5V				
3					
4	Retail Price	$15,500		Unit Increase	0
5					
6	Location	Units Sold	Tot. Sales		
7	Dublin	24	$372,000		
8	San Diego	123	$1,906,500		
9	San Jose	67	$1,038,500		
10	San Francisco	145	$2,247,500		
11	Sacramento	78	$1,209,000		
12					
13	Total	437	$6,773,500		

Figure 9-4 My slider model data

3. Leave the model open to complete Exercise 9.1.

Exercise 9.1: Use The Refresh Data Sources Option For Data Changes

In this exercise you will refresh the data in the My Slider model by using a spreadsheet that has different locations in the first column.

If you compare the data in the spreadsheet shown in Figure 9-5 to the data shown above in Figure 9-4, you will see that nothing else in the spreadsheet has been changed. Figure 9-5 shows the spreadsheet that will be used in this exercise.

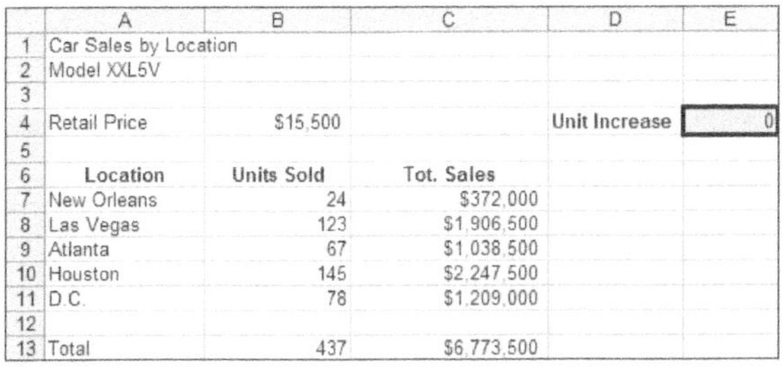

	A	B	C	D	E
1	Car Sales by Location				
2	Model XXL5V				
3					
4	Retail Price	$15,500		Unit Increase	0
5					
6	Location	Units Sold	Tot. Sales		
7	New Orleans	24	$372,000		
8	Las Vegas	123	$1,906,500		
9	Atlanta	67	$1,038,500		
10	Houston	145	$2,247,500		
11	D.C.	78	$1,209,000		
12					
13	Total	437	$6,773,500		

Figure 9-5 Spreadsheet with different data

1. Click the Browse button on the Import Model dialog box, then select the cx_refresh_data_sources spreadsheet.

2. Click OK.

   You will see the dialog box shown in Figure 9-6.

   Click Yes.

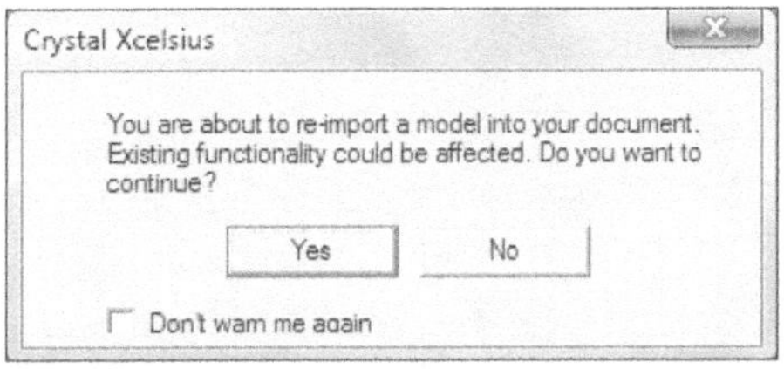

Figure 9-6 Refresh Data Sources warning dialog box

A few times my laptop that has Vista crashed after clicking the Yes button. I closed Crystal Xcelsius and reopened it. That seems to fix the problem temporarily.

3. Preview the model. It should look like the one shown in Figure 9-7.

   Notice that the locations across the bottom of the chart are different then the ones shown in Exercise 3.1, Figure 3-40.

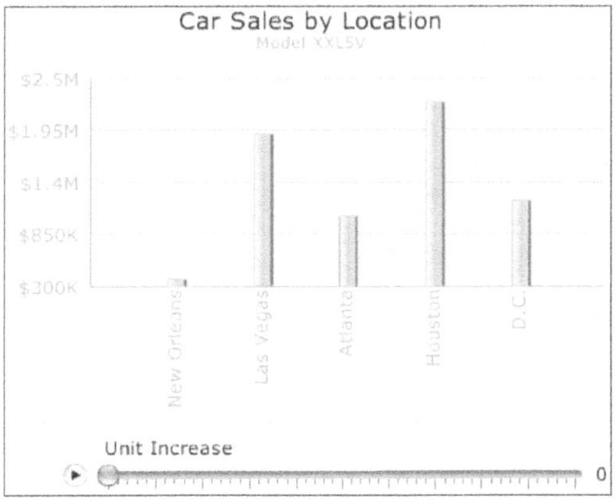

Figure 9-7 Location names changed

4. Save the model as `My slider refresh data sources model.`

Exercise 9.2: Use The Clear Data Sources Option For Structure Changes

In this exercise you will refresh the data in the My Slider model by using a spreadsheet that has a different structure. The structure change is rows have been added between existing rows of data, as shown in Figure 9-8. Compare this spreadsheet to the one shown earlier in Figure 9-4.

If the **CLEAR DATA SOURCES** option is selected on the Import Model dialog box and the spreadsheet shown in Figure 9-8 was used, the model would look like the one shown in Figure 9-9, because the original Data Range cell range on the General tab of the Properties dialog box has not been changed. As shown in Figure 9-10, the Data Range option for the chart is pointing to the range C7:C11. This is the range that the original model used.

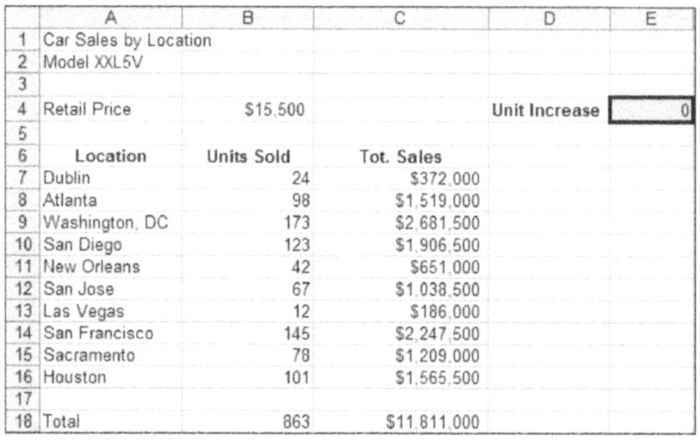

	A	B	C	D	E
1	Car Sales by Location				
2	Model XXL5V				
3					
4	Retail Price	$15,500		Unit Increase	0
5					
6	Location	Units Sold	Tot. Sales		
7	Dublin	24	$372,000		
8	Atlanta	98	$1,519,000		
9	Washington, DC	173	$2,681,500		
10	San Diego	123	$1,906,500		
11	New Orleans	42	$651,000		
12	San Jose	67	$1,038,500		
13	Las Vegas	12	$186,000		
14	San Francisco	145	$2,247,500		
15	Sacramento	78	$1,209,000		
16	Houston	101	$1,565,500		
17					
18	Total	863	$11,811,000		

Figure 9-8 Spreadsheet with structure changes

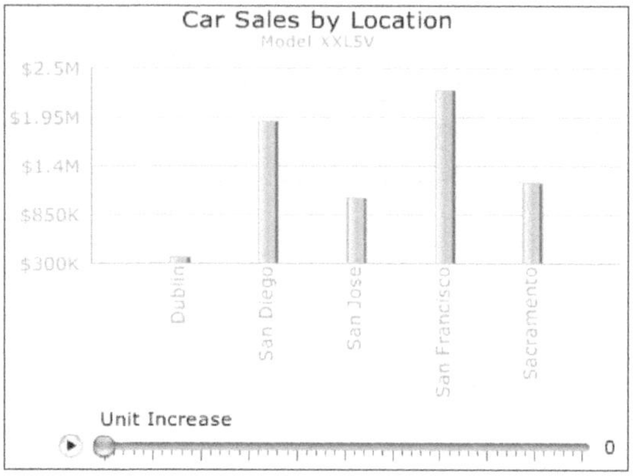

Figure 9-9 Spreadsheet structure changes without changing the Data Range

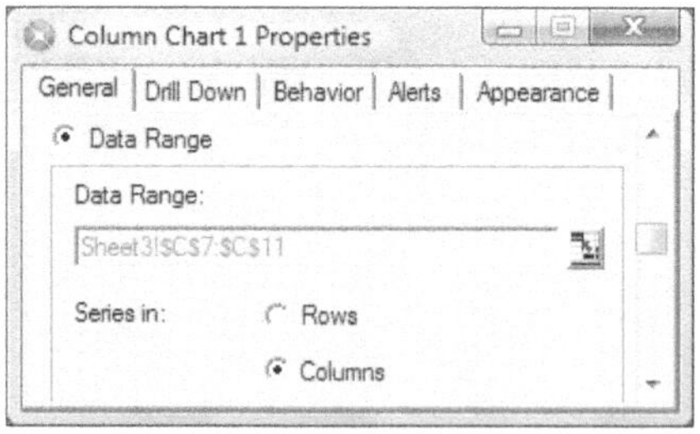

Figure 9-10 Data Range option for the original My Slider model

Interestingly enough, when the Use Clear Data Sources options is selected, the Data Range and Category Axis Labels options are cleared from the dialog box, but they are retained in memory until you change them or close the model. The Data Range would have to be changed to C7:C16 and the Category Axis Labels option would have to be changed to A7:A16, as shown in Figure 9-11.

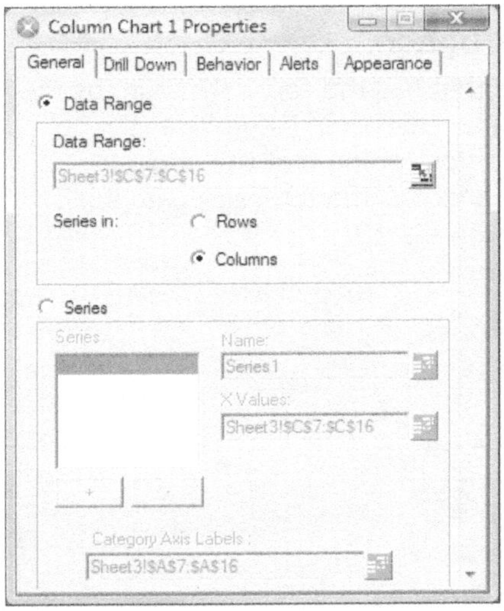

Figure 9-11 Data Range option that includes structure changes

1. Save the My Slider model as `My slider clear data sources.`
2. Click the Import Model button. Click the Browse button, then select the cx_clear_data_sources spreadsheet.
3. Select the **CLEAR DATA SOURCES** option. Click OK, then click Yes.
4. Open the Properties dialog box and change the Data Range option to C7:C16.
5. Change the Category Axis Labels option to A7:A16. You should have the options shown above in Figure 9-11.
6. Click on the slider. On the General tab, change the **LINK TO CELL** option to E4.
7. Save the changes.

   The model should look like the one shown in Figure 9-12.

   Notice that it displays all of the new locations that were added to the spreadsheet.

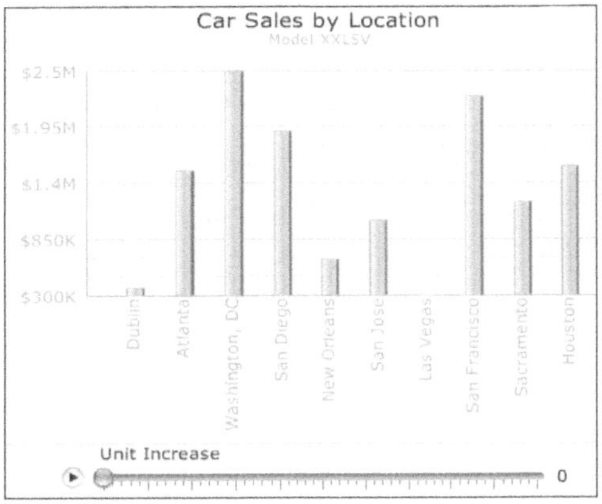

Figure 9-12 Model with new data structure

Exercise 9.3: Use The Refresh Spreadsheet Format Option

In this exercise you will import a spreadsheet into the model that has the same structure as the original spreadsheet that was imported into the model, as shown earlier in Figure 9-4. The difference is that the spreadsheet that you will import has cell formatting that the original spreadsheet does not have. The formatting that has been changed is the total sales amounts have been changed from currency to numeric, as shown in Figure 9-13.

	A	B	C	D	E
1	Car Sales by Location				
2	Model XXL5V				
3					
4	Retail Price	$15,500		Unit Increase	0
5					
6	Location	Units Sold	Tot. Sales		
7	Dublin	24	372,000		
8	San Diego	123	1,906,500		
9	San Jose	67	1,038,500		
10	San Francisco	145	2,247,500		
11	Sacramento	78	1,209,000		
12					
13	*Total*	*437*	*$6,773,500*		

Figure 9-13 Spreadsheet with formatting changes

1. Save the cx_slider_refresh_formatting model as `My slider refresh format model`.

2. View the model. It should have currency formatting on the Y-Axis, shown earlier in Figure 9-7.

3. Click the Import Model button, then select the Refresh Spreadsheet Format option.

4. Click OK, then save the changes.

   The model should look like the one shown in Figure 9-14.

   The format of the values on the Y-Axis have numeric formatting instead of currency formatting.

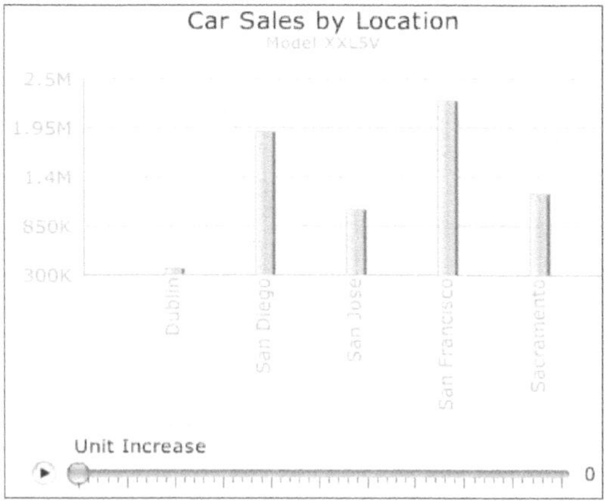

Figure 9-14 Model with modified formatting

Replace Data Selection

In Lesson 1 you read about two XML options that are only available in the Workgroup edition of Crystal Xcelsius. [See Lesson 1, Table 1-2] In Lesson 2 you read about the XML Map Option, which is used to connect to XML complaint databases. [See Lesson 2, Table 2-3] If you need to update data in a model but do not know XML or do not want to learn it (Don't feel bad, I don't want to learn XML either), the Replace Data Selection tool may fit your needs.

If users will need to update the data in the dashboard, using the options on the Replace Data Selection dialog box will make the process easier because you will not have to import the spreadsheet with the data changes. The options replace data in the model from an external spreadsheet that is not the one that was originally imported into the model. This option does not recognize new rows or columns because the options for the component are not changed.

For example, if the user needs to see the most current data in the dashboard every Tuesday, have them update the second spreadsheet before you export the model on Tuesday. During the export process, the options on the Export Settings dialog box are checked to see if the spreadsheet that was originally used to create the model should be used or if a different spreadsheet should be used. During the export process, the spreadsheet listed on the Export Settings dialog box is used to update the data for the dashboard.

It is probably safer to make a copy of the original spreadsheet that was used to create the model, for the users to change the data in. This copy should be placed on a server, especially if more than one person will need to provide the data changes.

Exercise 9.4: Use The Replace Data Selection Option

As you read in Lesson 2, the options on the Replace Data Selection dialog box are used to change the values from the spreadsheet that was originally used in the model. You can also import values using named ranges that are in the spreadsheet. In this exercise, you will learn how to create a range name in Crystal Xcelsius and Excel, then link the range to the cells in the spreadsheet. These are the cells that will be updated the next time the model is exported.

Creating range names is not a requirement to using the options on the Export Settings dialog box because the entire spreadsheet can be exported. I use range names when the spreadsheet has thousands of rows of data. Only having to update certain blocks of cells is faster than importing an entire spreadsheet. Another reason that I often use range names is in case a user makes changes to a part of the spreadsheet that they shouldn't.

1. Save the cx_actual_vs_projected model as `My replace data selection model`.

2. Data ⇒ Replace Data Selection.

How To Create A Range Name In The Model

In this part of the exercise you will create a range in the spreadsheet and give it an appropriate range name in the model. The range that you create will allow users to update the current sales amounts.

1. Click the **ADD** button on the Replace Data Selection dialog box.

2. In the **RANGE NAME** field, type `Current_Actual_Sales`.

3. Click the Cell Selector button, then select the range B12:B15.

   You should have the options shown in Figure 9-15.

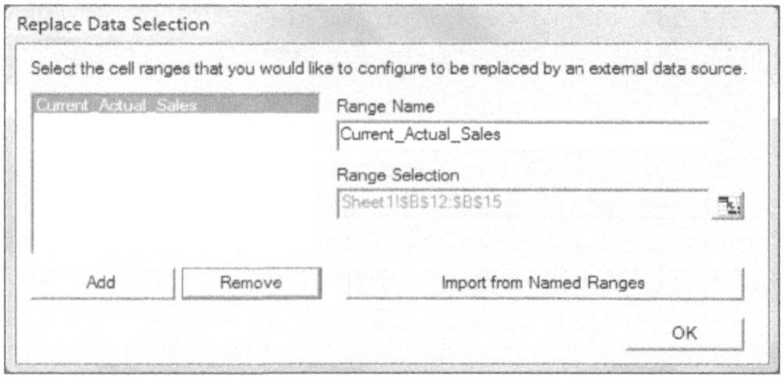

Figure 9-15 New range created

Create A Range Name In The Spreadsheet And Import It Into The Model

In this part of the exercise you will create a range in the spreadsheet and import it.

1. Leave the Replace Data Selection dialog box and Crystal Xcelsius open. Open the cx_actual_vs_projected spreadsheet in Excel.

2. Select the range C12:C15, then Insert ⇒ Name ⇒ Define.

3. Type `Current_projected_sales` in the **NAMES IN WORKBOOK** field.

   You should have the options shown in Figure 9-16.

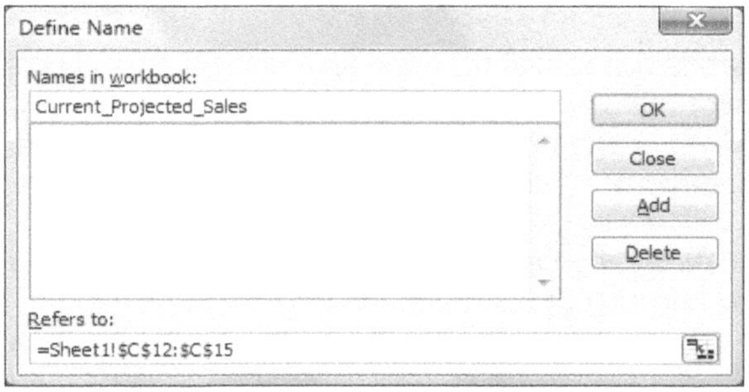

Figure 9-16 Range options in Excel

4. Click Add, then click OK. Save the changes and close Excel.

5. In Crystal Xcelsius, the Replace Data Selection dialog box should still be open.

   Click the **IMPORT FROM NAMED RANGES** button. You should see the range that you just created, as shown in Figure 9-17.

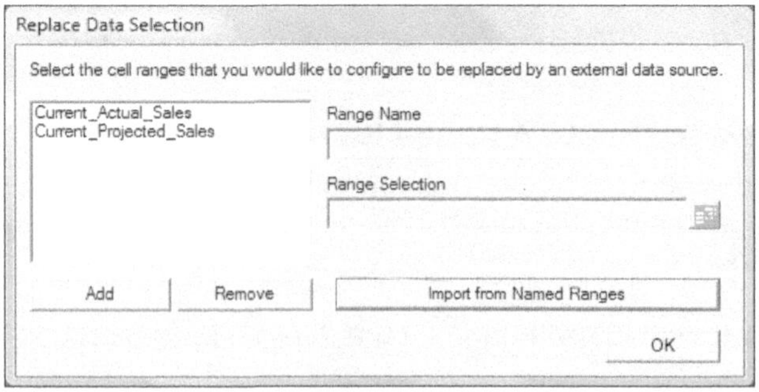

Figure 9-17 Imported range

6. You can now add the data from the ranges shown above in Figure 9-17 to the model. Click OK.

Add A Range To The Model

In this part of the exercise you will add one of the ranges shown above in Figure 9-17, to the model.

1. Open the Properties dialog box for the chart, then click on the General tab.
2. Click the plus sign at the bottom of the Series section.
3. In the Name field, type `Current Projected Sales.`
4. Click the X Values Cell Selector button, then select the range C12:C15.
5. On the Appearance tab, click the Series button, then make the changes in the table. The Series Markers section should look like the one shown in Figure 9-18.

Property	Change To
Use Custom Color	Select this option
Series	Current Projected Sales
Series Type	Line
Marker	Triangle

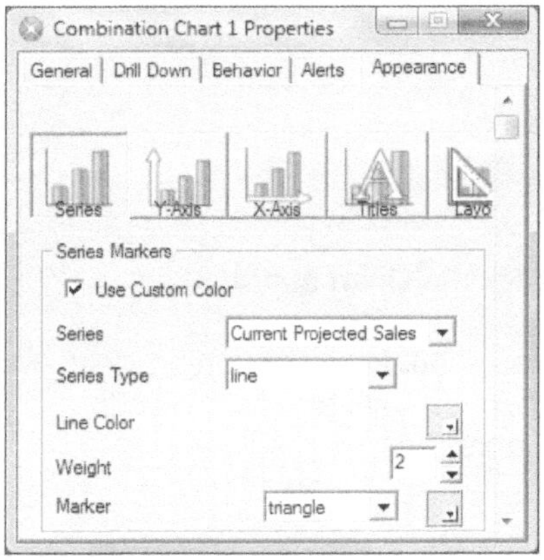

Figure 9-18 Series panel changes

6. Save the changes.

   When you preview the model, it should look like the one shown in Figure 9-19.

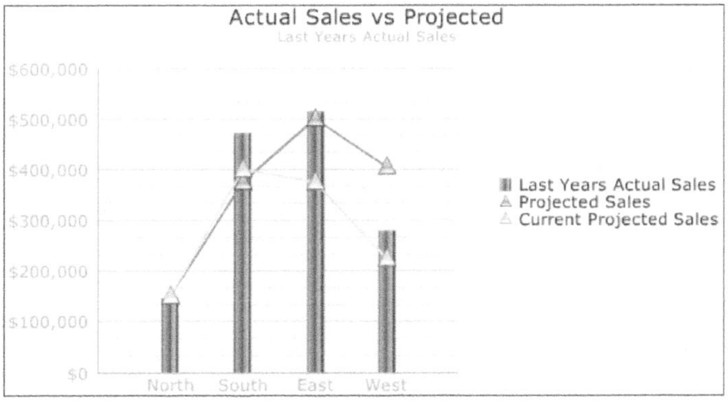

Figure 9-19 Model with data from a named range

Select The Export Settings

Now that you have selected the cells that will be updated the next time the model is exported, the last part of the process is to select the spreadsheet that will contain the revised data.

1. File ⇒ Export Settings.

2. Select the **USE ANOTHER EXCEL FILE** option.

3. Click the Browse button and select the cx_projected_sales spreadsheet, shown in Figure 9-20.

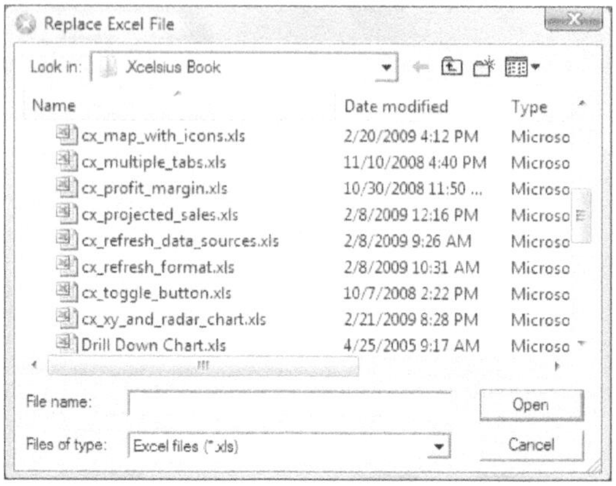

Figure 9-20 Replace Excel File dialog box

4. Click the Open button.

   You should see the spreadsheet that you selected, as shown in Figure 9-21.

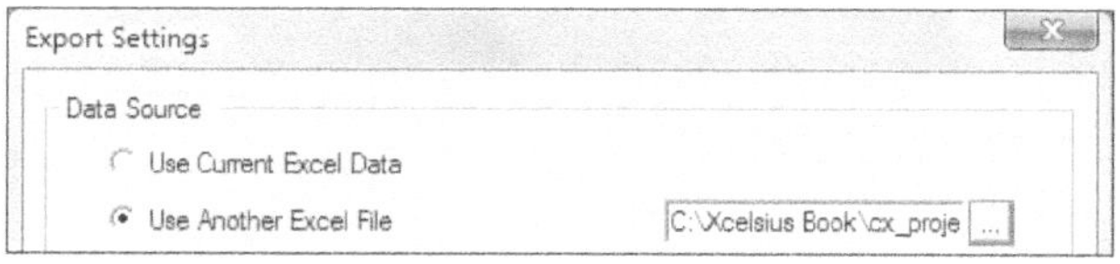

Figure 9-21 Export Settings dialog box

5. Click OK, then save the changes.

6. File ⇒ Export Preview.

   The chart should look like the one shown in Figure 9-22.

   When you compare it to the chart shown earlier in Figure 9-19, you will see that the Current Projected Sales values have changed.

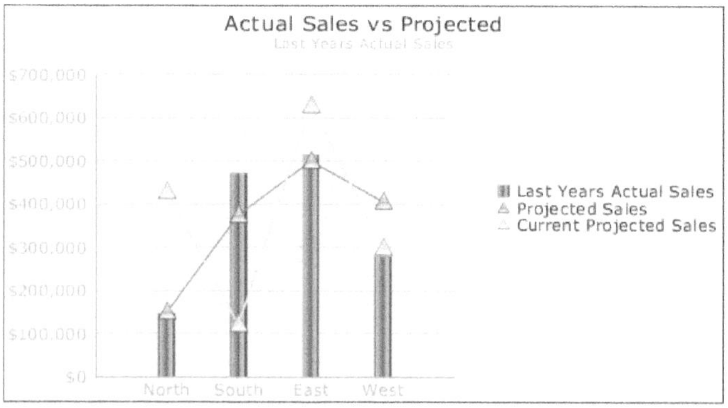

Figure 9-22 Changed Current Projected Sales values

Art And Background Components

These components are used to add more flair or personality if you will, to a dashboard to customize it. This is accomplished by adding other components to the model. All of the components in Table 9-1 have General and Behavior tab options that you can use to customize the component. The General tab options for these components are used to customize the component. The Behavior tab for these components have the Dynamic Visibility options that are covered in detail in Lesson 11. Table 9-1 explains the Art and Background components.

Component	Description
Background	Adds a background image or color to the model.
Ellipse	Adds an ellipse object to the model.
Image	Allows JPG image files, animations and videos to be imported into the model. This is how a corporate logo can be added to the dashboard.
Rectangle	Adds a square to the model. This component is often used as a border around components.
Vertical Line	Adds a vertical line to the model.
Horizontal Line	Adds a horizontal line to the model.

Table 9-1 Art and Background components explained

Background Component

General Tab Options

The options shown in Figure 9-23 are used to customize the background component.

CAPTURE MOUSE EVENTS Is used to prevent the user from using other components on the dashboard. For this feature to work, the background component has to be stacked on top of all other components.

BORDER SCALE Is used to adjust the width of the background components border.

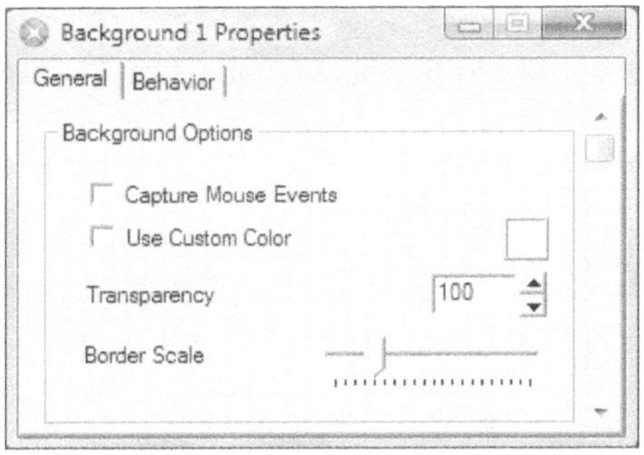

Figure 9-23 Background general tab options

Exercise 9.5: Adding A Background Component To A Model

In this exercise you will add a background component to a model that you created earlier.

1. Save the My filter drop-down list model as `My background`.

2. Add the Background-1 component, then make it larger than the two components already on the canvas.

3. On the General tab of the background component, move the **BORDER SCALE** slider to the right, past the half way mark.

4. Right-click on the background component and select **SEND TO BACK**.

5. Resize and adjust the background component as needed.

   Save the changes.

   The model should look like the one shown in Figure 9-24.

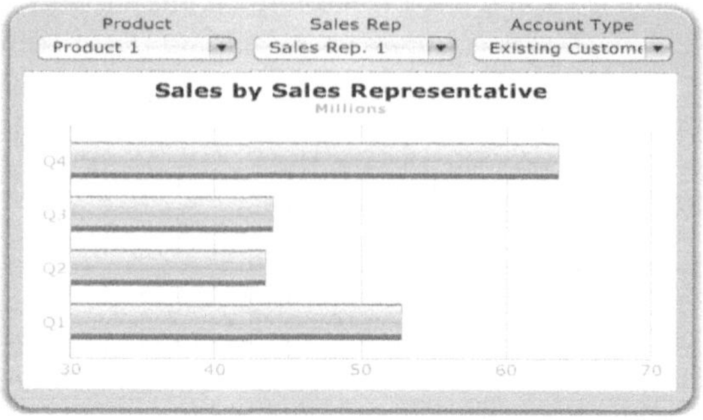

Figure 9-24 Background added to a model

Ellipse And Rectangle Components

These components are used to add shapes to a model. They have the same options on the Properties dialog box.

General Tab Options

The options shown in Figure 9-25 are used to customize the ellipse and rectangle components.

Border Appearance Options

The options in this section are used to select whether or not the ellipse or rectangle border should be displayed, as well as, the weight, transparency and color of the border.

SHOW BORDERS Select this option if you want the ellipse or rectangle to display a border.

COLOR Is used to change the color of the border.

Interior Appearance Options

The options in this section are used to select the color and shading of the interior (background) of the component.

FILL STYLE Is used to select one of the options shown in Figure 9-26. These options determine how the color is displayed in the ellipse or rectangle.

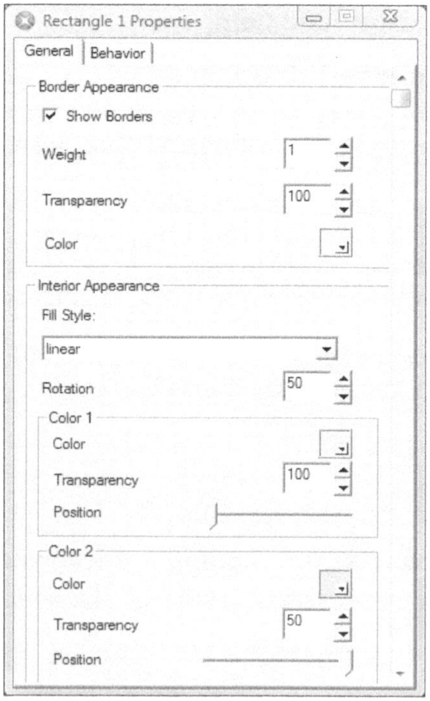

Figure 9-25 Ellipse and Rectangle general tab options

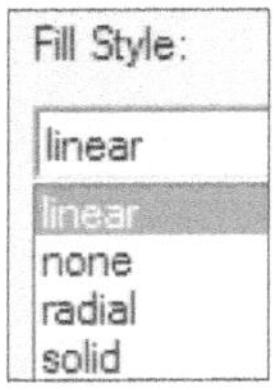

Figure 9-26 Fill Style options

ROTATION Is used to change how the Fill Style color is displayed. This option will remind you of the gradient option that many graphics software packages have.

Figure 9-27 shows the ellipse with the linear Fill Style option selected and the Rotation option set to 10.

Figure 9-28 shows the ellipse with the linear Fill Style option selected and the Rotation option set to 100.

Figure 9-29 shows the ellipse with the radial Fill Style option selected.

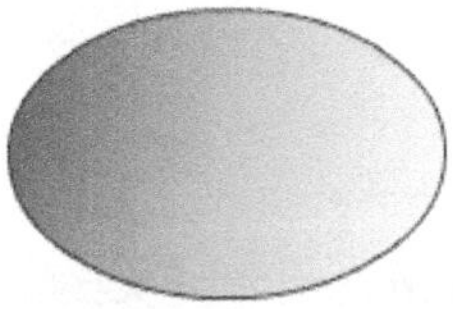

Figure 9-27 Ellipse component with Rotation set to 10

Figure 9-28 Ellipse component with Rotation set to 100

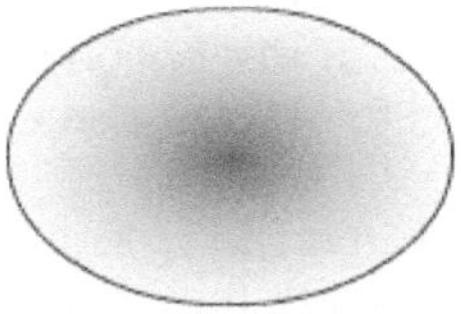

Figure 9-29 Ellipse with radial fill style

Color 1 And Color 2 Options
These options are used to select one or two colors for the interior of the ellipse or rectangle.

COLOR Is used to change a color of the interior of the ellipse or rectangle.

POSITION Is used to select how much of the interior area of the ellipse or rectangle the color should cover.

Image Component

By default, the Image Component is an empty container. You have to add a file to it before it has any functionality.

General Tab Options

As you read in Table 9-1, you can add images to a component, similar to how images are added to the Fish-Eye and Sliding Picture Menu components.

The options shown in Figure 9-30 are used to select, import and configure the image.

The following file types are supported: JPG and SWF. Progressive JPG, JPG with CMYK and Nested SWF files are not supported.

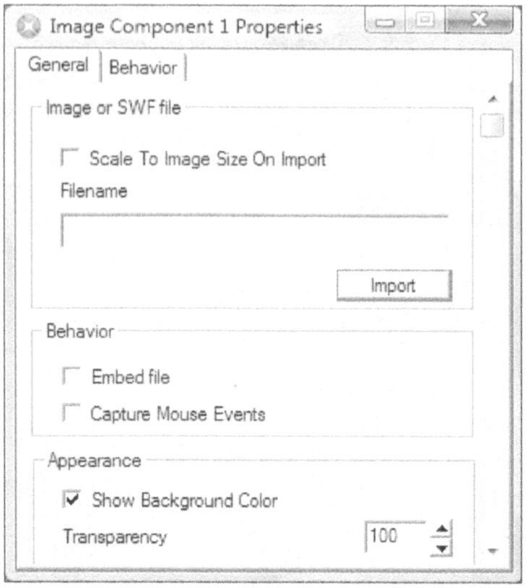

Figure 9-30 Image Component general tab options

Image Or SWF File Options

If checked, the **SCALE TO IMAGE SIZE ON IMPORT** option will import the JPG or SWF file that at its actual size. If this option is not checked, the image is resized to the size of the image component.

FILENAME You can type in the name of the image or you can click the Import button to select the file to import.

IMPORT BUTTON Is used to select the image file to be imported.

> When SWF files are imported using the Image component, the SWF file is an external file. When the dashboard is exported, the SWF files that were imported are placed in a folder with the final dashboard.

Behavior Options

EMBED FILE If checked, a copy of the image will be embedded in the model.

CAPTURE MOUSE EVENTS [See Background Component General Tab Options, earlier in this lesson]

Appearance Options

SHOW BACKGROUND COLOR This option is only available once a SWF file has been imported. It is used to select whether or not the background of the imported SWF file is displayed. If checked, the background color of the SWF file will be displayed in the image component.

Exercise 9.6: Using The Image Component

In this exercise you will add an image to an existing model. This is how you would add a corporate logo to a dashboard.

1. Save the My background model as `My image model.`

2. Add the Image Component to the top of the canvas.

3. On the General tab, click the Import button, then double-click on one of the image files in your folder.

4. Click the Fit canvas to components button on the toolbar.

5. Save the changes. You should see the image that you selected, above the chart, as shown in Figure 9-31.

Figure 9-31 Image added to the model

Vertical And Horizontal Line Components

The Vertical Line and Horizontal Line components have the same options. These components are used to add lines to the model.

General Tab Options

The options shown in Figure 9-32 are used to customize the vertical and horizontal components.

Appearance Options

LINE COLOR Is used to change the color of the line.

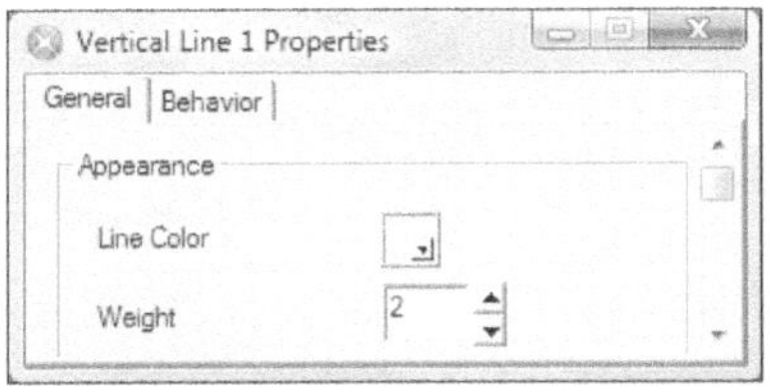

Figure 9-32 Vertical and Horizontal general tab options

Other Components

The components in this category can be used to enhance dashboards in a variety of ways. Table 9-2 explains the components in this category. The options on the Behavior tab are Dynamic Visibility options, which are covered in Lesson 11.

Component	Description
Trend Icon	Charts how the value in a cell on a spreadsheet changes, as shown in Figure 9-33. The direction that the arrow points in changes, as discussed below: ⇒ The arrow points up if the value in the cell is positive. ⇒ The arrow points down if the value in the cell is negative. ⇒ If the value in the cell is zero, a symbol is displayed instead of an arrow.
Local Scenario Buttons	This component allows users to save the current view of the dashboard. This is helpful if the user wanted to save several what-if scenarios. The saved scenario runs independently of the dashboard that it was created from.
Grid	Creates a dynamic table that displays rows and columns. You can display the data exactly like it is in the spreadsheet or you can change the appearance of the data. You can use the grid component instead of using several value components. In Exercise 7.5 you added this component to a model. [See Lesson 7, Grid Component]
Panel Set	Creates a series of frames that are used to navigate between the files in the dashboard. This component does not appear to work as intended. I could not find any information on how it should be used.

Table 9-2 Other component types explained

Figure 9-33 Trend Icon component

Trend Icon Component

This component is used to track the value in one cell and display a different color and arrow direction depending on the value. The Trend icon will remind you of an alert.

General Tab Options

The options shown in Figure 9-34 are used to customize the colors for the three value options.

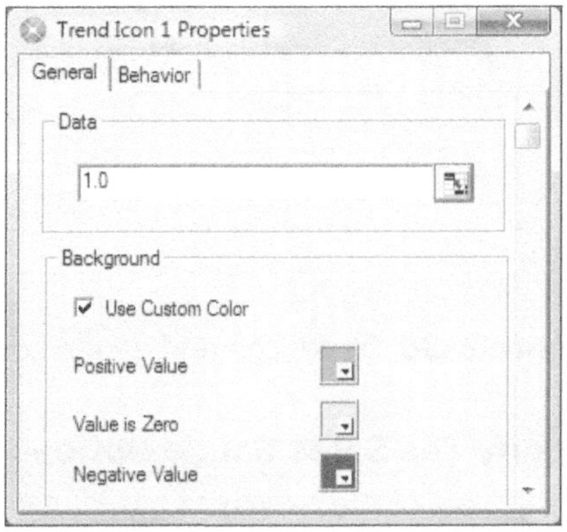

Figure 9-34 Trend Icon general tab options

Data Options

The option shown in this section is used to select the value that the Trend icon will represent.

Background Options

POSITIVE VALUE Is used to change the background color of the icon if the value is greater than zero.

VALUE IS ZERO Is used to change the background color of the icon if the value is zero.

NEGATIVE VALUE Is used to change the background color of the icon if the value is less than zero.

Exercise 9.7: Use The Trend Icon

In this exercise you will modify the Single Value alerts model by adding the Trend icon. The data range that the gauge and slider currently use is all positive. To demonstrate how the Trend icon changes based on negative numbers and zero, the value range on the slider will have to be changed.

Setup The Trend Icon

1. Save the My Single Value alerts model as `My trend icon`.
2. Add the Trend Icon-0 component to the middle of the sales gauge to cover the button that is there.
3. On the General tab for the Trend icon, select cell B5 for the Data option.

Modify The Sales Horizontal Slider Options

In this part of the exercise you will modify the sales slider to accommodate negative numbers.

1. On the Behavior tab of the Sales slider, change the Minimum Value to -100.
2. On the Appearance tab, click the Titles button, then make the changes in the table.

   These changes are necessary because you want the zero amount to be displayed and not just display a dollar sign as shown at the bottom of Figure 9-35.

Property	Change To
Numeric Format	Currency
Negative Values	-$1,234.10
Decimal Places	2
Prefix	Select this option. The $ should be visible.

Figure 9-35 Trend icon and gauge components not displaying a zero amount

Modify The Sales Gauge Options

In this part of the exercise you will modify the sales gauge to accommodate negative numbers.

1. On the Appearance tab, click on the Title button, then make the changes in the table.

   These changes are necessary because you want the zero amount to be displayed.

Property	Change To
Numeric Format	Currency
Negative Values	-$1,234.10
Decimal Places	2
Prefix	Select this option. The $ should be visible.

2. Save the changes.

Notice that when you preview the model and the slider is all the way to the left that it and the gauge display a negative number. Also notice that the trend icon component is red and pointing down, as illustrated in Figure 9-36.

When the slider reaches zero, the trend icon changes to a minus sign and displays the zero dollar amount, as illustrated in Figure 9-37.

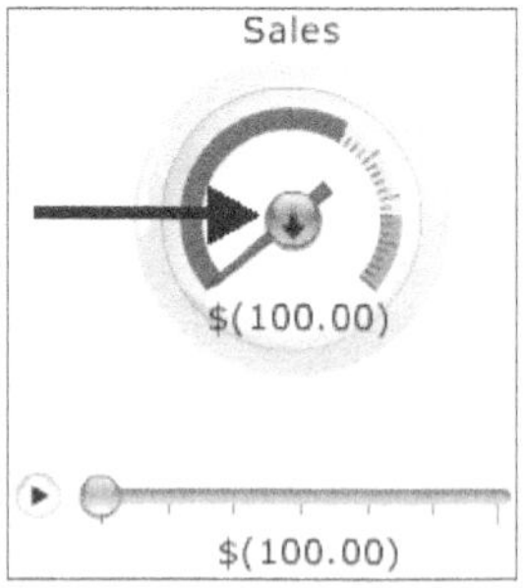

Figure 9-36 Gauge, slider and trend icon displaying a negative number

Figure 9-37 Trend icon and slider displaying a zero amount

Local Scenario Buttons Component

This component is used when users need to save their what-if analysis. Many of the models that you have created, allow the user to view data for several entities. For example, in Exercise 7.1, you learned how to create a List Box menu. This model lets the user select a branch from the menu. Once selected, the sales for the branch are displayed in the chart.

The Local Scenario Buttons component is unique in my opinion, for the two reasons discussed below.

① This component allows users to save their what-if scenarios.

② Once you add the component to the model, your job is done because the component does not need to have any options changed for it to work. However, you can change the default options, if needed.

General Tab Options

LABEL Type in or select the cell that has the data for the Local Scenario Button label, as shown in Figure 9-38.

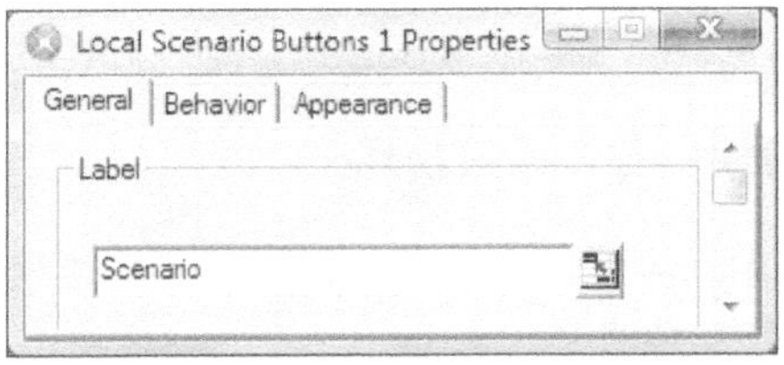

Figure 9-38 Local Scenario Buttons general tab options

Appearance Tab Options

The options shown in Figure 9-39 are used to customize the Local Scenario Buttons component.

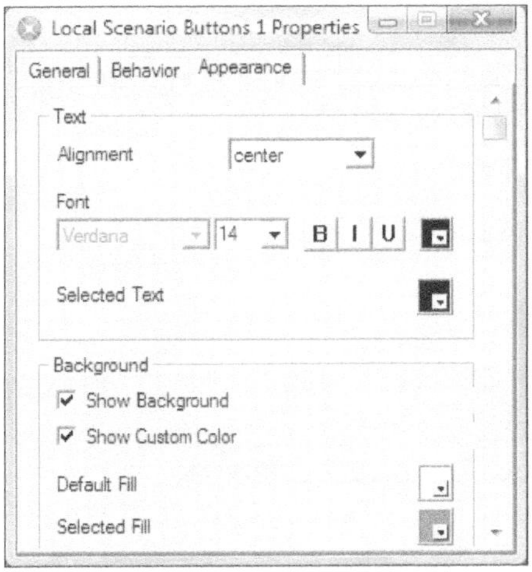

Figure 9-39 Local Scenario Buttons appearance tab options

Text Options

SELECTED TEXT Is used to change the color of the text on the scenario button.

Background Options

SHOW BACKGROUND This option must be checked to change the background color options on this tab.

SHOW CUSTOM COLOR This option must be checked to change the background colors of the scenario button.

DEFAULT FILL Is used to change the background color of the scenario button.

SELECTED FILL Is used to change the background color of the scenario button once the scenario button is clicked.

Exercise 9.8: Add The Local Scenario Buttons Component To A Model

In this exercise you will add the Local Scenario Buttons component to a model. You will also learn how to create, save and load scenarios from a users perspective.

1. Save the My radio button model as `My local scenario buttons`.

2. Add the Local Scenario Buttons component above the upper right corner of the chart, then save the changes.

3. File ⇒ Export ⇒ Adobe PDF. Type `My scenario button dashboard` as the file name.

How To Create A Scenario

In this part of the exercise you will create and save scenarios, just like a user would.

1. Open the Scenario button dashboard PDF file.

2. Select the Carmel branch.

3. Click the Scenario button, then click Save, as shown in Figure 9-40.

Figure 9-40 Local Scenario buttons on a model

4. Type `Carmel` in the field in the bottom left corner of Figure 9-41, then click the Save button.

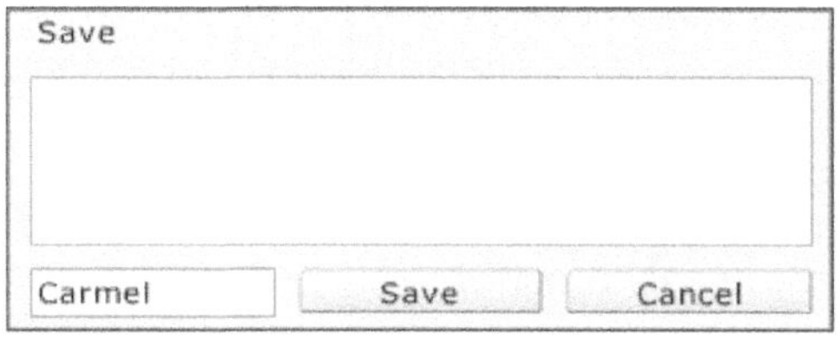

Figure 9-41 Save Scenario screen

5. Create and save a scenario for Irvine.

How To Load A Scenario

In this part of the exercise you will learn how to load saved scenarios from the dashboard file. When a scenario is loaded, it restores the model to the way it was, when the scenario was saved.

1. Click the Scenario button, then select Load.

2. Click on the Carmel scenario, then click the **LOAD** button, shown in Figure 9-42. You will see the data for Carmel.

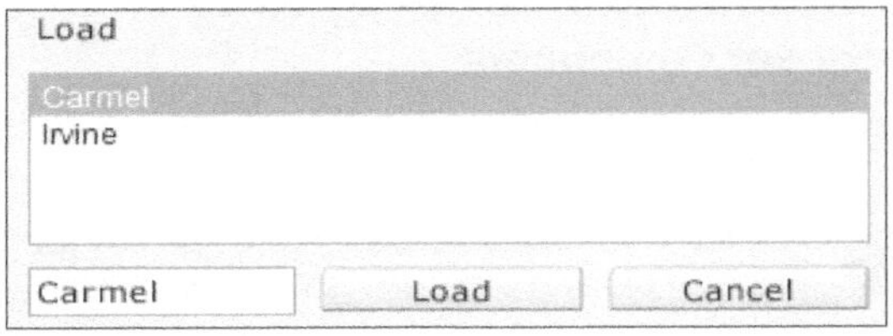

Figure 9-42 Load Scenario screen

> **Flash Player Impact On Local Scenario's**
>
> There is no limit to the number of scenarios that can be saved from a dashboard. The number of saved scenarios only becomes an issue if there is not enough hard drive space set aside for the Flash Player. In Lesson 12 you will learn how to change the local storage Flash Player Settings options to allocate more space.

The scenarios are not saved with the dashboard. This means that if one person uses the dashboard on multiple computers, each computer will only have the scenarios that were saved on that computer.

Each scenario that is saved creates a file. Over time they can build up. You can delete them from the Scenario component or you can delete them manually. The paths below are where the saved scenario files are stored. The temporary folder name is usually all caps with two numbers are the end of the folder name.

Windows Vista
C:\Users\username\AppData\Roaming\Macromedia\Flash Player\#SharedObjects\
<Temporary Folder Name>\localhost\<object name.sol>

Windows XP
C:\Documents and Settings\username\Application Data\Macromedia\Flash Player\
#SharedObjects\<Temporary Folder Name>\localhost\<object name.sol>

Panel Set Component

This component provides navigation between files through frames in the dashboard.

> I tried numerous times to get this component to work, but had no luck. After reading messages in the forum, I realized that I was not the only person that could not get it to work.

General Tab Options

The options shown in Figure 9-43 are used to select a layout and select the files that will be attached to each panel.

Layout Option

Select the layout for the Panel Set component.

Title Bars Options

The options is this section are used to select the options for the Panel Set Title bars.

SHOW TITLE BARS If checked, the frame titles will be displayed.

TITLES Is used to select or type in the title for each frame.

Content Options

PANEL Is used to select the panel that the JPG or SWF file will be linked to.

USE JPGS OR SWFS This option must be selected to be able to select the file to link to the panel. The SWFs cannot have been created in Crystal Xcelsius.

EMBEDDED Select this option to embed the JPG or SWF file that is imported.

IMPORT BUTTON Is used to select the file that you want to embed in the panel.

URL Select this option to link a file to the panel.

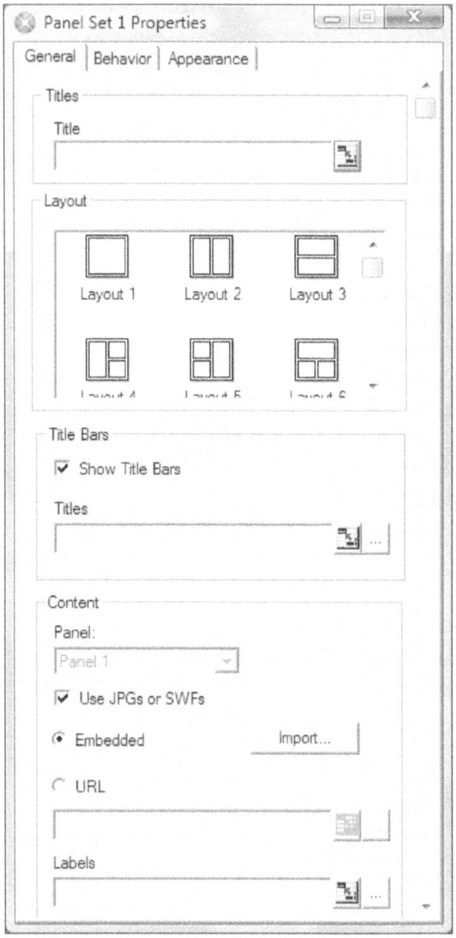

Figure 9-43 Panel Set general tab options

LABELS Is used to select or type in a name for the file that is linked or embedded in a panel.

Behavior Tab Options

The options shown in Figure 9-44 are used to select the options that will allow the user to expand one of the panels in the set.

Behavior Options

MAXIMIZED ENABLED If checked, the user can expand one of the panels in the set.

Default Options

The options in this section are used to select the default options for the panel set.

PANEL This drop-down list is used to select which panel will be displayed when the dashboard is first opened.

DEFAULT SELECTION This drop-down list is used to select the file that will be displayed in the panel selected in the Panel option.

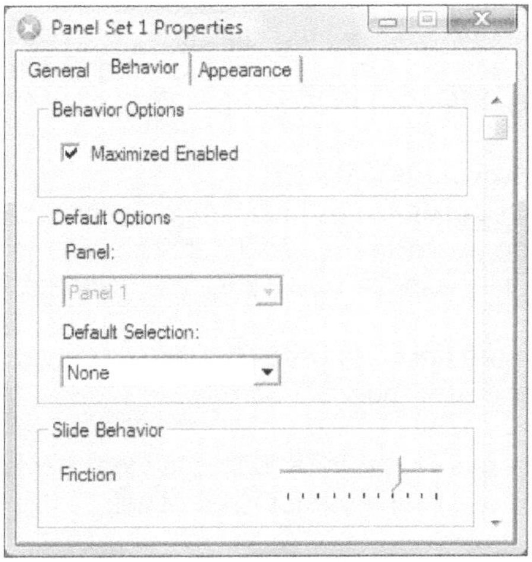

Figure 9-44 Panel Set behavior tab options

Slide Behavior Options

FRICTION Adjusts the scale to control the friction of the panel behavior.

Titles Panel Options

The Panel Set titles panel options are shown in Figure 9-45.

Drop-Down Labels Options

VISIBLE LABELS Is used to select the maximum number of options that can be displayed in the drop-down list for each panel.

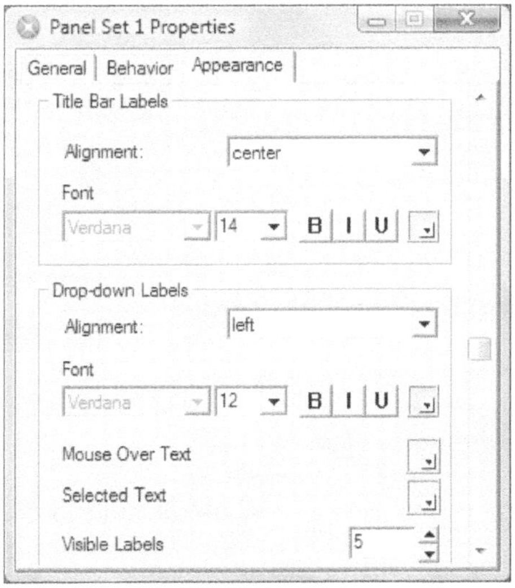

Figure 9-45 Panel Set titles panel options

Layout Panel Options

The options shown in Figure 9-46 are used to control whether or not the title on the Panel Set component is displayed.

Background Options

PANEL COLOR Is used to change the background color of the panels in the Panel Set. The color is for all of the panels in the layout that you selected.

BACKING COLOR Is used to change the background color of the Panel Set border.

TITLE BAR COLOR Is used to change the background color of the title bar for each panel.

Button Options

DEFAULT BACKGROUND Is used to change the background color of the buttons on the title bar.

DEFAULT SYMBOL Is used to change the color of the symbols on the right side of the title bar.

SELECTED BACKGROUND Is used to change the background color of the symbols in the title bar when they are selected.

SELECTED SYMBOL Is used to change the color of the symbols in the title bar when they are selected.

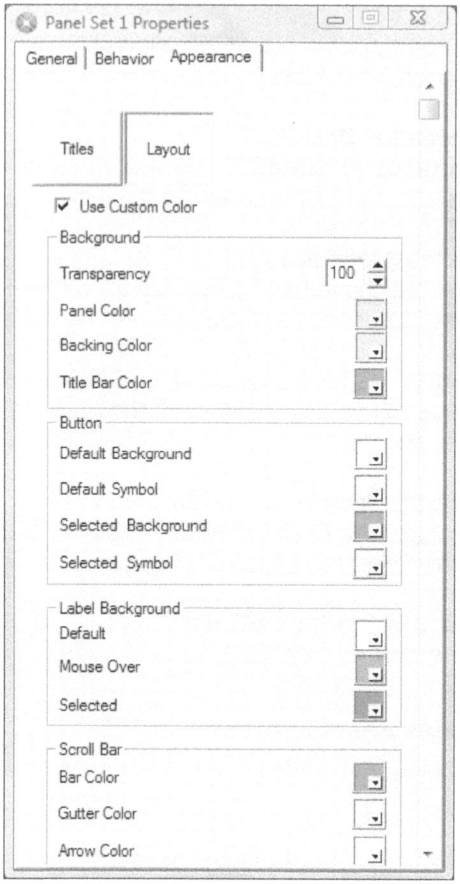

Figure 9-46 Panel Set layout panel options

Label Background Options

DEFAULT Is used to change the default color of the drop-down list.

MOUSE OVER Is used to change the color displayed when the mouse is hovered over an item in the drop-down list.

SELECTED Is used to change the color of the selected item in the drop-down list.

Scroll Bar Options

BAR COLOR Is used to change the color of the scroll bar slider on the drop-down list.

GUTTER COLOR Is used to change the color of the arrow of the scroll bar slider on the drop-down list.

ARROW COLOR Is used to change the background color of the arrow on the scroll bar slider on the drop-down list. Maybe it's me, but the gutter and arrow color options seem reversed.

Text Components

The components in this category are used to add free standing text and labels to the model. The values that are displayed in the **ENTER TEXT** option of text components do not change when the data in the model is updated. Table 9-3 explains both types of text components.

Component	Description
Input Text	Lets users type in the field. (1)
Input Text Area	This component is similar to the Input Text component. The difference is that the user can type multiple lines of text in the field.
Label	Users cannot type in this field. An unlimited amount of text can be entered in the field. This component is often used to create titles and help information for the component. Links for label components and the imported data are dynamic. (1)

Table 9-3 Text component types explained

(1) This component is covered in detail in Lesson 11.

Input Text Area Component

General Tab Options

The options shown in Figure 9-47 are used to select or type in the text for the field.

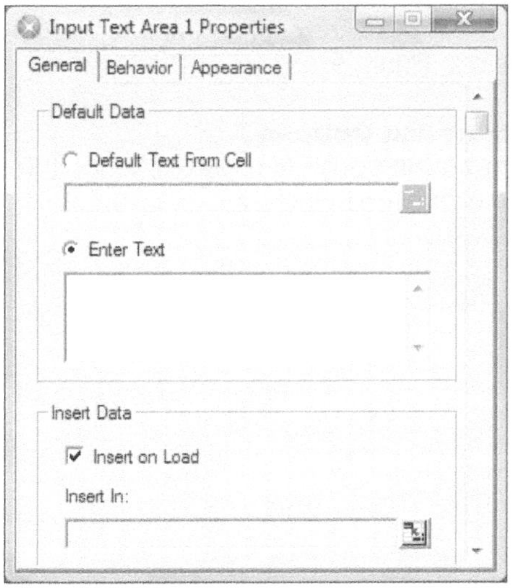

Figure 9-47 Input Text Area general tab options

Default Data Options

DEFAULT TEXT FROM CELL Is used to select the text from the spreadsheet that will be displayed in the Input Text field.

ENTER TEXT Is used to type in the default text that will be displayed in the Input Text field on the model. Select this option if the text that you need to initially display is not in the spreadsheet.

Insert Data Options

INSERT ON LOAD Is used to select the default text that will be added to the Insert In option when the dashboard is run.

INSERT IN Is used to select the cell where the text will be added.

Behavior Tab Options

The Input Text Area behavior tab options are shown in Figure 9-48.

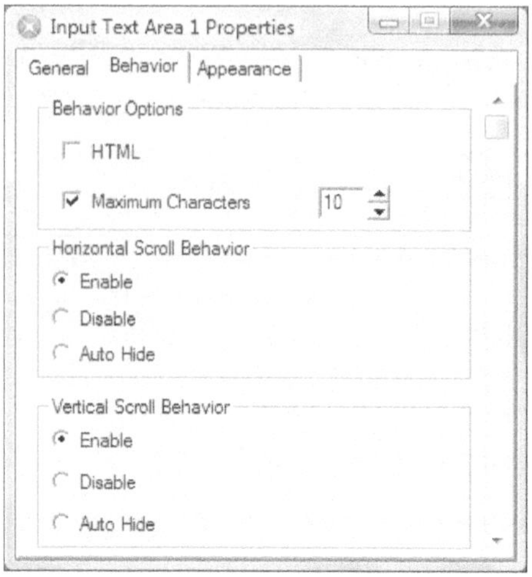

Figure 9-48 Input Text Area behavior tab options

Behavior Options

HTML If checked, the user can enter HTML tags so that the text will be displayed in HTML format.

MAXIMUM CHARACTERS Is used to select the maximum number of characters that the user can enter in the field.

Horizontal And Vertical Scroll Behavior Options

[See Lesson 7, Table Component Appearance Tab Options]

Appearance Tab Options

The Input Text Area appearance tab options are shown in Figure 9-49.

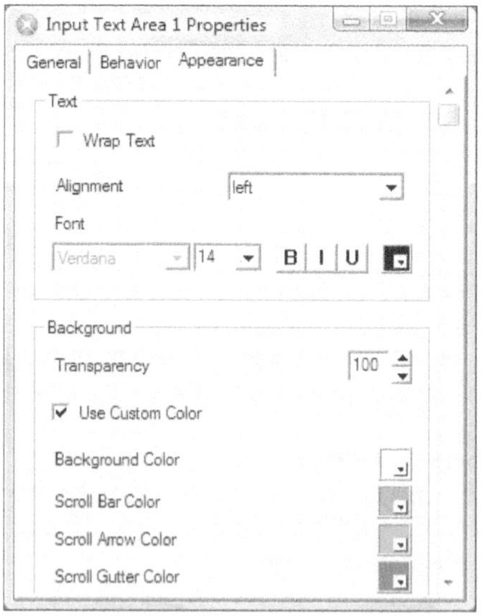

Figure 9-49 Input Text Area appearance tab options

Background Options

BACKGROUND COLOR Is used to change the background color of the area where a user enters text.

Web Connectivity Components

The components in this category allow Internet functionality to be added to a dashboard. Table 9-4 explains the Web Connectivity components.

Component	Description
External Slideshow	Creates a slideshow that uses images and SWF files that are stored on the Internet. The files do not have to be imported into the model. This component is only available in the Professional edition. [See Lesson 10, External Slide Show Component]
URL Link Button	This component is used to link a page on the Internet to a button on the model.

Table 9-4 Web connectivity component types explained

URL Link Button Component

General Tab Options

The options shown in Figure 9-50 that are specific to the URL Link Button component are explained below.

LABEL Is used to select the cell or type in the name that will appear on the button.

URL Is used to select the web site that you want the button to open when clicked.

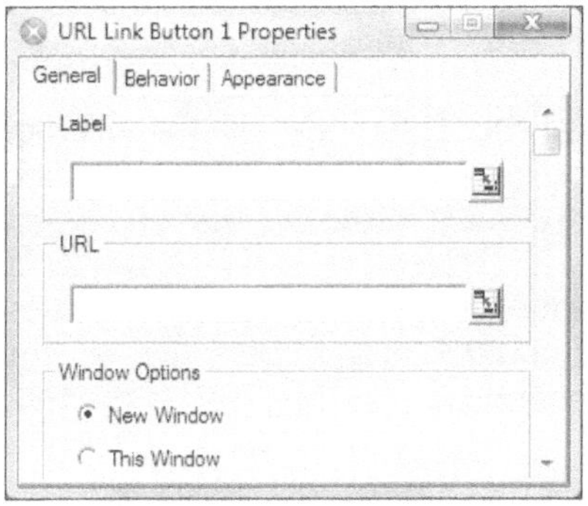

Figure 9-50 URL Link Button general tab options

Window Options

The options in this section are used to select whether or not the file or web site should be opened in a new browser window when the **URL LINK** button is clicked or if the file should be opened in the browser window that is already open.

Behavior Tab Options

The options shown in Figure 9-51 that are specific to the URL Link Button component are explained below.

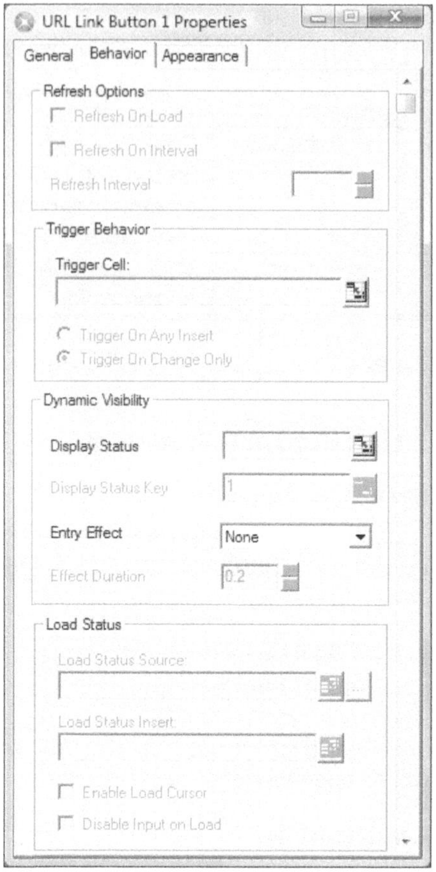

Figure 9-51 URL Link Button behavior tab options

Refresh Options

REFRESH ON LOAD If checked, the data will be refreshed when the dashboard is reloaded.

REFRESH ON INTERVAL If checked, the data will be refreshed at a specific interval that you select.

REFRESH INTERVAL Select the time in seconds when the data should be automatically refreshed.

Trigger Behavior Options

These options allow you to have the web site open if a value is added (inserted) in a specific field or if the value in a field is changed.

TRIGGER CELL Select the cell that will trigger the URL button. This means that the button will be triggered when the value in the cell that you select changes.

TRIGGER ON ANY INSERT Select this option if you want the URL button to be activated whenever a component changes the value in the trigger cell.

TRIGGER ON CHANGE ONLY Select this option if you want the URL button to be activated when the value in the trigger cell changes.

Load Status Options

These options are not available in Crystal Xcelsius 4.5.

Appearance Tab Options

The options shown in Figure 9-52 that are specific to the URL Link Button component are explained below.

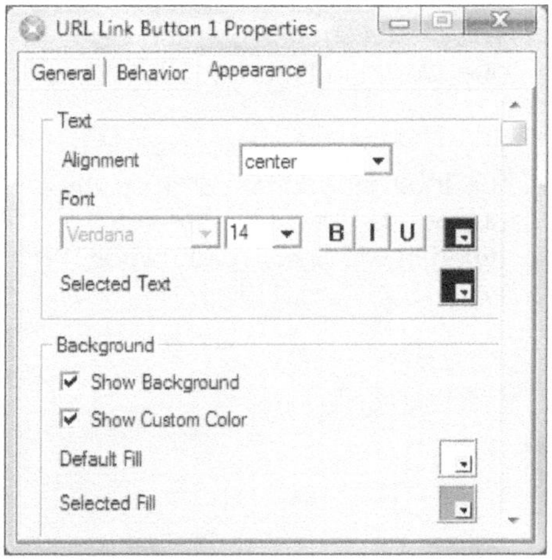

Figure 9-52 URL Link Button appearance tab options

Text Options

SELECTED TEXT Is used to change the color of the label when the button is clicked.

Background Options

SHOW BACKGROUND If checked, the background color of the URL Link Button will be displayed, otherwise you can create a text-only link. It also enables the Show Custom Color option.

SHOW CUSTOM COLOR Enables the Default Fill and Selected Fill options.

DEFAULT FILL Is used to change the default background color of the button.

SELECTED FILL Is used to change the background color of the button when it is clicked.

Exercise 9.11: Use The URL Link Button Component

If there is information on a web site that would be helpful to the user or information that would enhance the dashboard, you can create a button that is linked to the web site or specific page on a web site. You can also use this option to link to a file (like a spreadsheet) on the Internet or a server. Another popular use would be to link to a PDF file.

In this exercise you will add web connectivity to the filter drop-down list model that you created in Exercise 7.7. In this model, the URL could be used to view information about the products that the sales reps sell.

1. Save the My filter drop-down list model as `My URL product link`.

2. Move the chart down, then add the URL Link Button component right above the chart.

3. On the General tab, make the changes in the table.

Property	Change To
Label	View Products Online
URL	http://www.tolanapublishing.com

You have to type the http:// in the URL field.

4. Make the button larger so that all of the text on it is visible.

5. Save the changes.

   The model should look like the one shown in Figure 9-53.

   If your computer is connected to the Internet and you click on the button, the web site that you typed in will open in a browser window.

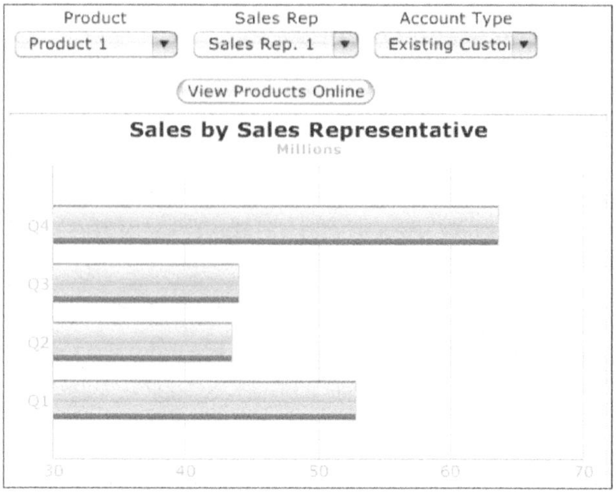

Figure 9-53 URL Link Button model

CRYSTAL XCELSIUS PROFESSIONAL

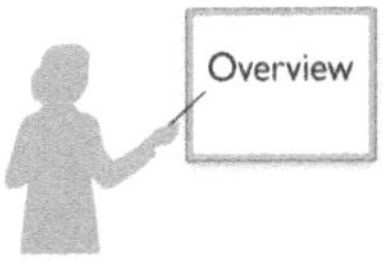

In this lesson you will learn about the following features that are only available in the professional edition of Crystal Xcelsius.

- ☑ Accordion menu
- ☑ Drill down chart
- ☑ Interactive Calendar
- ☑ Source Data component
- ☑ Fish-Eye Picture menu
- ☑ Sliding Picture menu
- ☑ External Slide Show

LESSON 10

Crystal Xcelsius Professional Overview

In this lesson you will learn how to use the features that are only available in the professional edition of Crystal Xcelsius. If you have the standard edition, you can read about these features to see if it is worth upgrading your software.

Accordion Menu Component

In Lesson 7 you learned that Accordion menus filter data based on the option selected in the menu. Components like the Accordion menu are designed to support a lot of data.

General Tab Options

The options shown in Figure 10-1 are used to select the categories and items for the menu.

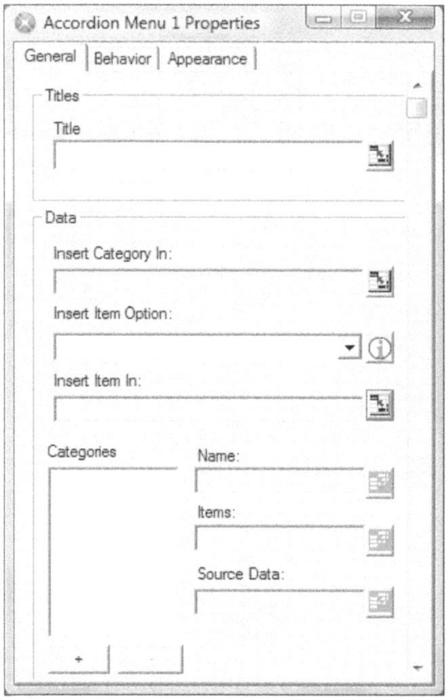

Figure 10-1 Accordion Menu general tab options

Data Options

INSERT CATEGORY IN Is used to store the destination of the data for the menu categories.

INSERT ITEM OPTION The options in this drop-down list are used to define the type of data or value that is delivered to the target destination (the Insert Item In option).

INSERT ITEM IN Is used to store the destination of the data for the item selected in the menu. The cells selected for this option should be empty.

CATEGORIES Is used to create the top level of each section of the menu.

The values in the **NAME** field are the category names on the menu.

The values in the **ITEMS** field are the items for the category selected in the Name field.

The values in the **SOURCE DATA** field is the range of data for the menu.

Behavior Tab Options

The options shown in Figure 10-2 are used to control how menu items open and close.

Open/Close Behavior Options

If the **FRICTION** scale is all the way to the right, the menu categories will open and close slowly.

Default Options

DEFAULT CATEGORY Is used to select the category that will be displayed when the dashboard is opened. The category selected filters the options that are available in the Default Item drop-down list.

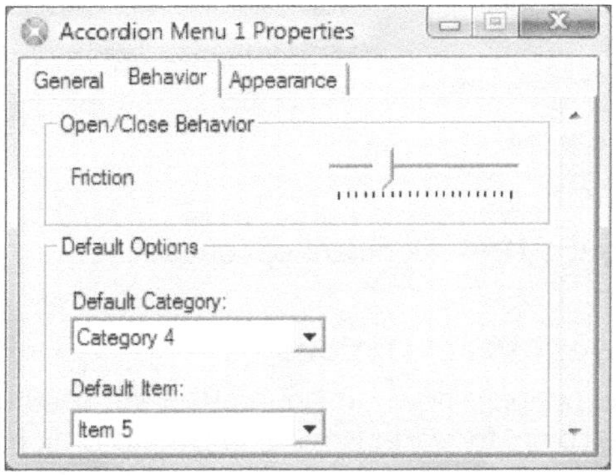

Figure 10-2 Accordion Menu behavior tab options

DEFAULT ITEM Is used to select the item that is displayed when the dashboard is opened. The options in this list correspond to the category that is selected.

Titles Panel Options

The options shown in Figure 10-3 are used to customize the category names and item labels on the menu.

Category Names

ALIGNMENT Is used to select how the categories are aligned (left, center or right). Figure 10-4 shows the Accordion menu with the category names alignment option set to left.

Item Labels Options

ALIGNMENT Is used to select how the items in the menu are aligned. Figure 10-4 shows the Accordion menu with the item labels alignment option set to center.

MOUSE OVER TEXT Is used to change the color to display when the mouse pointer is hovered over an item on the menu.

SELECTED TEXT Is used to change the color to display for the menu item that has been selected.

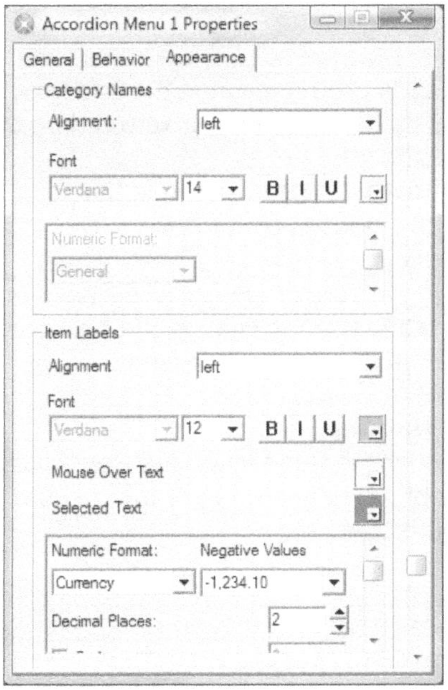

Figure 10-3 Accordion Menu titles panel options

The **NUMERIC FORMAT** options are only available if the Category Names or Item Labels options contain numeric values.

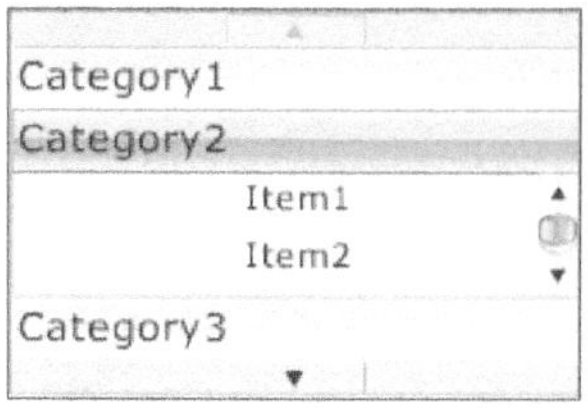

Figure 10-4 Alignment options set

Layout Panel Options

The options shown in Figure 10-5 are used to change the colors for various parts of the Accordion menu.

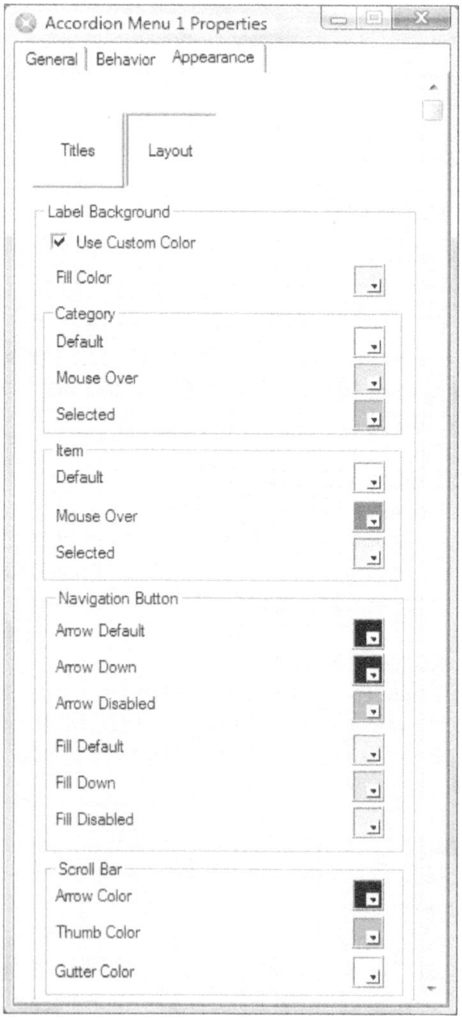

Figure 10-5 Accordion Menu layout panel options

Label Background Options

FILL COLOR Is used to change the color of the top and bottom portion of the menu where the navigation buttons are.

Category Options

The options in this section are used to change the colors of the category section of the menu shown above in Figure 10-4.

DEFAULT Is used to change the background color of the categories that are not selected on the menu.

MOUSE OVER Is used to change the color that is used when the mouse pointer hovers over a category on the menu.

SELECTED Is used to change the background color of the category that is selected.

Item Options

The options in this section are used to change the colors of the item section of the menu shown above in Figure 10-4.

DEFAULT Is used to change the background color of the items that are not selected on the menu.

MOUSE OVER Is used to change the color that is used when the mouse pointer hovers over an item on the menu.

SELECTED Is used to change the background color of the item that is selected.

Navigation Button Options

The options in this section are used to change the color of the arrow at the top and bottom of the menu.

ARROW DEFAULT Is used to change the default color of the arrow.

ARROW DOWN Is used to change the color of the arrow when it is clicked on.

ARROW DISABLED Is used to change the color of the arrow when clicking on the arrow will not display any more categories or items on the menu.

FILL DEFAULT Is used to change the background color of the arrow buttons.

FILL DOWN Is used to change the background color of the arrow button when it is clicked on.

FILL DISABLED Is used to change the background color of the arrow button when clicking on the arrow will not display any more categories or items on the menu.

Scroll Bar Options

The items in this section are used to change the color of the scroll bar on the menu.

THUMB COLOR Is used to change the color of the slider on the scroll bar on the menu.

GUTTER COLOR Is used to change the scroll bar slider background color.

Exercise 10.1: Create An Accordion Menu Dashboard

In this exercise you will design an Accordion menu that will be used to select a sales rep. When the sales rep is selected, their sales for the year will be displayed in a chart. Figure 10-6 shows the data for this exercise.

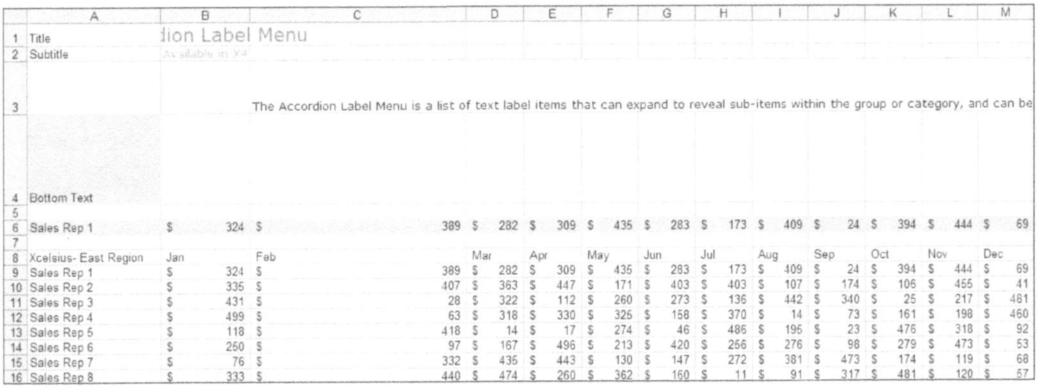

	A	B	C	D	E	F	G	H	I	J	K	L	M
1	Title	lion Label Menu											
2	Subtitle	Available in X4											
3			The Accordion Label Menu is a list of text label items that can expand to reveal sub-items within the group or category, and can be										
4	Bottom Text												
5													
6	Sales Rep 1	$ 324	$ 389	$ 282	$ 309	$ 435	$ 283	$ 173	$ 409	$ 24	$ 394	$ 444	$ 69
7													
8	Xcelsius- East Region	Jan	Feb	Mar	Apr	May	Jun	Jul	Aug	Sep	Oct	Nov	Dec
9	Sales Rep 1	$ 324	$ 389	$ 282	$ 309	$ 435	$ 283	$ 173	$ 409	$ 24	$ 394	$ 444	$ 69
10	Sales Rep 2	$ 335	$ 407	$ 363	$ 447	$ 171	$ 403	$ 403	$ 107	$ 174	$ 106	$ 455	$ 41
11	Sales Rep 3	$ 431	$ 28	$ 322	$ 112	$ 260	$ 273	$ 136	$ 442	$ 340	$ 25	$ 217	$ 481
12	Sales Rep 4	$ 499	$ 63	$ 318	$ 330	$ 325	$ 158	$ 370	$ 14	$ 73	$ 161	$ 198	$ 460
13	Sales Rep 5	$ 118	$ 418	$ 14	$ 17	$ 274	$ 46	$ 486	$ 195	$ 23	$ 476	$ 318	$ 92
14	Sales Rep 6	$ 250	$ 97	$ 167	$ 496	$ 213	$ 420	$ 256	$ 276	$ 98	$ 279	$ 473	$ 53
15	Sales Rep 7	$ 76	$ 332	$ 435	$ 443	$ 130	$ 147	$ 272	$ 381	$ 473	$ 174	$ 119	$ 68
16	Sales Rep 8	$ 333	$ 440	$ 474	$ 260	$ 362	$ 160	$ 11	$ 91	$ 317	$ 481	$ 120	$ 57

Figure 10-6 Accordion Menu data

1. Import the Accordion Menu spreadsheet.

2. Add the Accordion Menu component to the left side of the canvas, then add the Column Chart component to the right of the menu. Make the menu and chart the same length.

3. Save the model as `My accordion menu`.

Select The Chart Options

1. On the General tab, make the changes in the table.

Property	Change To
Chart title	A6 (1)
Chart subtitle	Thousands $
Data Range	B6:M6
Category Axis Labels	B8:M8

(1) The data in this cell will change when a different option is selected on the menu.

2. On the Behavior tab, make the changes in the table.

Property	Change To
Manual Scale	Select this option
Y-Axis Maximum Value	500
Auto Scale	Select this option

3. On the Appearance tab, click the Series button, then change the Bar Width option to 15.

Select The Accordion Menu Options

1. On the General tab, make the changes in the table.

Property	Change To
Insert Item Option	Rows
Insert Item In	A6:M6

Insert Item In This range of cells in the spreadsheet should either be empty or contain data that can be overwritten because the range will be used to store the selections made on the Accordion menu. As you saw when you selected the cells for the Insert Item In option, the range of cells was not empty. The values that you see in the range are for the sales rep whose data will be displayed by default.

2. On the General tab, add the following categories by clicking the plus sign button below the **CATEGORIES** list box. You should have the options shown in Figure 10-7.

Name	Items	Source Data
A8	A9:A16	A9:M16
A19	A20:A35	A20:M35
A39	A40:A62	A40:M62
A65	A66:A97	A66:M97

The Name field contains the regions.

The range in the Items field will display the sales reps for the region.

The Source Data field contains the sales reps monthly sales for a region.

Figure 10-7 General tab options

3. On the Behavior tab, make the changes in the table. You should have the options shown in Figure 10-8.

Property	Change To
Sound Enabled	Select this option
Default Category	Category 1
Default Item	Item 1

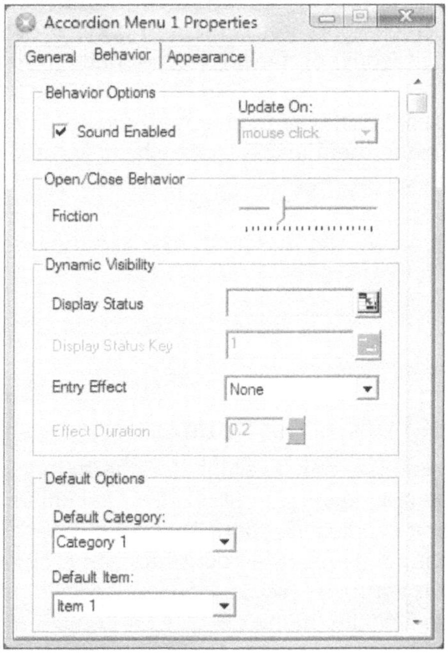

Figure 10-8 Behavior tab options

4. Save the changes. When an item in the menu is selected, the corresponding sales rep data is displayed in the chart. Click on the West region in the menu, then select Sales Rep 12. The model should look like the one shown in Figure 10-9.

When you select an option in the menu, you should hear a clicking sound.

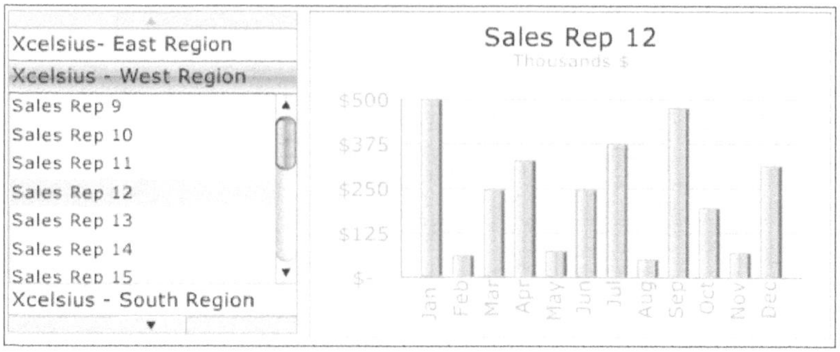

Figure 10-9 Accordion dashboard

If the number of items in the menu is longer than the space allocated for the menu, a scroll bar is automatically added, as shown above in Figure 10-9. The arrow at the top and bottom of the menu lets the user know that there are additional menu options that are not visible.

Modify The Menu Options

As shown above in Figure 10-9, the word Xcelsius starts each category in the menu. I don't know about you, but I would prefer not to see that.

The easiest way to change the category names is to change them in the spreadsheet and then re-import the spreadsheet.

If you do, the menu will look like the one shown in Figure 10-10.

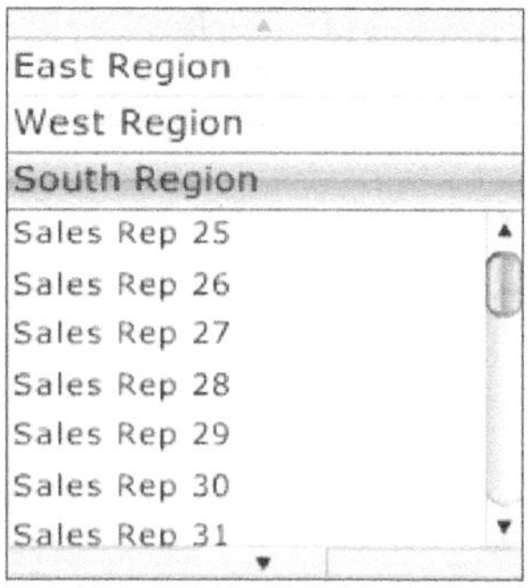

Figure 10-10 Modified menu names

Drill Down Tab Options

This tab is only available for charts that have more than one series of data. Figure 10-11 shows the drill down tab options for a combination chart. Figure 10-12 shows the drill down tab options for a candlestick chart. Drill down options add additional functionality to charts. When this feature is implemented, users can click on a part of the chart and view the detailed information that was used to summarize a specific part of the chart. The chart that has drill down functionality mimics a selector component because the chart is used to select the data that is displayed in another component on the dashboard. The options are explained below.

> Area, Stacked Area, Radar and Filled Radar are the only chart types that do not have drill down capabilities.

Combination Chart Drill Down Tab Options

The options shown in Figure 10-11 are used to set up drill down functionality for a Combination chart.

ENABLE DRILL DOWN Must be selected if you want to add drill down features to the chart.

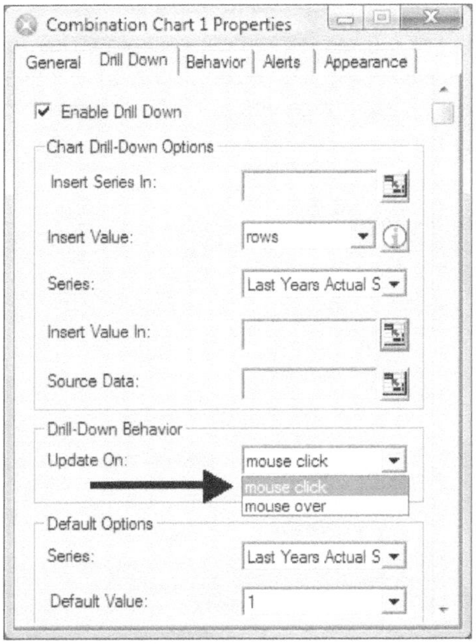

Figure 10-11 Combination chart drill down tab options

Chart Drill-Down Options

The options in this section determine what happens when a section of the chart is selected to be drilled down on. The options may look familiar from the selector component options that you learned about in Lesson 7.

INSERT SERIES IN Is used to select the cell where the selected series of data is added.

INSERT VALUE Is used to select the structure of the data that is added when a selection is made. [See Lesson 7, Common Selector General Tab Insert Data Options]

SERIES Is used to select the series of data to configure the drill down options for.

INSERT VALUE IN Is used to select the cells where the inserted data will be added.

SOURCE DATA Is only available if the Insert Value option is set to rows or columns. This option is used to select the range of data to display on the chart.

Drill-Down Behavior Option

UPDATE ON Is used to select how the chart should recognize that an option on the chart has been selected. The two options are illustrated above in Figure 10-11.

Default Options

The options in this section are used to select the default values for the chart when it is first displayed.

The **SERIES** drop-down list contains the series of data that the chart has. Select the series that you want displayed when the dashboard is first opened.

The **DEFAULT VALUE** drop-down list is used to select the value that will be selected automatically when the dashboard is first opened.

Candlestick Chart Drill Down Options

The options shown in Figure 10-12 are used to set up drill down functionality for a Candlestick chart.

Chart Drill-Down Options

SELECT VARIABLE Is only available if the Insert Value is set to open. The options shown are used to select which stock price you want to drill down on.

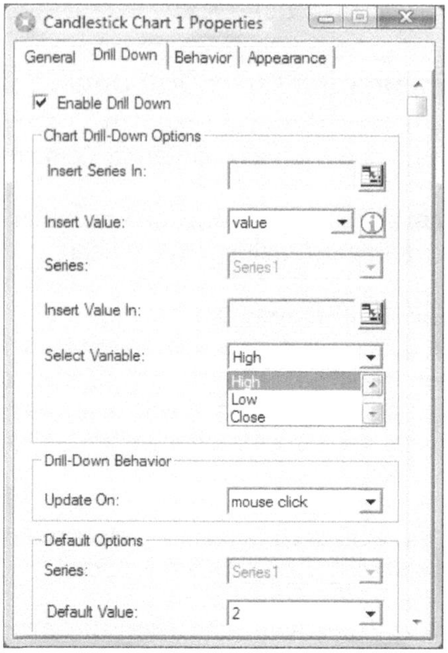

Figure 10-12 Candlestick chart drill down tab options

Exercise 10.2: Create A Drill Down Chart Dashboard

In this exercise you will add two charts to the model. You will add a pie chart that will be used to select a branch. Once selected, the sales data for the branch will be displayed in the column chart. Figure 10-13 shows the data for this exercise.

	A	B	C	D	E	F	G	H	I	J	K	L	M	N
1	**Insert In Range**													
2														
3														
4	**Actual Data**													
5	Sales by Branch	Jan	Feb	Mar	Apr	May	Jun	Jul	Aug	Sep	Oct	Nov	Dec	Totals
6	Atherton	$4.6	$3.0	$6.9	$5.4	$6.8	$9.0	$4.3	$5.6	$8.3	$8.9	$6.5	$3.0	$72.1
7	Berkeley	$13.0	$8.3	$11.3	$10.7	$8.8	$9.9	$7.8	$10.1	$7.1	$10.2	$10.0	$8.6	$115.8
8	Cupertino	$6.0	$6.4	$6.5	$5.5	$7.0	$6.1	$5.2	$7.8	$7.2	$5.0	$4.8	$5.9	$73.5
9	Fremont	$8.5	$6.2	$7.3	$9.7	$8.3	$11.0	$7.3	$9.5	$7.6	$6.1	$6.9	$8.8	$97.3
10	Milpitas	$9.9	$8.5	$9.2	$5.6	$8.1	$9.6	$9.3	$9.4	$5.7	$7.5	$5.9	$5.2	$93.9
11	San Francisco	$27.5	$28.4	$28.1	$27.6	$25.0	$25.9	$27.2	$29.3	$26.7	$29.0	$28.2	$29.4	$332.3

Figure 10-13 Drill down chart data

1. Import the Drill Down Chart spreadsheet.
2. Add the Pie chart component, then add the Column Chart component below it.
3. Save the model as `My drill-down chart.`

Select The Pie Chart Options

The pie chart will be used as a selector. The user will click on a slice of the pie and the corresponding sales data for the branch will be displayed in the column chart. The pie chart will have the drill down options.

1. On the General tab, make the changes in the table.

Property	Change To
Chart title	A5
Data Range	N6:N11
Category Axis Labels	A6:A11

2. On the Appearance tab, click the Series button, then make the changes in the table.

Property	Change To
Show Lines	Select this option
Weight	1
Data Point	Atherton

3. On the Appearance tab, click the Layout button, then make the changes in the table.

Property	Change To
Show Background	Select this option
Use Custom Color	Select this option

Select The Drill Down Options For The Pie Chart

The drill down options are used to link the two charts together. The pie chart is like a table of contents and will be used as a selector component. The column chart is used to display the detail information for the slice of the pie that is selected.

1. On the Drill Down tab, make the changes in the table.

Property	Change To
Enable Drill Down	Select this option
Insert Value	Rows
Insert Value In	A2:M2
Source Data	A6:M11

You should have the options shown in Figure 10-14.

Save the changes.

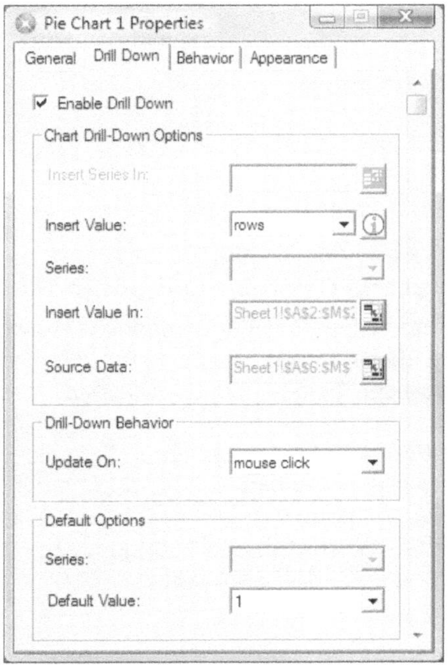

Figure 10-14 Drill Down tab options

Select The Column Chart Options

1. On the General tab, make the changes in the table.

Property	Change To
Chart title	A2
Chart subtitle	Monthly Sales
Data Range	B2:M2
X Values	B2:M2
Category Axis Labels	B5:M5

2. On the Behavior tab, make the changes in the table.

Property	Change To
Manual Scale	Select this option
Y-Axis Maximum Value	500
Auto Scale	Select this option

3. Save the changes.

   If you hold the mouse over the San Francisco slice of the pie chart, you will see the information shown at the top of Figure 10-15.

   If you click on the San Francisco slice of the pie chart, you will see the monthly sales in the column chart below, for San Francisco.

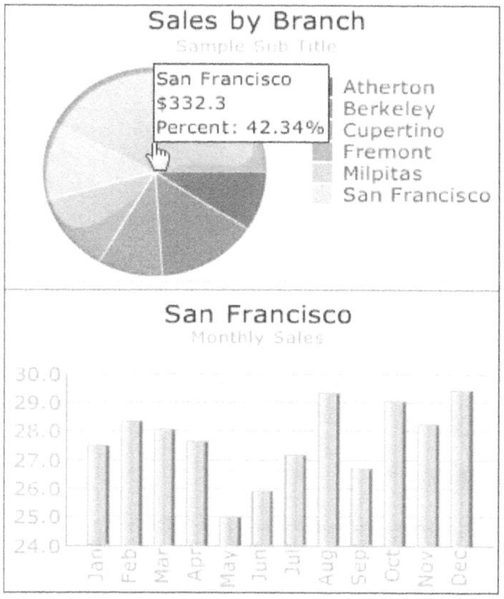

Figure 10-15 Drill down chart model

Interactive Calendar Component

The Interactive Calendar component shown in Figure 10-16 is used to browse the data from a spreadsheet, by day, month and year.

Once the user clicks on a date in the calendar, the corresponding data will be displayed in the another component on the dashboard. There are two ways to select the date range for the calendar component, as discussed below.

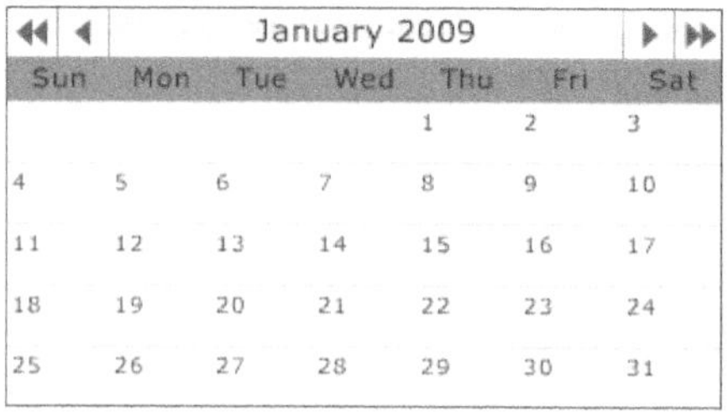

Figure 10-16 Calendar component

① Limit the range of dates that can be selected by setting a minimum and maximum value for the month and year.
② Do not put any limits on the dates that can be viewed.

General Tab Options

Insert Data Options

The options in this section are shown in Figure 10-17. They are used to select how the calendar will respond when a selection is made.

INSERT YEAR IN Is used to select the empty cell for the year.

INSERT MONTH IN Is used to select the empty cell for the month.

INSERT OPTION Select the **DAY** or **DATE** option from the drop-down list to indicate the format of the date that will be inserted.

INSERT SOURCE DATA IN Is used to select the cell that the date will be placed in.

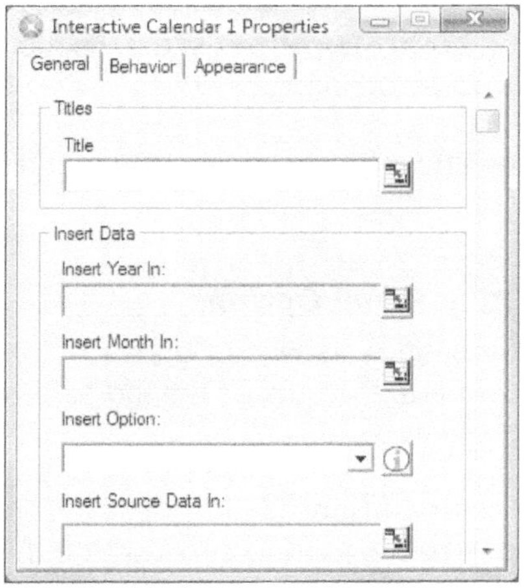

Figure 10-17 Interactive Calendar general tab options

Behavior Tab Options

The Behavior tab sets the default date and date range for the calendar. I find it easier to type in the day, month and year options, then to select them from the spreadsheet. That and the spreadsheet data is probably not in an appropriate format for the options on this tab <smile>.

Default Date Options

The options in this section are shown in Figure 10-18. They are used to select the day, month and year that are displayed when the dashboard is first opened.

Default Date Options

USE CURRENT DATE Select this option if you want the default date to be today when the dashboard is opened.

USE CUSTOM DATE Select the default date for the calendar when the dashboard is first opened.

The **DEFAULT MONTH, DEFAULT YEAR** and **DEFAULT DAY** options are used to select the day, month and year that is displayed on the calendar when the dashboard is first opened.

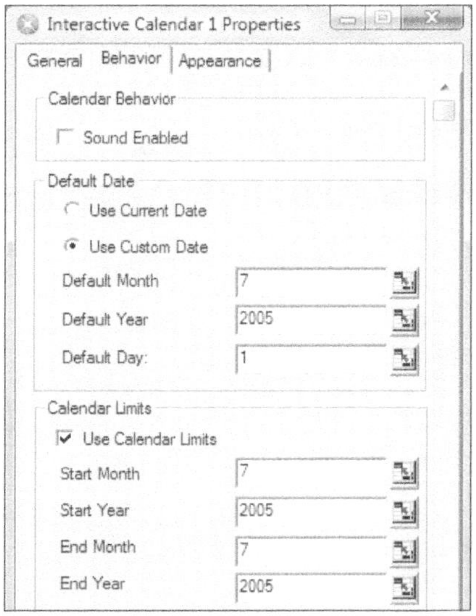

Figure 10-18 Interactive Calendar behavior tab options

Calendar Limits Options

The options in this section are used to select a specific date or range of dates that can be selected on the calendar.

USE CALENDAR LIMITS The option must be checked to select a date range for the calendar.

The **START MONTH** and **START YEAR** options are used to select the first month and year that can be accessed in the calendar.

The **END MONTH** and **END YEAR** options are used to select the last month and year that can be accessed in the calendar.

Titles Panel Options

The options shown in Figure 10-19 are used to customize the titles, days and dates on the calendar.

Month Options

POSITION Is used to select where the month and year at the top of the calendar should be placed.

Day Of The Week Options

POSITION Is used to select where the days of the week at the top of the calendar should be placed in their cells.

Date Options

The options in this section are used to customize the dates in the grid portion of the calendar.

MOUSE OVER TEXT Is used to change the background color of the cell in the grid when the mouse is hovered over a date.

SELECTED TEXT Is used to change the background color of the cell in the grid that is clicked on.

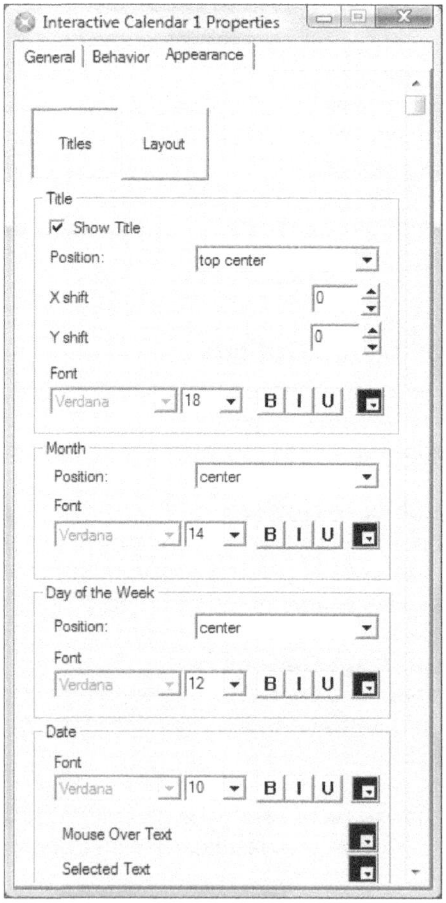

Figure 10-19 Interactive Calendar titles panel options

Layout Panel Options

The options shown in Figure 10-20 are used to select the colors for different parts of the calendar.

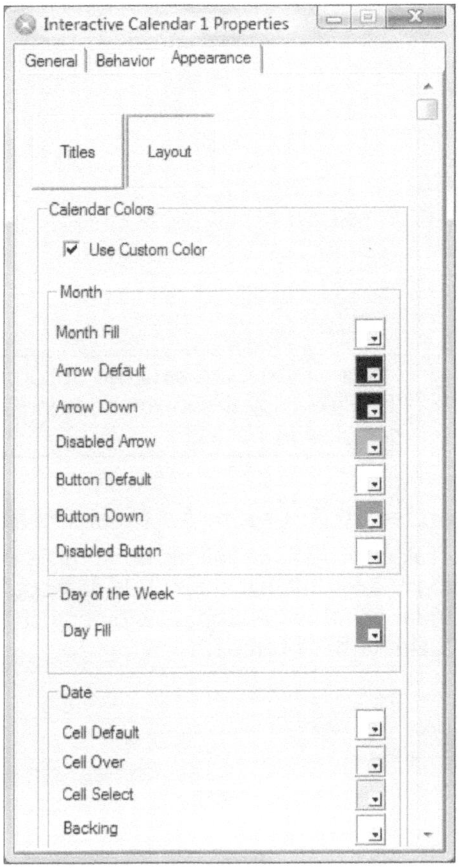

Figure 10-20 Interactive Calendar layout panel options

Month Options

The options in this section are used to change the appearance of the month and year at the top of the calendar.

MONTH FILL Is used to change the background color of the month and year at the top of the calendar.

ARROW DEFAULT Is used to change the color of the arrows next to the month and year.

DISABLED ARROW Is used to change the color of an arrow that is at the beginning or end of the calendar range. This means that clicking on the arrow will not display another month.

BUTTON DEFAULT Is used to change the background color of the arrow button.

BUTTON DOWN Is used to change the background color of the arrow button when the button is clicked.

DISABLED BUTTON Is used to change the background color of a button when it is disabled.

Day Of The Week Option

DAY FILL Is used to change the background color of the days of the week at the top of the calendar.

Date Options

The options in this section are used to change the color of the dates in the grid portion of the calendar.

CELL DEFAULT Is used to change the background color of the dates.

CELL OVER Is used to change the background color to display when the mouse pointer hovers over a date.

CELL SELECT Is used to change the background color of the date that is currently selected.

BACKING Is used to change the background color of the calendar, as shown in Figure 10-21.

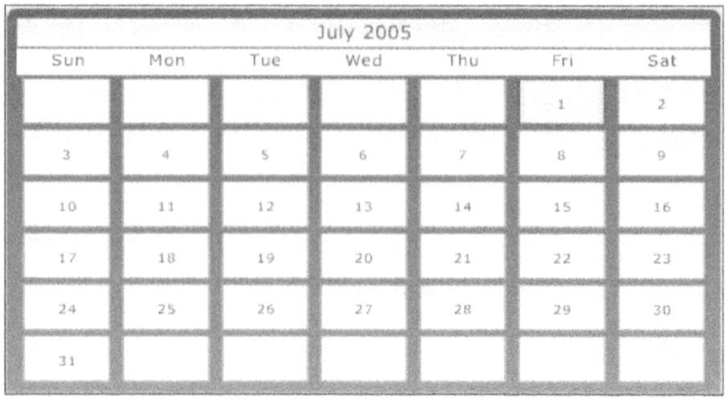

Figure 10-21 Backing option in the Halo skin

> I could not get the **BACKING** option to work with all skins. For example, it works with the Halo skin, as shown above in Figure 10-21, but not with the Aqua skin, which is the default skin.

Exercise 10.3: Create An Interactive Calendar Dashboard

The calendar that you will set up in this exercise will be used as an input component to display the daily sales in a bar chart. This dashboard will let the user select a day in July 2005 in the calendar and then see the sales by branch for the day that was selected. Figure 10-22 shows the data for this exercise.

	A	B	C	D	E	F	G	H	I	J
1										
2	Calendar Insert In Cell	7/1/2005								
3	Chart Data Range	$12.54	$12.65	$17.24	$10.79	$18.06	$15.98	$24.22	$9.92	$23.02
4	Chart Subtitle	7/1/2005								
5										
6										
7	Daily Sales by Branch	Atherton	Berkeley	Carmel	Cupertino	Fremont	Irvine	Milpitas	Orange Co	San Franc
8	7/1/2005	$12.54	$12.65	$17.24	$10.79	$18.06	$15.98	$24.22	$9.92	$23.02
9	7/2/2005	$11.02	$14.63	$17.33	$10.35	$20.13	$15.54	$23.61	$8.93	$22.00
10	7/3/2005	$12.77	$12.24	$19.50	$9.85	$19.43	$14.29	$22.50	$9.47	$23.10

Figure 10-22 Interactive calendar data

1. Import the Interactive Calendar spreadsheet.
2. Add the Interactive Calendar component.
3. Add the Bar Chart component below the calendar. Make both of the components larger.
4. Save the model as `My interactive calendar`.

Select The Bar Chart Options

1. On the General tab, make the changes in the table.

Property	Change To
Chart title	A7
Chart subtitle	B4 (2)
Data Range	B3:J3
Series Name	B4
Category Axis Labels	B7:J7

(2) Selecting this cell means that a different date will be displayed in the Chart subtitle field on the bar chart each time a different date is selected in the calendar.

2. On the Behavior tab, make the changes in the table.

Property	Change To
Manual Scale	Select this option
Y-Axis Maximum Value	500
Auto Scale	Select this option

3. On the Appearance tab, click the Series button, then make the changes in the table.

Property	Change To
Bar Width	15
Numeric Format	Currency
Decimal Places	2
Prefix	Select this option, then select the $, as shown at the bottom of Figure 10-23.

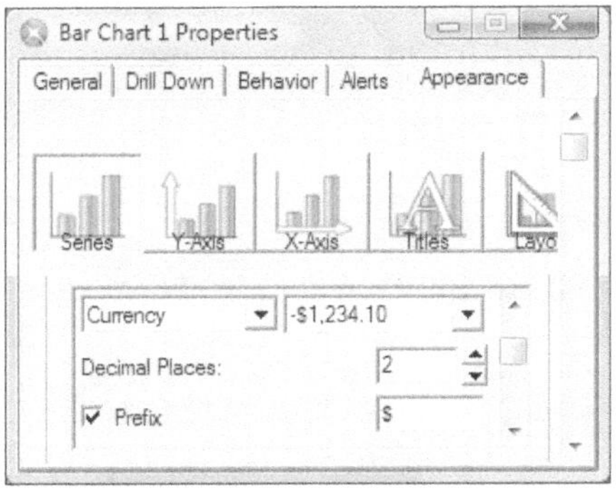

Figure 10-23 Prefix options

Select The Interactive Calendar Options

1. On the General tab, make the changes in the table.

Property	Change To
Insert Option	Date
Insert Source Data In	B2

2. On the Behavior tab, make the changes in the table.

   In this exercise the user can only select a day in July 2005.

   You should have the options shown earlier in Figure 10-18.

Property	Change To
Use Custom Date	Select this option
Default Month	7
Default Year	2005
Default Day	1
Use Calendar Limits	Select this option
Start Month	7
Start Year	2005
End Month	7
End Year	2005

3. Save the changes. The calendar should look like the one shown in Figure 10-24.

   When you click on a date in the calendar, the corresponding daily branch sales will be displayed in the bar chart.

   If you hold the mouse pointer over a bar in the chart, as shown at the bottom of Figure 10-24, you will be able to see the exact amount of the sales for the branch, for the date that is selected.

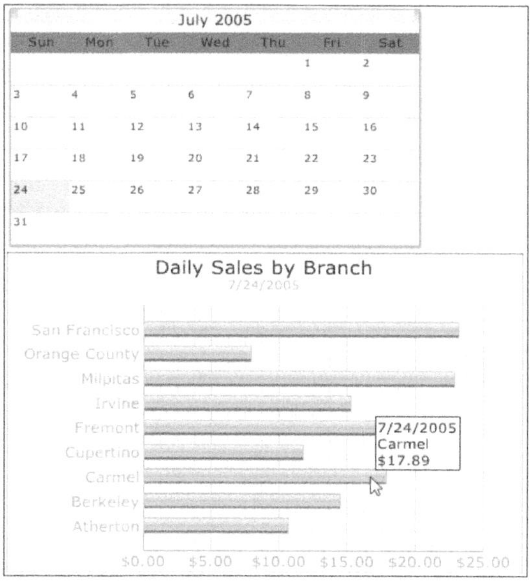

Figure 10-24 Interactive Calendar model

Notice that the calendar shown above in Figure 10-24 does not have any navigation options, which would allow the user to select a day in a different month. That is because the date range for the calendar is only one month.

Figure 10-25 shows a calendar that will allow dates from more than one month to be selected.

Figure 10-25 Calendar with navigation options

> **Using The Arrow Keys**
>
> In some calendars, you can use the arrow keys on the keyboard to select calendar options. In Crystal Xcelsius, the keyboard arrow keys do not work with the Interactive Calendar component.

Source Data Component

General Tab Options

[See Lesson 7, Common Selector General Tab Options]

Behavior Tab Options

The option shown in Figure 10-26 is specific to the Source Data Component.

INDEX CELL Is used to select the cell that will bind the Selected Index of the Source Data Component to the spreadsheet. If the value in the cell selected changes, it will be updated.

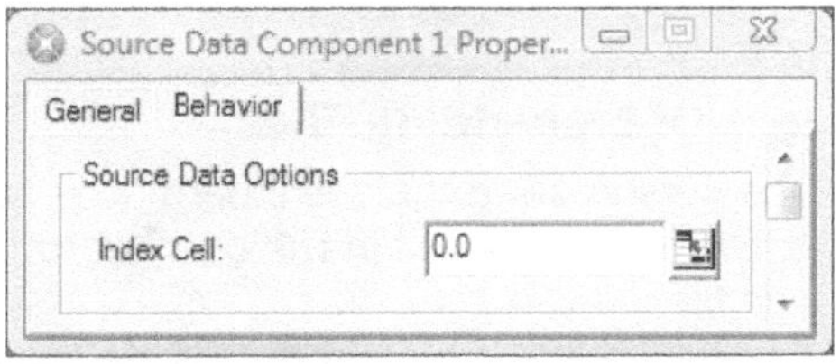

Figure 10-26 Source Data behavior tab options

External Files

More than likely, at some point you will have the need to use an external file for a dashboard that you create. Unlike the spreadsheet data which Crystal Xcelsius automatically embeds a copy of, you have the option of embedding other types of external files. Having the ability to incorporate external files into a model opens up a lot of possibilities for a dashboard. The next two sections discuss the external file types that you can use.

Nested Flash Files

The most interesting external file option to me is the ability to import a Flash file that was not created in Crystal Xcelsius into a model. This means that once you compile the model, the dashboard will have two SWF files. If this is something that you plan to do, if possible, embed all of the objects in the SWF file that you want to import into the model, so that you do not have to put a copy of any of the external files in the folder that the model uses for external file.

This is not a requirement. The reason to embed the objects is because the model can only look in one folder for files that are referenced. If the SWF file references files in the folder SWF/Images and you import the SWF file into a model, the model can only look in the folder that the saved the model in. This is where the files for the imported SWF file would have to be moved to, so that the model can find them.

Embedding Files

A good rule of thumb to follow in deciding whether or not to embed a file is who the user group is and how will they use the dashboard. If the user group will primarily use the dashboard on a desktop computer you can probably get away with not embedding the external files. Why? Because people tend not to move desktop computers around. If the user group will use the dashboard on a laptop, to me, that means that it is very possible that the dashboard could be used in a conference room, on a airplane or in a convention center, all of which may not have access to the server that the external files would be stored on.

The decision to embed files should be done on a dashboard by dashboard basis. Like a lot of things in life, there are advantages and disadvantages of embedding external files as discussed below. Depending on the environment that a dashboard will be used in, there could be more advantages or disadvantages than those discussed here.

Advantages Of Embedding Files

① The person using the dashboard does not need to have access to a server because all of the files are saved in the dashboard file. This means that you only have to distribute one file.

② Embedded files maintain their state (on or off) when hidden, using the dynamic visibility options.

③ Dynamic visibility functionality is faster because objects do not have to be reloaded.

Advantages Of Not Embedding Files

① The model does not have to be recompiled if a change is made to an external file.

② Load times are shorter because the external files are only loaded when needed. If all of the files are saved in the dashboard file, they are all loaded, whether or not they are accessed when the dashboard is run.

③ Run time performance can increase because external files are unloaded when dynamic visibility functionality is enabled to hide the files.

Picture Menus

Believe it or not, the Fish-Eye and Sliding Picture Menus are very similar to the other types of menus that you have learned how to create. They have many of the same options that other selector components have. The main difference is that pictures are used for the menu items instead of text. The steps required to create a Fish-Eye or Sliding Picture Menu are basically the same.

What Is The Difference Between Fish-Eye And Sliding Picture Menus?

In Lesson 7 you saw screen shots of the picture menus that you will create in this lesson. There are two noticeable differences between these picture menu components, as discussed below.

① By default, the Fish-Eye Menu displays all of the images. If you are using a lot of images, which makes the final display size of the dashboard larger than you need it to be, use the Sliding Picture Menu.

② The Sliding Picture menu has an option that controls the number of images that are displayed in the menu. This picture menu has arrows that are used to scroll through the pictures, one at a time or several at a time. The Sliding Picture Menu is better suited for menus that have a lot of images or if you need to control the display size of the menu.

Picture Menu Components

As stated earlier, the Fish-Eye and Sliding Picture Menu components are very similar. Options specific to either component are discussed later in this lesson.

Common Picture Menu General Tab Options

The options shown in Figure 10-27 are used to select and configure the image files for both picture menu components.

Titles Options

If you want to change the Label names from what they are in the spreadsheet, click the Browse button next to the Labels option to change the name, as shown in Figure 10-28.

Image Files Options

The options in this section are used to add images to the component.

EMBEDDED Is used to add a copy of the image to the model, so that it will always be available.

URL Is used to create a link to the image. The images do not have to be on the Internet to use this option. This option can be used to point to images on your hard drive (not the best option), on a network or shared drive.

Keep in mind that if the images are on a hard drive of any type and the drive is not working (is down), the images will not be available when the dashboard is run.

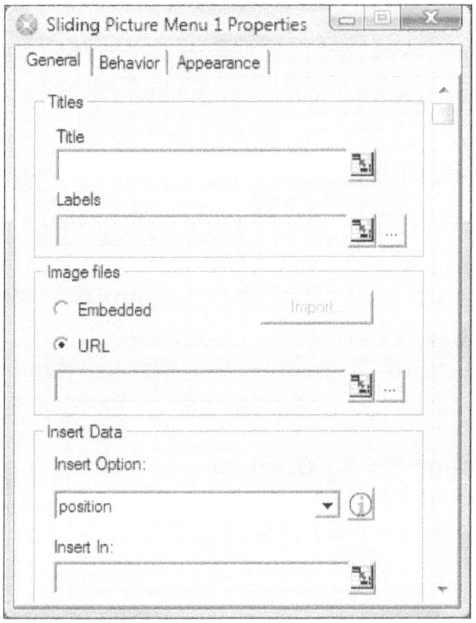

Figure 10-27 Fish-Eye and Sliding Picture Menu general tab options

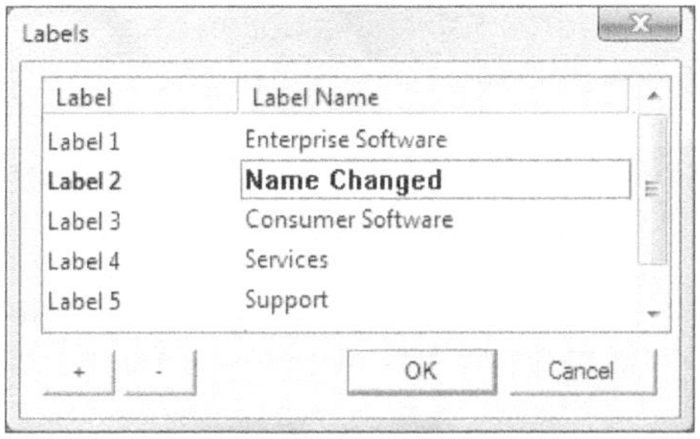

Figure 10-28 Labels dialog box

How To Determine Which Image Option Is Best

This decision should be made on a case by case basis. If the embedded option is selected and the images change, the model will have to be exported again and the dashboard will have to be redistributed. The options below are my summary of how to select the appropriate image option.

① Select the **EMBEDDED OPTION** if there are a small number of images or the images will not need to be changed on a regular basis.
② Select the **URL OPTION** if there are a lot of images or the images will change on a regular basis. With this option, when an image file changes, the model does not have to be exported again, unless the file name or location of the image changes.

Common Picture Menu Behavior Tab Options

[See Lesson 7, Common Selector Behavior Tab Options]

Common Picture Menu Titles Panel Options

[See Lesson 7, Common Selector Appearance Tab Options]

Common Picture Menu Layout Panel Options

The options on the Layout panel shown in Figure 10-29 are used to customize the image size, margins, colors and thumbnail background.

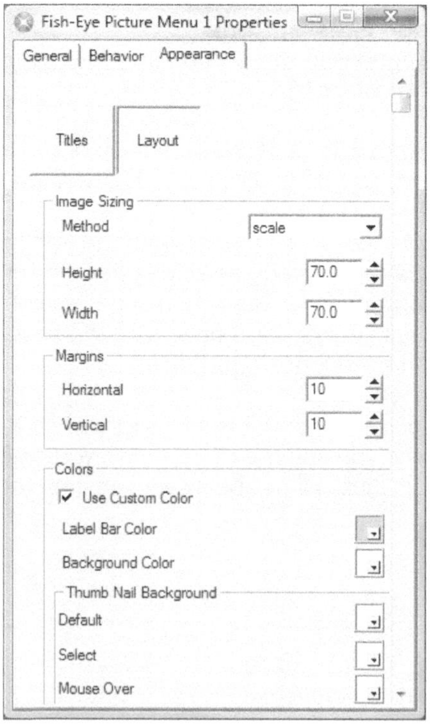

Figure 10-29 Fish-Eye and Sliding Picture Menu layout panel options

Image Sizing Options

The options in this section are used to resize the images for the menu.

The **METHOD** option is used to select how the image will be sized. The two options are explained below.

① **SCALE** Select this option to reduce the image to fit in the thumbnail area.
② **STRETCH** Select this option to resize the image to fit in the thumbnail area.

HEIGHT If necessary, select the height that the image needs to be resized to.

WIDTH If necessary, select the width that the image needs to be resized to.

Margins Options
The options in this section determine how much space is above, below and between the images on the menu.

HORIZONTAL The smaller the number, the closer together the images are, from left to right.

VERTICAL The larger the number, the more space there is above and below the images.

Colors Options
The options in this section are used to select the Label Bar, and background colors.

LABEL BAR COLOR Is used to change the color of the title bar at the top of the menu.

BACKGROUND COLOR Is used to change the background color behind the images on the menu.

Thumb Nail Background Options
The options in this section are used to select the default background color of the images, a different color when an image on the menu is selected and yet a different color when the mouse pointer is hovered over an image on the menu.

DEFAULT Is used to change the background color of the image when the model is first opened.

SELECT Is used to change the background color of the image when the image is selected (clicked on).

MOUSE OVER Is used to change the background color of the image when the mouse pointer is hovered over the image.

Fish-Eye Picture Menu Component

General Tab Options
[See Common Picture Menu General Tab Options, earlier in this lesson]

Behavior Tab Options
The options shown in Figure 10-30 are specific to the Fish-Eye component.

Fish-Eye Behavior Options
FISH EYE FRICTION Is used to set the popup effect for the Mouse Over option on the Layout panel.

FISH EYE MAX Is used to set the size of the image when the mouse is hovered over it.

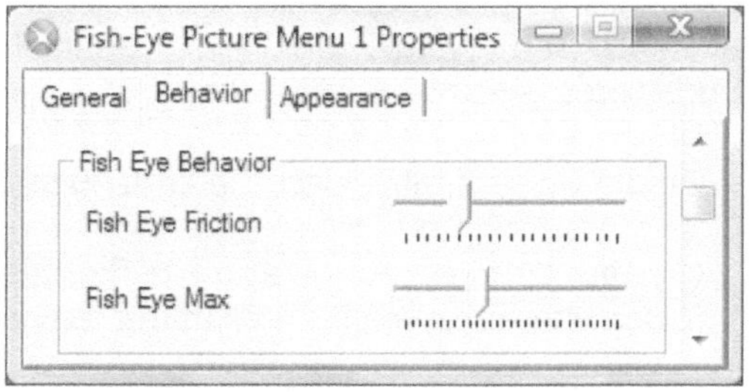

Figure 10-30 Fish-Eye Picture Menu behavior tab options

Titles Panel Options

[See Common Picture Menu Titles Panel Options, earlier in this lesson]

Layout Panel Options

[See Common Picture Menu Layout Panel Options, earlier in this lesson]

Exercise 10.4: Create A Fish-Eye Picture Menu Dashboard

The Fish Eye Menu that you will create in this exercise will display the sales by product for five years.

The options on the menu are the products. Figure 10-31 shows the data for this exercise.

	A	B	C	D	E	F
1	**Insert In Range**					
2						
3						
4	**Actual Data**					
5	Sales by Product	FY00	FY02	FY03	FY04	FY05
6	Enterprise Software	$19.7	$17.1	$18.3	$14.8	$19.8
7	Developer Tools	$14.4	$18.0	$16.4	$16.7	$19.3
8	Consumer Software	$18.8	$13.5	$18.7	$13.9	$15.7
9	Services	$12.0	$16.2	$17.5	$17.8	$13.8
10	Support	$19.2	$15.6	$19.6	$15.9	$14.4
11	Training	$18.9	$14.6	$16.7	$12.1	$13.9

Figure 10-31 Fish-Eye Picture Menu data

1. Save the cx_fish-eye model as `My fish-eye menu`.

2. Add the Fish-Eye Picture Menu component above the chart.

Select The Fish-Eye Picture Menu Options

1. On the General tab, make the changes in the table.

   The labels are the product names.

Property	Change To
Labels	A6:A11
Insert Option	Rows
Source Data	A6:F11
Insert In	A2:F2

How To Embed Image Files

The image files that you will use in this exercise are different then the ones in the sample model that comes with Crystal Xcelsius because the image files that are used in the sample are not included on the software installation CD.

1. On the General tab, select the **EMBEDDED** option, then click the Import button.

2. Click the disk icon button at the end of the **THUMBNAIL SOURCE** field, then navigate to the folder where the images are. In this exercise navigate to your folder.

3. Double-click on the image1.jpg file, as shown in Figure 10-32.

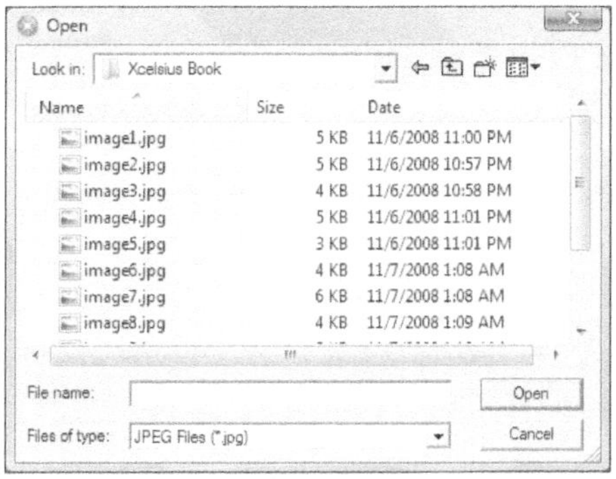

Figure 10-32 List of image files

4. Click the plus sign button at the bottom of the Import Thumbnail dialog box and add image2.jpg. As you see, the previous image file name is automatically copied to the new entry. You can click in the Thumbnail Source field and change the image name instead of clicking the disk icon to select each image.

> The order that you add the images in is how they will appear, from left to right in the menu. Notice that there is no option to rearrange the order of the images.

5. Repeat the previous step to add image files 3 through 6.

   When you are finished, the dialog box should look like the one shown in Figure 10-33.

   Click OK.

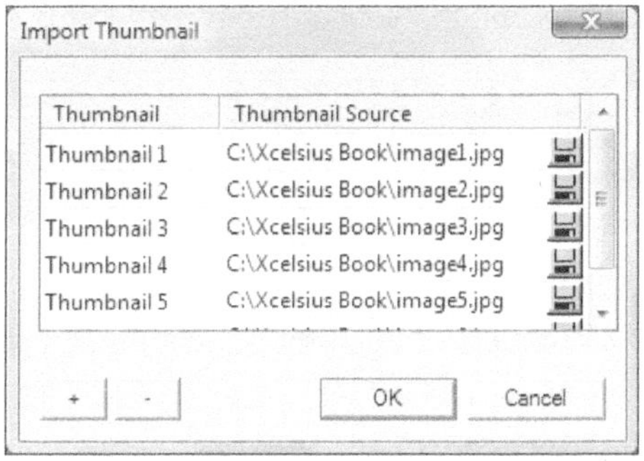

Figure 10-33 Import Thumbnail dialog box

6. On the Behavior tab, change the Default Selection option to Thumbnail 1.

7. On the Appearance tab, click the Layout button, then make the changes in the table.

Property	Change To
Method	Scale
Height	70
Width	70
Horizontal	10
Vertical	10
Use Custom Color	Select this option
Label Bar Color	Select a different color

Test The Fish-Eye Menu

1. Save the changes.

   The model should look like the one shown in Figure 10-34.

   When you click on an image in the menu, the text on the Title bar at the top of the menu will display the product name.

   The chart will display the data for the product that corresponds to the image that you clicked on.

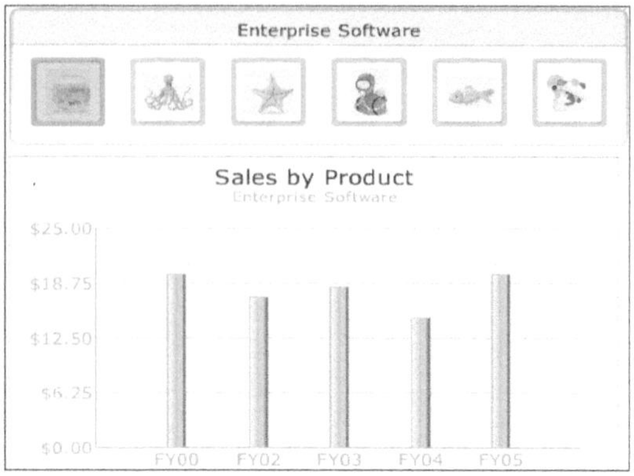

Figure 10-34 Fish-Eye Menu model

2. Hold the mouse pointer over an icon. It should look like the one shown in Figure 10-35. The closer the mouse pointer is to the middle of the image, the larger the image will appear.

   Figure 10-36 shows the image size when the mouse pointer is hovered over the upper right corner of the image. Notice that the image is smaller then the one shown in Figure 10-35.

Figure 10-35 Fish-Eye effect on an image

Figure 10-36 Different image size

Sliding Picture Menu Component

General Tab Options

[See Common Picture Menu General Tab Options, earlier in this lesson]

Behavior Tab Options

The options shown in Figure 10-37 are specific to the Sliding Picture Menu component.

Slide Behavior Options

SLIDE METHOD Is used to select the action used to scroll through the images. The two options are explained below.

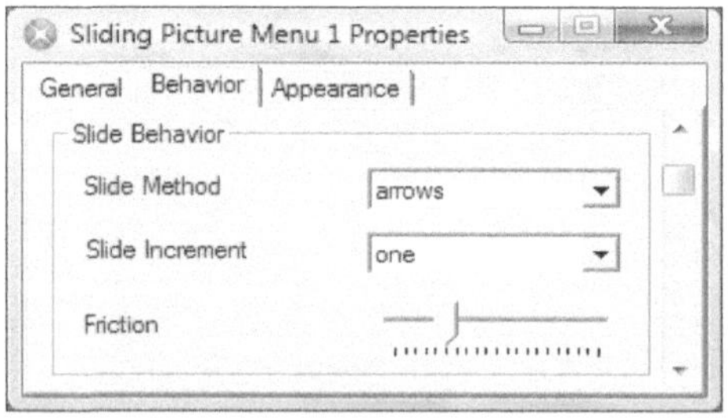

Figure 10-37 Sliding Picture Menu behavior tab options

① The **ARROWS** option will add arrows to the menu, that the user has to click on to view the images that are not currently visible in the menu.
② The **MOUSE** option uses the mouse pointer to scroll through the images in the direction that the mouse pointer moves. If the mouse pointer moves to the left on the menu, the first images will be displayed.

SLIDE INCREMENT Is used to select if the scroll is one image at a time or a page at a time. A page is equal to the number of images that are initially displayed on the menu. For example, if four images are initially displayed on the menu, when the arrow is clicked or the mouse pointer moves to the right, the next four images are displayed.

FRICTION Is used to determine how fast or slow the menu scrolls.

Titles Panel Options

[See Common Picture Menu Titles Panel Options, earlier in this lesson]

Layout Panel Options

The options shown in Figure 10-38 that are specific to the Sliding Picture Menu are explained below.
If the image does not clearly represent the product, the button image should have the name of the product to help the user know what item the button will display.

ARROW UP Is used to change the color of the arrows.

DISABLED ARROW Is used to change the color of the arrow when clicking on the arrow will not display any more menu options.

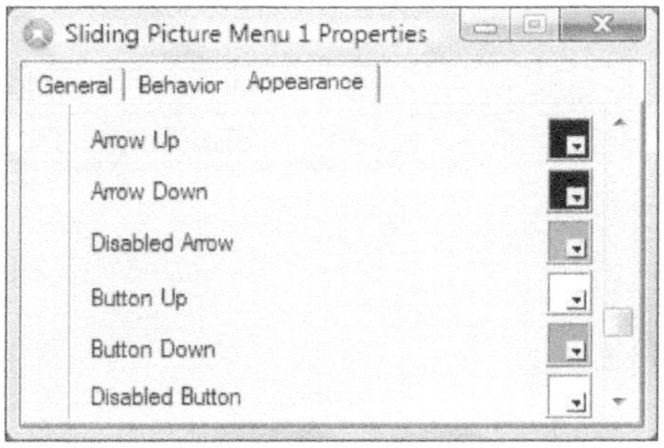

Figure 10-38 Sliding Picture Menu layout panel options

BUTTON UP Is used to change the background color of the arrow.

BUTTON DOWN Is used to change the background color of the arrow when it is clicked on.

DISABLED BUTTON Is used to change the background color of the arrow when clicking on the arrow will not display any more menu options.

Exercise 10.5: Create A Sliding Picture Menu Dashboard

In this exercise the Sliding Picture Menu will be used to select the specific product that you want to see the sales for, by clicking on the button on the menu that represents the product. The data for this model is the same as the Fish-Eye Picture Menu, shown earlier in Figure 10-31.

1. Save the cx_sliding_picture model as `My sliding picture`.

2. Add the Sliding Picture Menu component above the chart.

Select The Sliding Picture Menu Options

1. On the General tab, make the changes in the table.

Property	Change To
Labels	A6:A11
Insert Option	Rows
Source Data	A6:F11
Insert In	A2:F2

2. Follow the steps in the "How To Embed Image Files" section in the Fish-Eye Picture Menu exercise to add the images to the Sliding Picture menu. Use image files 7 to 12 for this exercise.

3. On the Behavior tab, make the changes in the table. When you are finished, you should have the options shown in Figure 10-39.

Property	Change To
Update On	Mouse click
Slide Method	Arrows
Slide Increment	Page
Default Selection	Thumbnail 1

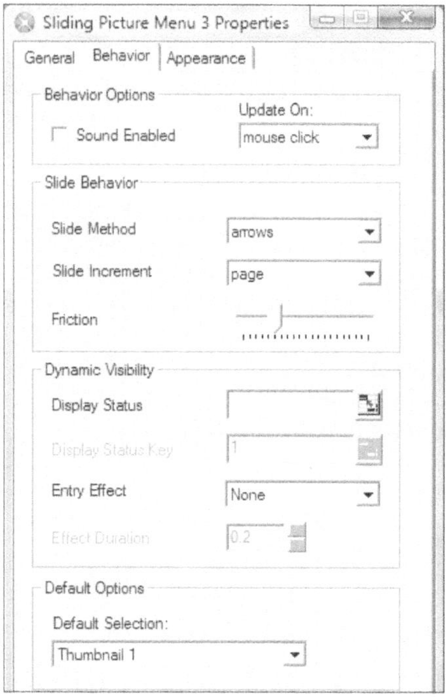

Figure 10-39 Sliding Picture Menu behavior tab options

4. On the Appearance tab, click the Layout button, then make the changes in the table. You should have the options shown in Figure 10-40.

Property	Change To
Method	Scale
Height	80
Width	80
Horizontal	10
Vertical	0

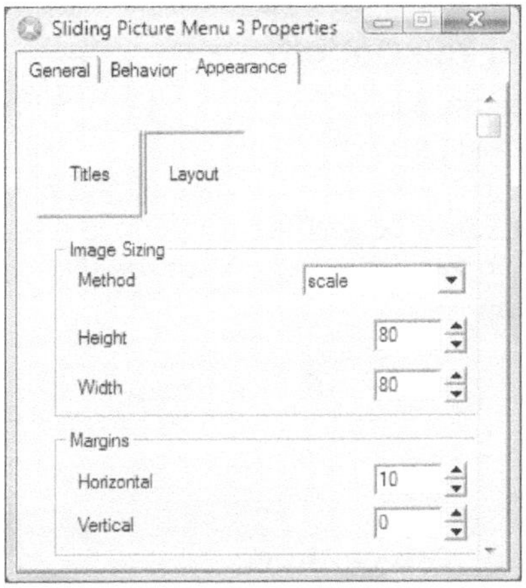

Figure 10-40 Sliding Picture Menu layout panel options

5. Save the changes.

   The model should look like the one shown in Figure 10-41.

   If you click on the right arrow button, you will see the next set of images.

Figure 10-41 Sliding Picture Menu model

External Slide Show Component

This component is used to create a slide show of images or SWF files that are on the Internet. Each time the dashboard is run, the component will load the images or SWF files that are in the location listed in the URL option on the General tab.

General Tab Options

The External Slide Show general tab options are shown in Figure 10-42.

The **URL (JPEG OR SWF FILE)** option is used to type in or select the location of the files for the slide show.

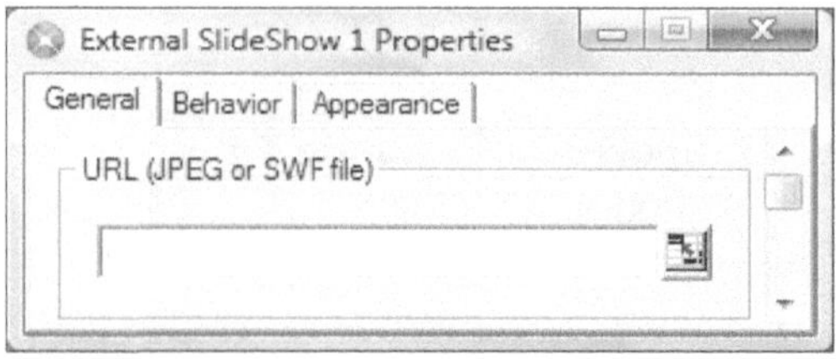

Figure 10-42 External Slide Show general tab options

Behavior Tab Options

The External Slide Show behavior tab options are shown in Figure 10-43.

Slide Show Behavior Options

The options in this section are used to set the style and timing of the transition.

EASE TYPE Is used to select how slow the slide show will open, close or both.

TRANSITION TYPE Is used to select the effect that should appear between each file.

INTERVAL TIME Is used to select the time in seconds between each frame.

Figure 10-43 External Slide Show behavior tab options

TRANSITION TIME Is used to select the time in seconds or a fraction of a second that the transition takes to run. 1000.0 is one second.

Appearance Tab Options

The options shown in Figure 10-44 are used to select the size and alignment of the file for the slide show.

Image Positioning Options

SIZING Is used to select how the file fits in the frame. The "default" option expands the file to its normal size.

HORIZONTAL and **VERTICAL ALIGNMENT** These options are used to select how the file is positioned in the frame.

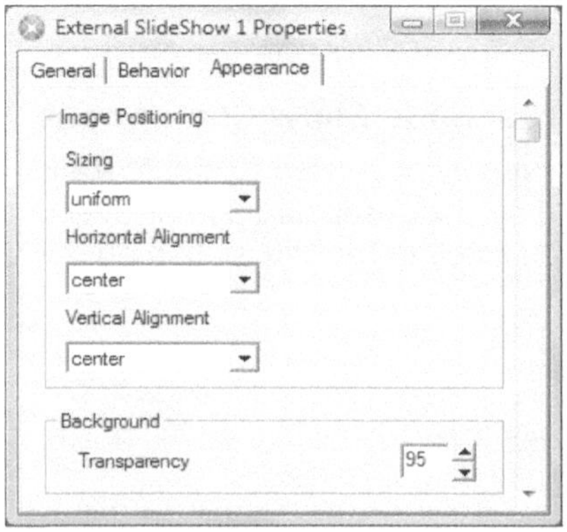

Figure 10-44 External Slide Show appearance tab options

ADVANCED FUNCTIONALITY

In this lesson you will learn about the following advanced functionality topics.

- ☑ Dynamic Visibility
- ☑ Password protecting a dashboard
- ☑ Use different components to display and hide other components
- ☑ Customize markers in a chart

LESSON 11

Advanced Functionality Overview

The topics covered in this lesson are not required to create most dashboards. Knowing that the topics covered in this lesson exist, will help you determine if they would enhance the dashboards that you create.

Dynamic Visibility

By now you have seen the dynamic visibility options on the Behavior tab of the Properties dialog box more times than you can remember. I hope that you are not annoyed that I waited until the next to last lesson to cover this topic. Hopefully, you will find the "cool" factor of this feature, worth the wait.

Simply put, dynamic visibility gives you the option of controlling when components are visible or hidden on the dashboard. The models that you have created in this book so far have not had an overwhelming number of components. But have no fear, users will ask for dashboards that need more components. There is but so much space available that you can use to display the components in a size that does not cause eye strain.

If you remember, you had to make the charts larger than the default size so that the values on the horizontal axis were easier to read. Usually, you can fit two or three charts plus a few selectors without a lot of sizing issues. If you have looked at the sample dashboards on the SAP web site, you have seen what I consider the best use of screen real estate for dashboards. Never mind that fact that they look great also. The graphics that are used on many of the sample dashboards on the web site are custom. I cannot tell you the number of hours that it takes to create dashboards that look like those from scratch, when you include the time to design the graphics.

If you do not have the time or artistic ability to create those dashboards, the dynamic visibility options will allow you to include all of the required components to meet the dashboard requirements, look good and have some "wow" functionality thrown in for good measure. I will say this about dynamic visibility, when I first started learning Crystal Xcelsius, there was not (and still is not) a lot of "how to" information for the software. Many people, including moiré, have spent countless hours trying to figure out what each option could be used for. Dynamic visibility is one of the topics that I just did not understand. I had no idea that four options could provide so much functionality!

Dynamic Visibility Options

The four options shown in Figure 11-1 are on the Behavior tab. They are the same on each component that supports dynamic visibility.

These options control when the component will be displayed on the dashboard. They are explained below.

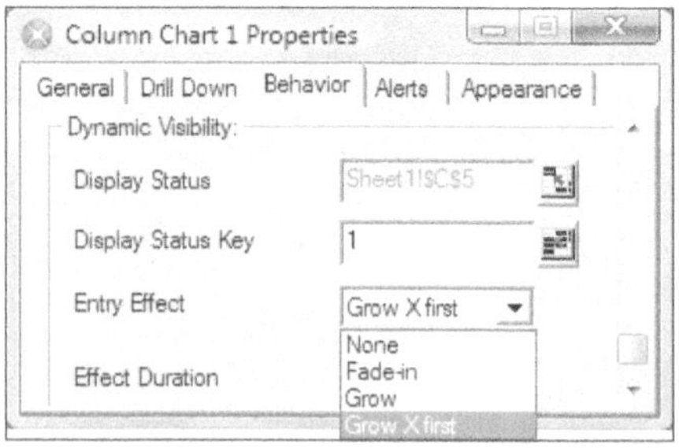

Figure 11-1 Dynamic Visibility options

DISPLAY STATUS This is the option that Crystal Xcelsius uses to determine if dynamic visibility is to occur for a component. If there is no cell in this field, Crystal Xcelsius ignores the other dynamic visibility options. This option is used to select the cell that is the trigger, to determine whether or not the component is visible.

DISPLAY STATUS KEY This option contains the value that the cell referenced in the Display Status field must match for the component to be visible on the dashboard. If the value in this field matches, the component is displayed. If not, the component stays invisible. The default value for this field is "1". Most of the time, you will not have to change this value. The number one signifies that the option is "on" and zero or any other value indicates that the option is "off". This field is case sensitive.

ENTRY EFFECT The options in this drop-down list are used to determine how the component should become visible. They are shown above in Figure 11-1. The default option is **NONE**. This option will display the component without any animation. The other options add animation to the component and are explained below.

① **FADE-IN** Select this option if you want the component to first appear semi-transparent and slowly become solid.
② **GROW** Select this option if you want the component to first appear small and gradually become its full size.
③ **GROW X FIRST** Select this option if you want the component to appear gradually reaching its full width, then its full height.

EFFECT DURATION This option is used to set how long (in seconds), the option selected in the Entry Effect field takes to complete. This option is not available if the Entry Effect option is set to None.

Check Box Component

General Tab Options

[See Lesson 7, Common Selector General Tab Options]

Behavior Tab Options

[See Lesson 7, Common Selector Behavior Tab Options]

DEFAULT SELECTION The options in the drop-down list shown in Figure 11-2 are used to select if the Check Box does or does not have a check mark when the dashboard is first opened.

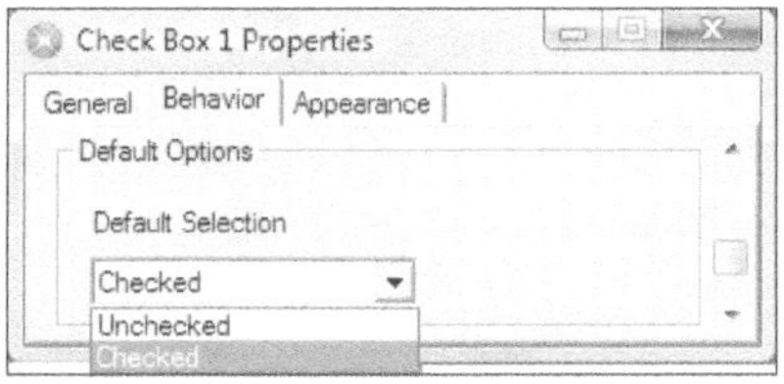

Figure 11-2 Check Box behavior tab options

Appearance Tab Options

Title Options

[See Lesson 7, Common Selector Appearance Tab Options]

Marker Options

USE CUSTOM COLOR As shown in Figure 11-3, this option is used to change the background color of the Check Box.

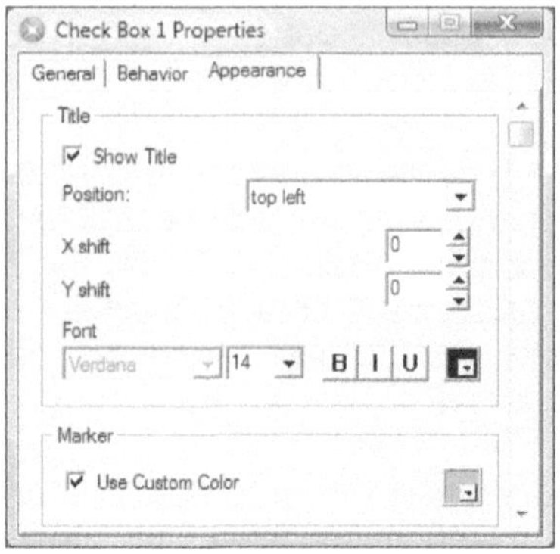

Figure 11-3 Check Box appearance tab options

Exercise 11.1: Display Or Hide A Chart

If the dashboard has several components and appears somewhat crowded or if there is something like a chart that does not always have to be displayed on the dashboard, you can hide it. To accomplish this, you will add a component that will let the user display or hide the chart as needed.

In this exercise you will modify an existing model to allow the user to select whether or not the chart is displayed.

1. Save the My line chart model as `My check box chart`.

2. Add the Check Box component above the upper left corner of the chart, then make the check box a little larger.

3. On the General tab, make the changes in the table.

Property	Change To
Title	View Chart
Insert Option	Value
Insert In	A7

4. On the Behavior tab, open the Default Selection drop-down list and select **UNCHECKED**. Selecting this option means that when the dashboard is first opened, the check box will be visible.

5. On the Appearance tab, make the changes in the table.

Property	Change To
Show Title	Select this option
Position	Right

6. On the Behavior tab of the line chart, change the **DISPLAY STATUS** to A7. This is the link between the check box and the chart to determine if the chart will be hidden or displayed when the button is clicked.

7. Save the model and preview it.

   Click the **VIEW CHART** button.

   You should see the chart.

   The model should look like the one shown in Figure 11-4.

   If you click the View Chart button again, the chart will be hidden.

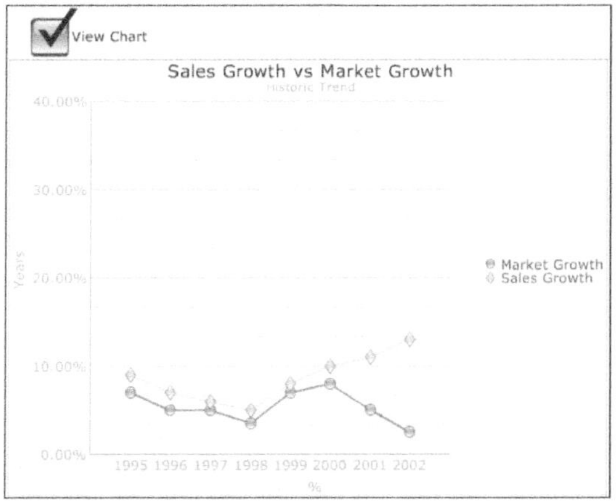

Figure 11-4 Check Box model

Input Text Component

General Tab Options

[See Lesson 9, Input Text Area General Tab Options]

Behavior Tab Options

The Input Text behavior tab options are shown in Figure 11-5.

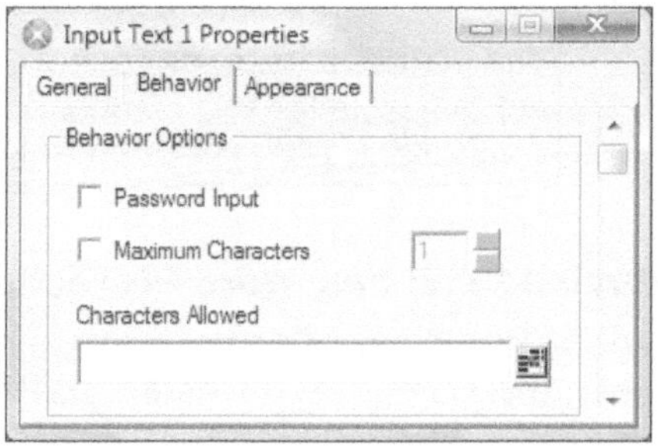

Figure 11-5 Input Text behavior tab options

Behavior Options

PASSWORD INPUT Selecting this option causes asterisks to be displayed instead of the password when it is typed in the field.

MAXIMUM CHARACTERS Type in the maximum number of characters that can be entered into the label.

NUMBER OF CHARACTERS Is used to select the maximum number of characters that can be entered for the password. Select a number that is at least the length of the password that you are using.

CHARACTERS ALLOWED Type in or select the characters that cannot be entered into the label. If the field is left blank, all characters can be entered in the field.

Appearance Tab Options

The Input Text appearance tab options are shown in Figure 11-6.

Background Options

BACKGROUND COLOR Is used to change the background color for the Input Text field.

Figure 11-6 Input Text appearance tab options

> **Background Options**
>
> The **SCROLL BAR COLOR**, **SCROLL ARROW COLOR** and **SCROLL GUTTER COLOR** options are not available for this component. They are available for the Input Text Area component. [See Lesson 9, Input Text Area Appearance Tab Options]

Exercise 11.2: Password Protection

There may be times when you want to restrict some people from viewing a dashboard. Usually, this is because the data is sensitive in nature. This type of functionality can be implemented using the Dynamic Visibility options. In addition to using these options, the component(s) on the dashboard that you want to protect have to be grouped.

In this exercise you will add password protection to a model. Users will have to enter the correct password before the dashboard will be displayed. While this exercise applies the protection to all of the components on the dashboard, you can set the protection for some components and allow access to other components all the time.

Group The Components For Password Protection

The components that have to be password protected have to be added to the same group, so that a password can be added to them. If there are several components on the model and only some of the components require protection, you have to select the ones that you want password protected when the dashboard is first opened and add them to the same group. Only components in the group that have a component with dynamic visibility enabled, will be hidden when the dashboard is run.

1. Save the My filter drop-down list model as `My password protection`.

2. Select both of the components in the Object Browser, then right-click and select **GROUP**, as illustrated in Figure 11-7.

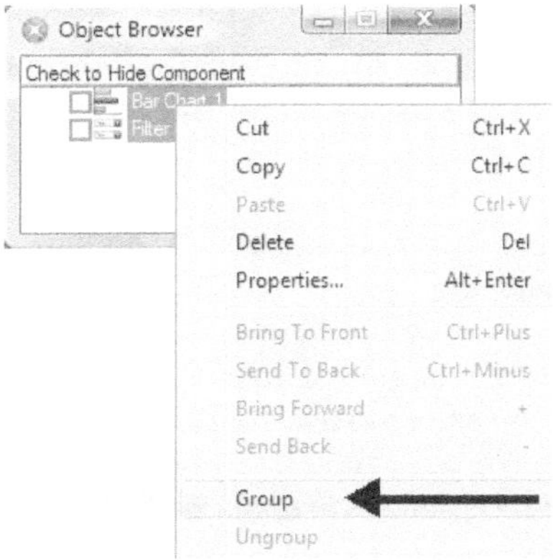

Figure 11-7 Group menu option illustrated

Set Up The Password

In this part of the exercise you will select the Display Status and Display Status Key options for the group. In this exercise the Display Status Key field will be used for the password.

1. Right-click on the group in the Object Browser and select Properties, as shown above in Figure 11-7. You will see the Dynamic Visibility Properties dialog box.

2. On the Behavior tab, (this should be the only tab) make the changes in the table. You should have the options shown in Figure 11-8.

Property	Change To
Display Status	H1 (1)
Display Status Key	Mypassword1 (2)

(1) You can use any empty cell in the spreadsheet for this option.
(2) The password is case sensitive because the Display Status Key field is case sensitive.

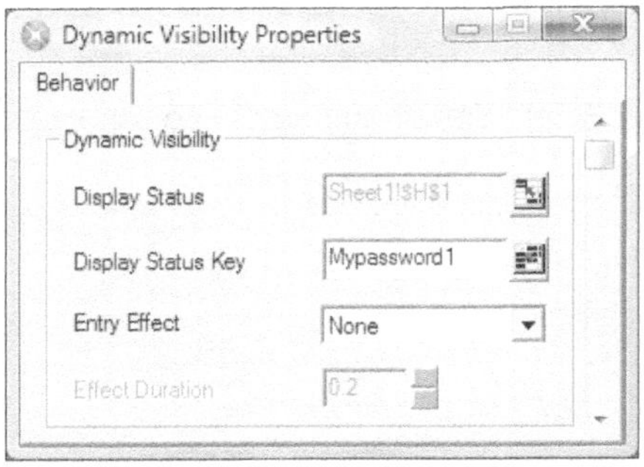

Figure 11-8 Dynamic Visibility Properties for the group

3. If necessary, move the components down so that there is room to add a component at the top of the model.

Select The Input Text Component Options

This component will be used as the field that the person running the dashboard will use to enter the password. While not done in this exercise, you should add another Input Text component to the model that informs the user to enter the password in the field, otherwise, they may not know what the field is for.

1. Add the Input Text-0 component above the filter component. Make the Input Text component longer.

2. On the General tab, change the Insert In option to H1. You have to select the same cell for this option that you selected for the Display Status option for the group.

3. On the Behavior tab, make the changes in the table.

   You should have the options shown Figure 11-9.

Property	Change To
Password Input	Select this option
Maximum Characters	Select this option
Number of characters	11

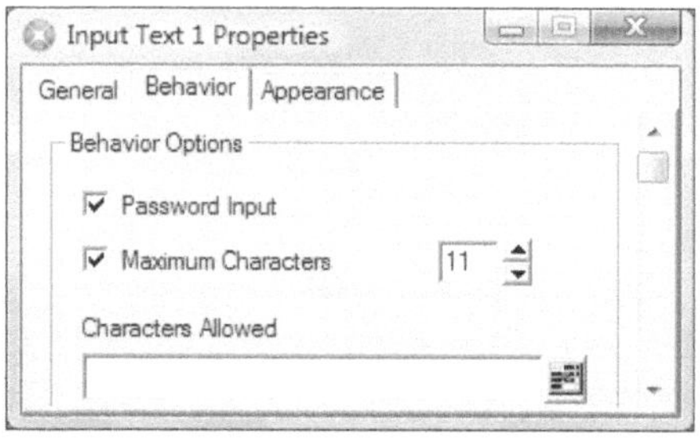

Figure 11-9 Input Text behavior tab options

Test The Model

1. Save the changes and preview the model. You should only see the password field on the model, as shown in Figure 11-10.

Figure 11-10 Password field

2. Type `testmodel` in the Password field and press Enter. This is not the correct password, so the other components in the group are not displayed.

3. Type `Mypassword1` in the field, then press Enter. You should now see the rest of the model.

Toggle Button Component

General Tab Options

[See Lesson 7, Common Selector General Tab Options]

Behavior Tab Options

[See Lesson 7, Common Selector Behavior Tab Options]

Appearance Tab Options

The Toggle Button appearance tab options are shown in Figure 11-11.

[See Lesson 7, Common Selector Appearance Tab Options]

Markers Options

OFF FILL Is used to change the background color when the button is clicked.

ON FILL Is used to change the default background color.

Figure 11-11 Toggle Button appearance tab options

Exercise 11.3: Use The Toggle Button Selector Component

Toggle buttons are used to display or hide an object on the dashboard. If you look at the chart in Figure 11-12, you see that it plots four series of data: Market growth, Sales growth, East region and West region.

This chart may look familiar because you created part of it in Exercise 6.1.

I added two series of data to the spreadsheet and chart.

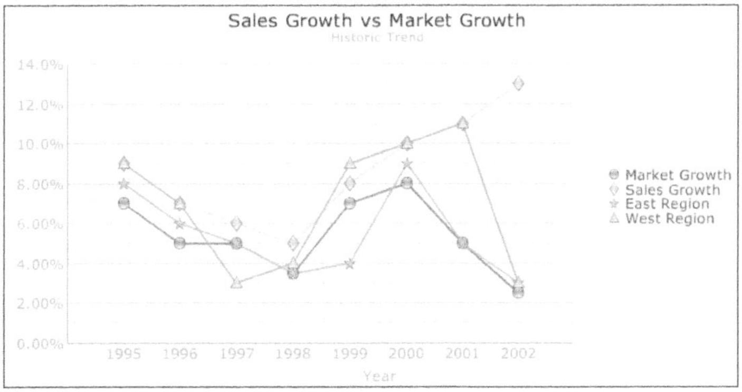

Figure 11-12 Line chart with four series of data

As you can see, it is somewhat difficult to see each series of data. If you added toggle buttons to the model, you could hide one or all of the series of data as needed, to make the chart easier to read.

1. Save the cx_toggle_button model as `My toggle button`.

2. Add the Toggle Button component above the chart on the left.

3. On the General tab, change the Insert In option to L4.

How To Customize The Text On A Button

By default, the text on a Toggle button is "On". If there is only one toggle button on the dashboard this may not be a problem because once the user clicked on it, they could tell what was hidden. This is not a good design choice though.

There are two options for changing the text on a button, as discussed below.

① **USE THE LABELS FIELD ON THE GENERAL TAB** If the text that you want to put on the button is in the spreadsheet, add the cell to the field.

② **USE THE LABELS DIALOG BOX** If you do not want to use data in the spreadsheet or the text that you want to use is not in the spreadsheet, select this option. A benefit that the Labels dialog box has is that you can select different text for the on and off states of the button.

How To Create A Custom Label For A Toggle Button

1. Click the **BROWSE** button at the end of the Labels field on the General tab.

2. Click in the **OFF** Label Name field. Type `Show Market Growth`.

3. Click in the **ON** Label Name field. Type `Hide Market Growth`.

4. You should have the options shown in Figure 11-13.

   Click OK.

   Make the button wider so that you can see all of the text.

Figure 11-13 Labels dialog box

5. Save the changes and preview the model. If you click the button, you will see that the market growth trend line in the chart disappears. If you click the button again the market growth trend line will reappear.

Add The Other Buttons

In this part of the exercise you will create buttons for the other three trend lines in the chart. To do that you will copy the existing button and only change what is necessary.

1. Right-click on the toggle button that you just created, then select **COPY**.
   Right-click on the canvas and select **PASTE**.
   Move the new button to the right of the first button.

2. Make two more copies of the button.

3. Select the options in the table below for each of the three buttons.

Property	Button 2	Button 3	Button 4
Insert In	L5	L6	L7
Label Off	Show Sales Growth	Show East Region	Show West Region
Label On	Hide Sales Growth	Hide East Region	Hide West Region

4. Save the changes.

   The model should look like the one shown in Figure 11-14.

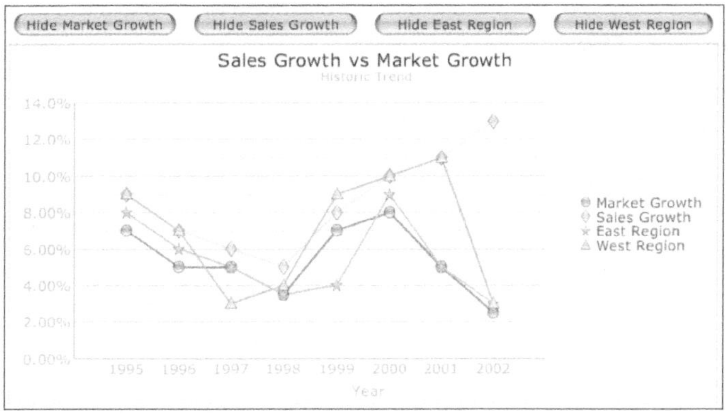

Figure 11-14 Toggle Button model

> By default, toggle buttons are first displayed in the On position. If you do not want a particular series of data to appear on the chart when the dashboard is first opened, change the **DEFAULT SELECTION** option on the Behavior tab of the Toggle Button to Off, as shown in Figure 11-15.

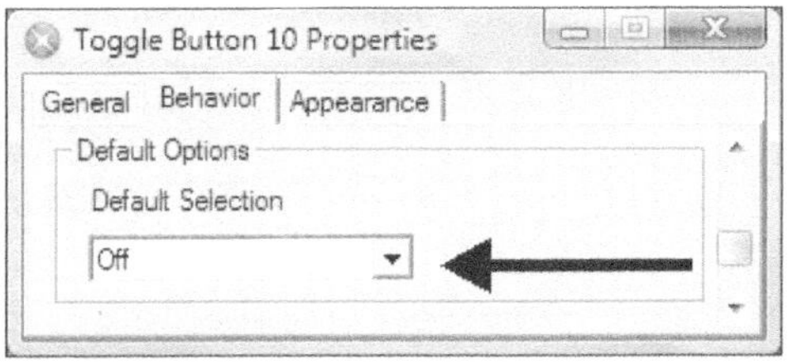

Figure 11-15 Option to hide a series of data by default

Figure 11-16 shows the model with the Market Growth and East Region data series turned off by default.

Figure 11-16 Model with two series of data hidden by default on start up

Label Component

General Tab Options

The Label general tab options are shown in Figure 11-17.

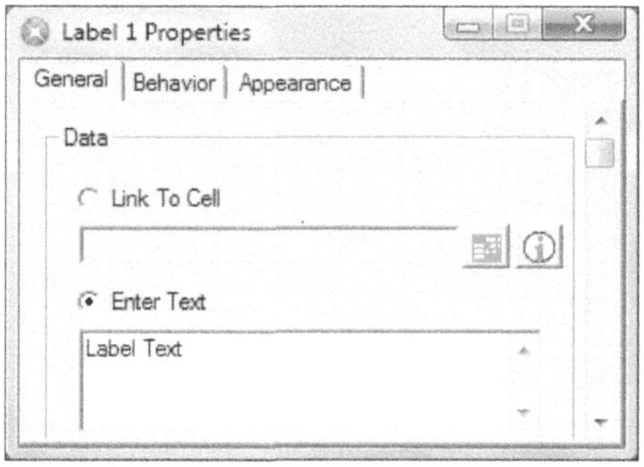

Figure 11-17 Label component general tab options

Data Options

LINK TO CELL Is used to select the cell that has the text for the label.

Behavior Tab Options

[See Lesson 7, Table Component Appearance Tab Options]

Appearance Tab Options

The Label appearance tab options are shown in Figure 11-18.

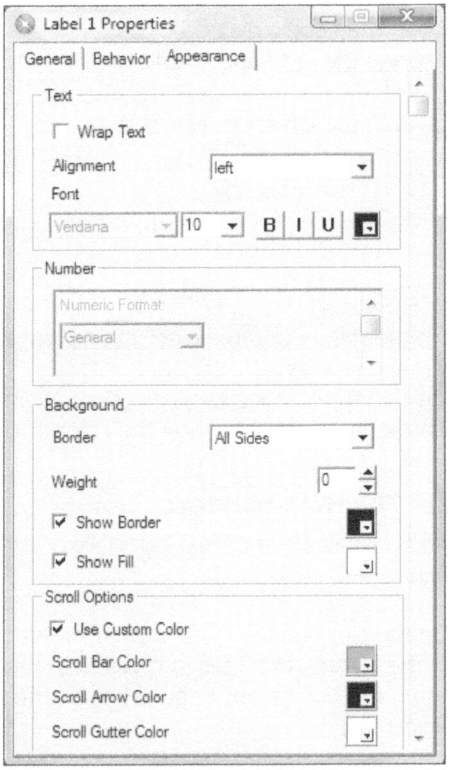

Figure 11-18 Label component appearance tab options

Text Options

WRAP TEXT If checked, the text will wrap to the next line of the label.

Background Options

BORDER Is used to select which sides of the label will display a border.

WEIGHT Is used to select the thickness of the border.

SHOW FILL Is used to change the color of the border.

Scroll Options

[See Lesson 7, Table Component Appearance Tab Options]

Exercise 11.4: Adding Help To A Dashboard

In Exercise 5.1 you created a dashboard that used a value component to get information from the user. This information is used to select the data to display on the chart. There are options about the field that a user may not know about. One way to help the people using the dashboard is to provide help, right on the dashboard.

Don't worry, the type of help that you will learn how to create will not detract from your visual master piece. In the previous exercise, you used a toggle button to display and hide series of data on the chart. In this exercise you will use a toggle button to display a help message for the Price per Unit field.

Create The Help Button

In this part of the exercise you will create the button that will be used to display and hide the help window that you will create later in this exercise.

1. Save the cx_help_button model as `My help button`.

2. Add the Toggle Button component to the left of the Price per Unit label.

3. On the General tab, change the Insert In option to E1.

4. Open the Labels dialog box.
   Change the Off Label Name to `Close`.

   Change the On Label Name to `Help`, as shown in Figure 11-19.

   Click OK.

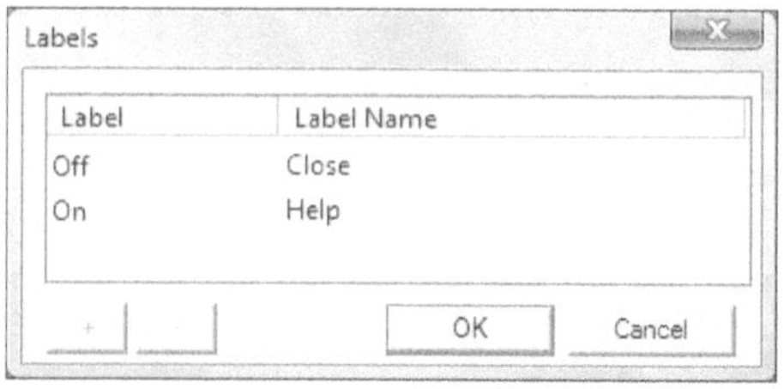

Figure 11-19 Toggle Button label names

5. On the Behavior tab, select the **SOUND ENABLED** option.

6. On the Appearance tab, select complementary colors for the **OFF FILL** and **ON FILL** options. These options will change the color of the button when it is clicked.

Create The Help Window

1. Add a Label (In the Text category of the Components dialog box) below the Price per Unit field.

2. On the General tab, type a brief message in the **ENTER TEXT** field that will help the person using the dashboard know what to enter in the field.

   My message is shown in Figure 11-20.

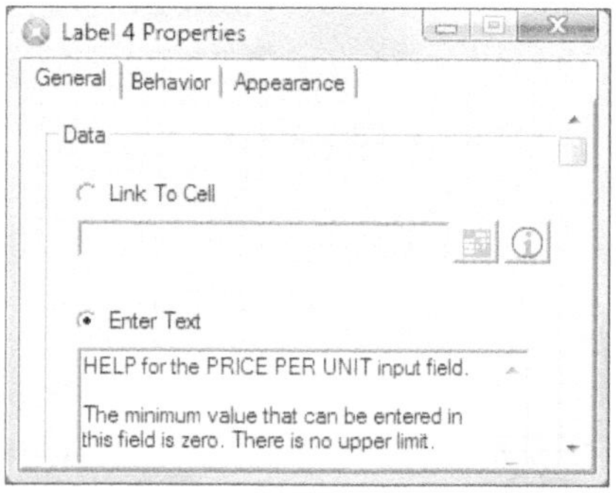

Figure 11-20 General tab options

3. On the Behavior tab, make the changes in the table. You should have the options shown in Figure 11-21.

Property	Change To
Vertical Scroll Enable	Select this option
Display Status	E1
Display Status Key	0

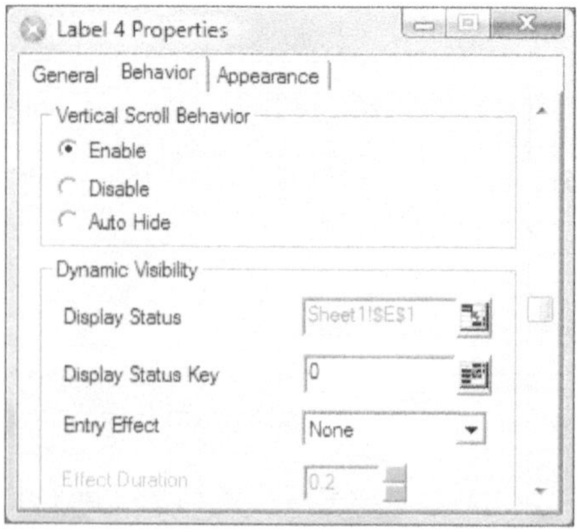

Figure 11-21 Behavior tab options

4. On the Appearance tab, make the changes in the table.

Property	Change To
Font size	9
Weight	1
Show Border	Select this option
Show Fill	Select this option
Use Custom Color	Select this option

5. Change the color of the following options: **SHOW FILL**, **SCROLL BAR COLOR** and **SCROLL GUTTER COLOR**.

6. Resize the Label component so that the scroll bar is displayed properly, then save the changes.

7. When you first preview the model, it should look like the one shown in Figure 11-22. When you click the Help button, you should see the help message that you entered, as shown in Figure 11-23. When you click the Close button, the help window will close.

Figure 11-22 Help button added to the model

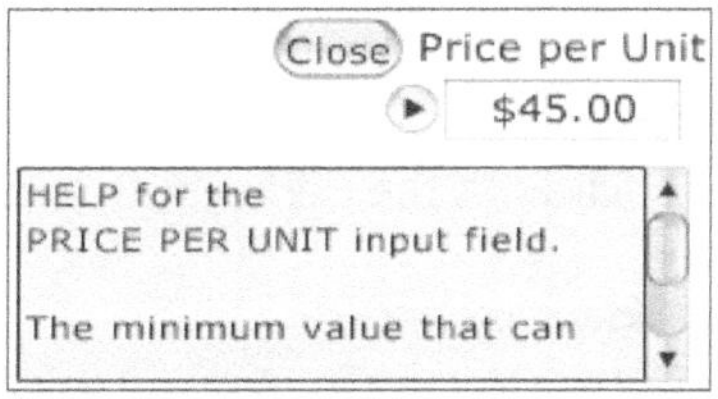

Figure 11-23 Help message

Exercise 11.5: Revise The XY Chart

In Exercise 6.9 you created an XY chart. The problem in my opinion, is that it is hard to tell which diamond marker is for which month of sales on the chart. To fix this, the data for each month has to be created individually, as its own series.

1. Save the My XY chart model as `My xy chart revised`.

2. On the General tab in the Series section, make the changes in the table.

Property	Change To
Name	Jan
X Values	B2
Y Values	C2

3. Click the **PLUS** sign button, then add the series of data in the table.

Property	Change To
Name	Feb
X Values	B3
Y Values	C3

The chart should look like the one shown in Figure 11-24.

Notice that the legend now has the month names. After you add all 12 series, you can change the symbol and/or color of the symbol for each month individually.

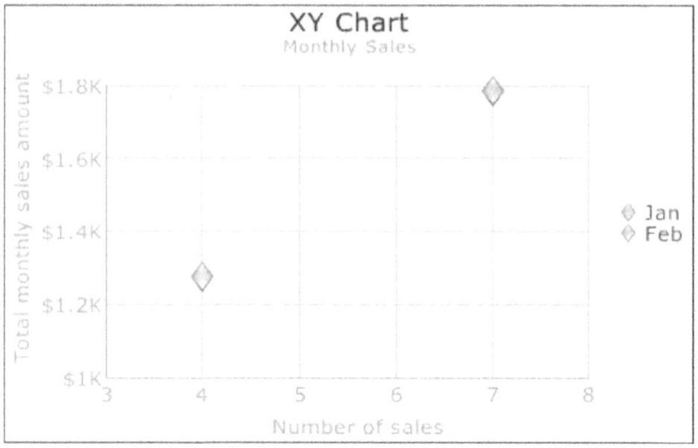

Figure 11-24 Chart with two months of sales shown in the legend

4. Repeat step three for each of the remaining months.

Customize The Markers

1. On the Appearance tab, click on the Series button. Select the **USE CUSTOM COLOR** option.

2. Open the **SERIES** drop-down list and select Feb.

   Select the symbol from the options shown at the bottom of Figure 11-25. Change the color for the symbol.

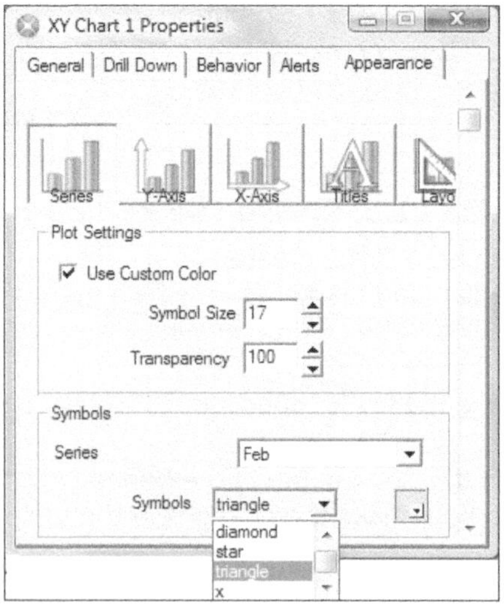

Figure 11-25 Symbol options

3. Repeat step two for each month. The goal is to make each month different on the chart. You can use the same symbol for all 12 months and select a different color for each month or any combination of symbols and colors that you want, as long as each month on the chart is uniquely represented.

4. Save the changes and preview the model.

   Figure 11-26 shows the options that I selected.

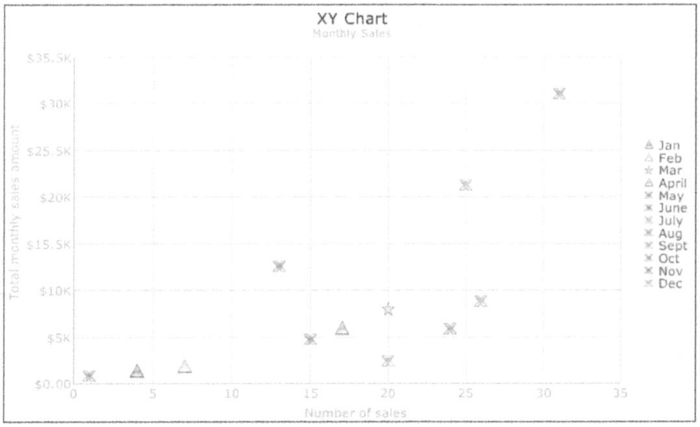

Figure 11-26 Modified XY chart

Displaying Multiple Charts

There will be times when a dashboard will require that more than one chart be displayed. There are several options available, including displaying all of the charts on the dashboard at the same time, displaying one or two charts at a time or letting the user select which chart they want to see.

Figure 11-27 shows five charts, displayed on the dashboard.

While this layout meets the users needs, it may not be very pleasing to the eye.

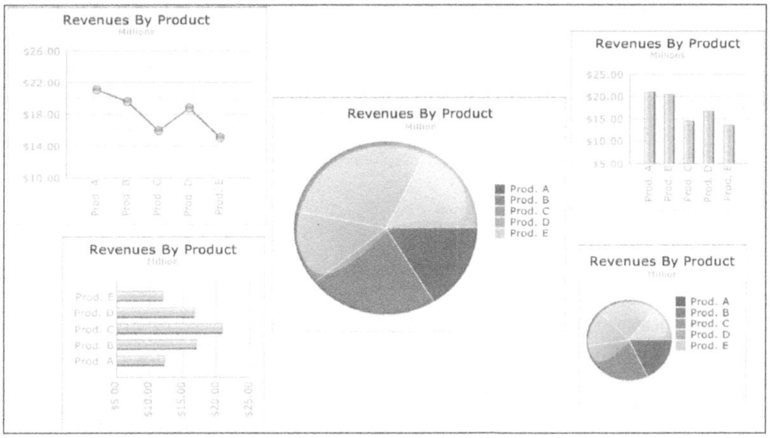

Figure 11-27 Five charts displayed on the dashboard

To display several charts on a dashboard at the same time may mean that you have to reduce their size. This could make the charts difficult to read. In Exercise 11.1 you added a Check Box component to the dashboard to display or hide a chart. You can link more than one chart to the same Check Box, by setting the Display Status option on multiple charts to the same value.

View A Better Layout For Multiple Charts

Believe it or not, the five charts shown above in Figure 11-27 came from one of the sample dashboards that come with Crystal Xcelsius.

1. Open the Samples dialog box.

2. Open the Status List model and preview it. If you click on each menu option, you will see a different chart.

If you go into design mode, it appears as though there is only one chart.

If you look in the Object Browser shown in Figure 11-28, you will see that there are five charts. I can't figure out why the two pie charts were not renamed. These are the same five charts shown above in Figure 11-27.

Yes, all five charts were created from data in the same spreadsheet, which is shown in Figure 11-29.

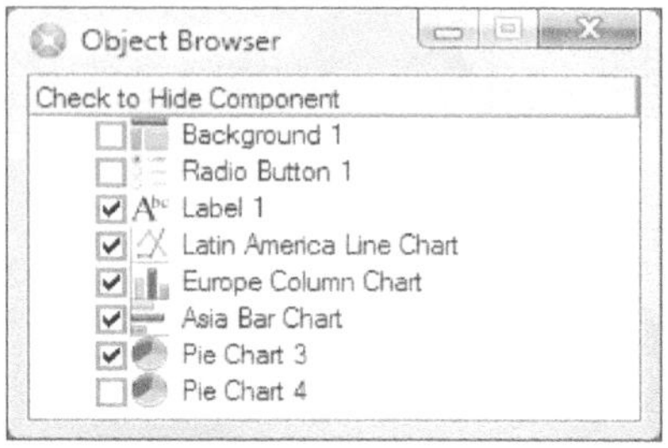

Figure 11-28 Object Browser with five charts

	A	B	C	D	E	F	G	H
1	Revenues By Product		Rev					
2								
3		Status List	Prod. A	Prod. B	Prod. C	Prod. D	Prod. E	Chart Type
4	North America		$ 14.22	$ 20.12	$ 12.18	$ 25.49	$ 15.64	Pie Chart
5	Latin America		$ 21.05	$ 19.54	$ 15.88	$ 18.73	$ 15.02	Line Chart
6	Europe		$ 21.06	$ 20.45	$ 14.49	$ 16.78	$ 13.61	Column Chart
7	Asia		$ 12.25	$ 17.12	$ 20.99	$ 16.79	$ 12.07	Bar Chart
8	Australia & Pacific		$ 15.36	$ 25.74	$ 13.17	$ 19.42	$ 12.70	Pie Chart

Figure 11-29 Data for the five charts

Icon Component

This component can be used to display and hide another component on the dashboard. This is useful if the dashboard needs to display several components on an as needed basis. By default, when an icon component is added to the model, the Alerts tab options are enabled. If the icon does not need alert functionality, disable this option. Disabling the alerts also will allow you to change the color of the icon.

General Tab Options

[See Lesson 7, Common Selector General Tab Options]

Behavior Tab Options

[See Lesson 7, Common Selector Behavior Tab Options]

Appearance Tab Options

The Icon appearance tab options are shown in Figure 11-30.

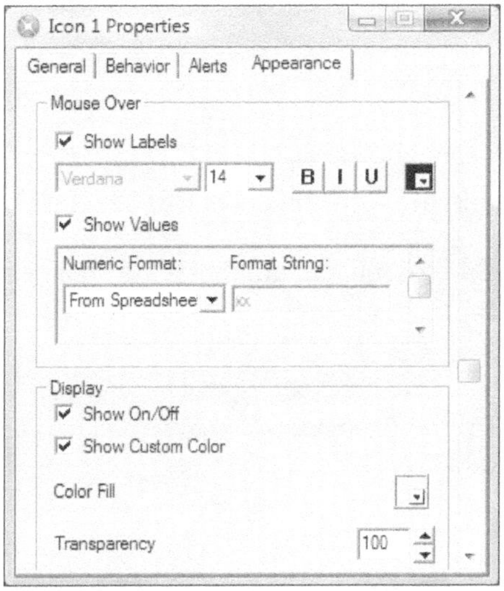

Figure 11-30 Icon appearance tab options

Mouse Over Options

SHOW LABELS Is used to display the label when the mouse pointer is hovered over the icon.

SHOW VALUES Is used to display the value when the mouse pointer is hovered over the icon.

Display Options

SHOW ON/OFF Is used to change the appearance of the icon when it is on (hovered over) and off (not hovered over).

COLOR FILL Is used to change the color of the icon.

Exercise 11.6: Display And Hide Charts Using The Icon Component

In this exercise you will use the icon component to display and hide two of the charts shown earlier in Figure 11-27. You will place an icon on two states on the map.

1. Save the cx_map_with_icons_model as `My icons model`.

If you look at the Object Browser you will see that three charts are hidden. After you complete this exercise, you can add icons to display and hide these charts also if you want to.

2. Add the Icon component to the state of Nevada.

3. On the General tab, make the changes in the table.

Property	Change To
Label	A4
Insert In	B4

4. On the Behavior tab, make the changes in the table.

Property	Change To
Update On	Mouse Over
Default Selection	Unchecked

5. On the Alerts tab, clear the Enable Alerts option.

6. On the Appearance tab, make the changes in the table.

Property	Change To
Show Labels	Select this option
Show On/Off	Select this option
Show Custom Color	Select this option
Color Fill	Red

7. Add the Icon component to the state of Florida.

8. On the General tab, make the changes in the table.

Property	Change To
Label	A4
Insert In	B4

9. On the Behavior tab, make the changes in the table.

Property	Change To
Update On	Mouse Over
Default Selection	Unchecked

10. On the Alerts tab, clear the Enable Alerts option.

11. On the Appearance tab, make the changes in the table.

Property	Change To
Show Labels	Select this option
Show On/Off	Select this option
Show Custom Color	Select this option
Color Fill	Blue

12. Save the changes. If you hold the mouse pointer over the icon on the state of Florida, you will see the chart shown in Figure 11-31.

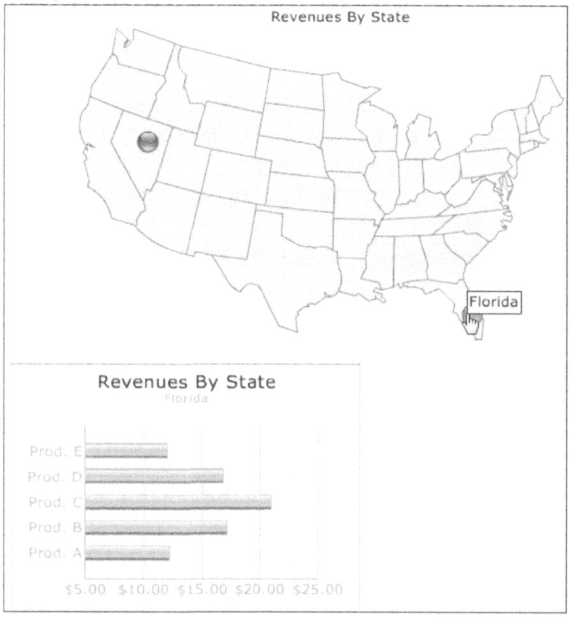

Figure 11-31 Map with icons

Exercise 11.7: Use A Menu To Display And Hide Charts

In this exercise you will start off with the model shown earlier in Figure 11-27. When you finish this exercise, you will have the Status List sample model that you viewed earlier.

As you saw earlier in Figure 11-27, the charts are not the same size. They have to be the same size to achieve the layout that you previewed. The other main task is to set up the dynamic visibility options.

Select The Dynamic Visibility Options

1. Save the cx_multiple_charts model as `My multiple charts menu`.

Compared to the Object Browser shown earlier in Figure 11-28 you will see that I renamed the two pie charts in this model. As you saw earlier in Figure 11-29, column B in the spreadsheet is being used to check the status of each chart. The cells in this column will be used to control when each chart is displayed.

2. On the Behavior tab, make the changes in the table for each chart.

   (**Hint:** When you open the Properties dialog box for a chart, you will see the chart name at the top of the dialog box.)

Chart Name	Display Status
North America	B4
Latin America	B5
Europe	B6
Asia	B7
Australia	B8

Resize The Charts

The pie chart in the middle of the model is the size that all of the other charts should be.

1. Click on the pie chart in the middle of the model, then press and hold down the CTRL key. Remember that the format options use the first component selected as the one that the others will be compared to and changed to match.

2. Click on each of the other charts.

3. Format ⇒ Make Same Size ⇒ Both. All of the charts should be the same size as the pie chart in the middle.

4. One by one, drag a chart and place it directly on top of the pie chart in the middle. The order that you place them in is not important. If they are not lined up exactly right, they will not be displayed properly in the dashboard.

Create The Menu

In this part of the exercise you will add the Radio Button component and attach each chart to an option on the menu.

1. Add the Radio Button component to the left of the charts.

2. On the General tab, make the changes in the table.

Property	Change To
Labels	A4:A8
Insert Option	Status list
Insert In	B4:B8

3. On the Appearance tab, make the changes in the table.

Property	Change To
Marker Size	17
X-Margin	20
Y-Margin	10

4. Resize the menu so that all of the items are visible.

Set Up The Background And Label Components

1. Add the Background-3 component to the canvas, then resize it so that it is large enough to cover the other components.

2. Right-click on the background and select **SEND TO BACK**.

3. Add the Label component above the menu.

4. On the General tab, in the Enter Text field, type `Status List Example`.

5. On the Appearance tab, select the Alignment Center option, then click the Bold button.

6. Save the changes.

   When you select an option on the menu, the corresponding chart should appear, as shown in Figure 11-32.

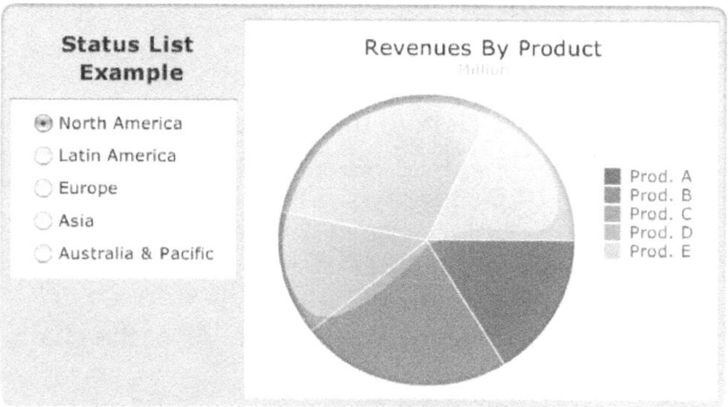

Figure 11-32 Status List example model

> **Using Unrelated Data In The Same Dashboard**
>
> What I hope that you gained from this exercise is that you could put unrelated types of data in the same spreadsheet and create a chart for each data set, if you will. For example, you could put the data from Exercises 11.1 to 11.5 on different sheets (tabs) in the Excel workbook, or you can put the data for all of the exercises on the same sheet, in the Excel workbook. This would allow you to create the same charts that you did in those exercises and combine them into one dashboard.

Exercise 11.8: Using A Spreadsheet That Has Multiple Tabs Of Data

In the tip box above, I discussed working with a spreadsheet that had multiple tabs of data. In this exercise you will import the spreadsheet discussed and create a chart.

1. Import the cx_multiple_tabs spreadsheet.

2. Add the Line Chart component. Make the chart larger. When working with a spreadsheet that has multiple tabs, the biggest difference is remembering to select the correct tab.

3. On the General tab, make the changes in the table. Click on the Line_Chart tab before selecting a cell. Figure 11-33 shows the **SERIES** section on the General tab. As illustrated, notice that the tab name is part of the data path.

Property	Change To
Chart title	A1
Chart subtitle	Historic Trend
Category X axis title	Years
Data Range	A4:I5
Category Axis Labels	B3:I3

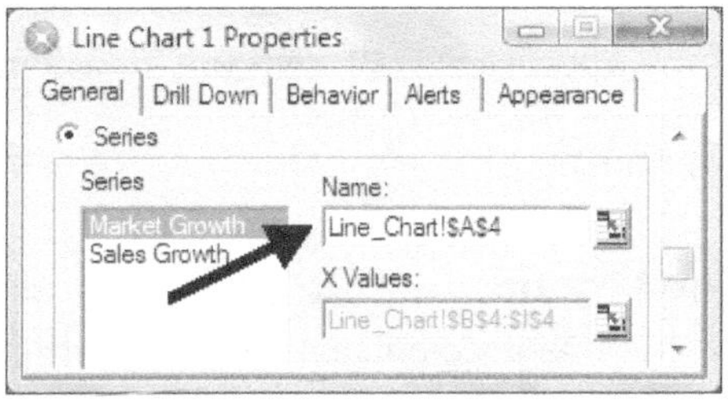

Figure 11-33 Series options

4. Save the model as `My multiple tab spreadsheet.`

Exercise 11.9: Create A Legend Using The Image Component

In Exercise 11.4 you used the Toggle Button component to display or hide another component on the dashboard. As you know, when you create a chart, you have the option of displaying a legend. If your dashboard contains a lot of components, you may decide to not display a legend for space reasons. The only time that the options on a legend change is if the structure of the data for a chart changes. For example, if you create a chart that displays data for three products and then six months later you add three more products to the chart, the structure has changed, which means the legend will change.

In this exercise you will use a Check Box component to display or hide the legend for a chart. You will not use the legend that is automatically created with the chart. You will use an image of the legend, which I have created for you. Using an image of the legend will allow you to place the legend any place on the canvas that you want, even over another component, because the visibility of the legend will be controlled by the Check Box.

Create The Pie Chart

1. Import the cx_annual_sales spreadsheet.

2. Add the Pie chart component, then make it larger.

3. On the General tab, make the changes in the table.

Property	Change To
Chart title	A1
Chart subtitle	Clear this option
Data Range	A3:B8

4. On the Appearance tab click the Series button, then select the colors for the countries in the table.

Data Point	Color
Australia	Orange
Japan	Light green
Canada	Red
Italy	Purple

5. On the Appearance tab, click the Series button, then change the Weight to 3.

6. On the Appearance tab, click the Titles button, then clear the Show Legend option.

7. Save the model as `My hidden legend`.

Add The Legend

1. Add the Image component. Place it partially over the orange slice of the chart, as shown in Figure 11-34.

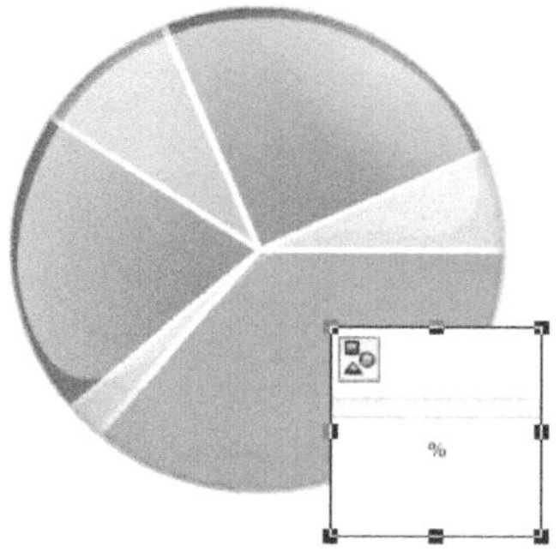

Figure 11-34 Image component added to the model

2. On the General tab, click the Import button, then select the legend.jpg file.

3. On the Behavior tab, make the changes in the table.

Property	Change To
Display Status	C2
Entry Effect	Select one

4. Save the changes.

> **How To Create The Legend Image**
>
> If you want to create a legend on your own, the steps below are how I created the legend.jpg file.
>
> 1. Create the legend in Crystal Xcelsius and format it when you create the chart.
> 2. Preview the model. Take a screen of the legend and save it in .jpg format.
> 3. Clear the **SHOW LEGEND** option on the Titles panel on the chart.
> 4. Save the model.

Add The Check Box

1. Add the Check Box component right below the word Sales in the chart title.
2. On the General tab, make the changes in the table.

Property	Change To
Title	Show Legend
Insert In	C2

3. On the Appearance tab, change the Use Custom Color option to light yellow.

Preview The Model

1. Save the changes.
2. When you click the Show Legend button, the legend will appear, as shown in Figure 11-35.

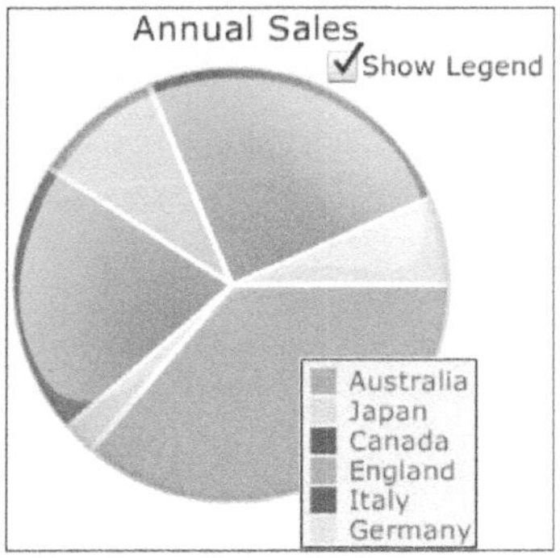

Figure 11-35 Chart with the legend as an image

GLOBAL CUSTOMIZATIONS & EXPORTING

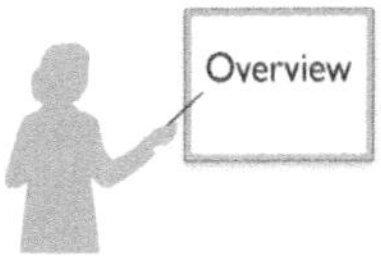

In this lesson you will learn about the following three types of global customization options:

- ☑ Skins
- ☑ Global styles
- ☑ Templates

You will also learn how to export models to several dashboard formats and how to adjust Adobe software options that can effect dashboards that you create.

LESSON 12

Global Customizations Overview

In Lesson 9 you learned enhancement techniques that are applied to individual components on dashboards. In this lesson you will learn about the customization options that are applied to the Crystal Xcelsius workspace and an entire dashboard.

If you have had to sit through what many, including myself, call boring PowerPoint presentations, keep all of the features of the PowerPoint presentation that made you cringe in the front of your brain, so that you do not wind up designing a dashboard that looks just like a presentation that was painful for you to look at <smile>.

I know that I have spent more time trying to figure out why the person that created the presentation used so many fonts on each slide or why the layout did not seem appropriate for the large amount of data, then I did paying attention to the actual information in the presentation. If you understand what I am talking about, this is your time to shine.

The majority of this lesson covers three ways that can be used to enhance the appearance of dashboards. And if you are graphically challenged like I am, you will like learning about the global customization options and how they will be helpful.

Skins

Crystal Xcelsius comes with five skins. Skins are used to change the appearance of components. Each skin has a different look and feel.

View ⇒ Change Skin, opens the dialog box shown in Figure 12-1.

Aqua is the default skin.

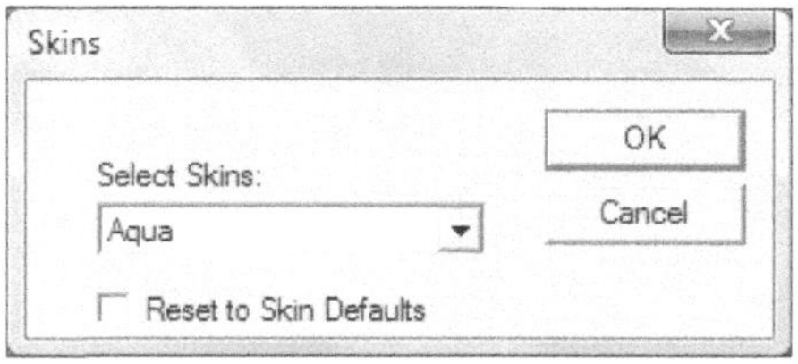

Figure 12-1 Skins dialog box

Select the **RESET TO SKIN DEFAULTS** option if you need to remove changes that you made to components and want to the default values for the skin that is selected in the drop-down list.

Figures 12-2, 12-3 and 12-4 show the same set of components (Combination chart, Accordion menu and Grid) in the three new skins in this version of Crystal Xcelsius. As you can see, the same component has a different look under each skin.

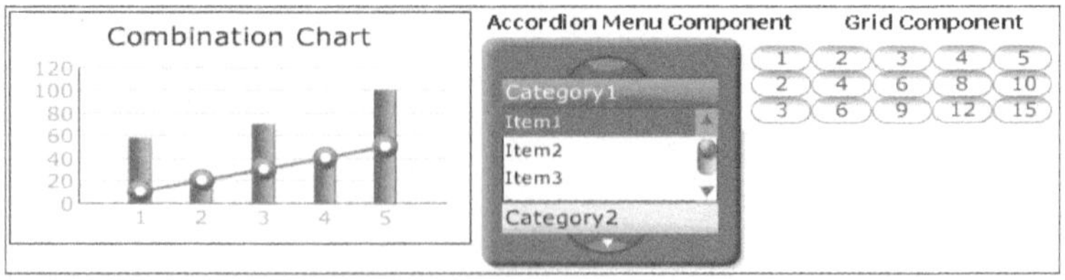

Figure 12-2 Graphite skin components

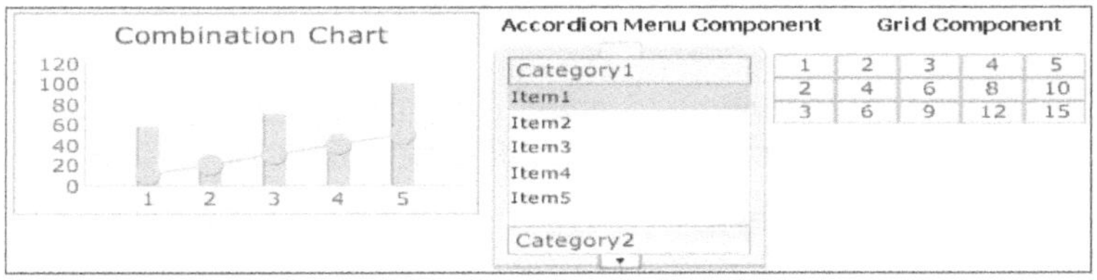

Figure 12-3 Halo skin components

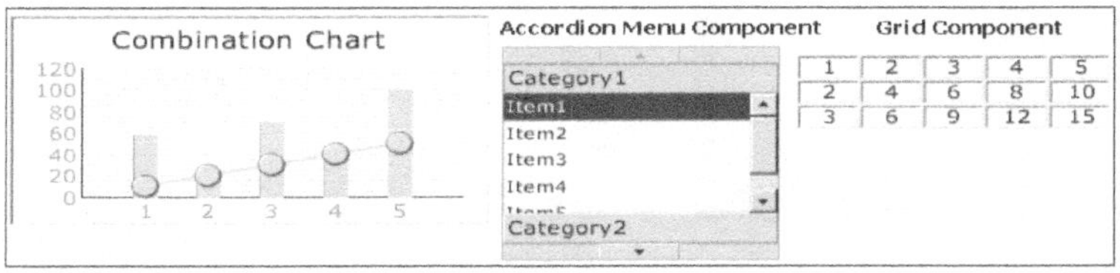

Figure 12-4 Windows Classic skin components

What I noticed is that all skins do not have all of the same components. For example, the Aqua skin has the progress bars shown in Figure 12-5 and the Graphite skin only has the progress bars shown in Figure 12-6.

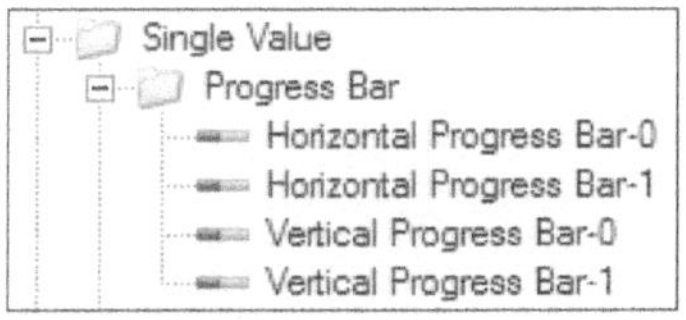

Figure 12-5 Aqua skin progress bar options

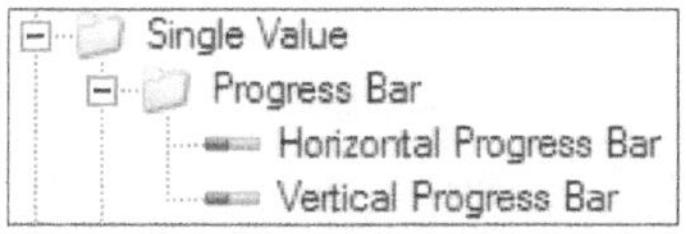

Figure 12-6 Graphite skin progress bar options

Changing Skins

As you just learned, each skin does not have the same number of options per component type. If you create a dashboard with one skin and later want to use a different skin on the dashboard, you could get unexpected results when the new skin is applied. For example, if the dashboard currently uses the Gauge-3 component in the Aqua skin, and you change the dashboard to use the Aero skin, the gauge component in the dashboard would go from the one shown in Figure 12-7 to the one shown in Figure 12-8. The reason this will happen is because the Aqua skin has four gauge components and the Aero skin only has one gauge component.

Figure 12-7 Aqua skin Gauge-3 component

Figure 12-8 Aero skin gauge component

Skin Backgrounds

I find the skin background options helpful when trying to customize the background of components. Figures 12-9 and 12-10 show the background components for two skins.

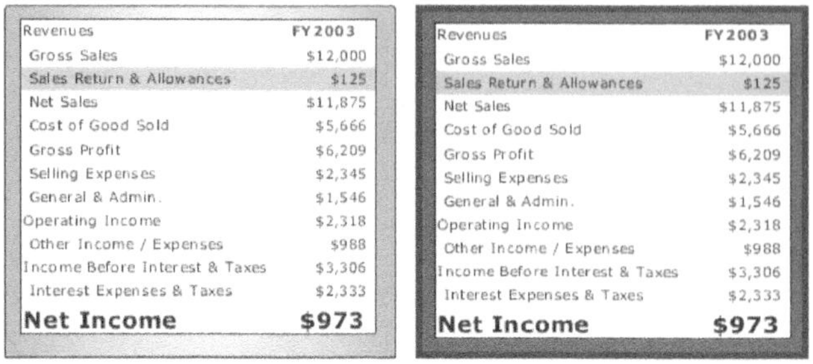

Revenues	FY2003
Gross Sales	$12,000
Sales Return & Allowances	$125
Net Sales	$11,875
Cost of Good Sold	$5,666
Gross Profit	$6,209
Selling Expenses	$2,345
General & Admin.	$1,546
Operating Income	$2,318
Other Income / Expenses	$988
Income Before Interest & Taxes	$3,306
Interest Expenses & Taxes	$2,333
Net Income	**$973**

Figure 12-9 Aero background components

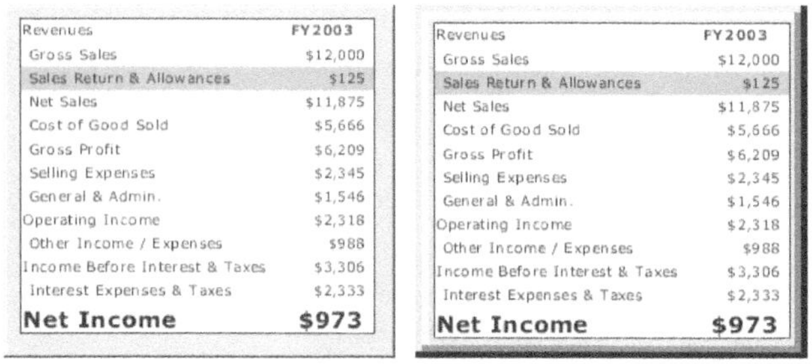

Revenues	FY2003
Gross Sales	$12,000
Sales Return & Allowances	$125
Net Sales	$11,875
Cost of Good Sold	$5,666
Gross Profit	$6,209
Selling Expenses	$2,345
General & Admin.	$1,546
Operating Income	$2,318
Other Income / Expenses	$988
Income Before Interest & Taxes	$3,306
Interest Expenses & Taxes	$2,333
Net Income	**$973**

Figure 12-10 Windows classic background components

Exercise 12.1: Change The Skin Of A Model

In this exercise you will change the skin of a model.

1. Save the My radio button menu as `My new skin background`.
2. View ⇒ Change Skin. Select Graphite from the drop-down list, then click OK.
3. Add the Background-3 component.
4. Delete the rectangle around the model.

5. Save the changes.

   The model should look like the one shown in Figure 12-11.

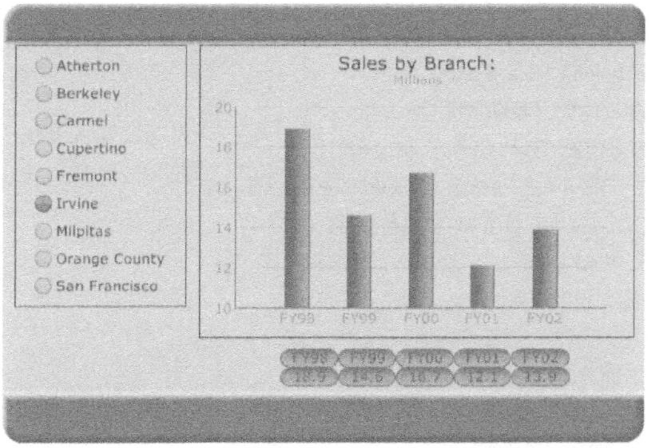

Figure 12-11 Model with a graphite skin background

Reset The Skin

1. View ⇒ Change Skin. Select Aqua from the drop-down list, then click OK.

2. Save the changes.

> **Skins Can Resize Components**
>
> If you apply a different skin to the model, depending on the components on the model, the size of the components will change. You may need to manually resize some of the components if the skin is changed after the components have been added to the model.

Global Styles

Global styles are used to change the color scheme of a dashboard. Each style is a collection of appearance options that are used to change the default colors for components. Global Styles do not change text formatting or fonts.

In some of the exercises in Lesson 9, you learned how to change the color of parts of a component. If you are color challenged like I can be sometimes, you will like the Global Styles tool because it contains several color schemes that can easily be applied to a model. You can also change the color for an individual item in a global style.

In addition to being able to apply the style to new models that are created, styles can also be applied to existing models that have a different style. If you open a model that has a style that is not on the computer that you open the model on, the model will still open and have the style that it was created with.

You have probably seen the **USE CUSTOM COLOR** option on the Properties dialog box more than a few times. While it may be necessary to select a custom color after selecting a global style, keep the following in mind, especially when using a global style other than the default global style. If you find yourself selecting the Use Custom Color option for several components on a regular basis in the model, you should consider creating your own global style, as they allow you to create a custom color scheme that will be applied to the components.

View ⇒ Change Style, opens the dialog box shown in Figure 12-12. The **DEFAULT** style cannot be modified because the color scheme comes from the skin that is currently selected. That is why there are no options that you can change on any of the tabs for this style.

Some of the options on the Styles, Text & Labels and Buttons & Backgrounds tabs, shown in Figures 12-12, 12-13 and 12-14 should look familiar from the Appearance tab on the Properties dialog box. The options on the Global Styles dialog box, are the default colors for the options on the Appearance tab.

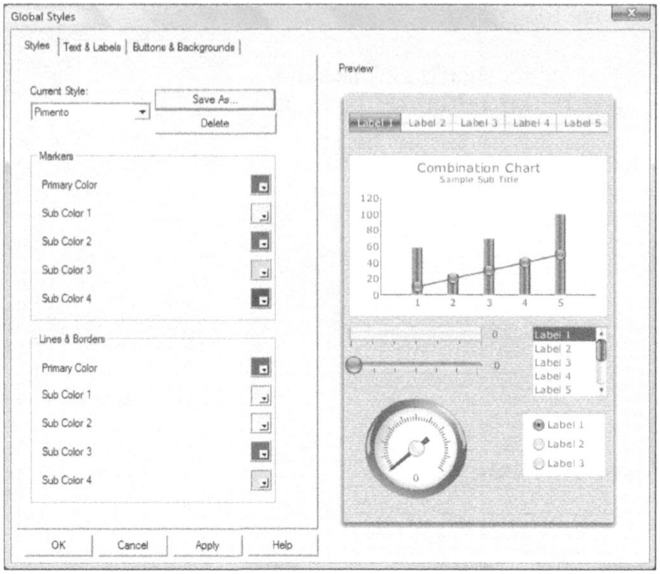

Figure 12-12 Styles tab on the Global Styles dialog box

Figure 12-13 Text & Labels tab on the Global Styles dialog box

Figure 12-14 Buttons & Backgrounds tab on the Global Styles dialog box

The good thing about creating your own global style is that if one of the global styles that comes with Crystal Xcelsius has many of the colors that you want to use, you can use that style as the starting point and change the colors that you need, then save the style with a new name.

Using Global Styles

There are two ways to apply a global style to a model, as discussed below.

① **TO THE CURRENT MODEL ONLY** Open the model that you want to apply the style to, then open the Global Styles dialog box and select the style that you want to use. Click the **APPLY** button on the Global Styles dialog box.

② **TO ALL NEW MODELS** Select the style on the Global Styles dialog box that you want to be applied to all new models that you create, then click OK. The name of the style that you select will appear at the top of the Components window, as illustrated in Figure 12-15, instead of the default style name shown in Figure 12-16.

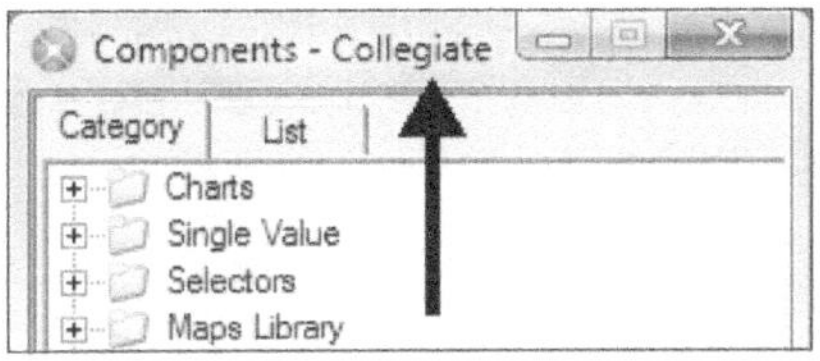

Figure 12-15 Style name change

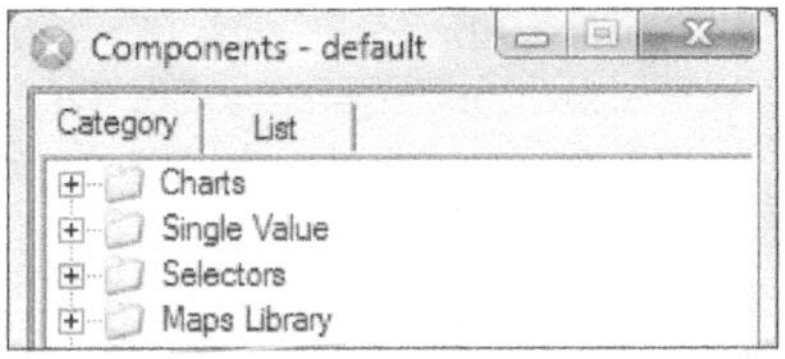

Figure 12-16 Default style name

Exercise 12.2: Apply A Different Style To A Model

In this exercise you will apply a different style to the model shown in Figure 12-17.

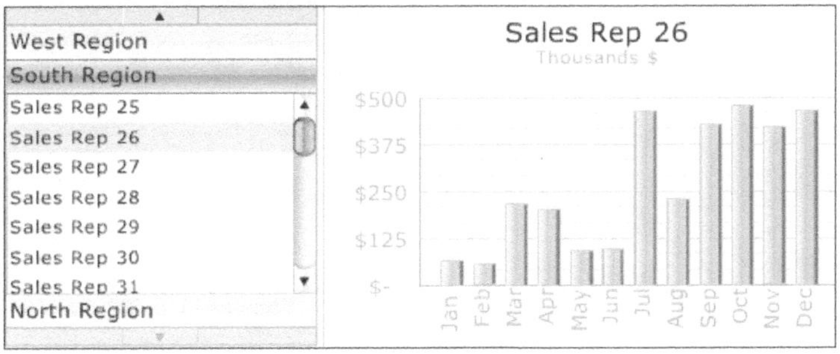

Figure 12-17 Accordion menu model

1. Save the My accordion menu model as `My new style.`

2. View ⇒ Change Style.

3. Open the Current Style drop-down list and select Pimento. Click Apply, then click OK.

4. Save the changes.

   The model should look like the one shown in Figure 12-18.

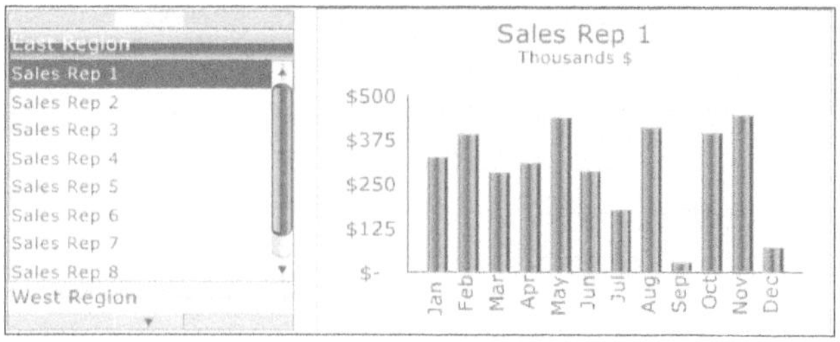

Figure 12-18 New style applied to a model

Create Your Own Global Style

You can change the color of any of the global style options. If you change any of the options on the dialog box, the style name will change, as illustrated in Figure 12-19.

If you want to keep the changes, click the **SAVE AS** button, then type in a name for the style on the dialog box shown in Figure 12-20. The style will be displayed in the **CURRENT STYLE** drop-down list on the Styles tab, with the styles that come with Crystal Xcelsius.

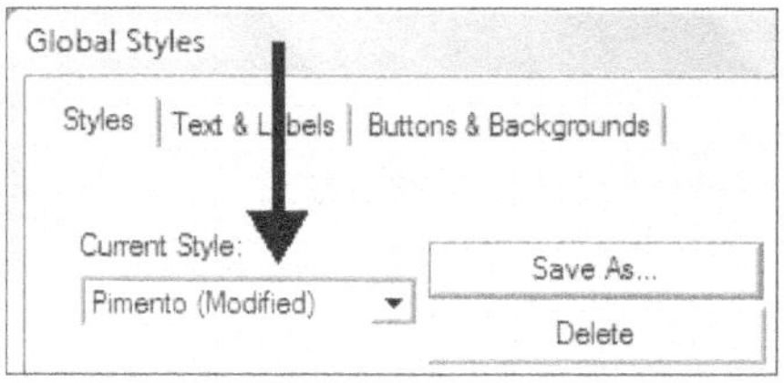

Figure 12-19 Style change notification

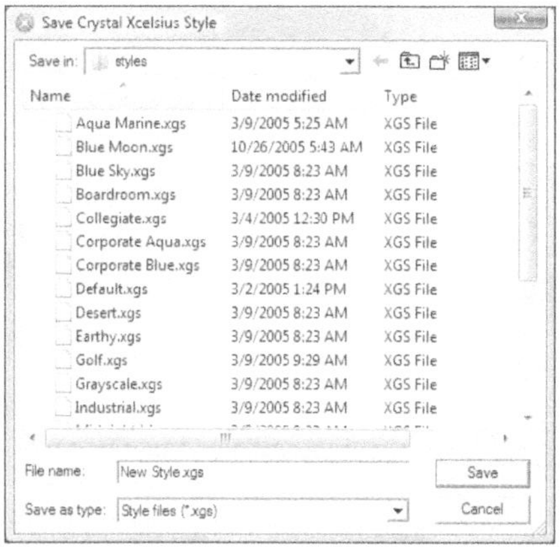

Figure 12-20 Save Crystal Xcelsius Style dialog box

The styles are stored in the Styles folder under the Crystal Xcelsius software folder. By default, styles that you create are saved in the same folder as the styles that come with the software are saved in.

Exercise 12.3: Using A Custom Style On A Different Computer

If you need to work on a model on a computer that does not have the custom style that you created or need, you have to copy the custom style file to the other computer.

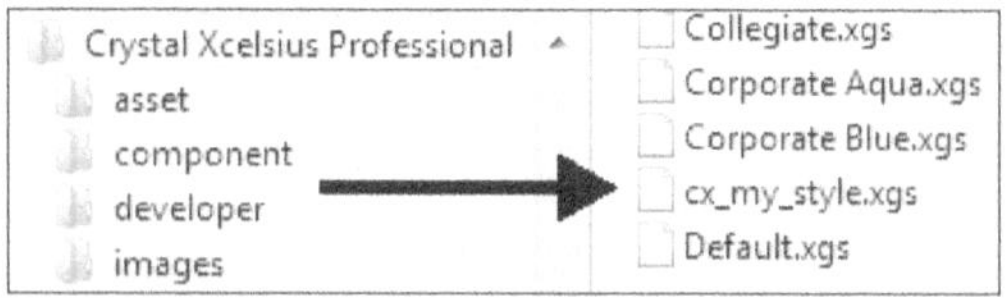

Figure 12-21 Styles folder

The Styles file extension is **.XGS**, as illustrated in Figure 12-21. I created the style cx_my_style, illustrated in the figure.

This is the file that I would copy to another computer. Follow the steps below to copy this custom style to your computer.

1. In Windows Explorer, copy the cx_my_style file in your folder to the Styles folder. The path for the Styles folder is shown in Figure 12-22. Your path may be slightly different if you are not using Windows Vista or do not have another Business Objects software package installed.

Figure 12-22 Path to the Styles folder

2. Save the My single value alerts model as `My custom style`.

3. View ⇒ Change Style.

4. Open the Current Style drop-down list and select the cx_my_style file. Click Apply, then click OK.

5. Save the changes. You should see the new style applied to the model.

Restore The Default Style

In this part of the exercise you will restore the default style so that the new models that you create will use the default style.

1. View ⇒ Change Style.

2. Open the Current Style drop-down list and select Default.

3. Click Apply, then click OK. Save the changes.

Troubleshooting Custom Styles

If you do not see the style that you copied to the Styles folder in the **CURRENT STYLE** drop-down list on the new computer, follow the steps below.

1. Open the Global Styles dialog box.

2. Open the Current Style drop-down list, then scroll to the end and select the Browse option illustrated in Figure 12-23. The dialog box shown in Figure 12-24 will open.

Figure 12-23 Current Style drop-down list

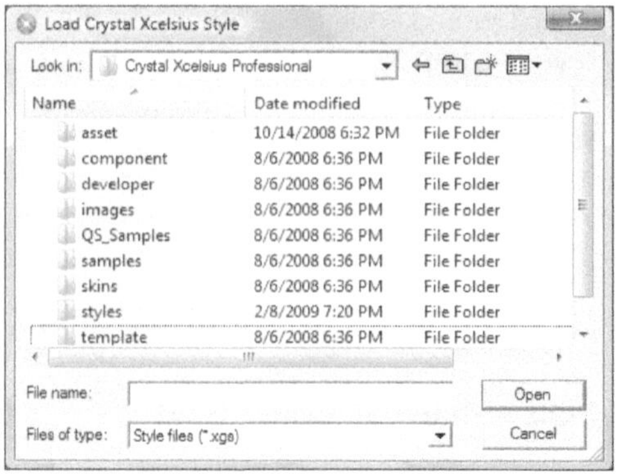

Figure 12-24 Load Crystal Xcelsius Style dialog box

3. Navigate to the main folder for the software. Double-click on the **STYLES** folder. Saving the style in this folder is optional. The reason that you should consider saving your style in this folder is if you want your style to appear in the Current Style drop-down list, shown earlier in Figure 12-23.

Templates

Crystal Xcelsius has eight templates that you can use to create the look and feel of the dashboard. Templates can save you time because you do not have to create the layout for the model from scratch.

File ⇒ New From Template, opens the dialog box shown in Figure 12-25. What is interesting about templates is that they are interactive on the dialog box, which means that you can click on the component displayed in the **PREVIEW** section and use it like you would use a dashboard.

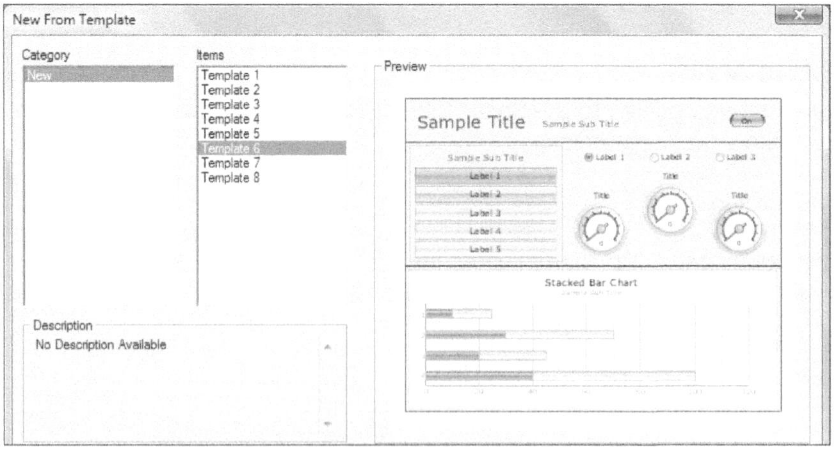

Figure 12-25 New From Template dialog box

Template Folders And Libraries

The default template folder is named template. On the left of the New From Template dialog box is a section named **CATEGORY**. In the documentation, the categories are called libraries. In addition to being able to create your own templates, you can create your own libraries, which are really folders.

One use that comes to mind for creating libraries is if you create dashboards for different departments in a company or if you create dashboards for different clients. The libraries would allow you to keep the templates separated. Figure 12-26 shows how the library structure that I created appears.

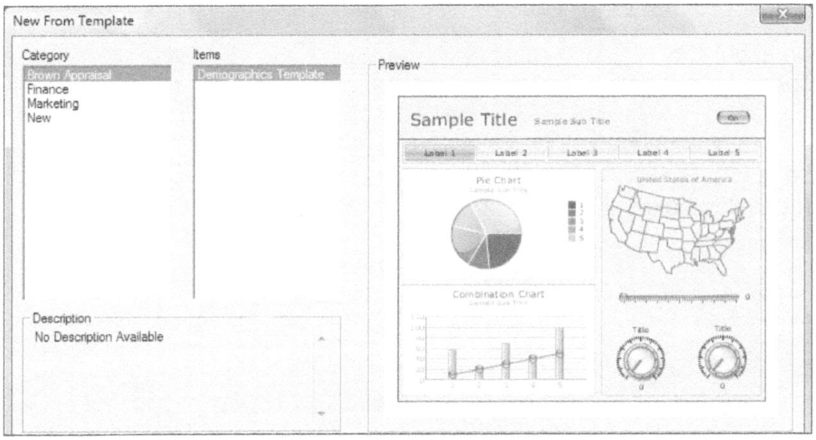

Figure 12-26 My library structure in the New From Template dialog box

How To Create Your Own Template Folder

If you need to create your own folder to store templates in that you create, follow the steps below.

1. Open Windows Explorer.

2. Navigate to the Crystal Xcelsius installation folder, then click on the Template folder.

3. File ⇒ New ⇒ Folder, then type in the name for your folder.

Create Your Own Template

If you create a model that has a layout that you think would be useful for future models, you can save it as a template by following the steps below.

1. Open the model that you want to save as a template, then File ⇒ Save As.

2. Navigate to the **TEMPLATE** folder, which is under the Crystal Xcelsius software folder or a template folder that you created.

3. Type in the name for the template, then press Enter. If you open the New From Template dialog box, you should see the template that you created.

Add A Description To A Template

If you use a lot of templates, you may find it helpful to add a description to the template to make it easier to remember important details about the template. If you want to add a description to a template, follow the steps below.

1. Open the template.

2. File ⇒ Document Properties.

3. Type in the information about the template in the Description field shown in Figure 12-27.

   This information will be displayed on the New From Template dialog box.

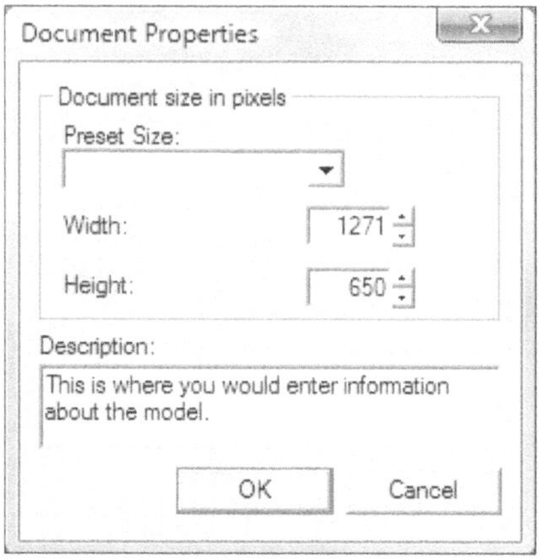

Figure 12-27 Document Properties dialog box

4. Click OK, then save the changes.

Make The Template Interactive

If you want your template to be interactive in the New From Template dialog box, follow the steps below.

1. Open the template that you created, then File ⇒ Export ⇒ Macromedia Flash (SWF).

2. Navigate to the folder that you saved the template in.

3. Type in the same file name that you used for the template, then press Enter.

Create A Data Snapshot

In the next section you will learn how to publish (export) the model to a variety of formats. There may be times when someone only needs the data that is currently being displayed on the dashboard, instead of the entire spreadsheet. The **SNAPSHOT** tool captures the data that is displayed. This is a subset of the data that is used to create the dashboard. Well, that is how this tool is suppose to work.

> The steps below show you how to take a snapshot of the data. The Snapshot tool is suppose to only export the data that is currently displayed. I did not find this to be the case. Instead, all of the data is included in the snapshot file.

1. Open the model that you want to take a snapshot of.
2. Click the Preview button, then display the data in the model that you want to capture in the snapshot.
3. File ⇒ Snapshot. You will see the options shown in Figure 12-28.

   The data is exported to the file type that you select on the snapshot submenu.

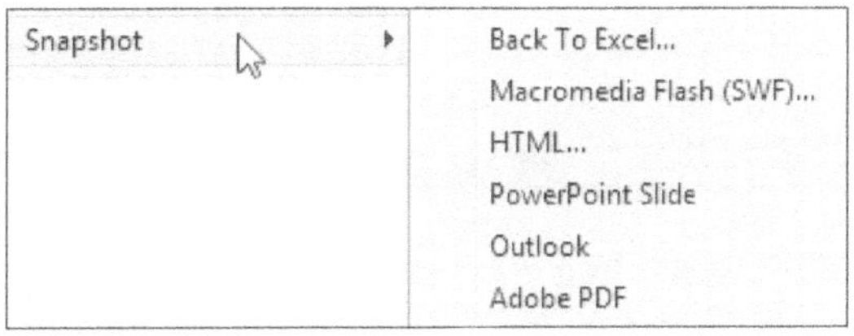

Figure 12-28 Snapshot output options

4. If necessary, navigate to the folder where you want to save the snapshot file, then type in the file name and press Enter. The snapshot file will be created.

> The one option that I found helpful is the **BACK TO EXCEL** option. The reason I found it helpful is if you have a model, but either cannot find the spreadsheet that was imported or you never had the spreadsheet, this option will recreate the spreadsheet, if you will.

Exporting

You have created a lot of models in this book, but you have only exported a model to a Flash file to create the dashboard. The rest of this lesson covers all of the exporting formats. Keep in mind that each export option creates a SWF file and then adds the SWF file to the export format that you select. Each export format retains all of the functionality that the model has.

The next to last step that I do before exporting the model is resizing the canvas, so that it is the right size for the dashboard. [See Lesson 9, Resize The Canvas] Exporting the model is the last step in creating the dashboard that will be distributed to users.

What may not be obvious is that the dashboard can be copied and pasted to another file. For example, when you export the model to PowerPoint, a file is created that has one slide that contains the dashboard. If you are creating a larger presentation, you can copy the slide with the dashboard to another PowerPoint file, by right-clicking on the slide that you want to copy. Open the presentation file that you want to copy it to. Select the slide that you want to paste it on, then right-click and select Paste. The same is also true for other export options.

Non Embedded Files

If there are files that are not embedded in the model, during the export process for all export options except Microsoft Outlook and Word, a folder is automatically created. The non embedded files are placed in the folder. The files must stay in this folder so that the dashboard will work properly.

Exporting Tip

If the images have not been embedded in the model, when you export a **SLIDING PICTURE MENU** model, the SWF file has to be exported to the same folder as the image files that the menu uses, so that the images will load properly.

Open the model that you want to create the dashboard for, before following the instructions below. Some of the export options will create two files: the SWF file and the export file type that you selected, as illustrated in Figure 12-29.

If the model is linked to external files that are not in the same folder that you select in step 2, a new folder will be created, as shown on the left of Figure 12-29, with the export file name that you create and the external files will be added to this folder.

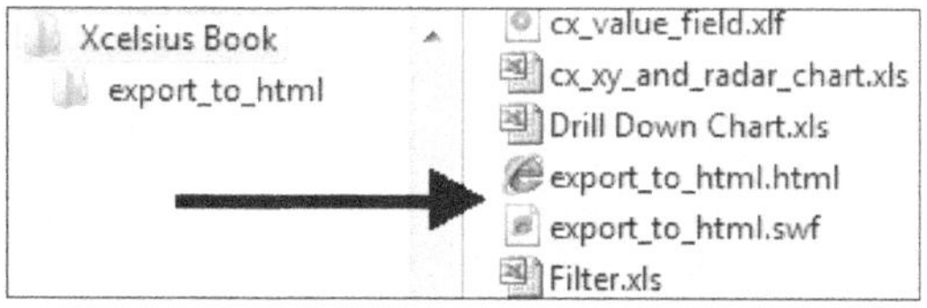

Figure 12-29 HTML export file with external files

Export The Model To Flash

This export option creates a SWF file. The Flash Player is usually used to view the dashboard created from this export option.

1. File ⇒ Export ⇒ Macromedia Flash SWF. You will see the Export To Macromedia Flash (SWF) dialog box.

2. Navigate to the folder where you want to save the dashboard file.

3. Type in the name for the Flash file, then press Enter or click the Save button.
   The dashboard in Flash format will be created.

Export The Model To HTML Format

This export option creates an HTML file (a web page) that automatically loads the SWF file. In Lesson 1, I discussed file naming conventions that will come into play with this export option. The SWF and HTML files that are created will have the same file name. It is best to use a name that does not have spaces. You can rename the HTML file after it is created. If necessary, if you need to rename the SWF file, you will have to change the code in the HTML file to point to the new name of the SWF file.

1. File ⇒ Export ⇒ HTML. You will see the Publish To HTML dialog box.

2. Navigate to the folder where you want to save the dashboard files.

3. Type in the name for the HTML file, then press Enter or click the Save button.
   The HTML dashboard file will be created.

Export The Model To A PowerPoint File

This export option adds the SWF file to a new Microsoft PowerPoint file. Like any other PowerPoint file, one with a dashboard can be emailed.

1. File ⇒ Export ⇒ PowerPoint Slide. You will see the Export PowerPoint (PPT) dialog box.

2. Navigate to the folder where you want to save the dashboard files.

3. Type in the name for the PowerPoint file, then press Enter or click the Save button.
   The PowerPoint dashboard file will be created.

How To Copy The Dashboard To Another PowerPoint File

As you read earlier, you can copy the dashboard to another PowerPoint file. If you have trouble using the copy and paste technique, the steps below explain another way to copy the dashboard to another PowerPoint file.

1. Open the PowerPoint file that you want to add the dashboard to.

2. On the Outline or Slides tab, click on the slide that comes before the location where you want to add the dashboard.

3. Insert ⇒ Slides From Files.

4. On the Slide Finder dialog box, click the Browse button, then navigate to and double-click on the dashboard PowerPoint file.

5. Click on the slide that has the dashboard.

6. Check the **KEEP SOURCE FORMATTING** option, then click the Insert button shown in Figure 12-30.

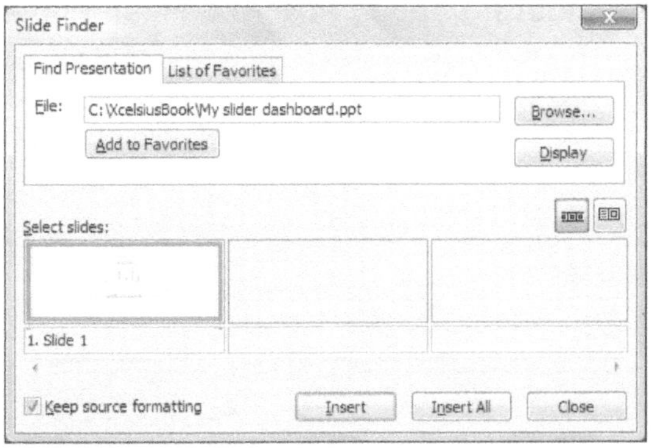

Figure 12-30 PowerPoint Slide Finder dialog box

7. Click Close, then make any changes that are necessary.

Export The Model To An Outlook Email

This export option adds the SWF file to a Microsoft Outlook email message that you can email to someone.

1. File ⇒ Export ⇒ Outlook. Outlook will open and a new email window will open. The SWF file will be attached to the email automatically.

Export The Model To A Word File

This export option adds the SWF file to a Microsoft Word document.

1. File ⇒ Export ⇒ Word. You will see the Export Word (DOC) dialog box.
2. Navigate to the folder where you want to save the dashboard file.
3. Type in the name for the Word file, then press Enter or click the Save button. The Word dashboard file will be created.

Export The Model To An Adobe PDF File

This export option adds the SWF file to an Adobe PDF file. This option is not available in the Standard edition of Crystal Xcelsius.

> Currently, the PDF export option only exports to a portrait layout. Landscape is not supported.

1. File ⇒ Export ⇒ Adobe PDF. You will see the Export Adobe PDF dialog box.
2. Navigate to the folder where you want to save the dashboard file.
3. Type in the name for the PDF file, then press Enter or click the Save button. The PDF dashboard file will be created.

Troubleshooting Adobe PDF And Flash Player Issues

If you are having problems exporting to a PDF file or you see the message shown in Figure 12-31, when you are trying to open a PDF file, it could mean that there are Flash Player options selected that are blocking .SWF files. Follow the steps below to see if they resolve the problem.

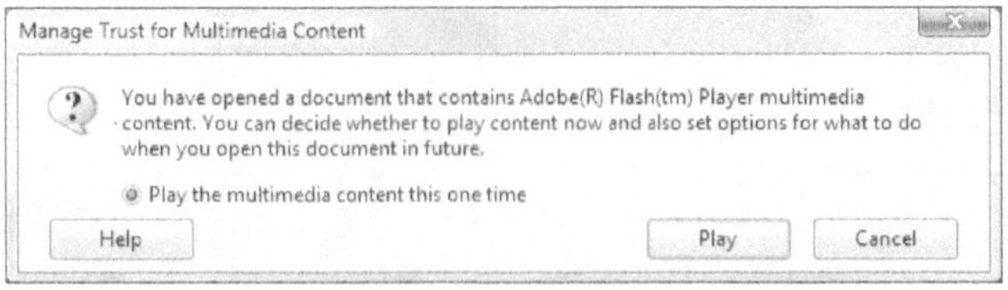

Figure 12-31 Manage Trust For Multimedia Content message

1. Open the Acrobat Reader.
2. Edit ⇒ Preferences. In the Categories list, click on the **MULTIMEDIA** option.
3. Select the **OTHER DOCUMENTS** option at the top of the dialog box.
4. Check the **ALLOW MULTIMEDIA OPERATIONS** option.
5. Select the **PERMISSION FOR ADOBE FLASH PLAYER IS SET TO PROMPT** option in the white box.
6. In the **CHANGE PERMISSION** drop-down list, select Always if you do not want to be prompted any more. If you select **PROMPT**, you will continue to see the message shown above in Figure 12-31.
7. You should have the options shown in Figure 12-32.

   Click OK.

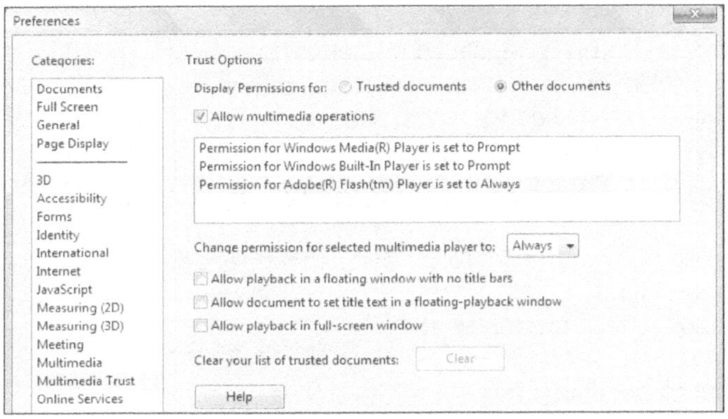

Figure 12-32 Multimedia Trust preferences

Adobe Flash Player Storage Settings

In Lesson 9 you created a dashboard that has scenario buttons. You learned that an unlimited number of scenarios can be saved as long as there is enough local storage space allocated in the Flash Player. The next section shows you how to increase the allocated space.

By default, the local storage for a flash (SWF) file is 100 kb. If the local storage has been disabled, the person using the dashboard will be prompted to enable local storage. The Flash Player will prompt the user to allocate more local storage. If no additional space is allocated, the scenario cannot be saved.

How To Change The Flash Player Local Storage Settings

If you want to follow the steps below to learn how to change the Flash Player local storage settings, open the My slider dashboard.swf file.

1. Right-click on the dashboard and select **SETTINGS**, as shown in Figure 12-33. You will see the dialog box shown in Figure 12-34.

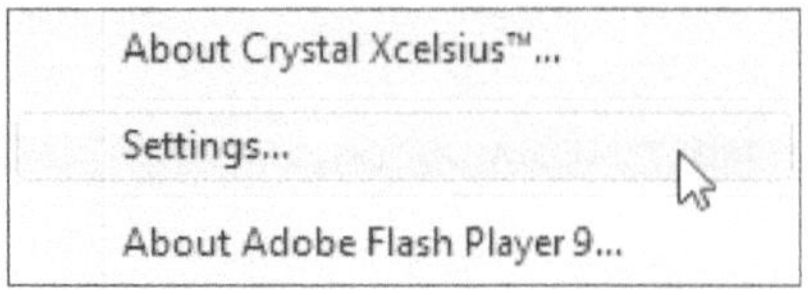

Figure 12-33 Flash file shortcut menu

Figure 12-34 Adobe Flash Player Settings dialog box

2. Click on the second icon (the folder) at the bottom of the dialog box.

3. Use the slider to select the amount of local storage that you want to allocate.

> If data (in this case, saved scenarios) has already been saved to the hard drive and you select an amount of local space that is less than the amount of space that has already been used for saved scenarios, you will be prompted that the scenarios that have already saved will be deleted. If this happens and you want to keep the scenarios that have already been saved, you will have to allocate more space.

4. If you do not want users to be prompted about local storage allocation, check the **NEVER ASK AGAIN** option, shown at the bottom of the dialog box in Figure 12-35.

Figure 12-35 Local Storage Adobe Flash Player Settings

5. Once you have made all of the necessary changes, click the Close button.

Configuring Security For The Flash Player

By design, Flash SWF files have default security settings that may or may not allow your dashboard to run properly. Some of the default security settings can cause run time errors. The steps below will show you how to make the dashboard a trusted SWF file.

1. From Windows Explorer, run the SWF file. (The dashboard should be running in Internet Explorer).

2. Right-click on the dashboard and select Settings. You should see the Adobe Flash Player Settings dialog box shown earlier in Figure 12-34.

3. Click the Advanced button.

4. Click on the **GLOBAL SECURITY SETTINGS PANEL** link, illustrated in Figure 12-36.

Figure 12-36 Flash Player Settings Manager

5. Select the **ALWAYS ALLOW** option shown in Figure 12-37.

Figure 12-37 Global Security Settings panel

6. Close all of the browser windows and rerun the dashboard. The dashboard should run properly.

Managing The Mayhem Of A Lot Of Data For A Dashboard

The process of creating complex dashboards can be overwhelming when there are a lot of components. The Object Browser allows you to hide components to get some of them out of the way so that you can work on others. If the dashboard requires a lot of data, to help keep the confusion to a dull roar, you can put different sets of data on different tabs in the spreadsheet.

In Exercise 11.7 you created a model that had six charts and a menu. What if you have to combine that model with all of the other models that you created in Lesson 11? That would add a lot more components and data to the dashboard.

I don't know about you, but I like to keep most things at a dull roar. I have a client that asked me if there way anything that I could do to make a PowerPoint presentation that had a little over 100 slides, most of which has spreadsheet data, look better. My first thought, due to lack of graphic and PowerPoint skills was to say "Put five bottles of liquor on each table in the conference room before the meeting starts", but I realized that if I said that, they would probably do it.

I looked at all of the software that I had installed on my laptop and at first glance I did not see anything that would work. I realized that I needed to put the data into smaller groups. Finally, it dawned on me that it may be possible to put it into Crystal Xcelsius. My biggest concern was that putting all of the data in a single dashboard may cause it to take a performance hit.

To make a long story short, I created several dashboards and a template with a main menu. The buttons on the main menu were linked to different dashboards, just like you have learned to do with charts. This is similar to building a mini application. The next exercise will show you how to tie everything that you have learned together.

Exercise 12.4: Handling Dashboard Overload

In this exercise you will create the framework for a main dashboard that runs several other dashboards.

Part 1: Create The Dashboards

Complete the steps in this part of the exercise for each of the following models:

⇒ My filter drop-down list
⇒ My toggle button
⇒ My multiple charts menu
⇒ My label based menu

1. Resize the canvas to fit the component.

2. Export the model to Flash. Use the same name as the model for the dashboard file.

Part 2: Create The Template For The Main Dashboard

This template will be used as a container to link all of the dashboards that you created in the previous part of the exercise. You will modify one of the templates that came with Crystal Xcelsius to use as the template for this exercise.

1. File ⇒ New From Template.

2. Select Template 7, then click OK.

3. Save the file as `My main dashboard`.

4. Delete the following from the template:

   ⇒ All of the objects at the bottom of the template, including the horizontal line.
   ⇒ The dials on the right side of the chart.

   When you are finished, the template should look like the one shown in Figure 12-38.

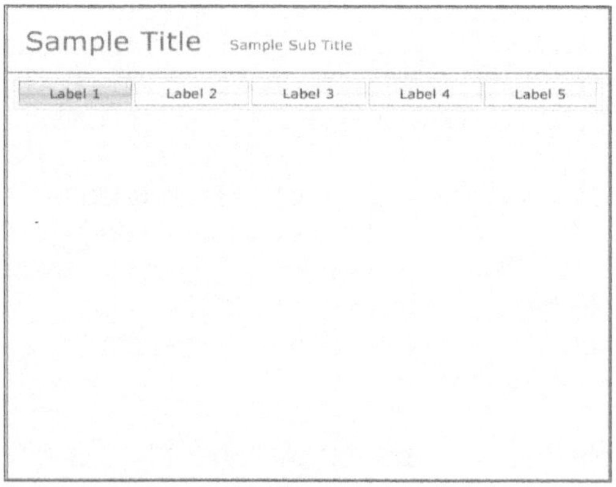

Figure 12-38 Empty template

Part 3: Import The Spreadsheet

The model that you are working with does not have an imported spreadsheet. That is fine because all of the dashboards that you will link to have the data that they need. The problem though, is that in order to attach a dashboard to a button on the menu and use the dynamic visibility options, you need to reference a cell in a spreadsheet.

Because the dashboards that will be added to this model (the main dashboard) will be in an image component, they will be able to access the spreadsheet linked to this model. The spreadsheet that you will import is empty, except for the cell where I state that the spreadsheet is empty.

1. Import the cx_my_main_dashboard spreadsheet.

Part 4: Modify The Label Based Menu

In this part of the exercise you will modify the menu and set up the dynamic visibility options for the menu.

1. On the General tab of the Label Based Menu Properties dialog box, click the Browse button at the end of the Labels option.

   Make the changes shown in Figure 12-39.

   (**Hint**: To delete the fifth label, click the minus button.)

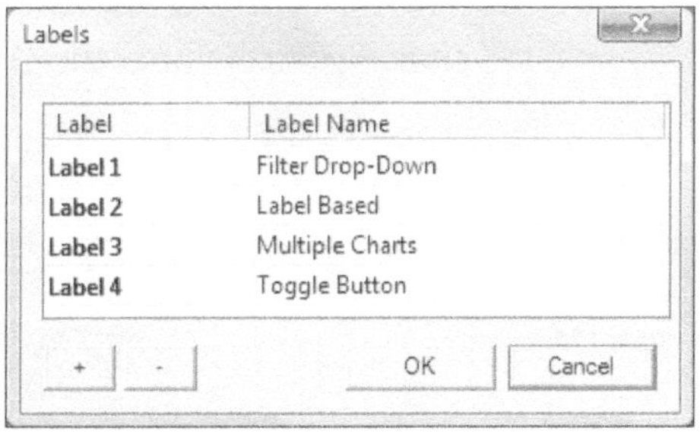

Figure 12-39 Label names

   If you were doing this for a production dashboard, you should use labels that denote what the dashboards display. I used the names shown above in Figure 12-39 so that you can easily tell which dashboard is which.

2. On the General tab, make the changes in the table.

Property	Change To
Insert Option	Position
Insert In	A1

3. On the Appearance tab, change the Label font size to 12.

4. Make the menu and rectangle around it smaller, then save the changes.

Part 5: Add The Dashboards To The Model

In this part of the exercise you will add an image component for each dashboard that you want linked to this model.

1. Add the Image component to the middle of the model.

2. Clear the **EMBED FILE** option.

3. Click the Import button. Select the My filter drop-down list Flash file.

4. When you see the message shown in Figure 12-40, click OK.

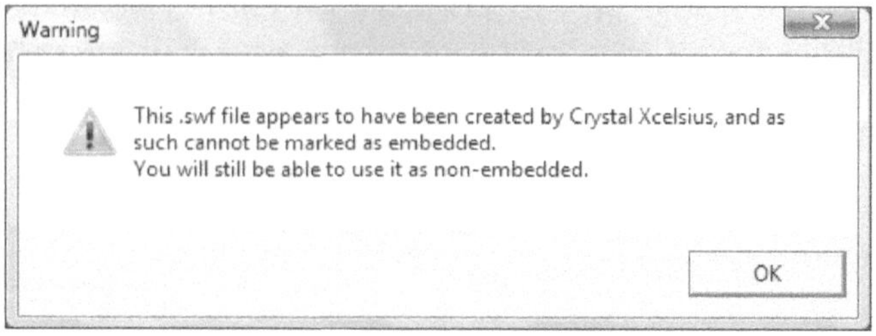

Figure 12-40 File cannot be embedded warning message

Because you cleared the Embed File option before clicking the Import button, I don't think that this message should appear because you are not trying to embed the file. So, I am not sure what the point of clearing the option first is for.

5. Rename the Image component in the Object Browser to the Flash file name.

6. Repeat the steps above to add the other three dashboards.

7. When you see the warning message in Figure 12-41, click OK.

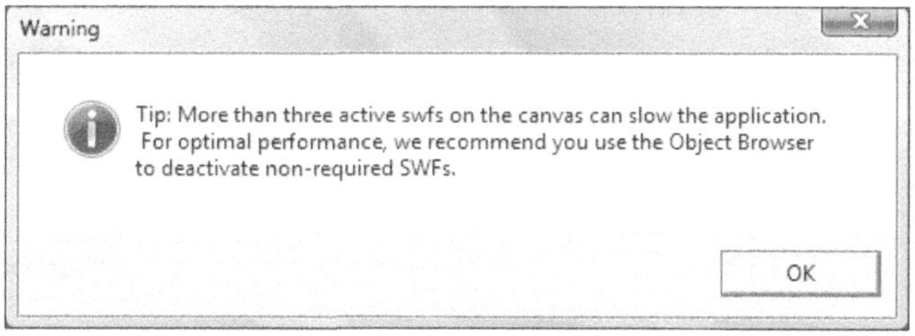

Figure 12-41 Optimal performance warning message

8. Your Object Browser should look like the one shown in Figure 12-42.

   Save the changes.

Figure 12-42 Object Browser

Part 6: Add Dynamic Functionality To The Image Components

Complete the steps below for each image component.

1. Change the Display Status to cell A1.

2. Change the Display Status Key option, as shown in the table.

Component	Display Status Key
Filter Drop-down	1
Label Based	2
Multiple Charts	3
Toggle Buttons	4

Part 7: Resize The Image Components

In this part of the exercise you will resize the image components. You should resize them to the size of the largest image component. For me, the largest image component is the Toggle Button component. Resizing the image components to all be the same size is optional. You should align all of the image components on the left and top so that they appear to be in the same location, when the user goes from dashboard to dashboard.

1. Select the largest image component.

2. Select the other three components.

3. Format ⇒ Align ⇒ Left.

4. Format ⇒ Make Same Size ⇒ Both. This step is optional.

5. One by one, move the image components to the center of the model, so that they are on top of each other.

Part 8: Change The Titles

1. Click on the Sample title label at the top of the model.

2. On the General tab, type `My Main Dashboard` in the Enter Text field.

3. Resize the title so that all of the text is visible.

4. Change the subtitle to `4 Dashboards In 1.`

5. If you want to make any changes, make them now, then save the changes.

Preview The Model

The model should look like the one shown in Figure 12-43. As you can see, all of the functionality in each dashboard works as it did in the original exercises that you created them in.

Remember that even though the dashboards are external files (the dashboards that you created in Part 1) that were added using the Image component, the changes are not automatically picked up by the main dashboard the next time that it is run.

Figure 12-43 My main dashboard model

To have the changes picked up by the main dashboard, open the Properties dialog box for the image component that has the dashboard that was changed and click the Import button on the General tab.

The End!

If you are reading this paragraph, I hope it means that you have completed all of the exercises in this book. If so, congratulations because you have covered a lot of material. If some topics seem a little fuzzy right now, that is to be expected. Hopefully you have gained some valuable Crystal Xcelsius dashboard creation skills and techniques. If so, I would greatly appreciate it if you would post a short review on Amazon (www.amazon.com). I hope that you enjoyed the book.

INDEX

D

E

F

G

H

I

K

L

M

N

S

T

U

V

W

X

Y

Z

No Stress Tech Guides

ISBN-13: 978-1-935208-02-0
ISBN-10: 1-935208-02-0

ISBN-13: 978-0-9773912-9-5
ISBN-10: 0-977391-29-9

ISBN-13: 978-1-935208-07-5
ISBN-10: 1-935208-07-1

ISBN-13: 978-1-935208-00-6
ISBN-10: 1-935208-00-4

ISBN-13: 978-1-935208-01-3
ISBN-10: 1-935208-01-2

ISBN-13: 978-0-9773912-7-1
ISBN-10: 0-977391-27-2

ISBN-13: 978-0-9773912-8-8
ISBN-10: 0-977391-28-0

ISBN-13: 978-0-9773912-1-9
ISBN-10: 0-977391-21-3

ISBN-13: 978-0-9773912-4-0
ISBN-10: 0-977391-24-8

Other Titles	ISBN-13:		ISBN-13:
Microsoft Works 7	978-0-9773912-2-6	ACT! 2007	978-0-9773912-5-7
Windows XP	978-0-9773912-0-2	Crystal Reports/Visual Studio 2005	978-0-9773912-6-4

Visit us on the web at www.tolanapublishing.com

Made in United States
Cleveland, OH
06 November 2026

47789600R00198